Emergency Money

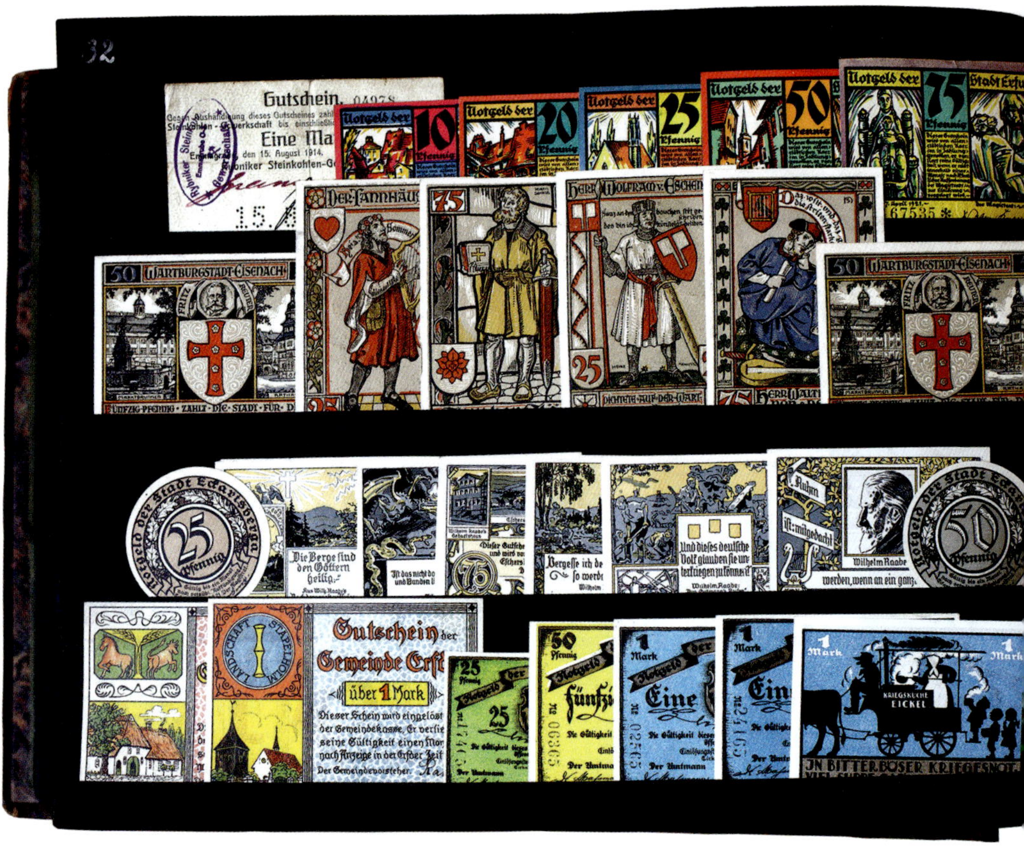

Notgeld album owned by Aby Warburg. Warburg Institute, London.

Emergency Money
Notgeld in the Image Economy of the German Inflation, 1914–1923

Tom Wilkinson

THE MIT PRESS
Cambridge, Massachusetts . London, England

For Owen Kyffin
1961–2023

The decisive actions can involve an—apparently—trivial matter. For here we can see in operation the truth that in the dialectical totality the individual elements incorporate the structure of the whole.
Lukács, "Reification and the Consciousness of the Proletariat," 1923

Any scrap of paper will do.
Goethe, *Faust: Part One*, 1808

Introduction: Full Pockets, Empty Signs

Paper has value because it circulates.
Marx, *A Contribution to the Critique of Political Economy*, 1859

A 1921 banknote from the north German town of Itzehoe shows a figure squatting in a garden or meadow, shirt hitched up and pipe in mouth, serenely shitting. The turd, caught mid-flight by the artist's brush, forms a number "1," the denomination of the note. A small bird looks on curiously, as well it might. "Not kennt kein Gebot!," the inscription tells us, "Necessity knows no command!," as if to excuse the obscenity of the image—to cover the arse of the artist, we might say, borrowing his own idiom. It is in any case a reference to the perilous economic situation, the *Not*, distress or emergency, that had called forth this *Notgeld*, emergency money. An equivalence is thereby asserted between the indomitable urgency of the bowel and the printing of notes. The latter response is posited as natural, reflexive, unstoppable—and explosively scatological. What had things come to when a note such as this—a note whereon money was rendered as excrement—could be considered legal tender? Put another way, why had a governmental body promulgated a visual autocritique in mass-produced form? And what had induced its designer, the expressionist painter Wenzel Hablik, to descend from his habitual, airy realm of utopian crystalline constructions to this earthily humorous and somewhat cynical scene, an image that seems to express its maker's contempt for the currency and thus for his own work in this medium?[1]

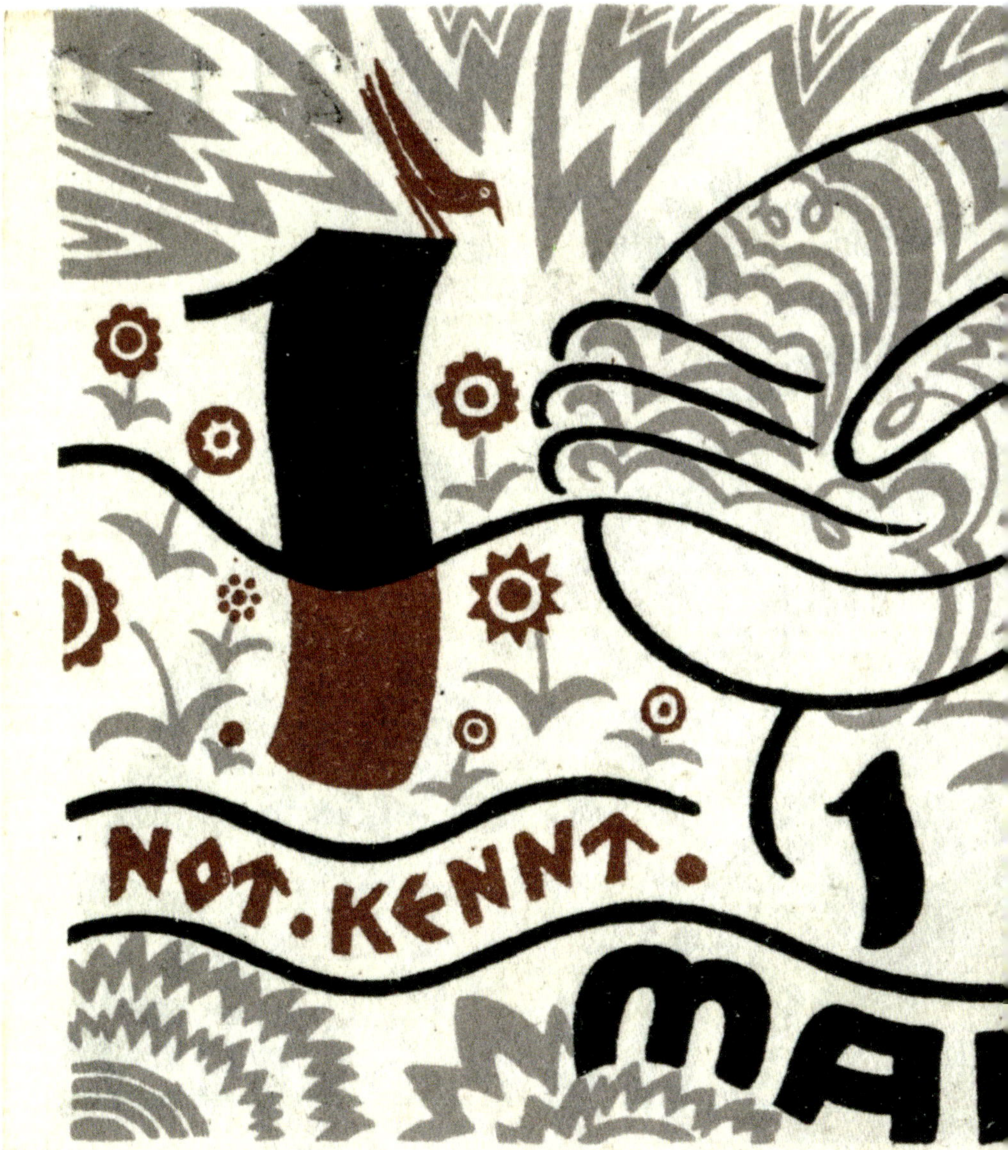

Notgeld designed by Wenzel Hablik for Itzehoe, 1921. Collection of the author.

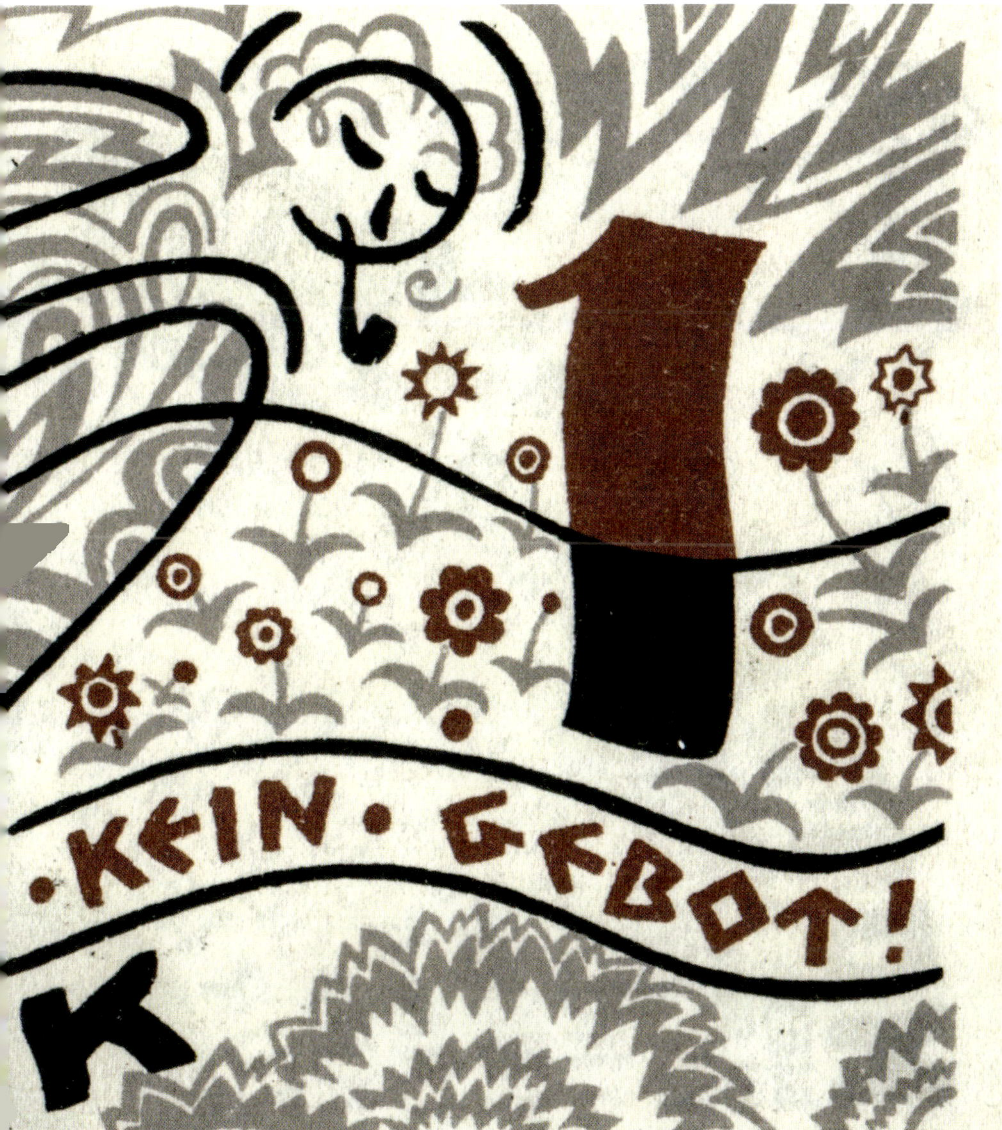
1
KEIN GEBOT!
K

Notgeld was issued in Germany during the inflation that began with the First World War in 1914 and ended in 1923. The baskets of notes heaved to the shops, bundles of notes stacked by children at play, the immiseration of the middle classes and the chiseler's feast day—these images of the fever's critical phase, the hyperinflation that lasted from 1922 to 1923, are familiar ones. However, the phenomenon was much more drawn out than is usually remembered. It began when the Wilhelmine authorities uncoupled the mark from the gold standard so that they could print money to finance the war, hoping that victory would allow them to restore the nation's finances. The value of the currency halved over the course of the conflict, which of course ended in defeat. Following the revolution, in the early years of the republic, this policy of monetary production was intensified to reconstruct the nation; at the same time, the burden of reparations damaged the economy yet further. These factors led to another burst of inflation in 1919. Yet, by suppressing the mark's value, the government also produced an export-led boom, leading to the partial stabilization of 1920–1921; as an additional benefit, this brought in foreign currency that could be used to satisfy the demand for reparations, at least in part. But this was not enough: the country defaulted on its payments, and, in 1923, the French invaded the Ruhr in order to extract payments in kind from the industrial region. In response, the German government instituted a policy of passive resistance, backed by printing yet more money. Their expansionary approach had already begun to produce the inevitable consequences: from 1922, the value of the mark collapsed on international markets, and at home prices went stratospheric. The cost of a loaf of bread rose from half a mark in 1918 to 700 marks at the beginning of 1923, and reached 200 billion marks by November that year. These repeated waves of inflation meant that increasing quantities of money were required to purchase goods, and the Reichsbank met this demand by printing ever-greater numbers of notes in ever-higher denominations, culminating with a 100,000,000,000,000-mark note dated February 1924. Before this could be put into circulation, however, the inflation had been abruptly and, from a historiographic perspective, somewhat mysteriously brought to an end with the introduction of a new currency, the Rentenmark, on November 15, 1923.[2]

Until his timely death that month, the director of the Reichsbank, Rudolf Havenstein, publicly defended this strategy of

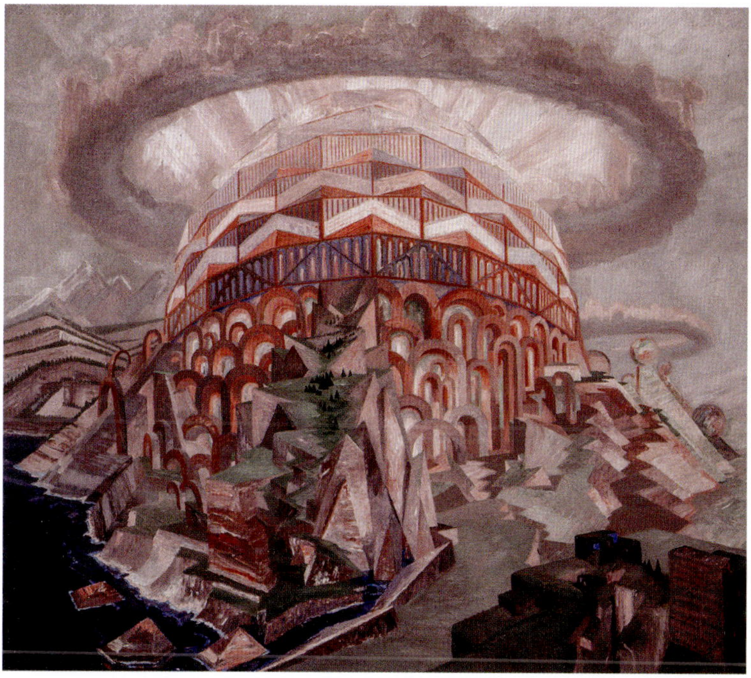

Wenzel Hablik, *Cantilever Cupola Supported on Five Hilltops*, 1918–1924, oil on canvas, 166 × 191 cm. Wenzel Hablik Museum, Itzehoe.

pecuniary hyperproduction as an essential means of combating the inflation—an assertion that has since seemed, to orthodox monetarists at least, akin to madness.[3] Others have conjectured that it was not mere irrationality but rather an underhand means of liquidating the government's debts at the cost of the population's savings, one that may have seemed expedient at the time, but which fatally undermined trust in the republic. Others yet have pointed out that this strategy was actually a factor in the successful postwar reconstruction of the economy, allowing for the inauguration of an unprecedented welfare state, and maintaining employment while the rest of the world endured a recession—until, that is, the final, fatal phase of hyperinflation, when jobs evaporated as rapidly as value. In the absence of conclusive explanations, we might turn instead to that most heterodox of economic thinkers, Georges Bataille, whose notion of nonproductive expenditure appears in some ways congruent to the phenomenon: "human societies can have ... an *interest* in considerable losses, in catastrophes that, *while conforming to well-defined needs*, provoke tumultuous depressions, crises of dread, and, in the final analysis,

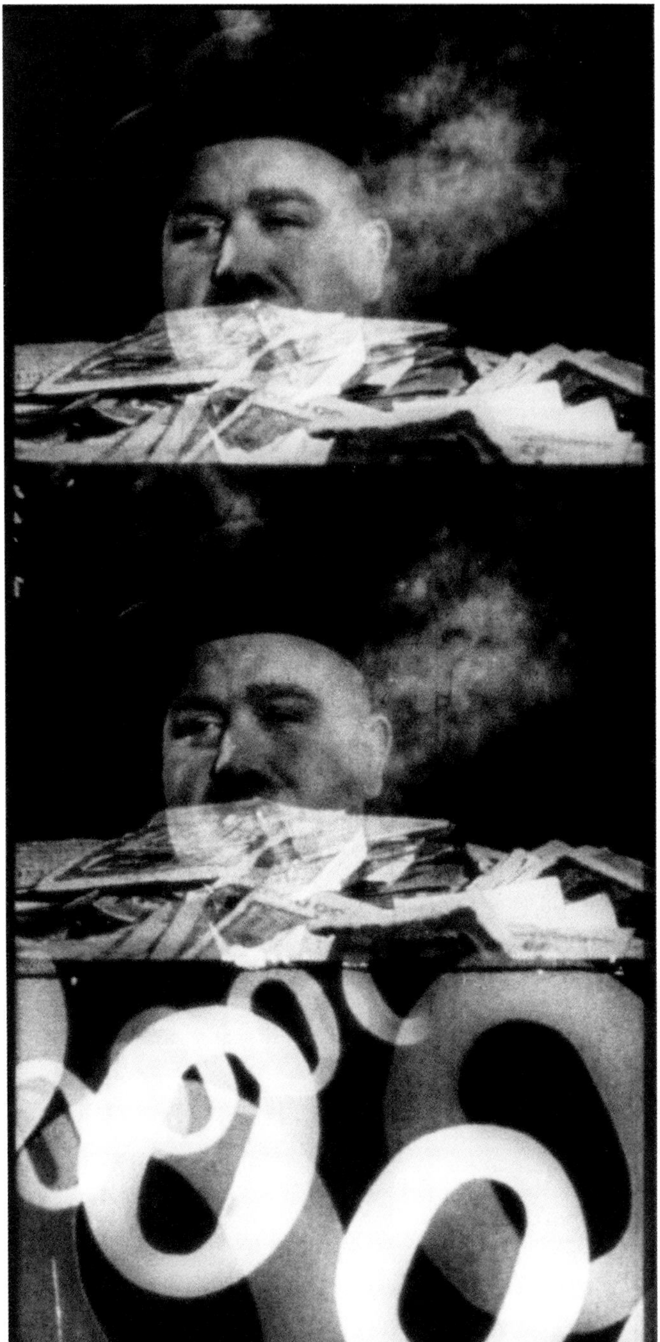

Stills from Hans Richter, *Inflation*, 1928. Centre Pompidou, Paris.

a certain orgiastic state."[4] The needs to which Bataille refers are those of energetic discharge, which can in his opinion be achieved negatively via wars (and, we might add, inflations) or, less destructively, through potlatch, festivals, orgies, and revolutions.

Whatever the motivations of the economists and policy makers of the empire, and of their successors during the early years of the republic, we can say that the detachment of the mark from the gold standard and the creation of vast quantities of fiat money had repercussions far beyond the realm of the economic. There were analogous impacts in culture and perception. A short film by Hans Richter titled *Inflation*, made in 1928 as an incongruously avant-garde B movie to accompany a melodrama on the same subject, demonstrates some of these. Hands counting out piles of money are doubled, tripled, and quadrupled, transforming the orderly practice of accounting into a morass of chaotic activity. Coins, banknotes, and numerals—especially zeroes—swirl before the eyes of the viewer in a dizzying, disorienting manner, and human faces observing this scene also appear in a confused mass of superimpositions. The subject is blurred and multiplied along with the growing piles of money and, it is implied, is similarly devalued. The film ends with the collapse of a building, as the very material real is demolished by the apparently insubstantial dancing zeroes. Despite these pervasive impacts of the inflation on culture, this conjuncture has been discussed at length only once, by Bernd Widdig; however, he concerns himself with texts, touches only briefly on images, and hardly mentions Notgeld itself.[5] In an earlier essay on the same problem, Anton Kaes concluded, "In the eye of contemporaries, the proliferation of 'empty signs,' of denominations without substance, extended into the cultural market as much as into the money markets."[6] Kaes gets close to the crux of the matter here, but in his essay, too, the visual remains untouched. By contrast, the objects under consideration here provide a panorama of this region.

However, while the notes that are the focus of this book certainly participated in the inflationary situation, they are not examples of money issued by the central government; rather, they are a coterminous and not unrelated phenomenon. As well as rising prices and concomitantly climbing monetary production, the inflation was also marked by the episodic dwindling of coinage. At the outbreak of war this was tugged in two directions as the public, apprehensive of the consequences of war, hoarded its cash, and the government, facing the same situation, melted it down for

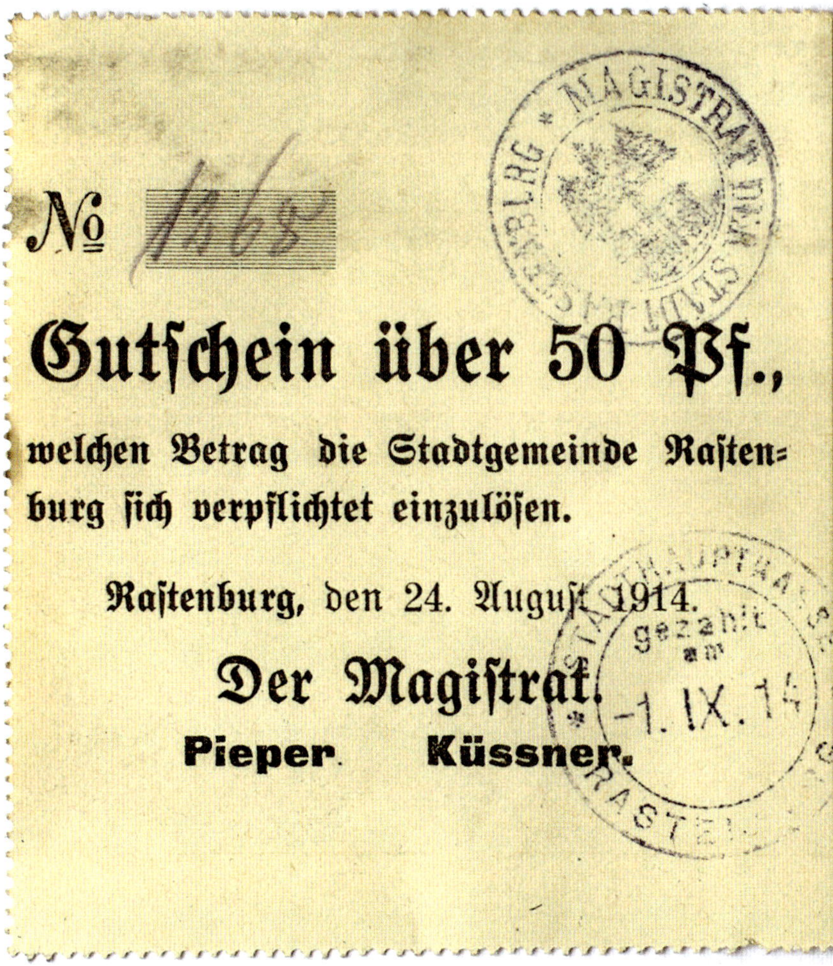

Notgeld from Rastenburg, 1914. Warburg Institute, London.

its metallic content, or withdrew it for the purchase of materiel. In response to this lack, businesses began to issue crude tokens in order to give change to their customers. They also printed them to pay their staff, a strategy with obvious economic benefits. Municipalities did the same, hoping to thereby keep their local economies going. In doing so they had at first the approval of the central government, which insisted on a nominal backing—a principal that was increasingly honored in the breach. The strategy certainly had immediate benefits, but eventually its attendant dangers became apparent, too.

Starting in 1916 and continuing until after the defeat, another shrinkage of the supply of small change led to a second wave of

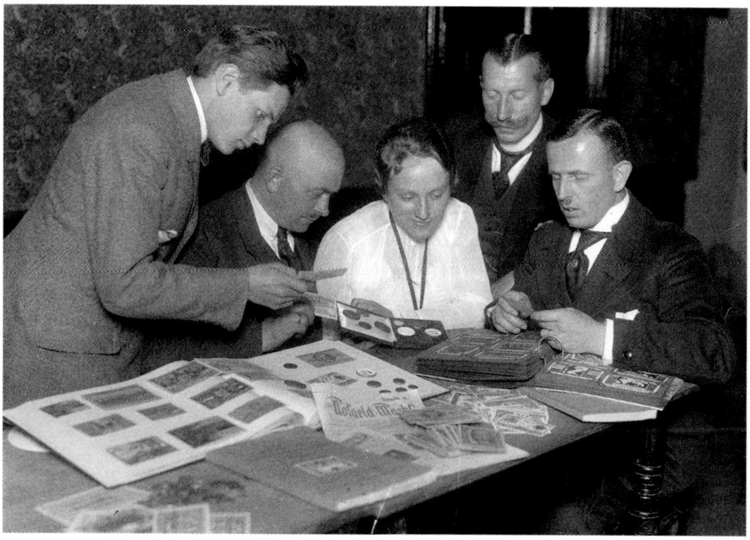

Willy Römer, Members of the Berlin Notgeld Collectors' Association, 1923. Kunstbibliothek, Berlin.

Notgeld issues, often more elaborately designed than those of 1914. A collector's market began to develop around these objects, along with fairs and magazines, and so enterprising parties started producing notes aimed directly at these buyers. When the economic situation briefly stabilized between 1920 and 1921, visually striking notes were printed in enormous quantities by municipalities hoping to improve their finances. In order to prevent their redemption, these often had no validity at all. In response to this proliferation, and in the context of rising inflation, Notgeld was suppressed by government decree on July 17, 1922. However, when the French invaded the Ruhr the next year, the rules regarding Notgeld were relaxed in order to support the policy of passive resistence, and examples with huge denominations appeared. At the climax of the crisis there were around 5,800 points of issue, and something in the order of 500 trillion marks' worth of unbacked emergency notes had been brought into circulation.[7]

As well as being extraordinarily plentiful, Notgeld was also very varied in appearance, and strikingly dissimilar to conventional currency in these terms—as Hablik's excremental note demonstrates. The growing peculiarity of the money, what we might call its aesthetic inflation, was driven in large part by the aim of appealing to collectors. In several cases emergency currency was not even printed on paper, with some issuers making

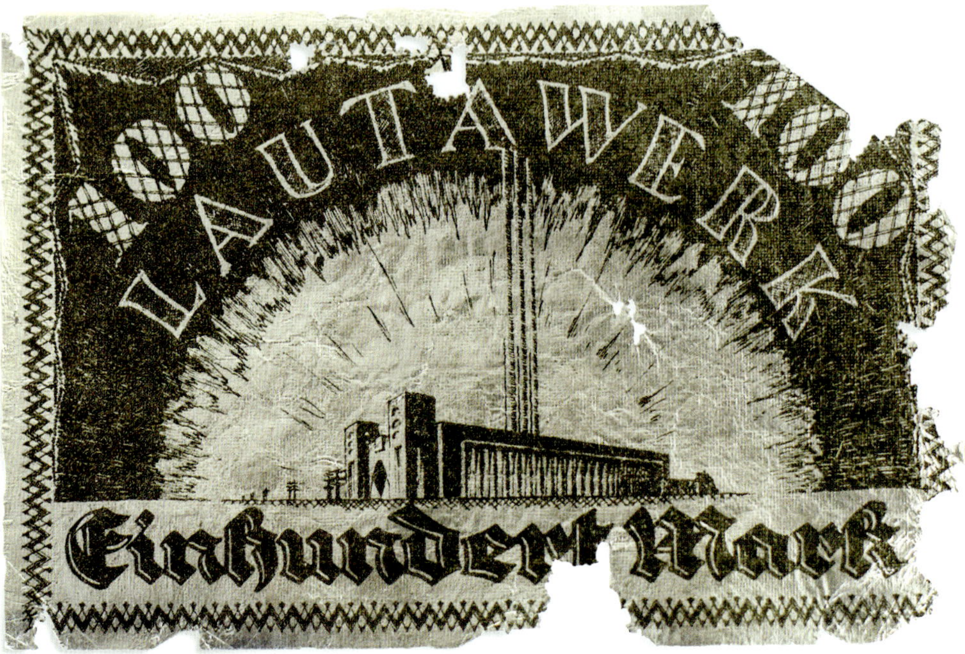

Notgeld from the Lautawerk aluminum factory, Lauta, 1922. Fitzwilliam Museum, Cambridge.

money out of the commodities produced by their local industries. In Dresden there were porcelain coins, for example; in Bielefeld, rectangles of brightly colored silk; a coal company based in Röthenbach in the Ruhr issued coins made from disks of compressed coal dust (few of these have survived, as their use value soon exceeded any other factors encouraging their retention); and an aluminum factory printed notes on extremely friable foil. As well as images of bodily functions, these objects were adorned with depictions of witches, skeletons, and demons, and also humorous or sometimes bitter references to the crisis itself, in the form of empty purses, piles of worthless money, and the dance around the golden calf.

These were quite unlike the banknotes of the preceding imperial period, the clichéd attributes of which Walter Benjamin enumerated in his book *One-Way Street* (this was published in 1928, but Benjamin had begun working on the manuscript at the height of the inflation): "Nowhere more naively than in these documents does capitalism display itself in solemn earnest. The innocent cupids frolicking about numbers, the goddesses holding tablets

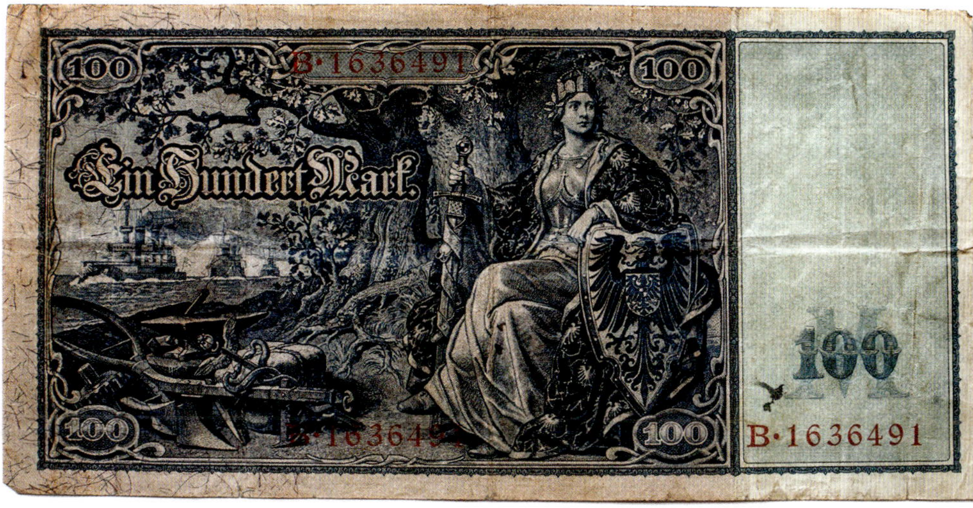

Flottenhunderter, 1908. Warburg Institute, London.

of the law, the stalwart heroes sheathing their swords before monetary units, are a world of their own: ornamenting the facade of hell."[8] The allegorical jumble delineated by Benjamin evokes Wilhelmine paper money like the so-called *Flottenhunderter*, "fleet hundred," a jingoistic note of 1908 on which the figure of Germania, reminiscent of Dürer's *Melencolia*, is cheered up by the arrival of some new warships;[9] and his sulfuric peroration may simply be a reiteration of the conventional figurative terms of the left—there was, after all, something hellish about capitalism to Marx.[10] However, given that these words were written shortly after the inflation, it seems quite possible that the diabolical facade to which Benjamin refers may in fact have been emergency money, which was in many cases literally hellish, swarming with supernatural beings.

Benjamin introduced his monetary iconography by stating that "a descriptive analysis of banknotes is needed." This demand—which was surely piqued by the era's proliferating currency—has often been cited by commentators on the aesthetics of money.[11] It has rarely been satisfactorily fulfilled. Furthermore, Benjamin and the other writers associated with the Frankfurt School have rarely been invoked in discussions of the culture of the inflation, though the relationship between culture and economics was central to their inquiries, and despite their lives and ideas having been forged in this crucible. Admittedly, there is a hole in the pocket of Benjamin's own analysis. As Marc Shell has pointed out,

> Benjamin mentions coinage only once in his essay ["The Work of Art in the Age of Its Technical Reproducibility"], although it serves better than photography as a case study of the relation between or confusion of reproduction and production. ... Coins are themselves both artful reproductions and active participants in the sum total of the relations of production. They are things ontologically equal to each other as products of the same die, and money, which they symbolize, equalizes *in potentia* all (other) things. ... Coinage ... heralded the modern age of mechanical reproduction.[12]

This book is an attempt rectify these lacunae. It does so in part by fulfilling Benjamin's demand for analytic description, but beyond this, and the familiar art historical questions posed earlier regarding the motivations of Notgeld designers and their patrons, the distinctiveness of emergency money also raises some broader questions about the aesthetics of currency, the way it functions as a circulating medium, and how these two fields intersect. These multitudes of emergency notes moved in a complex image economy that incorporated the wider world of image production but also frequently ran in the same circuits as that of the so-called real economy. These pieces of paper were both money, albeit of a peculiar sort, and also, in a modest sense, works of art. Like the real economy, in this period the German image economy also experienced recurrent stoppages and leaks, eruptions and regurgitations; indeed, it was convulsed by paroxysms as never before. Complex feedback loops developed between the two spheres of activity, with the result that this material, Notgeld, is not just a site in which the impact of economic forces can be traced in the visual realm. It is also a test case for the hypothesis that the current can be reversed: that the visual can determine the economic.

In arguing this point, it should be noted, I am not making a case for the inversion of the economic and cultural spheres but rather for a nuanced mediation between the two, one that, as we shall see, cleaves closely to material factors. Before we come to these questions, and the degree to which—and routes whereby—the movements of these two parallel economies were linked, an explanation is owing regarding the phrase *image economy*.[13] By this I mean a network for the production, circulation, and use of images, and the intertwinement of this system with flows of capital.

Crucially, although the term might suggest submission before the disciplinary imperialism that has attempted to bring all domains of inquiry beneath the flag of economics, I am not asserting an absolute identity here—that is, the reduction of images to economics, or indeed vice versa. Instead, I insist on the difference of these two spheres, which partake, nevertheless, of a closely mediated relationality. I thereby wish to reassert the material aspect of the study of the image and its movements.[14] The constituent parts of image economies have of course been examined elsewhere; however, by employing this material as a lens, a particularly sharp picture can be developed of such a nexus.[15] Motifs and figures circulate here, moving between picture postcards, notes crumpled in people's pockets, and canvases hung in galleries. Images serve as a medium of exchange and become stores of value; these phenomena are particularly eye-catching from our own vantage point, when blue chip art collections are stored in high-security free ports, entirely shorn of what Benjamin called their "exhibition value" and reduced instead to pure exchange value; meanwhile, the most up-to-date monetary technology, the blockchain, has fused with the artwork in the form of the nonfungible token (NFT).[16] Equally familiar is inflation—indeed, uncomfortably so, since on the hundredth anniversary of the hyperinflation's peak, this exorbitant tendency stalks the globe once more. This force affected the image economy of the German inflation, too, when images mounted up in quantity and were inevitably devalued. Yet despite the heuristic potential of Notgeld, and despite the fact that it offers one of the most extensive funds of visual material regarding one of the most remarked episodes of twentieth-century history, in art historical terms it remains almost unstudied, excepting two essays by Erin Sullivan Maynes and Christine Künzel.[17] These contain suggestive reflections on the material, and call, in the latter instance, for an "iconography of Notgeld"; something along these lines will be attempted here, but not only this.[18] I will also ask about the particular characteristics of this strange medium.

The Political Economy of the Sign

Money behaved in some very peculiar ways during the inflation. In order to measure how far it strayed from its customary functions, we must first establish how the latter are constituted. This question opens a can of extremely lively worms; writers on the subject are scarcely able to agree on the most basic principles regarding what money is and does.[19] In accordance with the emphasis of this book, I will focus on two aspects of monetary theory: its dual status as sign and medium. These categories are by no means clear-cut: money is a sign of value, but arguably of other things, too—indeed, it has been called *the* sign, the structure of which determines all other signs. And while it is conventionally called a medium of exchange, it is also a medium of value and of other signs. It has been used as an artistic medium, too, as we shall see later.

Reflections on money's semiological status flourished following Jean-Joseph Goux's work in the late 1960s, when he theorized that money's structure was paralleled by the organization of what he saw as the other dominant signifying systems, "father, phallus and language."[20] Shortly afterward, Jean Baudrillard mapped the structure of the commodity onto the structure of the sign, arguing against "the artificial distinction between the economic and the ideological."[21] That the sign is a commodity is persuasive, as is Baudrillard's parallel point, that the commodity is a sign, and these ideas would influence a number of art historians, stimulating a productive refocusing on the realm of circulation, especially in the historiography of modern design. I am thinking here in particular of Frederic Schwartz's book on the Werkbund, in which he argues convincingly for the trademark as a Baudrillardian commodity-sign.[22] Notgeld occupies a similarly ambiguous position, being simultaneously commodity and sign, artwork and money, and so Baudrillard's theory has some bearing here. However, the radical nature of his claim—his assertion that the "very form [of the commodity] establishes it as a total medium, as a system of communication administering all social exchange"—has problematic implications.[23] These are sketched at his essay's conclusion, where calls for revolution in the realm of production are superseded by a demand for revolution in the realm of signification. Seen from a distance of 50 years, these theorists appear to have something in common with their neoliberal context, in which money was viewed as a language, a means of conveying information (so-called price signals). Furthermore, the question of causality was bracketed by this approach, a move that allowed its proponents to avoid the pitfalls of vulgar Marxism but tended to throw the baby of history out with the bathwater of determinism.[24] I will return to these questions in chapter 2.

More recently, following the flourishing of media theory in the 1990s (and especially the "media archaeology" inaugurated by Friedrich Kittler), attention has begun to turn to the question of money as medium. In an essay on the subject, Jens Schröter observed that while money was frequently described as such in the works of the classical economists, the idea has not been taken up by media theorists.[25] However, he notes what he regards as a striking congruence between Friedrich Kittler's tripartite definition of the medium and the three functions of money as it is conventionally understood: on the one hand, a technology for the transmission, storage, and processing of information, and, on the other, a medium of exchange, a store of value, and a unit of account. This comparison, which echoes Goux's correlation of these functions to the three Lacanian orders, seems to me rather facile and to partake—as Goux and his followers had done—too readily of the tendency to overemphasize money's role as a bearer of information. Furthermore, I would suggest that attempting to map one schema directly onto the other conceals the reason for Kittler's "surprising" neglect of money, despite his readiness to see other artifacts as media. Any investigation in this direction would have required a confrontation with the kind of questions his account programmatically circumvents—matters of political economy, in other words. Kittler's media are unquestionably more substantial, more materially constituted than those of many writers in the field; nevertheless, without a political economy his remains an incomplete materialism. And however useful his approach has been for describing the behavior of other media, when it comes to money, such questions cannot simply be ignored. An approach to money from this angle, while taking money's media status seriously by using the best available tools for analyzing the discursive functions of media technologies, would also force a productive engagement of such theory with matter beyond the realm of discourse—from which Kittler, despite his proclaimed intentions, never escapes. Putting these reservations aside, Schröter has nevertheless uncovered a fecund stratum for a media archaeology of money, proposing that the particular task of such an investigation would be to understand the way in which the material of the medium is used to stabilize its value. Coming at the question from a different angle, Gottfried Gabriel has asked how the images and inscriptions on money shore up belief in its value.[26] Stabilization, employing what we might think of as techniques for the inculcation of faith, was particularly important in a moment in which value had come into question as never before. Schröter and Gabriel have opened promising lines of inquiry in terms of the media archaeology and political iconography they respectively espouse; I suggest that these approaches, alongside the Baudrillardian emphasis on the ambiguous commodity-sign, can be taken further by looking beneath the skin, to the value congealed in these objects—and its sources.[27]

To rebalance the account, we must return to Marx, but—in view of Hablik's scatology—I go to him via Bataille, borrowing the latter's base materialism as a bulwark against the idealist tendencies outlined above.[28] For Marx, money's medium status was subtly—and, of course, materially—constituted. In his view, under capitalism money is one stage of the metabolic process whereby capital is transformed into commodities and back again. It is therefore not simply a medium facilitating the exchange of commodities but the alpha and omega of the money-commodity-money equation. Furthermore, though it is, like the commodity, a medium of value—albeit one that conceals the source of this value—it is no mere sign. It is instead, to borrow Marx's viscous terminology, a *congealment* of value, that is, of a relation between humans and nature. This is why Marx adopts the biochemical term *Stoffwechsel*, metabolism—literally, "material exchange"—to designate the fundamental economic process of capitalism. It has been objected that, because Marx was concerned with the "money commodity," that is, with gold, his analysis has been rendered obsolete with the obsolescence of the latter as currency. In Marx's words, token money (like banknotes) is the symbol of money, but it maintains the characteristics and functions of its antecedent just as long as it is backed by commodity money and its currency is enforced by the power of the state.[29] This is a peculiar type of sign, then, functionally identical with what it signifies—and the signification of which is maintained by violence. In light of the above, the psychological component of money's function also becomes evident: the users of money must be convinced of its value, by force if necessary. However, in the situation under consideration here, this backing was absent and the power of the state disintegrated into thousands of local money-issuing bodies. The story of Notgeld-as-medium is the story of these disintegrations, and it therefore allows, from its borderline status, a critical reflection on money's customary functions and their failures. As well as plotting these deviations throughout the course of this text, I will return to Marx's concept of the medium when Hablik's note showing a shitting figure drags idealist conceptions of money back down to earth—not with a conservative or mystificatory grounding, as in some other cases, but with an unstoppable scatological explosion. It thereby forces us to reconsider the economic process as part of what Georges Bataille called "general economy," that is, the cosmic circulation of energy of which the economy, understood in its limited sense, is only a small part (images are another).[30]

This book groups Notgeld into four iconographic categories, each of which corresponds to major thematic questions regarding these objects and the period in which they were made. In dividing my analysis thus, I run the risk of emphasizing image over value, but in each case I have bound these two aspects as closely as possible. It must also be admitted that this division, though responding to the predominant motifs on this money, is nevertheless (inevitably) somewhat whimsical, not least because many instances of Notgeld could be fitted into more than one of the categories. It might be asked why I have elected not to organize my book according to the periodization established by the earliest collectors of Notgeld; though useful, this schema was inspired by the question of what constitutes "true" Notgeld (i.e., issued as a medium of exchange, and not as a collectible), and this is not my concern. Instead, it is structured in a way that allows me to interrogate methods of stabilization, or techniques of faith, working from those notes that conform to this apparently essential characteristic of the medium to those that confound and even countermand it. The first chapter deals with images of place, the most common category of stabilizing motifs on these notes. Here I have gathered, alongside landscapes, all those motifs that refer to the area in which the Notgeld was produced, for instance landmarks, famous people, episodes from local history, and so on, producing a panorama of the conventional iconography of Notgeld and establishing a benchmark against which deviations and critique can be measured. The second chapter is concerned with images of labor, another common category of stabilizing motifs. I also take this opportunity to depart from iconography and discuss the labor of the artists who designed these objects. The third chapter focuses on quite a different sort of note, this time apparently destabilizing: those featuring supernatural beings such as ghosts and witches, and also demonizing caricatures of Jews, which were all too common a feature of this money. I incorporate a discussion of expressionistic Notgeld into this chapter, as this tendency—which was frequently employed by designers of emergency money—is conventionally understood as being concerned with the realm of spirit. The fourth chapter looks at images that explicitly refer to the inflationary crisis, especially those depicting acts of defecation, asking how these images can be squared with the media theory of money outlined in this introduction: that is, the demand for stabilization. Indeed, as well as abrogating this demand, these excremental notes—especially those designed by Hablik—appear as a comment and critique on the most common techniques of stabilization, references to land and labor. I conclude chapter 4 by proposing a speculative, base-materialist theory of money in response to these notes. Finally, in the epilogue I turn to the afterlife of Notgeld in the work of the artist Karl Hermann Trinkaus, who employed the material to retrospectively critique money as a medium following the catastrophe of 1933.

1 *Land*

Where nature bears the imprint of history, that is to say where it is a setting, does it not have a numismatic quality?
Walter Benjamin, *The Origin of German Tragic Drama*, 1928

On August 11, 1919, the provisional German government—then in exile in Weimar due to street fighting in the capital—signed a new constitution into law. Besides confirming that Germany was no longer a monarchy but a democratic republic, the document transformed the legal status of German territory. Article 155 of this document proclaimed that the state would oversee the use of land with the aim of ensuring a home for every citizen. To that end, properties could be expropriated, and "the entailed estates are to be dissolved." These words announced that inherited lands were to be salable, that is, soluble by the power of money: it was, in other words, the end of feudalism—at least on paper.[1] The reality on the ground was more complicated, and these complications worked their way into people's pockets.

One of the most popular stabilizing strategies employed by designers of emergency money was the representation of place; indeed, notes featuring such images constitute the majority of this material. In this, they did not entirely depart from the conventions of the medium: banknotes of all countries feature national personifications, heraldic symbols, and the like. However, whereas on standard money the place in question was the nation as a whole, now the burden of stabilization devolved to more localized referents: to the region, city, town, and even to the county or village. In view of the circumscription of these notes, which could only be redeemed in the places they were issued, this is unsurprising. As a consequence of this situation, banknote designers, who had previously had a stock of well-worn signifiers to hand, were faced with a challenge: they now had to concoct new means of referring to place. These included coats of arms, landscapes and landmarks, significant figures associated with the region, and episodes from local folklore and history. More topical events were also shown, and at a council meeting in Halle in 1921 it was even jocularly suggested that scenes of the recent communist uprising be illustrated on the city's notes.[2]

Beyond its iconographic ramifications, the localization of money also had frustrating practical consequences, and anecdotes abound regarding the difficulties that ensued. In an article on Notgeld published in 1923, Siegfried Kracauer relates a type of incident that is familiar from accounts of the time, "a true tale of woe involving ten million-mark notes from the Kassel Railway." These, their bearer finds, are useless when he arrives at his destination, Frankfurt, where he is sent from pillar to post in order to try to resolve the difficulty—without success. Hence "emergency money is not only the result of emergency, it also causes emergency, too."[3] How much truer must this have been on a macro level, where the brake this localization put on the national economy can only be speculated about, not to speak of the psychological effects on bearers of these dubious notes.

Later, when Notgeld began to be printed specifically for sale to collectors, such practical difficulties no longer arose. The redemption of these notes was often no longer possible at all, since they were intended to be retained by their purchasers, thereby guaranteeing their issuers the sum paid for them. Nevertheless, they often retained a strong local flavor. This was partly an attempt to appeal to local buyers, who would, it was hoped, be moved to support their municipalities by purchasing such issues, and also to collectors further afield, whose interest might be piqued by the relatively exotic imagery, as well as by the desire to assemble a geographically representative collection.

In this chapter, I discuss some examples of this localizing Notgeld, setting it in the context of discourse around place that occupied the period during which it was produced, and I measure it against the requirements of stabilization inherent to the medium. Place was highly contested at the time, both in discursive and physical terms, and emergency money was one of the key arenas in which this discourse was elaborated.[4] The relationship between the local and the national that is constructed on these notes oscillates between yearning and resentment, reflecting the centripetal and centrifugal forces that tugged the Weimar Republic this way and that. This tension was not new to Germany, which had only been united in 1871; from the outset, the country's federal structure was disputed by particularist factions. In the tumultuous inflationary period, enemies of the republican government often turned to their local *Heimat* or homeland as an antidote to what they perceived as an illegitimate and chaotic state; others pined for the supposed unity of the prewar empire, for the Heimat as a national entity. These tendencies were not necessarily exclusive. The notion of Heimat is a slippery one: it could be at once local and national, and it could serve liberal and even socialist demands. Yet, as expressed on Notgeld, these localizing strategies were almost exclusively animated by a conservative impetus toward rootedness. This was in part an attempt to cancel out the solvent power of money, which was widely perceived to be one of the main factors disturbing connections to place, and indeed the possibility of place itself. However, this anchoring strategy was enacted using the very medium the effect of which it was intended to counteract.

The first wave of emergency money, which was issued shortly after the war began in 1914, consisted of simple slips of paper. These had very low denominations and were often printed with the word *Gutschein*, token, to distinguish them from "real" money. They were usually also stamped with the municipal crest, which symbolized the local origin of the note, alongside the signature of a magistrate or some other official to authenticate them. These bureaucrats must surely have been exhausted by the incessant demand on their money-producing powers—hence, perhaps, the development of more elaborately printed notes toward the end of the war, when these symbols were joined by views of town and country. These were often designated *Kriegsnotgeld*, war emergency money, and frequently showed landscapes defended by soldiers. Sometimes these figures were dressed in antiquated armor, as in a note from Villingen issued in 1918, which features a local hero of the sixteenth century, Remigius Mans. He stands guard before an aerial perspective of Old Villingen, barring the way of foreign attackers but also, the anachronistic vision implies, protecting the nation's past from the chaos of the present. Otto

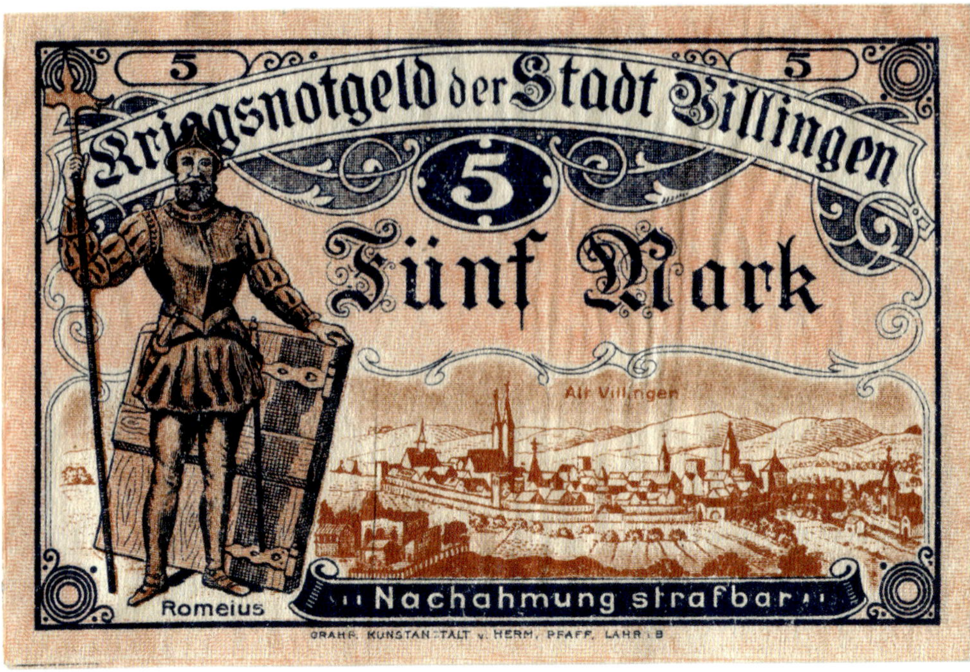

Notgeld from Villingen, 1918. Collection of the author.

Dix spent the inflation's most tumultuous years, from 1920 to 1923, working on a more modern perspective of war: his scandalous painting *The Trench*, a landscape composed of piles of rotting human flesh. This was the new landscape of conflict in the early twentieth century, one viewed from the stinking thick of things; on the Villingen note, by contrast, we see things from the ruler's viewpoint.[5]

The general intent behind these images of land is made explicit on a note designed for Genthin by the Erfurt-based expressionist Alfred Hanf in 1921. The note shows the town on either side of its canal, a waterway joining Berlin to Hamburg and hence an important economic landscape; the image was topical as the government had legislated to extend the canal to the Ruhr the previous year. Above this scene is written: "Your belief makes this scrap of paper into money, so believe in the *Vaterland* and build your world for yourself." Like all localizing strategies of stabilization, this coupling is perilous. Jochen Hörisch has remarked that conventional coins join crowned head and value in an inextricably circular economy, where each one props up the other; but as

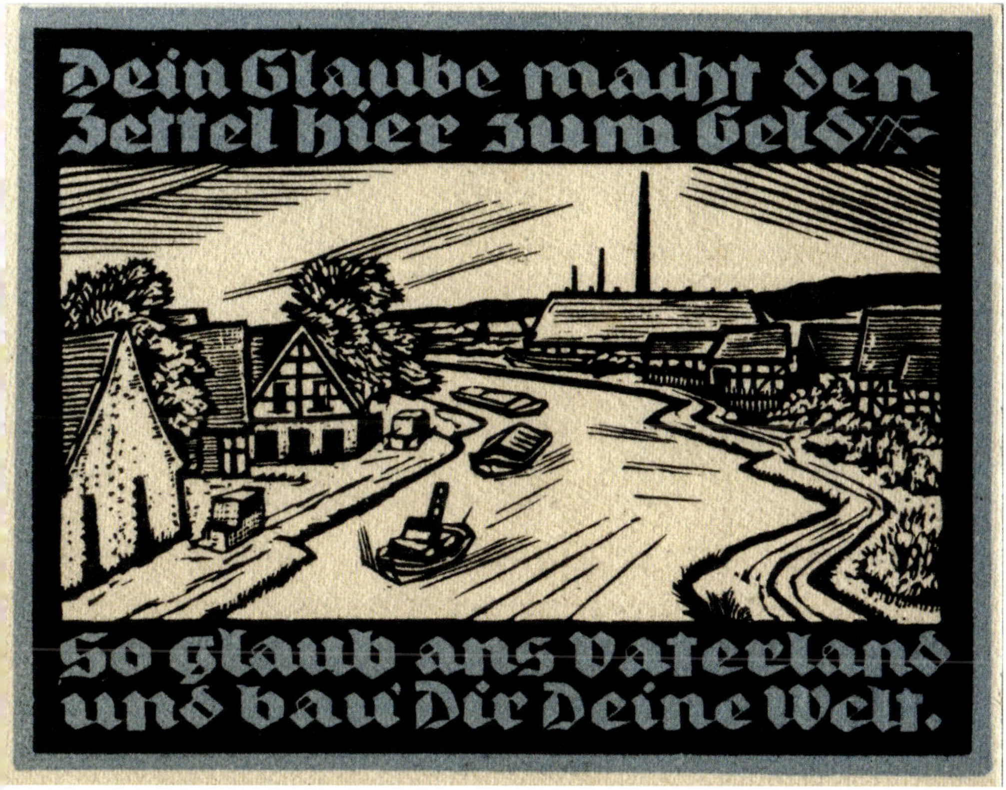

Notgeld from Genthin, designed by Alfred Hanf, 1921. Collection of the author.

a result of their connection, the devaluation of one likewise leads to the other's depreciation.[6] So too with Notgeld that identifies with its place of issue. In the case of Genthin, if you were to stop believing in the value of the local money, the implication is that you will also stop believing in the *Vaterland*—and hence, its ability to cover the money it issues, thus leading to a spiral of mistrust. Such vicious circles, though psychological in nature, have very real economic effects: they lie behind most stock market crashes, when contagious fear leads to cataclysmic destructions of value. When it comes to Notgeld, this strategy is worse than risky, since the image of land is fatally conjoined to a value that is already almost valueless, and promises to evaporate yet further.

Perhaps this explains the rather plaintive quality of the imperative expressed on the Genthin note. While the message is unusual in its frankness, its iconography is not. Most of these localizing notes adhere closely to the conventions of picturesque landscape

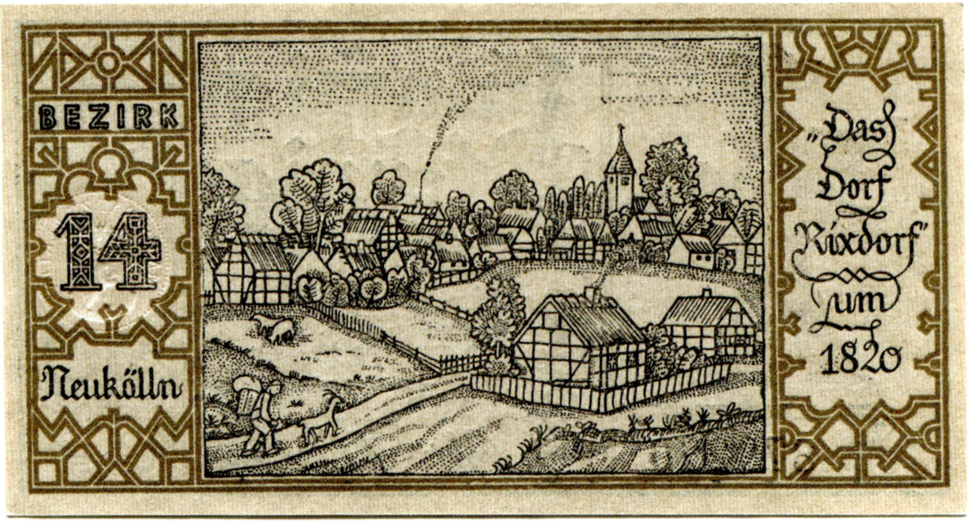

Notgeld from Berlin, 1921. Collection of the author.

and quaint townscape, although they vary widely in terms of the quality and style of the image. Sometimes, however, the scenes selected to represent places are somewhat less predictable, and all the more revealing for that. When in 1921 Berlin issued a series of notes showing each of its districts, it chose to illustrate the city before industrialization, a time when Berlin was hardly a city at all. To give one example, Neukölln, which in the 1920s was notorious for its louche morals, is represented by an idyllic depiction of Rixdorf, which had been the name of the area when it was still a village (ironically, the name had been changed in order to shake off the district's dubious associations, which were long-standing). Though strikingly anachronous in the context of Germany's most modern city, in their nostalgic affect the Berlin notes are very much of their moment. A large proportion of Notgeld notes hark back to idealized earlier periods; in this moment of crisis, the cities—especially Berlin—were widely seen as being dissolute, and as threatening to infect the healthy and moral countryside. But whereas medieval centers could call on a well-stocked supply of gothic architecture, the much newer city of Berlin had to look back to a more modest history, and one that had since been all but eradicated—in other words, it had to exhume a usable past from beneath the morass of late nineteenth-century speculative development. In doing so, it sought to provincialize the metropolis: to Heimatize that which threatened the Heimat.[7]

Yet more modern scenes were sometimes depicted as well. Industrial landscapes were not uncommon on notes from Germany's manufacturing centers, especially those issued by towns located in the coalfields of Silesia and the Ruhr Valley. Here, though land is still a guarantor of value, it is no longer valuable in quite the same way as in the old, conservative sense. It no longer has that numinous form of land value that appears ontologically inherent but in fact derives from long-standing, exploitative modes of value extraction, by the scythe and by rent, which have been enveloped in mystery following centuries of encrustation by law, tradition, and representation.[8] Here, instead, the mode is novel and lies very close to the surface, the smokestack serving as a symbol for the extraction of value out of the earth. New and disturbing though they may be, these industrial structures are thereby still signs of the value-stabilizing function of place and, if represented with sufficiently steely romanticism, can be rooted in the soil, as in an example from the "industrial city" Pößneck. In 1922, even a

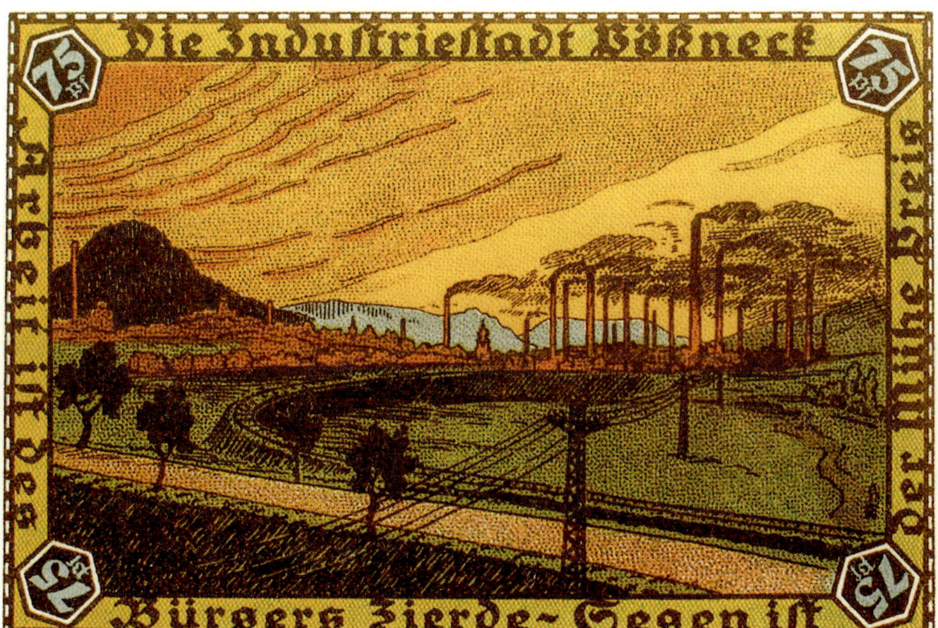

Notgeld from Pößneck, 1921. Fitzwilliam Museum, Cambridge.

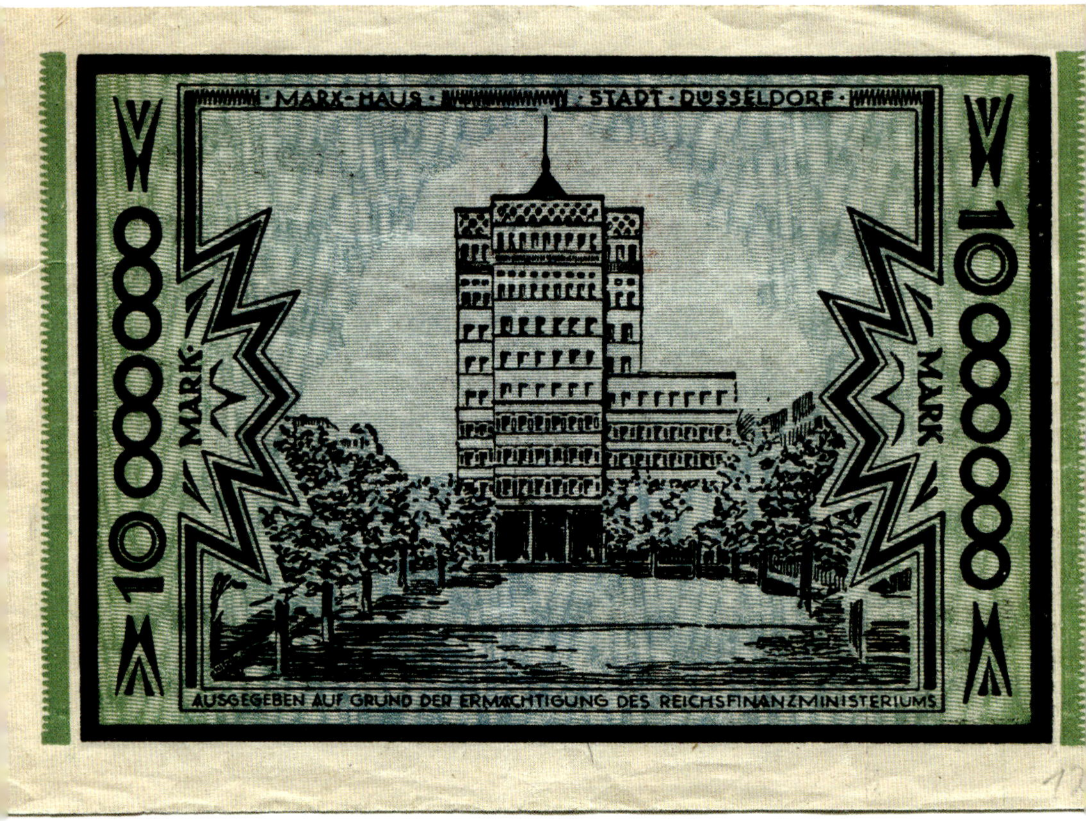

Notgeld from Düsseldorf, 1923. Collection of the author.

reactionary such as Oswald Spengler could say that "industry, too, is earth-bound like the yeoman. It has its station, and its materials stream out of the earth."[9]

Occasionally, modernist landmarks were also employed to signify place, as in a 1923 note showing the new Wilhelm-Marx-Haus in Düsseldorf, one of Germany's earliest skyscrapers. Such a boosterish insistence on modernity is rare, but hardly incongruous in the context of an industrial region. In the construction boom of 1922, industrialists in the prosperous west built many new plants, office buildings, and workers' housing using profits derived from dumping cheap German goods on international markets over the course of the preceding year; however, by the time this note was printed, the Ruhr was under French occupation, inflation had turned into hyperinflation, and the regional economy was in total stasis.[10] Sometimes, notes were successfully used to raise money for building projects, so-called *Bausteinscheine*. The town hall in Naumburg was renovated using funds raised by the sale of Notgeld; so too was the Volkshaus in Leipzig, a large trade unions facility that had been bombed by the Reichswehr during the Kapp Putsch in 1920, under the pretext of suspicions that the Spartacists were operating out of the building. Thanks in part to Notgeld sales it was reopened in 1921, a rare instance of an oppositional space made, or remade, by these means.

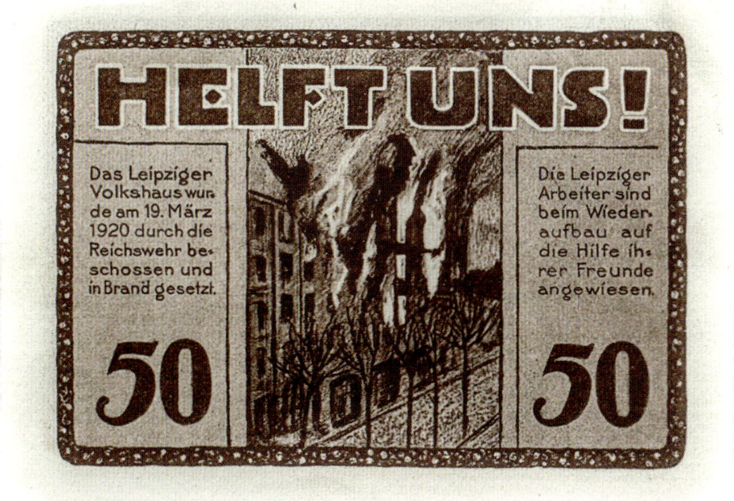

Notgeld depicting the Volkshaus, Leipzig, 1920. Warburg Institute, London.

Local People, Local Voices

As well as landscapes and townscapes, local people of note are also a regular feature of Notgeld. These figures are often also of national significance, and so this emergency money is able to simultaneously assert both the significance of the local and its participation in the national. Bismarck, as a figurehead of the old Reich, was a particularly effective mediating term in this relation, and thus ubiquitous: he appeared on a series designed for Genthin by Alfred Hanf (where he is depicted at different stages of his life), and also on individual examples from Hamburg (which shows the Bismarck monument in that city); Stroebeck (where he appears with a chessboard, and is labeled the "world chess master"); Jerichow (where the other side shows the local house in which he was born); and Jever (where he is paired with the local Bismarck Tower, one of many such monuments that were erected around the nation in his memory). Via such linkages the image of Bismarck—who was himself celebrated for producing a unitary place, namely, the German Reich—is deployed in the attempt to reaffirm a link between the nation and the particular locale. It hardly needs to be added that he also mediates between the past and present, as he stood for the erstwhile empire, and not the dubious new republic.

At the other end of the political spectrum, August Bebel, cofounder of the Social Democratic Party (SDP), is shown on a series of notes issued by Glauchau, which was located in the first constituency to elect him (indeed, it was the first constituency to elect any member of his party). These retell a humorous anecdote regarding the local police force's surveillance of Bebel, who was seen as posing a danger to the state at the time of his election. Annoyed by this harassment, the story goes, the politician sought his revenge by walking back and forth across the town holding an enormous blood sausage behind his back. His police guard was forced to follow him and the sausage, and so, infuriated at being made a spectacle, they detained him in the county courthouse. This note demonstrates that, though usually conservative in tenor, localizing emergency money sometimes—albeit, very rarely—evinced sympathies with oppositional elements. Bebel appears once more on a series of notes issued by the SDP in Emden in 1921; other examples show Engels, Karl Liebknecht, and Marx. The local is not necessarily reactionary, these notes suggest, and can in

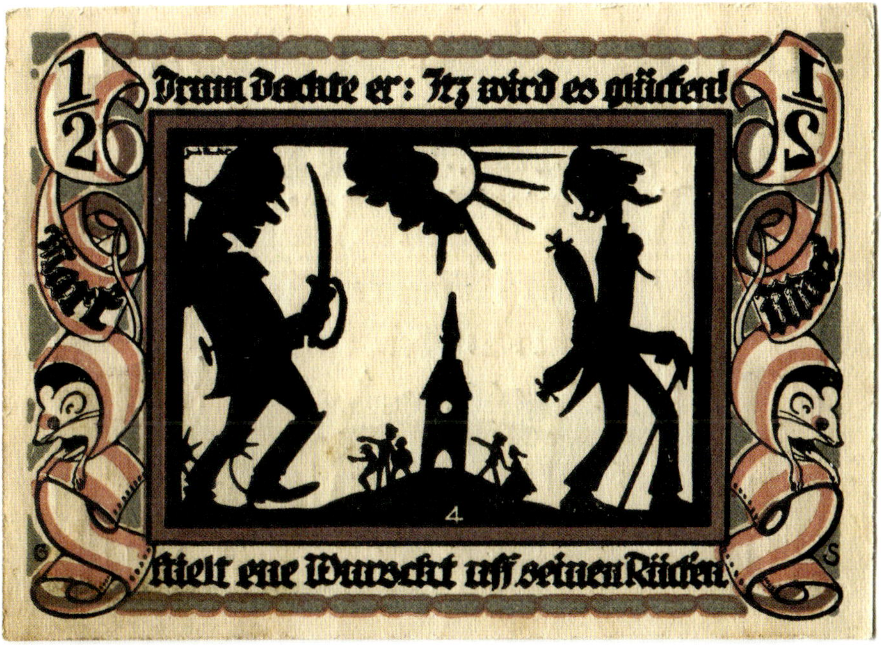

Notgeld from Glauchau, 1921. Collection of the author.

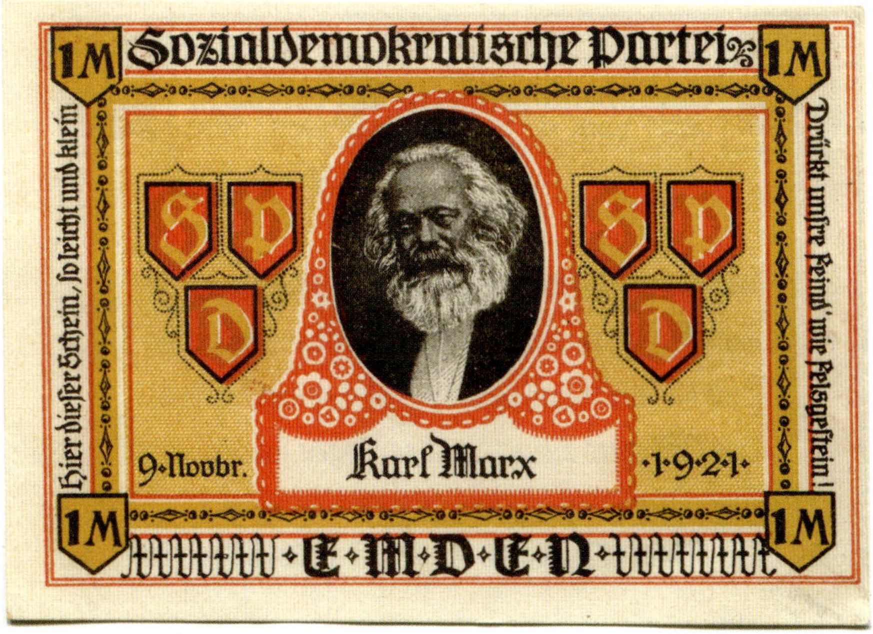

Notgeld from Emden, 1921. Collection of the author.

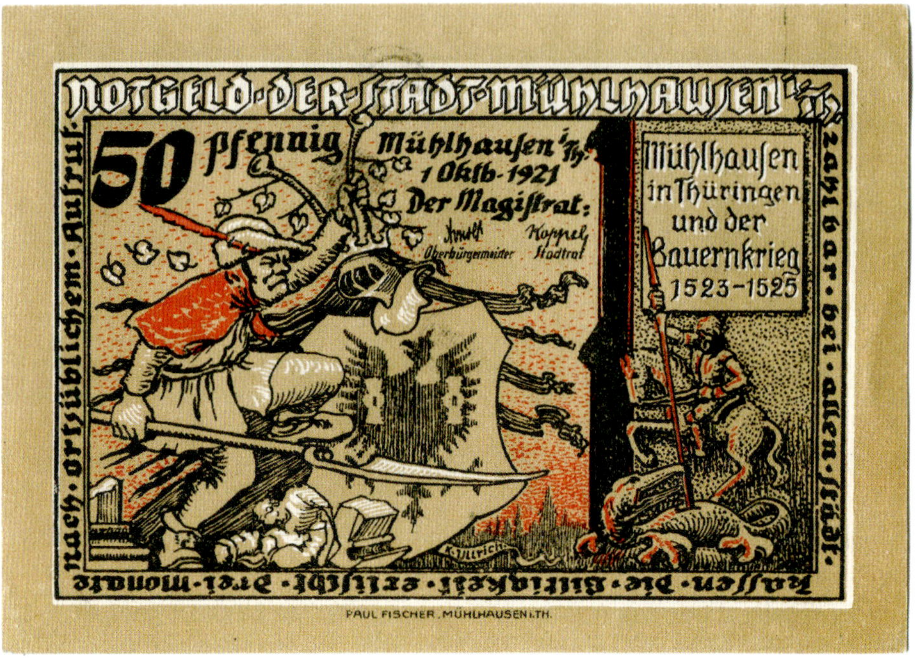

Notgeld from Mühlhausen, 1921 (front and back). Collection of the author.

fact be a source of opposition against repression. More common, however, were series that recalled historical uprisings such as the Peasant's War, with an emphasis on the gruesome end that came to their participants; the latter were rarely depicted with any sympathy. At a time of widespread food riots, the pertinence of these cautionary tales regarding the consequences of social unrest could hardly have gone unnoticed.

As well as politicians, artists also appear on many examples of Notgeld. The aspiration behind such notes was diagnosed with acuteness by the author Ernst Jünger, although he was thinking of the official banknotes of the republic, which likewise attempted to shore up their value with images of cultural heroes. "There is hardly a stamp, hardly a banknote, on which we do not encounter this kind of thing," he wrote, a phenomenon that he attributed to "the bourgeois lack of instinct in relation to value. It is a question of a kind of opium through which danger is disguised and the deceptive sense of a kind of order is evoked."[11] Jünger was writing from the far right, and in 1932: a moment in which danger was to be embraced, in his view, and not smothered beneath monuments to Dürer, whose works were a constant presence on the republic's

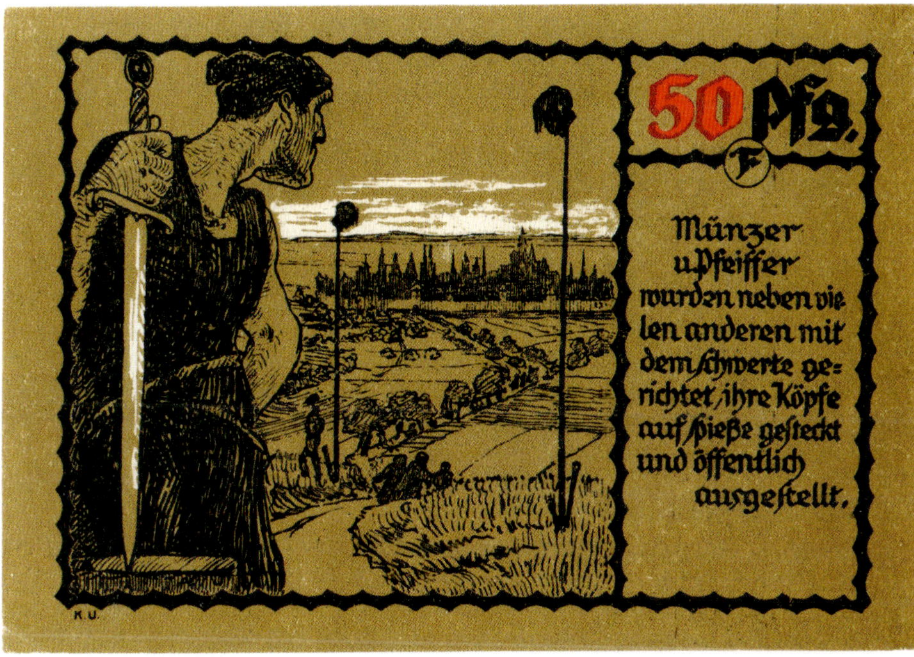

banknotes. Yet his observation that these classical figures decorating dubious notes are intended to disguise and even to evade the crisis of value is not without merit. In attempting to produce itself as a *Kulturnation* via images on money, the republic enlisted aesthetic value to support exchange value, with the result that, as the value of the notes in question evaporated, the culture it was using as a prop was also bankrupted.

This self-defeating strategy was also employed by Notgeld designers. Goethe is depicted on a number of notes, as are scenes from his works (I return to these in a later chapter). He usually appears in some place associated with him, but, as with Bismarck, he figures at the same time for the entire German nation, thanks to his role as a national cultural hero. He is, unsurprisingly, to be found on several notes from Weimar, where he lived, and he is also represented by his famous garden house in that city. A different structure associated with the writer appears on one particularly striking note, part of a series issued by the resort town of Ilmenau, where Goethe stayed on numerous occasions. On one of these visits, which probably took place in 1780, Goethe spent a night in a little shelter on a hill, where, moved by his surroundings, he wrote a poem—one of his most famous—directly onto the wooden wall of the building. In Longfellow's translation:

> O'er all the hilltops
> Is quiet now,
> In all the treetops
> Hearest thou
> Hardly a breath;
> The birds are asleep in the trees:
> Wait, soon like these
> Thou too shalt rest.

On the piece of emergency money in question, we see the famous writer sitting on a bench before the hut, gazing (we presume) at the landscape beneath him; the iconography had by that point become standardized. At either side, the lines of "Wanderers Nachtlied II" are reproduced in a pseudo-facsimile of the author's own script. This was poetry inscribed very literally in place, although the medium to which it is affixed here, money, is intended to circulate freely, thereby peeling it away from its site and scattering it across the country.

A less poetic aspect of Goethe's presence in Ilmenau is the fact that his visits were made at the behest of the duke of Weimar, who sent him there to revive the local mining industry. It was a task to which he applied himself with zeal, although he met with little success. This connection with the landscape—extractive and instrumental, rather than disinterested and contemplative—shows his literary activity there in a somewhat different light. His official labors are absent from this contemplative note, and indeed from most notes featuring Goethe—although he visits a mine on one example from nearby Roda. In any case, the presence of the poem on the note is itself highly revealing in this regard. Poetry is a common feature on emergency money, albeit usually in the form of doggerel. Here, on the other hand, the very apex of German poetry is coupled with the sign of denomination—a mere 20 pfennigs, in this case. Although this may recall Jünger's critique regarding "the bourgeois lack of instinct in relation to value," the note in question, dubious though its numismatic status may have been, stands in fact in an ancient tradition. In his book *The Economy of Literature*, Marc Shell remarks of the inscriptions on ancient coins that this was the first medium by which poetry was reproduced.[12]

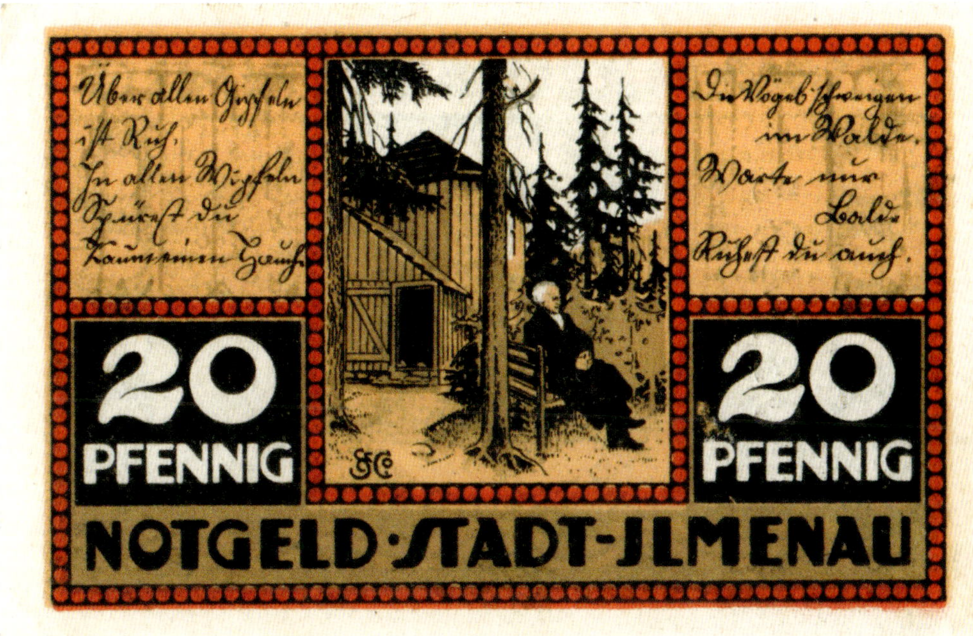

Notgeld from Ilmenau, 1921. Collection of the author.

Shell's central thesis is that money and literature developed in tandem, both being structured around the central mechanism of exchange; in the case of poetry, this exchange takes the form of metaphor. So although poetry often protests its opposition to the flattening power of money, which makes all things equivalent, it is in fact bound up with its logic from the very start. In light of this, Jünger's critique itself is therefore revealed as partaking of the bourgeois delusions he excoriates. This is supported by Goethe's trip to Ilmenau, where he gazes at the landscape with a view that is at once that of a surveyor and a poet. He says as much in a letter of 1824, in which he wrote that "Ilmenau has cost me much time, trouble and money, but I have also learned something thereby and acquired a view of nature that I would not exchange for any price."[13] This contradictory statement tells us that he has in fact already paid for this priceless view of nature: that it is, in fact, eminently exchangeable. Poetic vision is a commodity, and it commodifies what it alights upon.

Another literary figure to whom reference was made by numerous examples of Notgeld, Fritz Reuter, has quite a different position in the world of German letters. Reuter, who was born in the small north German town of Stavenhagen in 1810, wrote a number of popular novels in the local Plattdeutsch, or Low German, dialect. His work in preserving and elevating the status of the vernacular, which was, like dialects across Germany, already beginning to die out at the time, made him an obvious candidate for representation on Notgeld in the state in which he lived, Mecklenburg-Vorpommern. Such notes—Reutergeld, as they are often labeled—were very numerous: they were issued by no fewer than 70 towns in 1922, although they were all printed by the same publisher in Schwerin at the request of the Reuter Society, so they cannot be considered spontaneous manifestations of affection (though the fact that they were made at all surely attests to the fact that Reuter was considered a marketable figure). Many of them bear vignettes from the writer's stories, often of a comic nature, and quotations from his works—in Plattdeutsch, naturally—are also a common feature.

In the instance of Reutergeld, and on many other notes besides from the north of the country, dialect is used to signify locality. Here we see the local pulling away from the national, rather than an attempt to reassert the connection between the two, as was the case with notes featuring images of Bismarck or Goethe, and as had also been the case with the reproduction of Goethe's poetry, which, although fixed in space in Ilmenau, was also readily detached and circulated, thanks to its perfectly standard Hochdeutsch. The centrifugal tendencies evinced by Notgeld with Plattdeutsch inscriptions were a common enough phenomenon during the Weimar Republic, when the newly formed federation often felt as if it were coming apart at the seams. As Kurt Tucholsky noted in 1928, the "republican ideal ... is to be found only spottily out there in the countryside."[14] Provincial resistance to the central government is explored in novels by Hans Fallada, including his Schleswig-Holstein-based *Farmers, Functionaries and Fireworks*, published in 1931, and by Lion Feuchtwanger, whose 1930 novel *Success: Three Years in the Life of a Province* is written partly in the dialect of Bavaria, where it is set. It is telling that these writers should have turned from the cities, which had been the focus of much of Weimar's earlier culture, to the provinces in these last, ominously fractious years of the republic. They were far from unique in doing so, and, although most *Heimatliteratur* of the time was conservative, if not strongly reactionary, they were not entirely alone in their critical stance, either.[15]

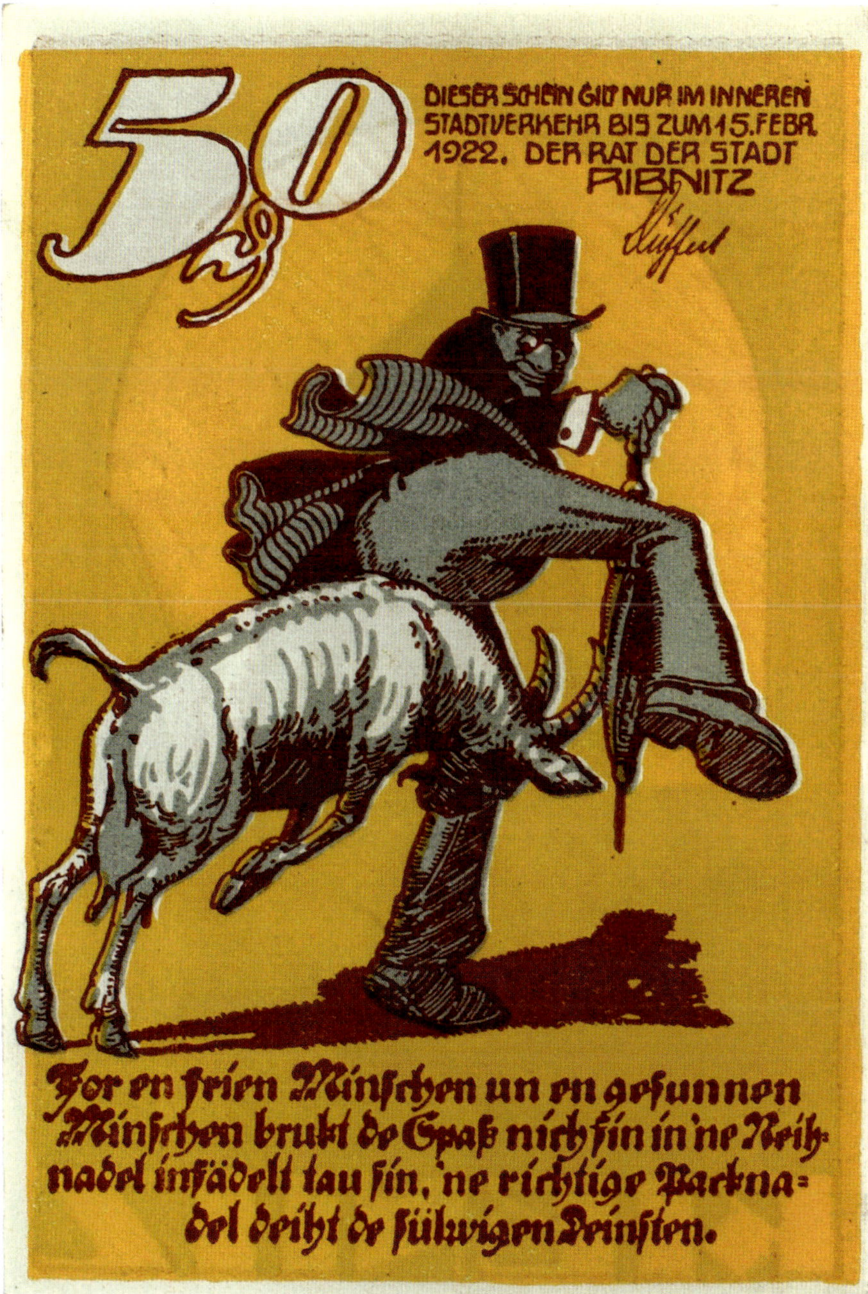

Reutergeld from Ribnitz, 1922. Warburg Institute, London.

Feuchtwanger's tale is set at the peak of the inflation, and it reflects on the political consequences of the crisis, which leads to the rise of a Hitler-like figure. He observes that, while the central government was far from popular in these years, especially among local politicians who "would not admit that their countries [*Länder*] were dwindling into provinces of the republic," nationalism of another sort was brewing among the populace.[16] Despite the fact that "the property of the peasants did not melt away beneath them like the wealth of the townspeople," many of them nevertheless grew to feel that

> their ancient ways were doomed. Their private existence was too expensive, they would have to conform to the Reich. ... From instinct they became nationalists, for they felt that the only thing that supported the German farmer was the necessity for food supplies in case of war. So from instinct these peasants, a mixture of Slavonic and Latin blood, became the champions of a pure racial Germany.[17]

The relationship between town and country during the inflation years is explored in another novel by Fallada, who had worked as a farm bailiff after the war. *Wolf among Wolves*, which was published in 1937, plays out between Berlin and the fictional village of Neulohe on the Polish border.[18] The plot is set in motion when the tenant of the estate at Neulohe is forced to go to the city to seek laborers to bring in the harvest, a state of affairs reflecting the increasing urbanization of formerly rural populations. This situation is bemoaned by the farmer, who wonders why people would give up the advantages of the countryside for Berlin, that "accursed city" where the inflation was making life impossible; as another character ruefully remarks, "land is the only real thing today."[19] However, the rural is by no means as solid or as idyllic as it appears from the city: agricultural laborers are being dislodged from their customary stasis by the economic chaos; shadowy figures roam the landscape, plotting a putsch; and the farmer is constantly squeezed for more rent by his landlord, who is also his father-in-law (thus the economic basis of aristocratic family relations is laid bare by the crisis). The farmer's own character eventually disintegrates under the strain, and his friend remarks that "the earth sweats fear instead of corn ... the peace of the fields is an illusion."[20]

Rural-urban relations were also occasionally a feature of Notgeld, though they were hardly observed with the dialectical subtlety of Fallada's middlebrow novel. A series of notes issued in 1921 by the villages of Altenwerder and Finkenwerder, which lay on islands in the Elbe across from Hamburg's docks, express quite unambigously the way some rural people felt about the big city during this period of heightened tensions. Here the metropolis appears as a monstrous amphibian crowned with Hamburg's heraldic crest. In one image, it reaches its enormous hand from the city to grab the milk and fruit produced by its rural hinterland; in another, the creature places its webbed hands on the villages, and the Plattdeutsch inscription says, "Greater Hamburg would love to snatch us up, we islands as juicy morsels"; finally, the creature holds the villages in its arms, exclaiming, "Oh, if only you were mine!" These images reflect the specific political circumstances of the day, when Hamburg was considering the incorporation of the villages in order to expand its docks (this did in fact eventually happen, albeit not until the 1970s). The economic relationship between town and country is clearly of equal concern: another note shows an open-mouthed cow attached to Hamburg via the tubes of a milking machine, while a farmer hurls apples at the distant city; beneath is the inscription, "Hamburg, you our neighbor city, we fill you up with milk, fish and apples!" This was not how things appeared from the cities, however, where there was widespread resentment regarding the "profiteering" of the peasants; the latter preferred to hoard produce rather than sell it at government-dictated prices. When the situation worsened, and desperate workers faced food shortages, this resentment began to break out into literal raids. On August 16, 1923, to give just one example, 500 employees of a porcelain factory in Radeberg marched on a nearby village, where they confiscated large quantities of dairy produce from farms.[21] Firefights often broke out between looters and farmers, and, in the cities, citizens and policemen were regularly killed in food riots.

The Vanishing Landscape

The prevalence of references to land on Notgeld, whether centripetal or centrifugal, pastoral or industrial, should not only be seen in the context of novelistic representations of place; it must also

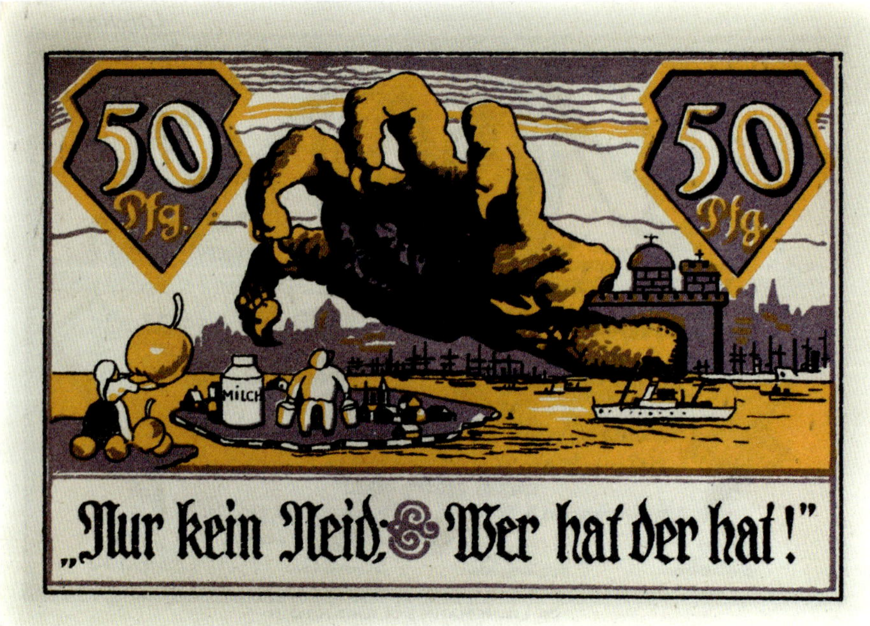

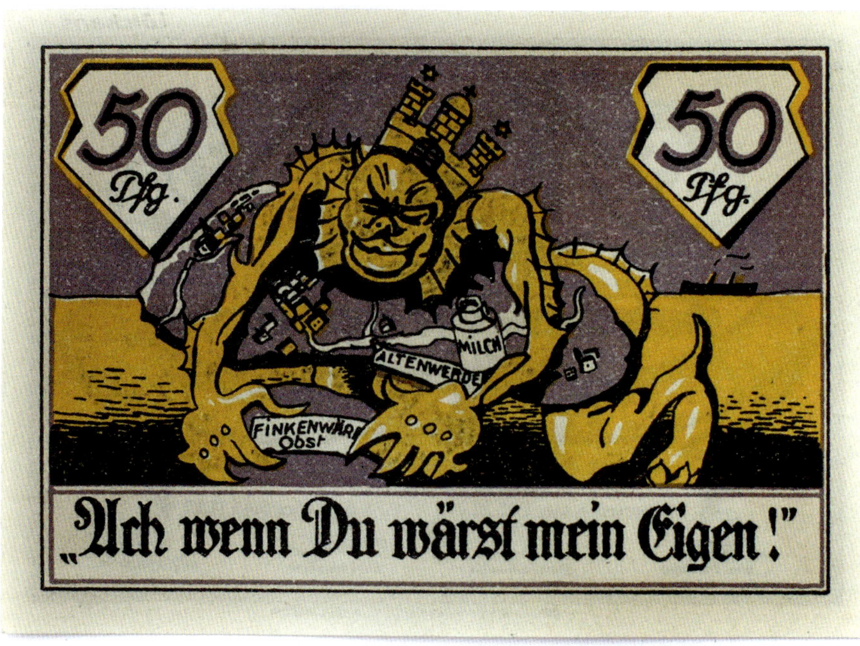

Here and facing page: Notgeld from Altenwerder, 1921. Warburg Institute, London.

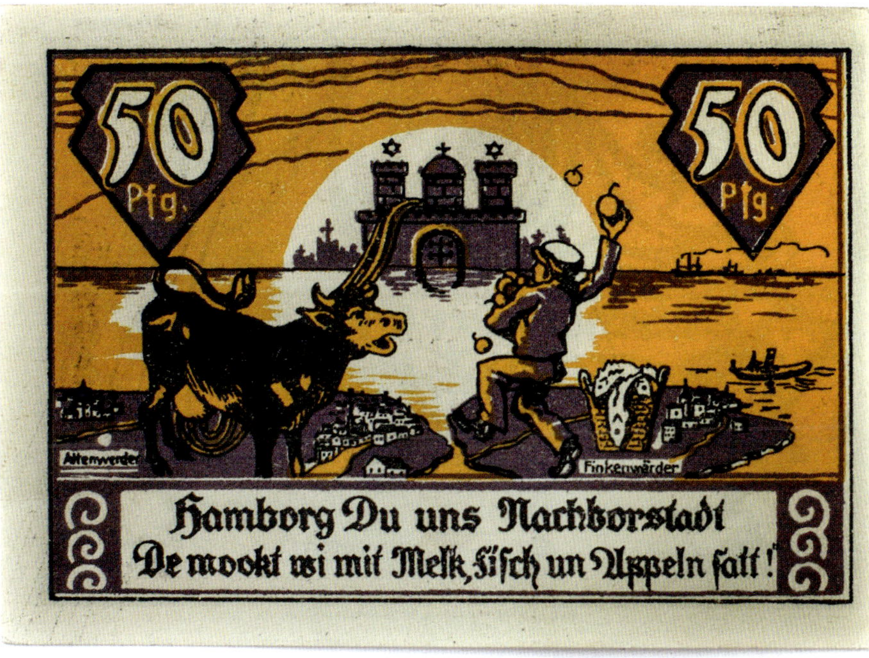

be set in the context of the wider image economy of the early Weimar Republic. In the inflation period, however, representations of landscape had all but disappeared from advanced art in Germany.[22] Before the war the expressionists had repeatedly envisioned new life in rural settings, but the trenches put paid to such pastoral idylls. This change of focus also reflects the increasing concentration of the nation's art market in Berlin: one of the pioneers of this tendency, Ernst Ludwig Kirchner, had already abandoned the lakes at Moritzburg for the capital's street corners in 1911. At around the same time, other expressionists began to launch themselves from the springboard of landscape into the aerial realm of abstraction, most notably Wassily Kandinsky. During the war and its immediate aftermath, references to the land were rejected by the Dadaists (with one notable exception, to whom I turn shortly), along with all the other remnants of the academic tradition that they perceived the expressionists as having preserved. And yet, while landscapes were being purged from the studio, they proliferated elsewhere, in those reservoirs of popular imagery constituted by the cinema and by printed items such as Notgeld, postcards, photobooks, and illustrated magazines.[23] The tone of these was overwhelmingly conservative.

Two films by F. W. Murnau, both released in 1922 near the inflation's height, can be taken as exemplars of such popular landscapes in their most elaborated form. One of these, *Nosferatu*, remains well known today; the other, *Der brennende Acker* or *The Burning Soil*, much less so. The plot of *Nosferatu* concerns a Transylvanian vampire, Count Orlok, who purchases some buildings in the fictional Hanseatic city of Wisborg. In the course of the sale, it becomes clear that he is obsessed by the agent's wife, but, in the famous, final scene, in which he attempts to suck her blood, he is defeated by the rising sun, which reduces him to a wisp of smoke. The film has been widely understood as expressing fears regarding the invasion of Germany by the eastern, probably Jewish, Other, which brings death and disease in its wake. It has also been more jocularly remarked that *Nosferatu* takes property speculation as a central theme.[24] But there is more to this wisecrack than meets the eye: the buildings are not just any buildings but early modern warehouses in Lübeck with stepped gables—in other words, exactly the sort of vernacular architecture that appeared on Notgeld (a series representing similar structures was issued by Lübeck the same year, 1922)—and their sale is a prostitution of sacred German land for foreign money. Indeed, during the inflation it was widely feared that foreign plutocrats were buying up cheap German real estate with their hard dollars.[25] It is precisely this betrayal that invites the vampire's curse.[26] To ram the point home, on traveling to Germany, Orlok brings with him a cartload of coffins filled with Transylvanian earth. German soil itself will be made foreign, and it is clear that this alien ground is the vector through which the plague arrives, along with the rats that creep from the coffins. But the rootlessly cosmopolitan is in the end defeated by the steadfastly local, as, when the vampire dissolves into daylight, it is the reflection of its light by the warehouses that strikes the fatal blow. The radiant solidity of these ancient buildings evaporates the nebulous count, and land triumphs over capital.[27]

While *Nosferatu* deals with anxiety regarding the vernacular architecture—the urban local, in other words—that often represents place on Notgeld, *The Burning Soil* turns to the countryside, that other, seemingly more reliable anchor. Yet here too capital threatens an earthquake. The melodrama centers on a tract of land in a Silesian village, popularly known as the Devil's

Field, which has long been haunted by association with demonic forces. Discovering that the ground actually conceals an unsuspected oilfield—whence the mysterious rumblings that lie behind its baleful reputation—an ambitious peasant inveigles himself into the household of the landowner. Once ensconced there, he begins his campaign by seducing the landowner's daughter, but, following the death of the old man, he marries his widow instead, knowing that she has inherited this apparently inconsequential property. However, when he begins to develop the oilfield, she becomes aware of her new husband's ulterior motives, and drowns herself; then at the film's climax the scorned daughter sets fire to the pitheads that had been erected on the Devil's Field, also dying in the conflagration. The film concludes with the peasant returning, chastened and penniless, to his family home.

In this film, land itself is transformed directly into gold—the black gold of oil—but the price of this alchemical operation is that the peasant must sacrifice true love, a betrayal that ends in catastrophe. The similarities to the plot of Wagner's *Ring* cycle are clear; however, in the *Ring*, the challenge made by the upstart Mime to the gods of the ancien régime is not unjust, as they are corrupt and must die, whereas in this reactionary tale, it seems that the real sin is not so much the betrayal of true love by the antihero—and certainly not the oath-breaking of the gods—but rather the destruction of the countryside *and the transgression of class boundaries*. It is the peasant's ambition to join the aristocracy, and to conduct a necromantic-industrial transmutation of sacred German soil, that summons nemesis. Order is ultimately restored by a cleansing fire: the land is returned to its original state, and the peasant is returned to his hut.[28] In both of Murnau's films, German land is menaced by the solvent power of money, whether of foreign origin or the money of the industrial nouveaux riches, and in both films German land prevails over these unsettling forces, a wish that was clearly shared by many designers of localizing Notgeld in this period.

Such conservative views of the land have a long history. Like conservative thought in general, they developed in reaction to the French Revolution and the upheaval of feudal land relations and traditional territories that ensued. In Germany, bourgeois dislocations were unusually protracted, as was the reaction they elicited. The unification of the country in 1871 (which was partly accomplished in order to construct a unitary internal market; in other words, it was another demonstration of capitalism's solvent power) was resisted by adherents of the ancien régime, and by others besides, who resented the provincialization of their former sovereign states. There resulted a swathe of local imagery in the form of *Heimatkunst*, novels and paintings idealizing the peasants and their relationship to the soil. These tendencies intensified following the defeat of 1918, which was accompanied by a significant shrinkage of Germany's territorial extent, and the revolution of 1918–1919, which transformed the legal status of German land. It was in this tumultuous context that the localizing iconography of the preceding 50 years was resurrected and distributed to a wide public via Notgeld. As Wolfgang Kemp put it, "The *Heimat* movement had collected the material of fairy tales, sayings, customs and legends; now it was put into circulation."[29]

But these motifs did not go unchanged in the process. The localizing tendencies of conservative thought were radicalized in the Weimar period, when they were conjoined with burgeoning racial theories and propagated by writers such as Oswald Spengler, who explicitly posited place as the antipode of money. In the second volume of his enormously popular *Decline of the West*, published in 1922, he argues: "Through the economic history of every culture there runs a desperate conflict waged by the soil-rooted traditions of a race, by its *soul*, against the spirit of money. ... Money aims at mobilising all things. World-economy is the actualised economy of values that are completely detached in thought from the land, and made fluid."[30]

Spengler notoriously concludes the book with a prophecy: money had "thrust into the life of the yeoman's countryside and set the earth a-moving ... but ... the last conflict is at hand in which the Civilization receives its conclusive form—the conflict between money and blood."[31] This mystically conceived blood will be championed by what Spengler calls Caesarism, a concept that many on the right took to foreshadow the rise of Hitler. Spengler's emphasis on the connection between race and place was hugely influential and contributed to the *Blut und Boden*, or blood and soil, ideology of the National Socialists. While much localizing Notgeld is of a fairly anodyne, nostalgic character, and conservative in a moderate sense, we can detect the shoots of the more radical thinking to come in certain notes, especially those that are explicitly concerned with the numerous political crises affecting Germany's territory in these years.

Before I turn to this subject, I want to conclude this section by examining another visual critique of the financialization of the countryside, albeit one made from a political position diametrically opposed to that of Murnau (or Spengler). The idea that capital disrupted traditional social structures was hardly confined to the right, after all: the *Communist Manifesto* famously states that "all that is solid melts into air," and, from a liberal perspective, Simmel observed in 1900 that "money is involved in the general development which in every domain of life and in every sense strives to dissolve substance into free-flowing process."[32] Yet for Marx and Simmel, and the many cultural critics who followed in their wake, this solvent quality of money was by no means entirely negative: for Marx, it dislodged the calcified social formations of feudalism, and for Simmel, it made possible a kind of freedom, although this was admittedly an ambiguous one. During the inflation, however, the tremors unloosed by money resulted in an avalanche, bringing forth strange and disastrous effects. Discourse regarding money's solvent power grew correspondingly more trenchant on both the right and the left, and Marx's hopeful addendum, that "man is at last compelled to face with sober senses his real conditions of life," proved to be far from accurate.

A particularly stark left-wing critique of the financialization of the countryside during the inflation is made by Georg Scholz's 1920 painting *Industriebauern* (Industrial Farmers), which he exhibited at the First International Dada Fair in Berlin that year. Scholz was a resident of Karlsruhe—in other words, he was a provincial, and he remained one throughout the republic. His location informed his work in this period, which is more inclined to landscapes than that of his fellow Dadaists. *Industriebauern*, the most vituperative of these paintings, shows a monstrous farming household in a parodic recreation of a Biedermeyer family portrait. The heavily scarred paterfamilias sits bolt upright clutching a Bible, the mother cradles a piglet, and their human child tortures a captive frog. Each of them is rendered visibly brainless in some way, or rather, their brains have been replaced by symbols of capitalist modernity: the child's cranium is empty apart from an advertising slogan, the mother has a screw driven into her head, and the father's face, already a collage of scar tissue, is broken up yet further by real banknotes, which are collaged into a wound in his skull. In the background, a bust of the Kaiser stands on a sideboard, while through the window a modern straw-baling machine

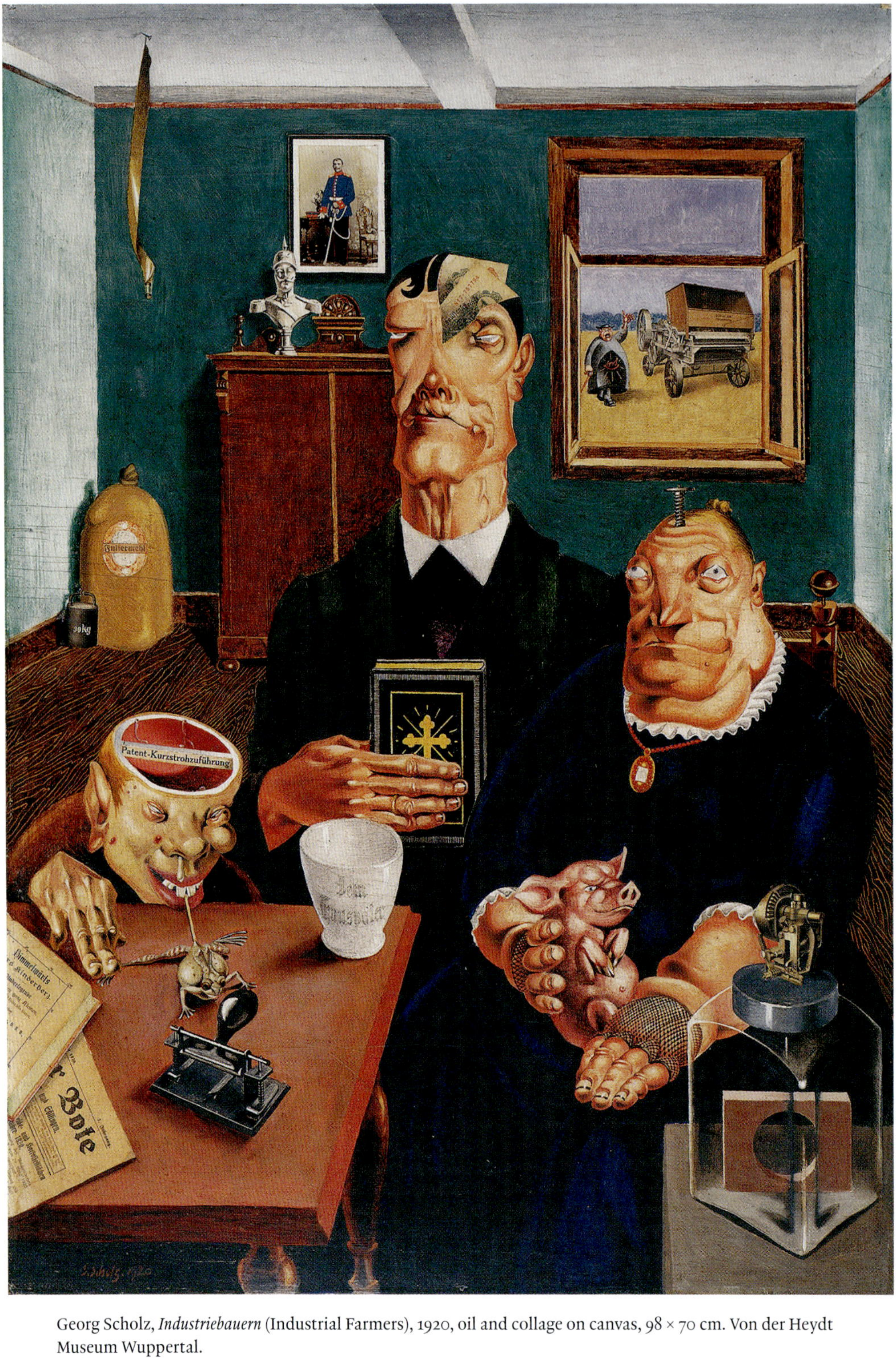

Georg Scholz, *Industriebauern* (Industrial Farmers), 1920, oil and collage on canvas, 98 × 70 cm. Von der Heydt Museum Wuppertal.

(another collaged element) dominates the landscape. The presence of this apparatus is a reference to the material transformation of the countryside that had occurred due to the inflation, when the rural economy was increasingly industrialized and prosperous. It produced *Sachwerte*, after all, tangible assets, and thanks to these, in Feuchtwanger's words, "many farmers did not consider that they were complete without their car and their racing stable."[33] Scholz was a card-carrying communist, and, as the juxtaposition in its title suggests, his painting is an attempt to expose the underlying structures at work in the town-country dialectic: the process of real subsumption by which farming was industrialized. In doing so, he also exposes conservative myths of the rural as an island in the raging ocean of finance.

This exposure hinges on the "real" elements inserted into the picture, especially the banknotes that fill the father's brain—or rather, to be specific, *Darlehnskassenscheine*, which were issued by special loan banks that had ostensibly been set up to finance the regional governments at the outset of the war. These notes could be purchased with treasury bills, which were not permissible as coverage for the issuance of money, and then exchanged for war bonds, which were; this allowed the government to escape the suspicion that they were printing unbacked money.[34] This none-too-subtle subterfuge was one of the key mechanisms behind the inflation, so the central position of these notes in this work can be seen as a kind of material punctum whereby actuality, in the form of printed money, penetrates the membrane of ideology, the outmoded oil portrait. But, of course, the money itself is hardly "real," in a classical sense—it is devoid of all backing and therefore stands for a fateful uncoupling of the signifier from the signified. This makes for a stark contrast to the notes on which images of Goethe and Dürer serve to prop up devalued currency. Here instead the image of the bourgeois family, together with its noncontemporaneous accoutrements comprised of technological apparatuses and imperial trinkets, is revealed to lie on a substrate of money, and false money at that, which emerges from beneath the surface of the oil paint through the smashed head of the father. The notes therefore function not as an interruption of the unreal by the real but as a *mise en abyme*, whereby the empty head of the father—and of traditional modes of representation—is filled by equally empty money, the empty medium that has emptied out all other media.

The perception that the ground beneath one's feet was being undermined was more than just a local reflection of the phenomenon Marx had identified as being central to capitalist modernity, and which had intensified during the inflation as money destabilized relations yet further. For Germans in this period, the question of land also had a very particular political resonance, since they had lost one-eighth of their prewar territory and all of their overseas empire as a result of the war. The nation continued to shrink in peacetime, too. The Allies dictated plebiscites on national affiliation in the border region of Schleswig-Holstein and the exclave of East Prussia in 1920, and another in Upper Silesia in 1921. The Saarland was occupied by the French and British in 1920; in 1923 the Memelland was annexed by Lithuania; and, in the same year, the French occupied the Ruhr, remaining there until 1925. These events nibbled away at the edges of the state and contributed to a general sense that Germany was disintegrating.

The threat to the territorial integrity of Germany during the war was the subject of several notes. I have already mentioned one example of *Kriegsnotgeld*, or war Notgeld, on which an image of a town was defended by a medieval warrior. More contemporary iconography was also occasionally deployed in this context, with decidedly mixed results. In 1918, Füssen in Bavaria issued a note showing a soldier in a loincloth defending the town's medieval fortress from a dragon with several heads. While this creature, presumably representing the Allies, is straight out of Dürer, and the seminude warrior strikes a classicizing contrapposto, his face is modern, with a fashionable moustache and a *Stahlhelm* on his head. The result is eloquent of the complex temporality of conservative reaction to defeat, and utterly bathetic.[35] More successful was an issue from Bielefeld, on which the heads of two young soldiers are collaged against a text enumerating the battles fought by the local garrison; at the bottom is a paraphrase from the Lutheran hymn "A Mighty Fortress Is Our God": "And if the world is full of devils, we must still succeed!" Such religious relics do nothing to disguise the fact that the embattled landscape has been translated from the ruler's perspective of feudal tradition to its bureaucratic codification as a list of military engagements.

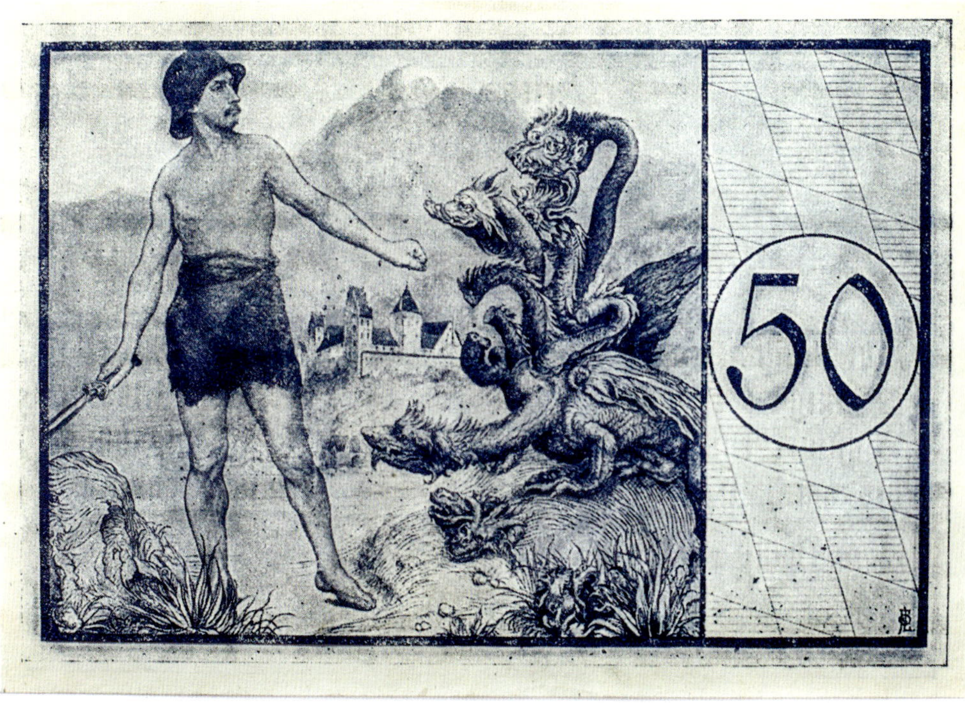

Notgeld from Füssen, 1918. Warburg Institute, London.

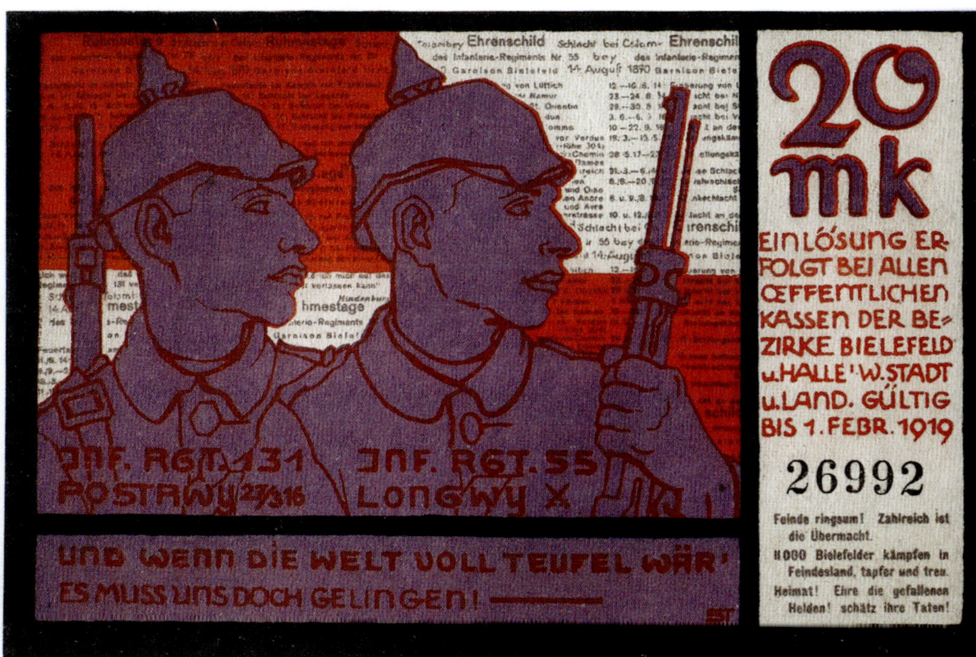

Notgeld from Bielefeld, 1918. Warburg Institute, London.

The loss of Germany's overseas possessions was also widely mourned during the Weimar Republic. Popular novels such as 1920's *Heia Safari!* by General Paul von Lettow-Vorbeck, the celebrated "lion of Africa," cast a rose-tinted look back at the relationship between the colonizers and their subjects. Lettow-Vorbeck also acted on his dissatisfaction: he was discharged from the Wehrmacht following his involvement in the Kapp Putsch the same year his book was published. A number of organizations likewise agitated for the return of the colonies, albeit less violently. One example of such activity was a German-Hanseatic Colonial Memorial Day, which took place in Berlin, Hamburg, and Bremen in 1921. Two series of notes were issued to commemorate the occasion; one of these showed a map of Germany's former possessions on one side and notable figures from the nation's colonial history on the other. Among these can be found Carl Peters, who was notorious for the brutality with which he administered Kilimanjaro Region. His actions led to local uprisings, and as a result he was recalled to Berlin, where in 1897 he was dishonorably discharged. He then fled to London to evade prosecution for abuse of state power; nevertheless, he was regarded as a hero by German imperialists in the years that followed, and he was later pardoned by Hitler. His celebration on this note demonstrates the use of such material to propagandize against the republican government, which was seen by revanchists as having surrendered territory too easily, or even as having been complicit in its loss.

Another series on this theme shows a palm tree silhouetted against a setting sun and the dates 1682–1884–1918, respectively referring to the establishment of the first German overseas territory in Ghana, the Berlin Conference at which the partitioning of Africa between the European powers was formalized, and the loss of the colonies at the end of the war. The reverse sides of these notes show picturesque scenes in which coloniality is signified by the juxtaposition of local people and flora against European-style buildings. Among these are images representing Dar es Salaam in German East Africa, with a distant church incongruously framed by palm trees; Kiatschou in China, represented by a traditional Chinese gate in the foreground and a large Western structure, probably the governor's residence in Qingdao, across the bay; and Swakopmund in German South West Africa, where a man in colonial garb stands among palms before a selection of German-built landmarks. The latter colony was the site of the genocide of the

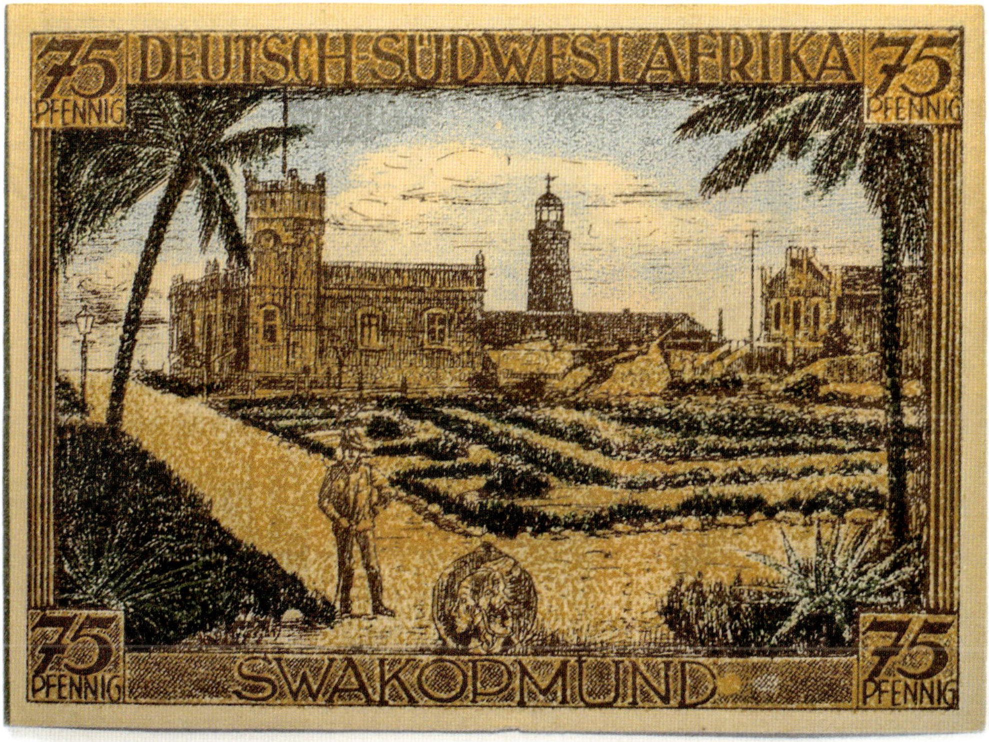

Notgeld produced for the Deutsch-Hanseatischer Kolonialgedenktag, 1921. Fitzwilliam Museum, Cambridge.

Herero and Nama people, the first such atrocity of the twentieth century, which is now seen as having been a precursor of the Holocaust. At the time, however, accusations of abuses by the German colonial authorities were dismissed by revanchists as *Schuldlüge*, "guilt lies," concocted by the Allies.

These notes are a special case of locational money, since they show not the place in which they were produced, but rather a distant place that was once to some degree local, thanks to the logic of imperialism. These wish-images of the reincorporation of lost colonies into the Reich are a form of sympathetic magic, expressing the desire for Dar es Salaam or Swakopmund to take their place alongside Bielefeld and Hannover as valid candidates for representation on German money. This wish sometimes took more explicit form: to mention one final example of Notgeld relating to this subject, Neustadt in Mecklenburg issued a series of notes in 1922 that were likewise decorated with scenes from Germany's former

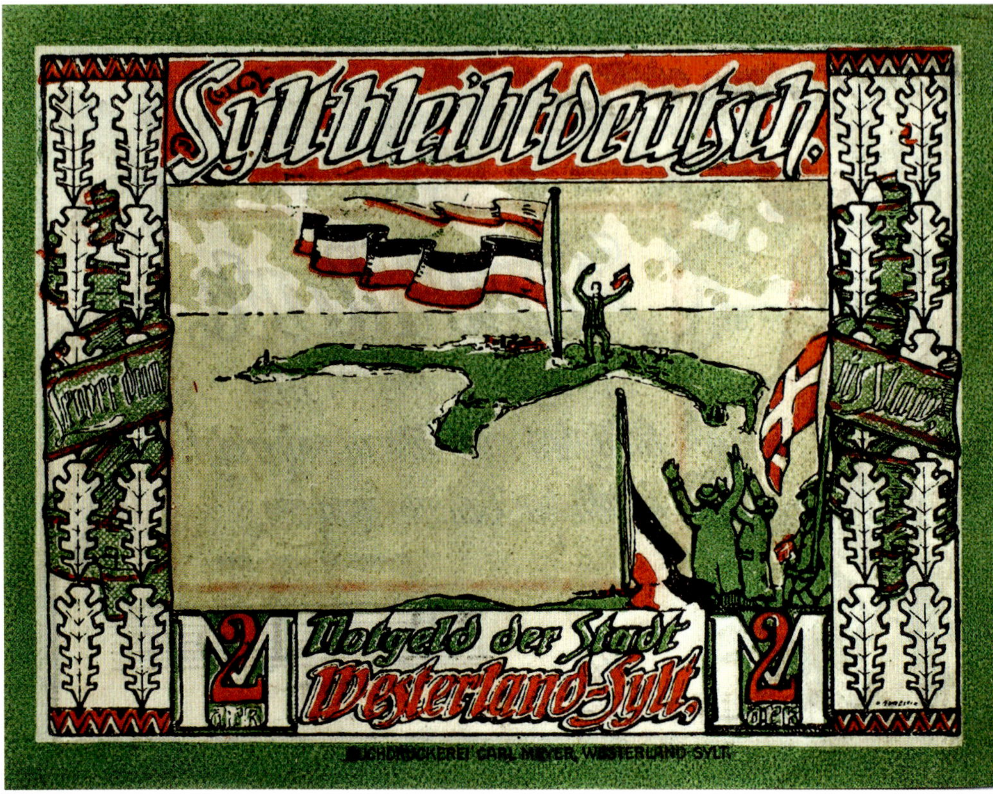

Notgeld from Sylt, 1920. Warburg Institute, London.

overseas possessions. The tone here is fiercer: the notes featured the slogan "Give us our colonies back!" In fact, this position was to become official policy in 1923, when Stresemann became foreign minister—albeit expressed sotto voce, so as not to upset the delicate negotiations regarding reparations.

Closer to home, the territorial plebiscites were likewise the subject of numerous notes. Many examples printed in Schleswig-Holstein refer to the two referenda that took place there in February and March of 1920. The disputed area was divided into two zones for the purposes of the vote. The first referendum addressed the population of the northern Zone 1, which chose to join Denmark, while in the second referendum the southern Zone 2 voted to remain German. The irredentist German view on these matters is succinctly demonstrated by a note from Sylt, which shows the island under the tricolor of the German empire (a flag that had been rejected by the republican government amid much controversy).

A man waves to his compatriots on the mainland, while a figure holding a Danish flag turns dejectedly from the scene. The slogan reads "Sylt stays German."

An opposite stance is taken by two notes from the commune of Gramby, which was located in the northern zone. The first of these marks the second referendum by showing a map, which French and British soldiers are on the verge of cutting in half at the border of the lower, second zone. However, the Danish Prime Minister, Carl Theodor Zahle, indicates a border significantly more advantageous to Germany, and instructs, "Cut here." This refers to Zahle's perceived acquiescence to the result of the plebiscite, which made him unpopular in Denmark; indeed, he was deposed by the king as a result. Another note from Gramby refers to the so-called Easter Crisis, as the ensuing constitutional upset was known, by showing the king putting his hand on the shoulder of a consternated Zahle while the latter attempts to interpose himself between Mother Denmark and two girls labeled Zone 1 and Zone 2.

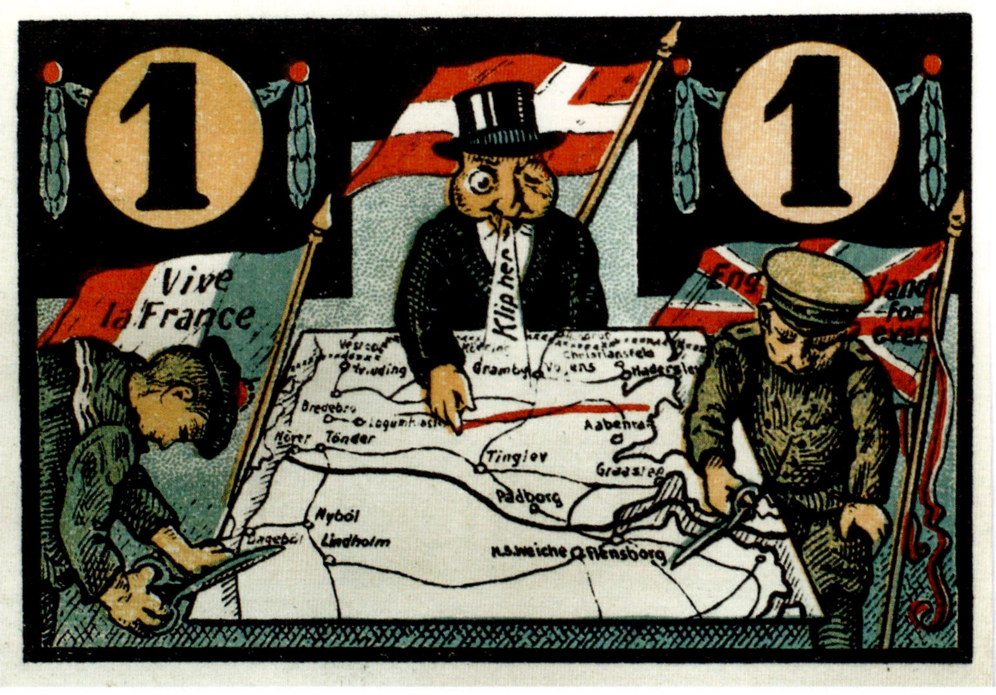

Notgeld from Gramby, 1920. Warburg Institute, London.

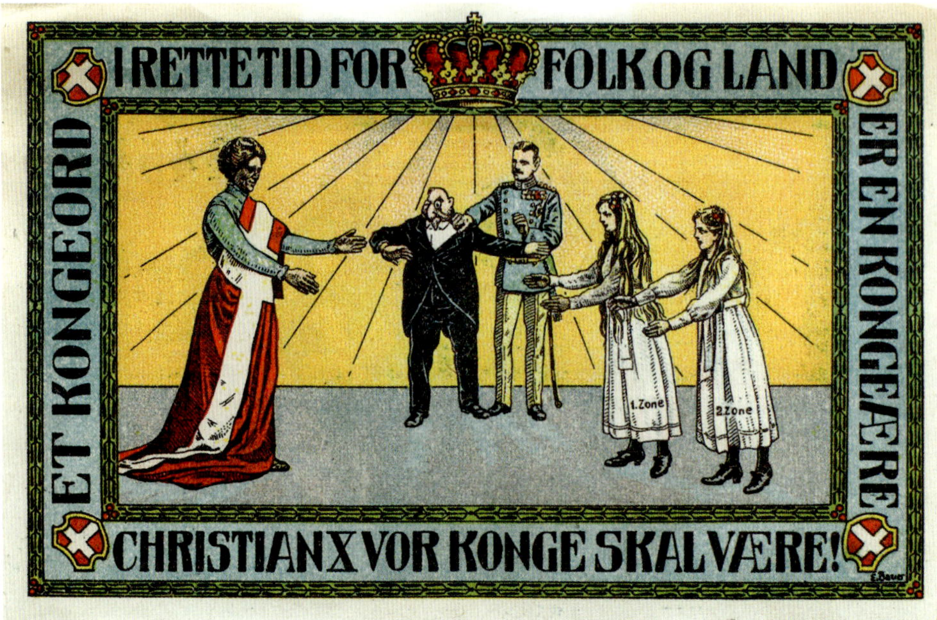

Notgeld from Gramby, 1920. Warburg Institute, London.

The Silesian plebiscite of 1921 was also marked by a number of notes, none more histrionic than an example printed by the Glauchau branch of the German Defense League, or Deutsche Schutzbund, an irredentist organization formed in 1919. The note, which was issued to raise money to support Upper Silesia, features an image of a skull wearing the Polish military headdress known as the *czapka*, which had become a symbol of that country's struggle for independence. This is half-buried under an enormous heap of paper; in the background, tiny figures can be seen adding more to the pile. The inscription reads, "Die Zettel zahl bannt Tod und Qual" (The number of slips of paper [*Zettel*] prevents death and suffering). The paper here figures ambiguously as both the voting slips in the upcoming referendum but also as the Notgeld itself, which, it is suggested, would help ward off the supposed Polish menace if purchased in sufficient quantities. Indeed, the run-up to the vote was marked by violence, with three nationalist uprisings, violently suppressed by German troops, leading to numerous deaths in the area. The equation of voting slips with pseudo-money—this very piece of money, in fact, which had been produced to raise funds for the region—does little to support belief in either of these paper objects, however.

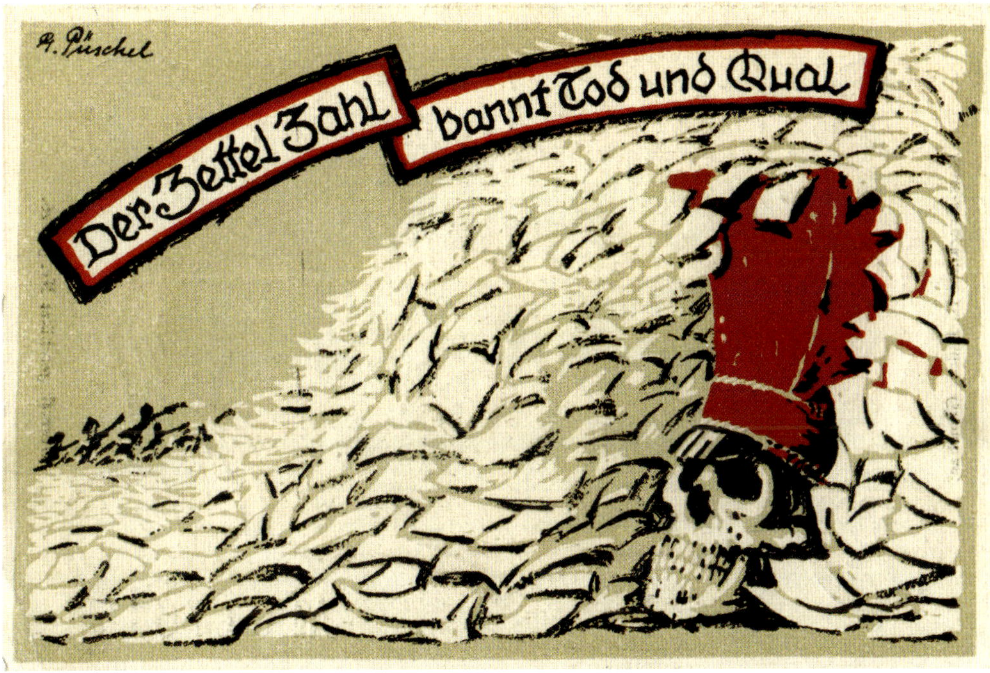

Notgeld issued by the Deutsche Schutzbund, Glauchau. Collection of the author.

Even before they had been lost, it was precisely in these border regions that Notgeld first developed: it had originated in Germany's threatened fringes when war broke out, first in East Prussia and shortly afterward on the other side of the Reich in Leverkusen on the Rhine.[36] "Nowhere is Germany more genuinely, essentially present than in those places where it had ceased to exist politically," as Wolfgang Kemp sardonically remarks.[37] Beyond the iconographic concern with local identity that fairly straightforwardly follows from threat, this suggests the operation of a curious form of self-fulfilling national anxiety: faced with the possibility of attack, the populace hoarded coins, forcing local governments to issue money that, in its localization, enacted the de facto dissolution of the Reich—if we consider a unified currency to be one of the essential attributes of the modern nation—long before this was accomplished de jure.

This process reached a climax when, on January 11, 1923, the French invaded the Ruhr in retaliation for Germany defaulting on its reparations. In response, the Cuno government—composed of ostensibly nonpartisan technocrats—instigated a policy of "passive resistance," in effect a cessation of all economic activity in the occupied zone. This was made possible by printing yet more money, a strategy that was also partly motivated by the desire to keep workers and industrialists onside. Huge Reichsbank credits were made available to industry so that wages could continue to be paid, and as a result, the value of the mark collapsed on the international currency markets. The inflation, already galloping, now became hyperinflation. Unemployment soared, food riots broke out around the country, and, in Bavaria, Hitler attempted a putsch. Notes were printed with exorbitant denominations—in the millions, billions, trillions, even hundreds of trillions. Contrary to conservative beliefs about money, the dissolution of land preceded and in fact produced this tidal wave of currency; but this was a dialectical process, and the resulting tide of money fed back into this catastrophe. Far from stabilizing value, land functioned as a short circuit in the process of its destruction.

As the hyperinflation reached its peak, the danger of binding belief in the locality to belief in the currency, the fundamental strategy of all locational money, became ineluctable. The humor drained out of notes, which were once again being issued as functional currency, since the government could not keep up with demand for means of payment while prices rocketed upward. But references to place remained, and they became ever more problematic. I turn to notes that explicitly addressed the crisis in a later chapter, but even Notgeld that attempted to maintain a land-based value-support strategy confirm the worst. An example issued by the town of Weißenhorn in 1923 shows a blue-tinted photographic image of the town square, a quaint medieval architectural ensemble with a church spire and an old city gate, over which the denomination is plastered in a bold red sans-serif typeface: 2 million marks. The modern, advertising-style lettering contrasts jarringly with the antiquated and peaceful scene beneath it, which it dominates and partially obscures. This label suggests a price—indeed, it screams it, like an advertisement for a cut-price sale—but here the price was ever-increasing, while the value of the goods on offer plummeted. In October of that year, Siegfried Kracauer observed the situation with deep regret, writing that it "symbolizes the disintegration of our state in all too vivid a manner."[38] However, as this chapter has shown, emergency money did not just symbolize dismemberment: it was a material factor in this process, in which it played the role of both scalpel and corpse.

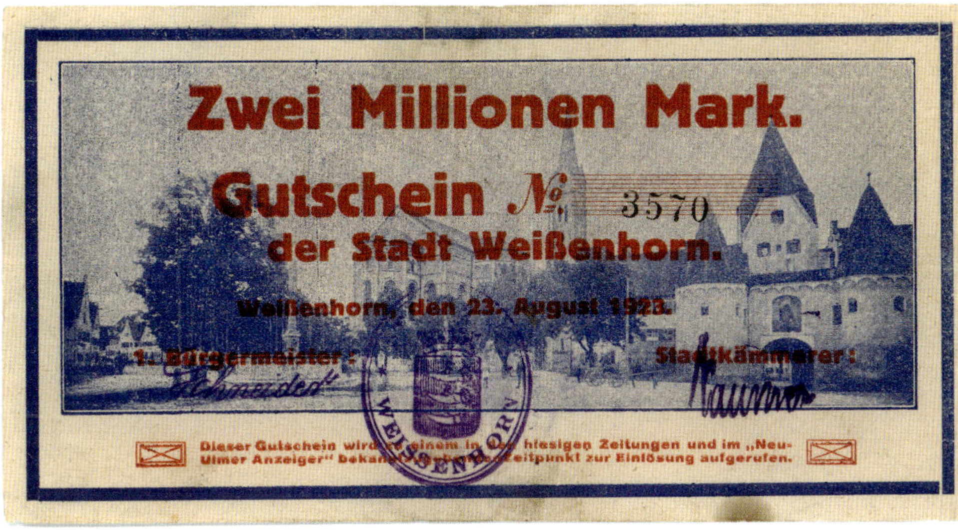

Notgeld from Weißenhorn, 1923. Giesecke+Devrient Geldscheinsammlung, Munich.

Reterritorialization

On November 15, 1923, a new currency named the Rentenmark was put into circulation, bringing the inflation to an end. How this succeeded remains a matter of debate: it is obscure enough for the contemporaneous phrase, "the miracle of the Rentenmark," to retain its felicity. Particularly curious, in the context of the preceding discussion, is the fact that the Rentenmark was backed by land (indeed, one alternative proposed solution went one step further, and was to be called a *Bodenmark*, "earth mark").[39] The real estate of agricultural and industrial concerns was mortgaged by a newly created bank, the Rentenbank (*Rente* means mortgage), and the interest paid on these mortgages was to provide the nominal backing for the new paper. The success of this strategy, despite historic failures in this line (such as the French "assignats" of the revolution, supposedly backed by land confiscated from the church and crown) and the recent total collapse of the German currency, must be attributed to psychological factors. These were partly bound up with the arrival of a new government, which instituted these changes, as well as the proclaimed backing of the new currency by *Sachwerte*, "real values." However, the exact mechanism by which this succeeded remains obscure.

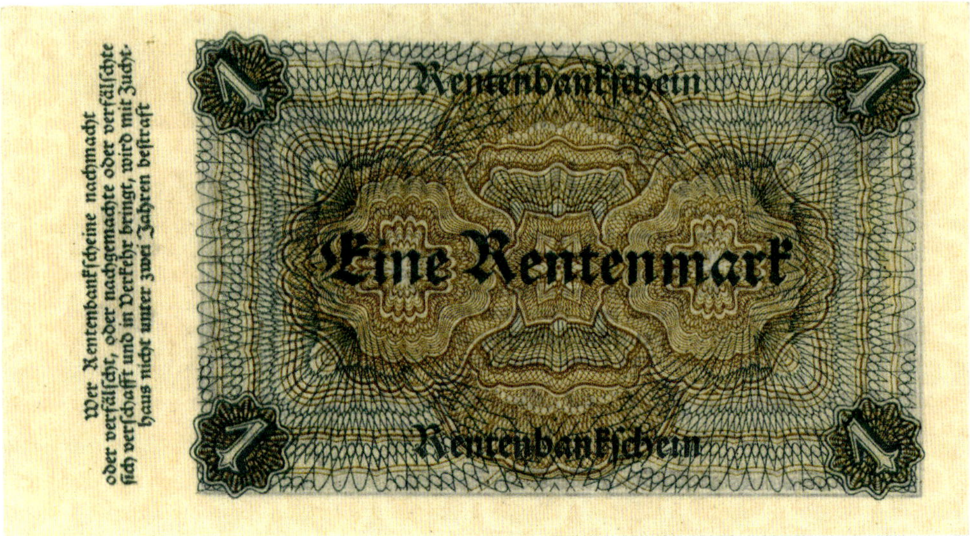

Rentenmark, 1923. Giesecke+Devrient Geldscheinsammlung, Munich.

In their 1980 book *A Thousand Plateaus*, in a chapter titled with the date of the Rentenmark's introduction, Deleuze and Guattari placed this event in the context of speech act theory: "a semiotic transformation of the Reichsmark into the Rentenmark, making possible a reterritorialization";[40] however, a few pages earlier they had argued that "the sum of the 'circumstances' suddenly made possible a semiotic transformation that, although indexed to the body of the earth and material assets, was still a pure act or incorporeal transformation—*November 20, 1923*." Which came first—the chicken of circumstance or the egg of semiotics? They answer that it is a case of "each intervening, each operating in the other."[41] This circular explanation does not take us very far, but their notion of reterritorialization, the process by which capital attempts to halt its own runaway motor of deterritorialization via techniques of relocation, does I think have explanatory value in this context.[42] The circumstances have been the subject of this chapter: a situation in which land and location were thrown into total disarray. The introduction of the Rentenmark, this semiotic abracadabra, represents a massive, state-backed reterritorialization of the currency, which had been preceded, in fact, by Notgeld issues on which we see a naive expression of the same impulse, applied directly to the wound through which the flows of the economy were leaking.

Reterritorialization did not stop with the printing presses, however. In the years following the stabilization of the German economy, though Notgeld had ceased to be produced, images of land continued to proliferate, and these were colored by increasingly radicalized ideas of *Blut und Boden*. To give one example: the Bund Heimatschutz, or Homeland Protection Association, which had been founded in 1904 to protect landscapes and traditional buildings, veered increasingly to the right from the mid-1920s. Eventually, its leader, the architect Paul Schulze-Naumburg (who had renamed himself after the Thuringian city of his birth), would fuse his rhetoric with anti-Semitic race "science." His popular series of books of photographs of vernacular German buildings were joined by texts such as *The Face of the German House* (1929), which set the firmly rooted peasant hut in opposition to modernist architecture's rootless degeneracy. Schulze-Naumburg was a reactionary in both political and aesthetic terms, and as I mentioned earlier, advanced art had largely disposed of land as a motif by the early 1920s; yet it remained central to the oeuvre of one particular artist, Emil Nolde, who, like Schulze-Naumburg, had named himself after the place in which he had been born, and who also turned to the extreme right. Unlike Schulze-Naumburg, however, he operated in a mode that was not in the end amenable to the Nazis. Significantly, Nolde was located in Schleswig-Holstein, that mystical source of the German "race"; however, following the plebiscites of 1920, Nolde—both the village and the artist—became Danish. He was radicalized yet further by this turn of events, and his paintings of the early 1920s include vicious anti-Semitic caricatures.[43] He also continued to depict the local landscape in paintings filled with vitalist pathos.

While Nolde kept the expressionist beacon burning at the northern border, long after it had been extinguished in Germany's more up-to-date salons and journals, the *retour à l'ordre* commonly referred to as Neue Sachlichkeit that had followed on the heels of the Dadaist purge brought with it a flood of landscapes. These were sometimes made by painters who were politically of the left, as in the case of Georg Schrimpf, but such precise renderings of German place, which cast a glance back to *altmeisterisch* precedent in terms of both their iconography and technique, were easily adopted by National Socialists (Schrimpf himself was given a professorship in 1933, although this was rescinded in 1937 in view of his political hinterland).[44] This resulted in such reactionary images as the queasy anti-Semitic kitsch of Austrian Franz Sedlacek, and Werner Peiner's 1933 painting *German Soil*, a portentously titled view of a peasant plowing a field beneath a lowering sky. The latter was hung by Hitler in the Reich Chancellery and distributed across the nation on thousands of postcards—but similar imagery had long preceded it along these circuits, whence it was carried by countless pieces of emergency money. Bloch observed these developments in 1929, when he wrote that "from the country old sap rises into long-forgotten shoots, it nourishes National Socialists and folkish mythologists, in short, arises as *pastorale militans*."[45] However, this militant pastoralism was not the only attempt to resolve the problem of place under modern conditions to emerge out of Notgeld's image economy, and in the final chapter I turn to a more utopian view of landscape that envisioned a different relationship with the earth—one that did not depend on race or nation.

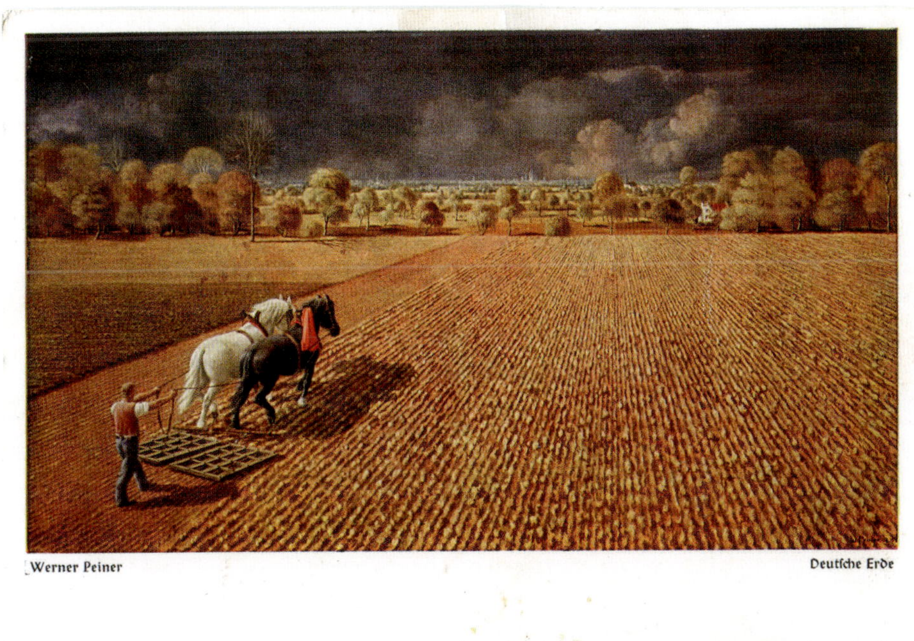

Postcard showing Werner Peiner's 1933 painting *German Soil* (original lost). Collection of the author.

2 *Work*

The painter, perhaps unwillingly, is a banknote factory.
George Grosz, "Instead of a Biography," 1920

A double-page spread in a 1923 issue of the satirical magazine *Die Pleite*, "Bankruptcy," shows twelve cartoons by George Grosz responding to the question, "How can I get rich?" It is a rogues' gallery illustrating the many possibilities available to scammers during the hyperinflation. Among the more obvious of these, such as "Become a middleman," "Make a career in politics," and "Become a film star," there are some acutely vicious answers: "Win battles, lose wars, write memoirs and coin it in dollars and pounds," and "Become a fascist, speculate on pogroms and collect Jewish fortunes." For ordinary people, meanwhile, the prospects were grim. One of the figures stoops down to grasp something lying on the pavement, above the advice "Collect cigarette butts," and the final image depicts a shirtless and underfed miner wielding a pick. The punchline to the question "How can I get rich?," it is captioned: "By working, never!"

As Grosz's smorgasbord of dubious career options demonstrates, work became a serious problem during the inflation. It was freely available—this was, for the most part, a time of full employment—but wages didn't keep pace with the price of goods. Yet while workers went hungry, profiteers seemed to be having the time of their lives, and this inevitably led to a great deal of social unrest. Despite the apparent devaluation of work during the period, it was nevertheless one of the primary means by which

Wie werde

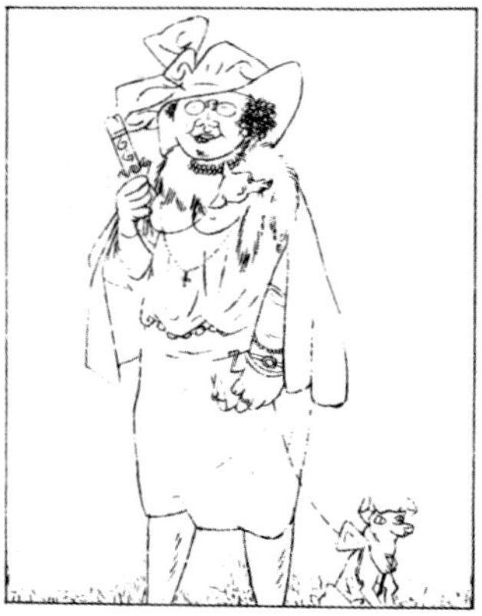

Wähle die richtige Frau

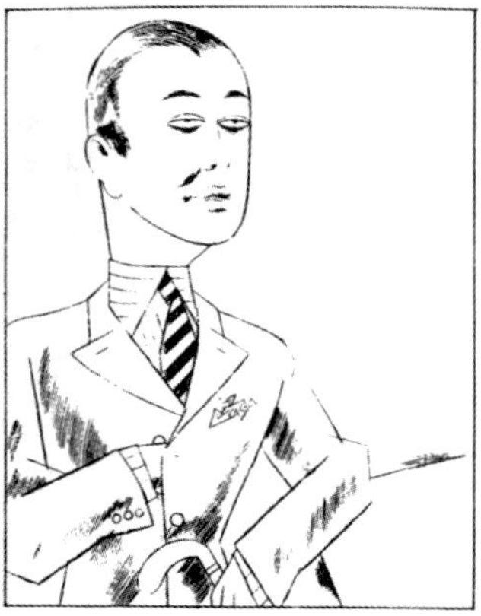

Werde Filmstar

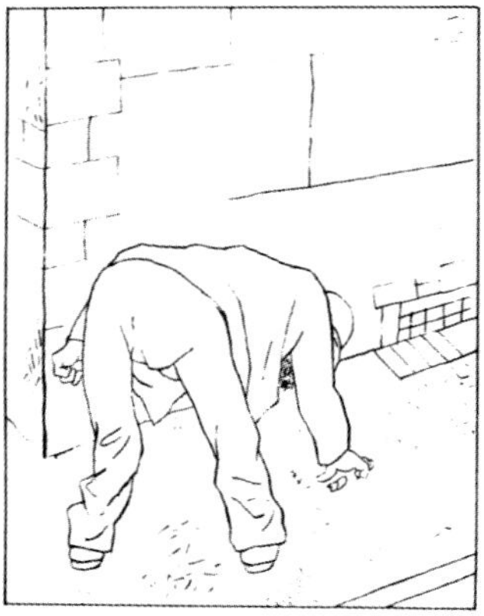

Sammle Zigarrenstummel

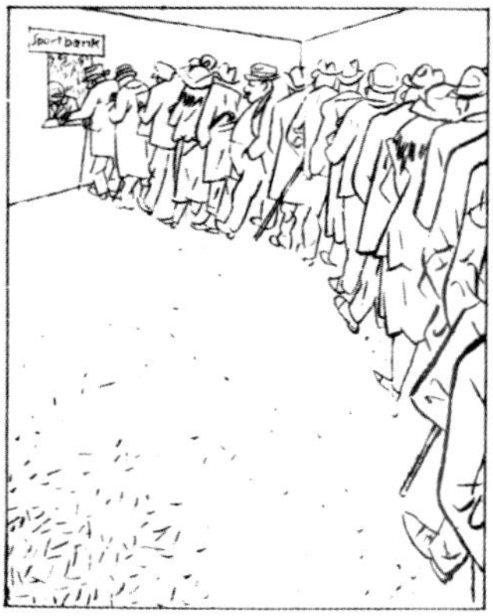

Gründe eine Sportbank

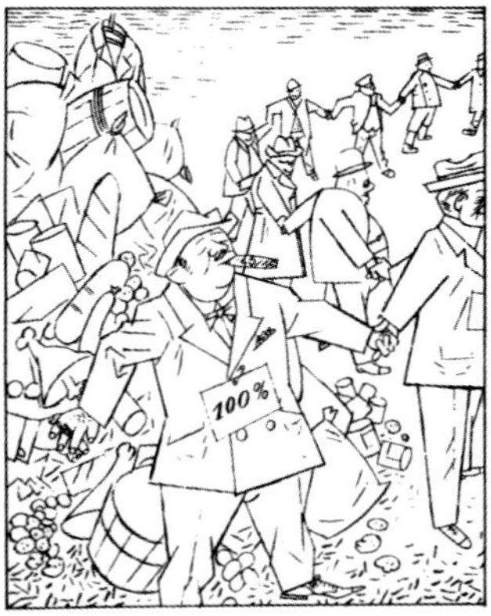

Werde Zwischenhändler

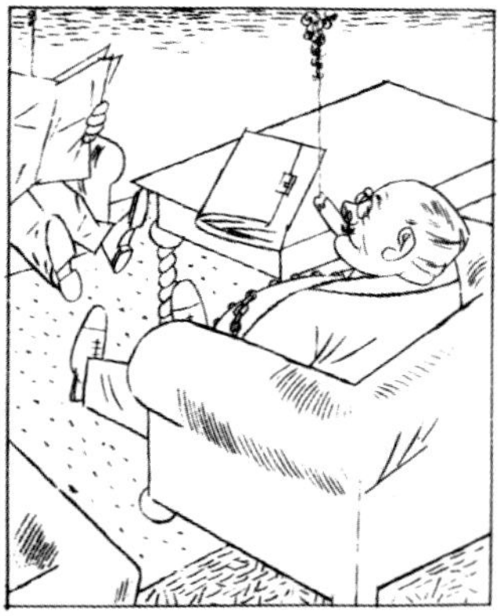

Laß Dich ins Parlament wählen

. . . reich?

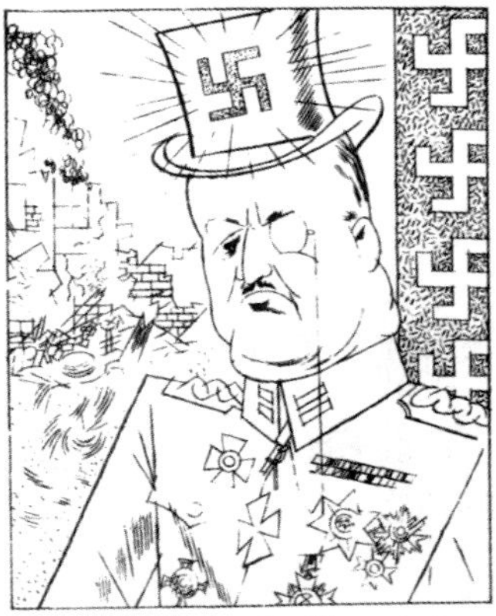

Gewinne Schlachten, verliere Kriege, schreibe Memoiren und versilbere sie in Dollar und Pfund

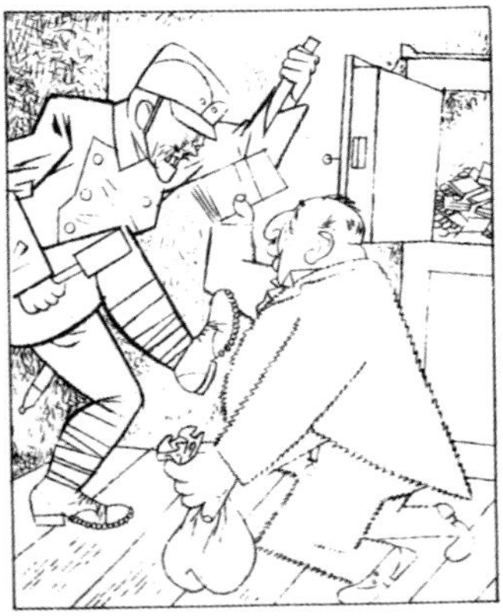

Werde Faschist, spekuliere auf Pogrome und sammle die jüdischen Reichtümer

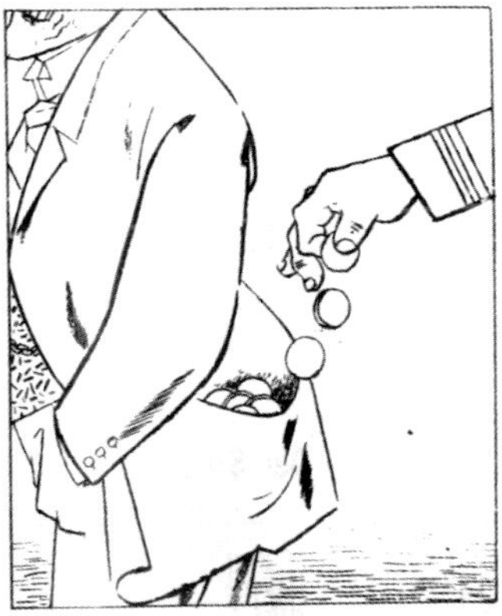

Werde Separatist, dann rollt der Frank von selbst in deine Tasche

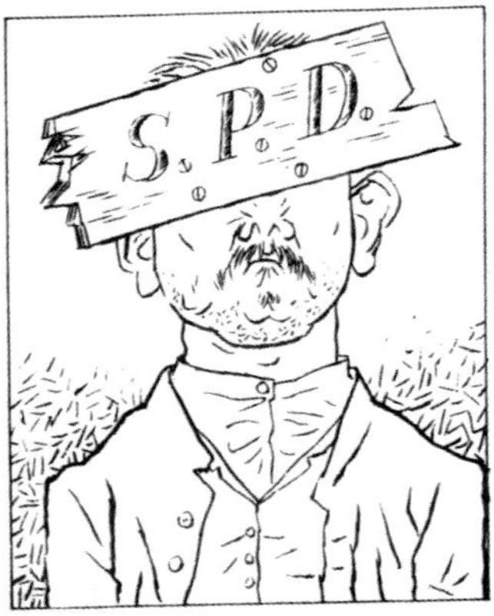

Mache in politischer Karriere

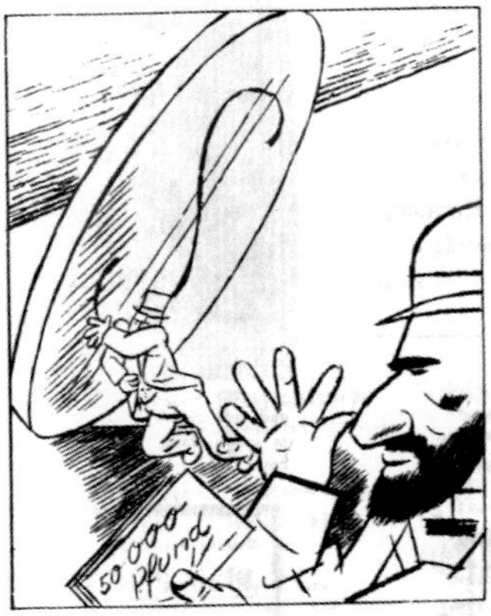

Stütze den Dollar und laß Dich von der Regierung anpumpen.

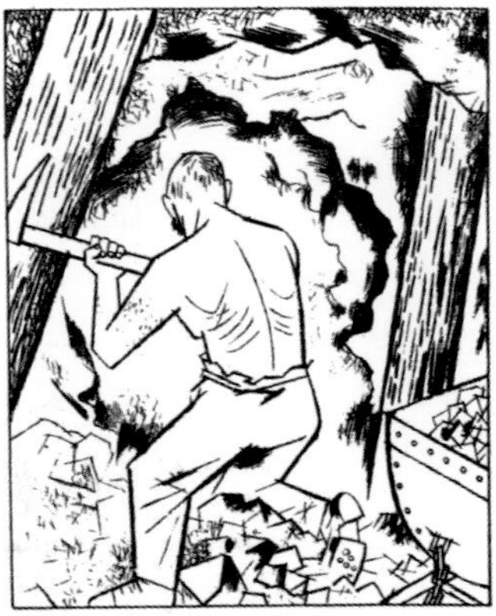

Durch Arbeit nie!

Zeichnungen von George Grosz

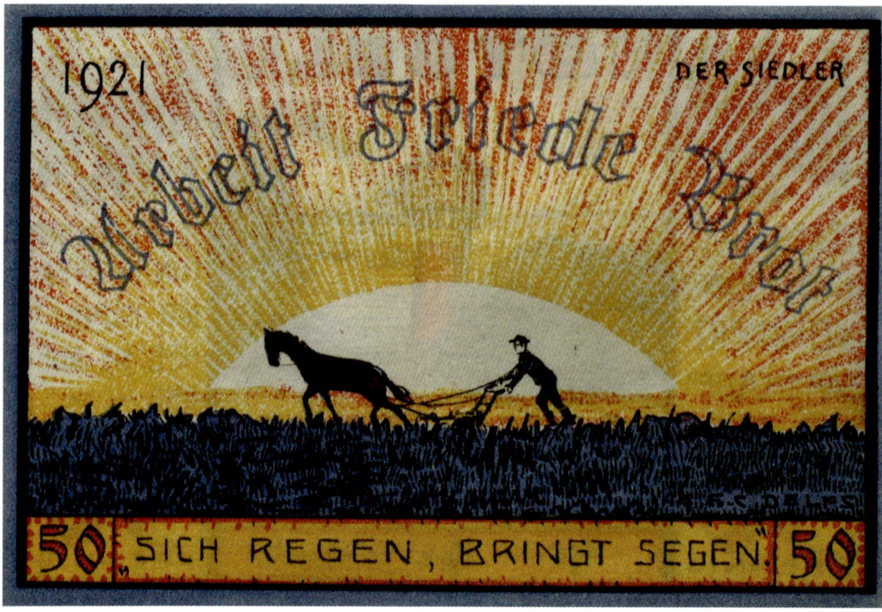

Notgeld from Lockstedter Lager, 1921. Warburg Institute, London.

the makers of Notgeld sought to prop up belief in these questionable slips of paper. Second only to land as a stabilization technique, the designers of emergency money referred time and again to the labor that ostensibly produced its value, and value in general. In many instances, these images are closely related to locational Notgeld, with the locale depicted beneath the till or the scythe of the farmer. These diligent peasants are often accompanied by exhortations regarding the benefits of work. An example issued in 1921 by the Schleswig-Holstein barracks of Lockstedter Lager shows a field being plowed together with the proverb, "Sich regen bringt Segen" (hard work pays off). The other words on the note, "Work Peace Bread," were a reactionary slogan; the barracks was closely associated with right-wing militias.[1]

The majority of such notes likewise depict the preindustrial agricultural technologies that still prevailed in rural Germany. Industrial labor does appear on Notgeld, too, however. Two examples issued by Dortmund in 1920 show workers manufacturing steel, the town's dominant industry. As is usual in such cases, these are classic worker-hero types; caught in dramatic action, the isolated figures dominate the composition. Other notes show small- to medium-scale production of the sort carried out by the

Previous: George Grosz, "How Can I Get Rich?," *Die Pleite*, 1923. Private collection.

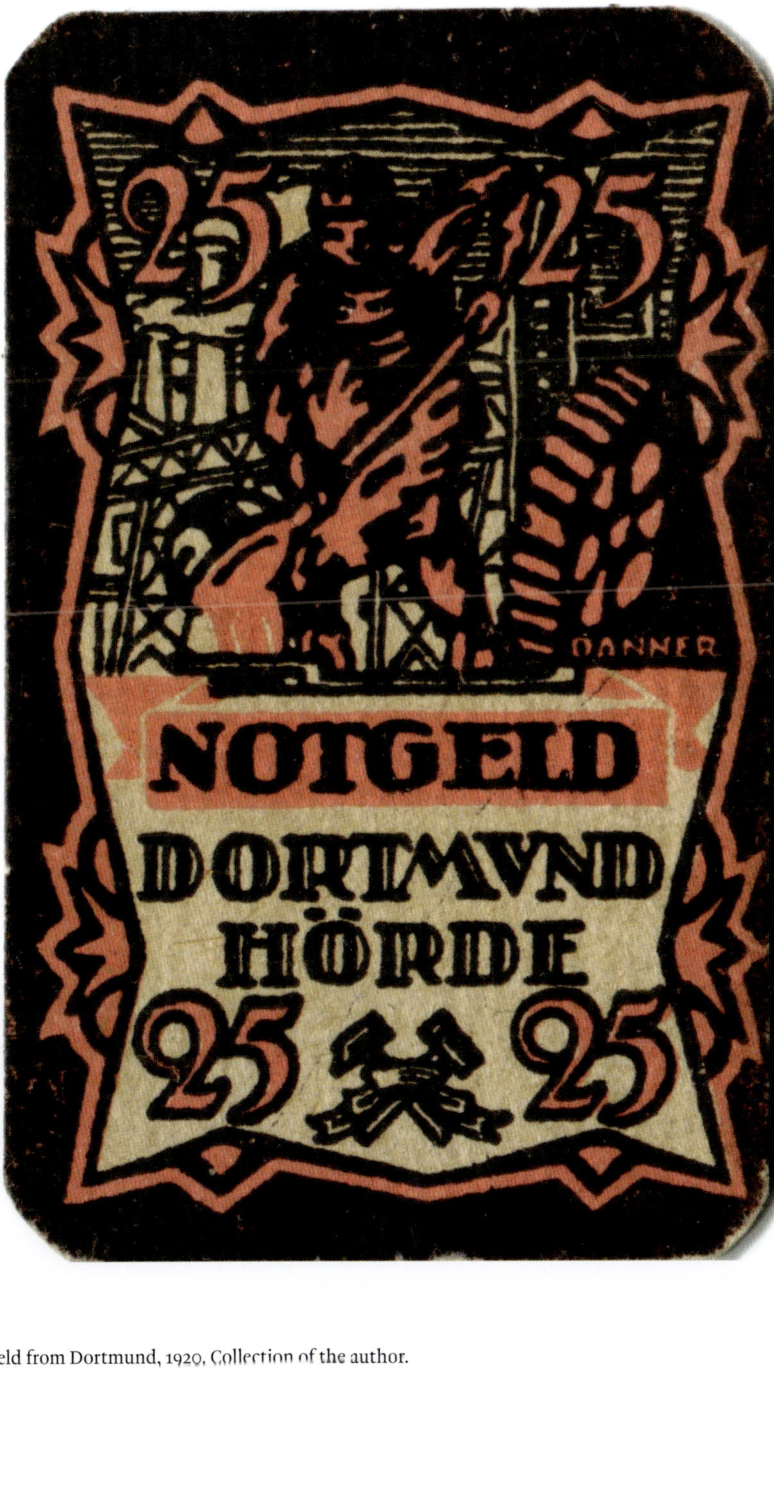

Notgeld from Dortmund, 1920, Collection of the author.

traditional *Mittelstand*, such as glass manufacture and weaving. In the latter case, we see a woman operating the mechanical loom, the complicated machinery of which almost crowds her out of the picture. The inscription reassures us, however, that "whether woven by hand, as once was the case, or produced by machine, Pößneck's flannel was and will always be the best goods in the world."

To a large extent, the basis of the local economy determined the type of labor illustrated on Notgeld, and in towns dominated by one particular industry this can sometimes be very specific. Such references often have a boosterish intent; sometimes they are more straightforwardly an advertisement for the goods in question, in the case of notes issued by firms that depict the activity undertaken in their factories. In every instance, however, these depictions were highly idealized, in no sense corresponding to the actuality of work in the period. Alex Potts has written that "the labouring featured in artistic representation at any historical moment changes, even as it often functions for the society in which it originates as the image of what labour is as a material

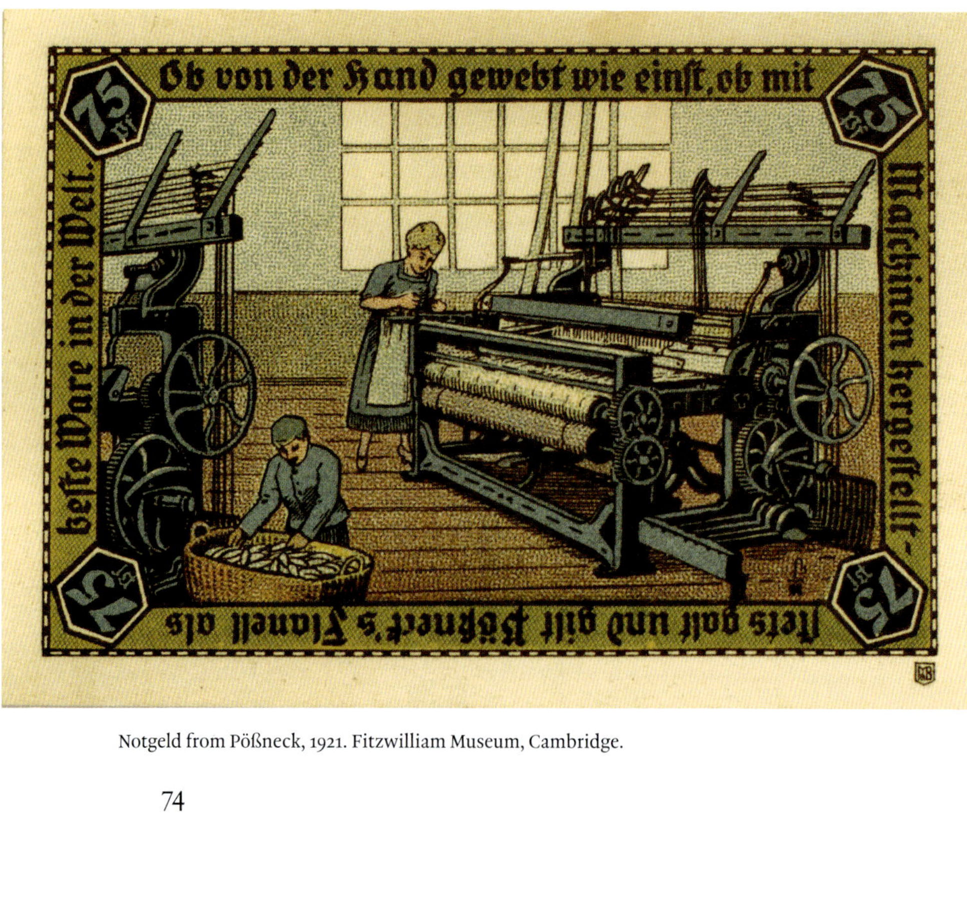

Notgeld from Pößneck, 1921. Fitzwilliam Museum, Cambridge.

practice."[2] In this moment, however, the image of labor—at least, as it appeared on Notgeld—remained static, bound up with the legacy of nineteenth-century realism, when workers first took on heroic scale in advanced European art, along with popular iconography of the sort to be found on religious prints and needlework samplers. All the while, labor itself was going into violent flux. Yet despite being out of sync, these notes do tell us what the bodies and artists who commissioned and designed these notes thought labor ought to look like. Furthermore, the notes themselves are products of a very particular type of labor—artistic labor—and as such, they are indexical traces of the conditions of that activity during this period of crisis.

As mentioned above, work was violently contested throughout the Weimar Republic. During most of the period under consideration here, an export-led boom created full employment, but prosperity did not necessarily ensue, and this discrepancy was a source of strife. Changes in the class composition of the nation also caused widespread unease. These developments had begun long before the war, with industrialization, but they were catalyzed by the inflation—and thrown into stark relief by the birth of the first workers' state to the east. For most, the period seemed dominated by the growing power of the industrial working class, and, depending on one's position, this was grounds for fear, resentment, or frustrated anticipation. Germany had avoided going the same way as Russia in its own partial revolution of 1918–1919, when the monarchy was deposed but the radical left failed to seize control of the government. However, the rights and benefits introduced by the Social Democrats did improve the prospects of workers, and they could feel themselves a rising class. Furthermore, the dumping of cheap German goods on the world market meant that the people who made them were guaranteed a source of income, but this was inadequate, and they had to fight for their wages to keep up with prices. Despite widespread and repeated strikes, they never achieved this, and rocketing costs and shortages meant that they often went hungry. It was their employers, the big industrialists, who were the real winners of the inflation, as their debts evaporated and they invested profits denominated in foreign currency into new plants and machinery.

For others, the period was one of decline and its attendant anxieties. The situation was especially stark for those who lived from fixed salaries, from pensions, and from rents. Among these were the

Bildungsbürgertum, the educated middle classes, such as academics and other higher-ranking civil servants. Their salaries plummeted in real terms: in 1913, a higher official earned seven times as much as an unskilled worker, but by 1922, the figure was only double.[3] Furthermore, any savings and additional income they received from investments dwindled away. As a result, they felt themselves becoming proletarianized, and much was written about "Die Not der geistigen Arbeiter," the distress of the intellectual workers, to cite the title of a famous speech given by Alfred Weber in 1922. In response to their changed circumstances, some members of this class, such as Walter Benjamin and other figures associated with the Frankfurt School, turned to the left; many more turned to the right.[4] In contrast to their superiors, the new middle classes of office workers and junior bureaucrats had no investments to lose; instead, they had to live from salaries that had been small to begin with, and which did not keep pace with rising prices. While this made their kinship to the industrial proletariat unmistakable, they could not detach their loyalties from the bourgeoisie to which they aspired, and so for them the inflation was a time of spiritual homelessness, to borrow Kracauer's later diagnosis.[5] Finally, though farmers and landowners did well out of the inflation on the whole, they felt their political power diminish during this period. Confronted by the *douceur de vivre* of certain sectors of society, these groups succumbed to envy and resentment regarding the profiteer, or *Schieber*, a ubiquitous hate-figure at the time; profiteers enriched themselves through idle speculation, making a mockery of honest toil. These suspicions were not always misplaced, but their targets often were. Especially vulnerable in this regard were Germany's Jews.

Faced by the changing balance of forces in these years, numerous reformers proposed schemes for improving work. It had long been feared that the rise of the industrial proletariat was destabilizing society and that the nature of their work was alienating and hence degrading to their humanity, and to German culture more widely. In the revolutionary moment, while workers' councils agitated for the socialization of the firms that employed them, reformers dreamed up utopian projects to return a state of *Arbeitsfreude*, joy in work, a notion that had a long history in Germany.[6] Most of these ideas remained speculative, but a few were put into practice, for example at the artist's colony at Worpswede, which had been founded at the end of the nineteenth century. One of the houses in the village evolved after the war into the Arbeitsschule ("work school") Barkenhoff, an anarcho-syndicalist experiment in self-sufficient communal living led by Heinrich Vogeler, an artist radicalized by his war experience. The idea of a return to the land was also popular on the right: in 1923, at the height of the hyperinflation, an anti-Slav Artaman movement was proposed that sought to "recolonize" the eastern fringe of the nation with *Wehrbauer*, soldier-peasants. (Richard Walther Darré drew his theory of *Blut und Boden*, which would shortly be adopted by the National Socialists, from the movement.)[7] Others, meanwhile, sought to reform industrial labor itself through further "rationalization": this was the era in which Taylorism and psychotechnics were developed, although these ideas would gain a wider reception in Germany only following the stabilization of the economy.

The Laboring Image

Visions of *Arbeitsfreude* are ubiquitous on emergency money, with its relentlessly industrious farmers and hammer-wielding factory workers. This rose-tinting also extends to the question of strife between economic sectors: on one note from Hoym, both peasant and proletarian are present, and the rhyme instructs the bearer that "Agriculture and industry must shake hands / Or misery will never leave this land." In other words, conciliatory fictions were rampant, and few of the realities of contemporaneous labor appear on Notgeld. In its anachronicity it had much in common with the wider iconography of work during the Weimar period, even in the left-wing press, where, unsurprisingly, images of labor are most frequently to be found.[8] As was the case with Notgeld, these publications were dominated by idealized heroes, for instance Hans Baluschek's 1920 drawing of a gigantic solitary worker striding from a factory on the cover of the first issue of *Der Proletarier*, the organ of the antiparliamentarian communist party the KAPD.[9] Immiserated workers did make an appearance elsewhere, in the work of artists such as Käthe Kollwitz and Heinrich Zille, but the readers of socialist publications expressed a preference for idealized rather than realist depictions.[10] In 1928, educator and art historical popularizer Paul Brandt published a two-volume survey of the figure of the worker in art (in the introduction he dedicated his book to the cause of *Arbeitsfreude*). Discussing recent developments, Brandt noted that, although mechanization was transforming work, "in the middle of enervating metropolitan life, it is not just the artist's eye that turns with certain affection to these work forms and rhythmic movements which demand healthy physical strength and which lie so much closer to nature."[11] In his opinion, the traditional image of labor—he mentions smiths and reapers in this connection—survives because it soothes the nervous overstimulation of the modern city. Six years later, when the path from such fantasies to the swastika had become clear, Bloch wrote: "The employee's *desire* not to be proletarian intensifies into an orgiastic desire for subordination, for a magical bureaucratic existence under a duke."[12]

Not all artists who concerned themselves with the image of labor were delusional reactionaries or aesthetic conservatives. In 1920, expressionist Conrad Felixmüller won the prestigious Saxon Rome Prize; rather than using the money to spend two years in Italy, as was the custom, he went to paint workers and factories in the Ruhr, which was then in the midst of a communist uprising. The same year, he wrote a barely veiled autobiographical article in *Die Aktion*, the anarchist-expressionist journal to which he regularly contributed graphics, titled "The Proletarian (Pönnecke)": "This Pönnecke was one of millions like him and of the same mind. One who now saw and understood everything: that he, even if he was praised as an 'artist,' was nevertheless a proletarian, and so he was a revolutionary."[13] For all their left-wing fervor, his Ruhr pictures were well received, and they were exhibited in the national gallery's modern wing at the Kronprinzenpalais in Berlin in 1923.

George Grosz, though he affected a cooler stance regarding the revolution, attempted to speak more directly to the workers than Felixmüller and the other expressionists. He returned again and again to the worker during the inflation, a time of almost frenzied productivity for him. His proletarians were often juxtaposed with industrialists or profiteers; he also depicted the unemployed, with a special focus on disabled veterans of the recent war. While Grosz's agitational images are intentionally unambiguous (his erstwhile collaborator, Carl Einstein, called them "banal"), his workers are not idealized and they are rarely straightforwardly heroic.[14] With their haggard faces and shabby clothes, they might almost be pathetic, but they bear up under the strain; often, this determination is signaled by furrowed brows and clenched fists. Many of Grosz's depictions of work and worklessness were collected in his inflation-era publications for Wieland Herzfelde's Malik Verlag,

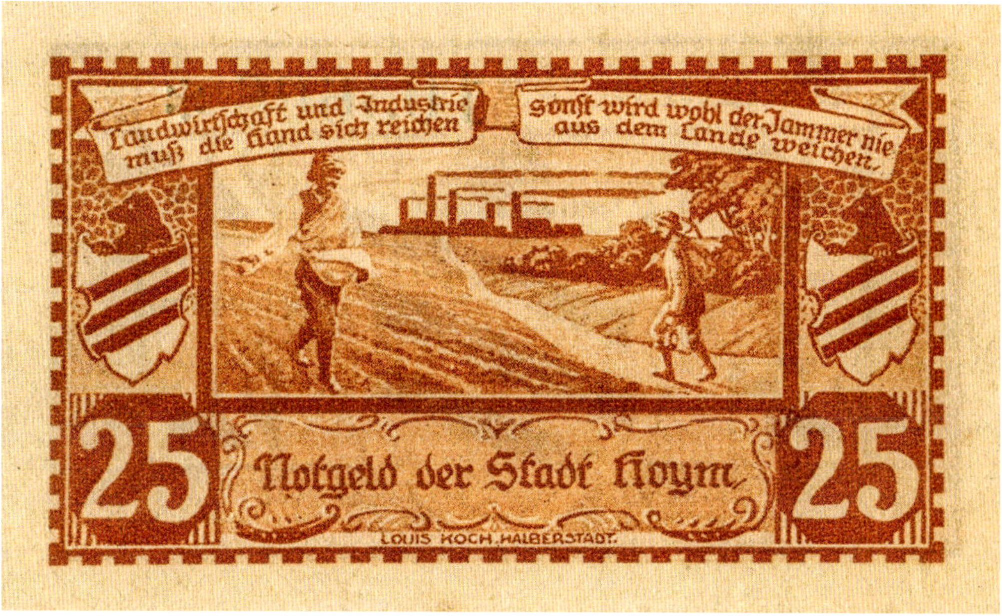

Notgeld from Hoym, 1921. Collection of the author.

such as *Das Gesicht der herrschenden Klasse*, "The Face of the Ruling Class," of which 25,000 copies were printed in three editions in 1921. His images were also used on the placards and posters of the communist party.

Somewhat incredibly, in 1921 Grosz also illustrated a book of communist fairy tales for children by Hermynia zur Mühlen.[15] In *Was Peterchens Freunde erzählen*, "What Little Peter's Friends Say," the friends in question are objects in the bedroom of a poor, convalescent boy, which relate the stories of their own production. In one of these, titled "What the Coal Said," a lump of coal explains its discovery to another: "I fell into a narrow passageway, it was so small and so low that a man could not stand upright in it. A man was there, bent completely double he struck at the wall. He gasped, and sweat flowed from his brow. But he didn't rest, he struck and struck for many hours. Oh, how tired he was, the poor man!" The other piece of coal replies, "That's nothing," and goes on to describe an underground explosion in which several men had suffocated to death. Finally, a particularly black and clever piece of coal explains that all this suffering occurs to make money for the bosses.[16] This cheery tale is accompanied by a drawing of miners working beneath the surface of the earth. They are strong, but

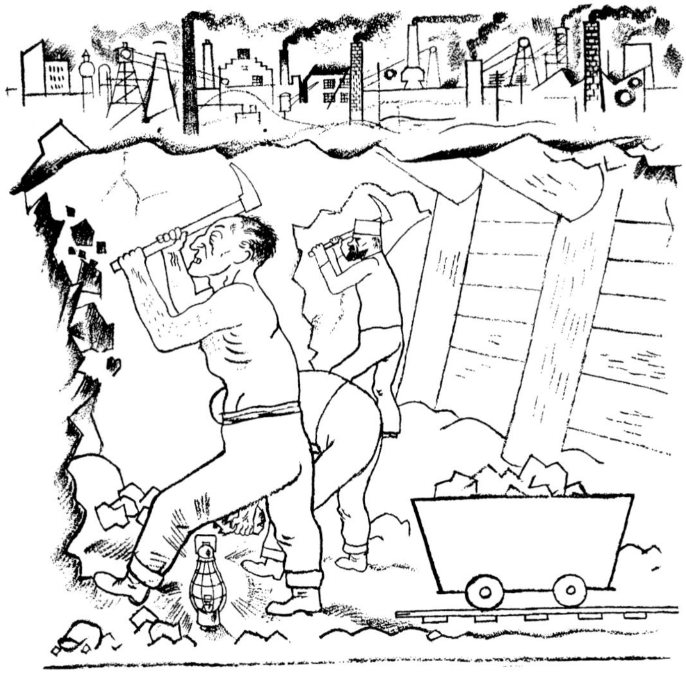

George Grosz, illustration from Hermynia zur Mühlen, *Was Peterchens Freunde erzählen* (Malik Verlag, 1921). Collection of the author.

they are not heroes; the man in the foreground is no longer young, his hair is receding, his ribs are visible, and he closes his eyes to protect them while he attacks the coalface. Above them, on the surface, stretches a vast and empty industrial landscape. Grosz's image appears to be a direct riposte to a cartoon by Thomas Theodor Heine that had appeared on the cover of *Simplicissimus* in January 1919; this shows the red devil of communism rising up from a mineshaft to destroy the factories above, along with "homeland earth" itself, as the caption informs us. More broadly speaking, it also responds to a type of image prevalent in the period: the depopulated representation of the factory that forms the upper register of his image was common at the time. In 1912, Krupp had staged a jubilee exhibition in Essen of paintings of industrial buildings, in which the workers, when they were present at all, appeared as tiny marks, "powerless against the elementary natural force" of the machinery, as Brandt put it.[17] During Weimar these structures were completely evacuated by the new photography, most notably in the work of Albert Renger-Patzsch. Such images were famously assailed by Brecht in 1930: "a photograph of the Krupp works or

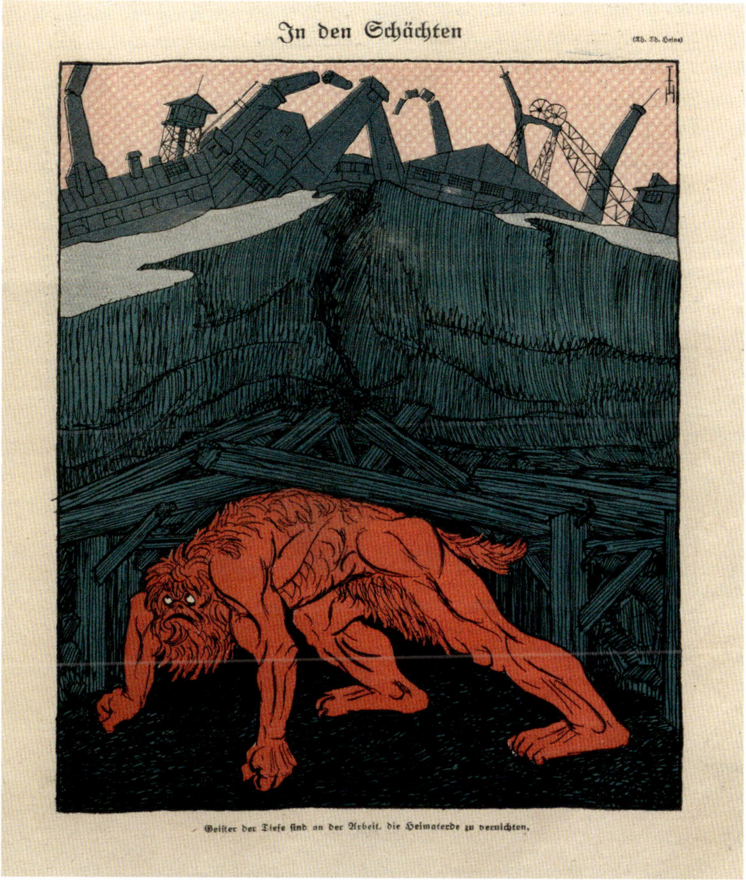

Thomas Theodor Heine, "In the Shafts," *Simplicissimus*, January 21, 1919. Private collection.

the AEG shows almost nothing about these institutions. ... The reification of human relations, such as the factory, for example, no longer surrenders the latter."[18] In contrast, Grosz's stratified composition returned labor to the commodity (as do the talking commodities of the story it accompanied), with the chimneys and pitheads appearing to grow out of the workers beneath the earth.

Grosz's strategy makes for a similarly stark contrast to comparable images of labor on Notgeld. An example issued in Freital in 1923 depicts the local coal-mining industry. As in Grosz's drawing, we are shown both the industrial architecture and the worker, who pushes a truck full of coal in the foreground. However, he is silhouetted and so we cannot tell how old, tired, underfed, or unhappy he is. Furthermore, the truck itself is labeled with the denomination of the note, 200,000 marks. This makes clear the link between

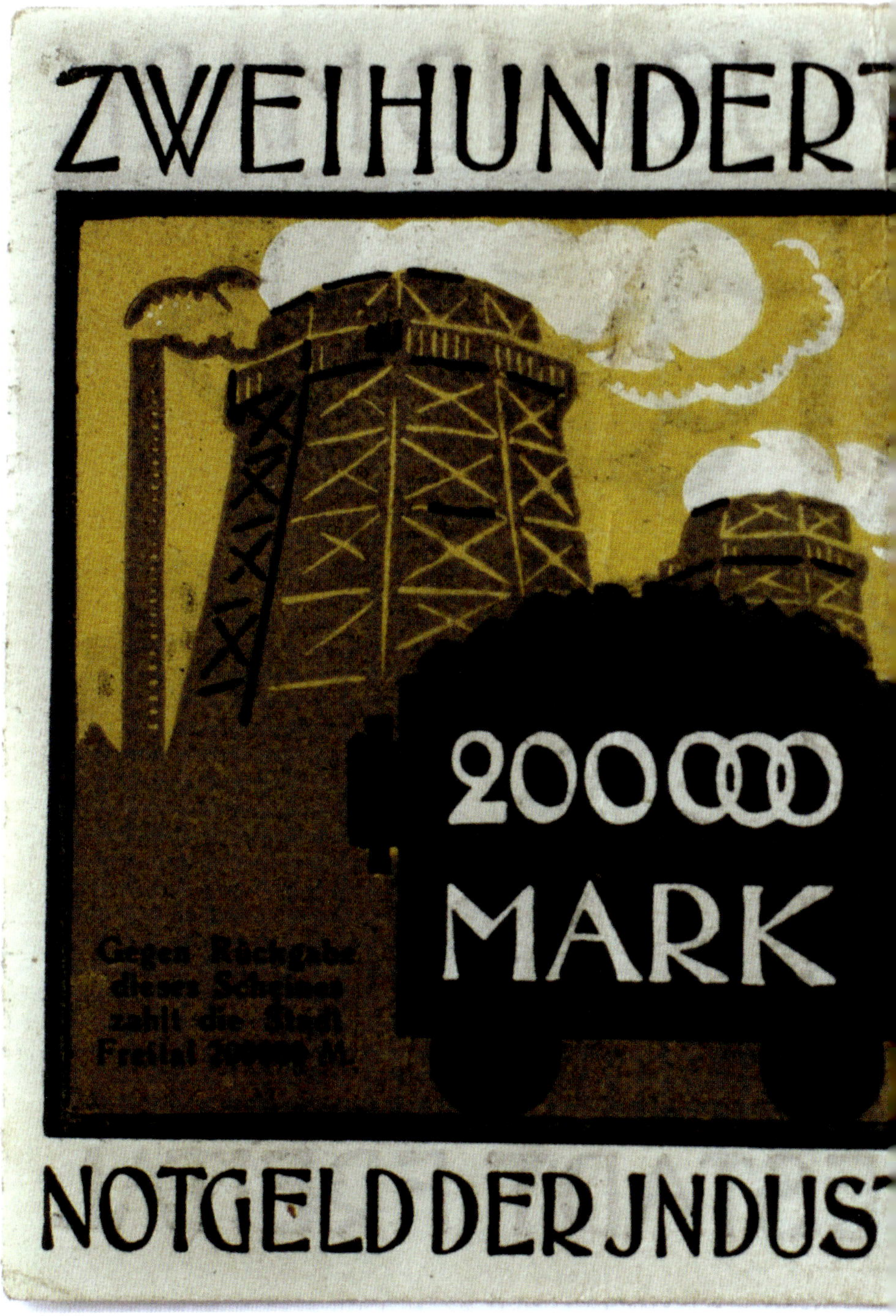

Notgeld from Freital, 1923. Warburg Institute, London.

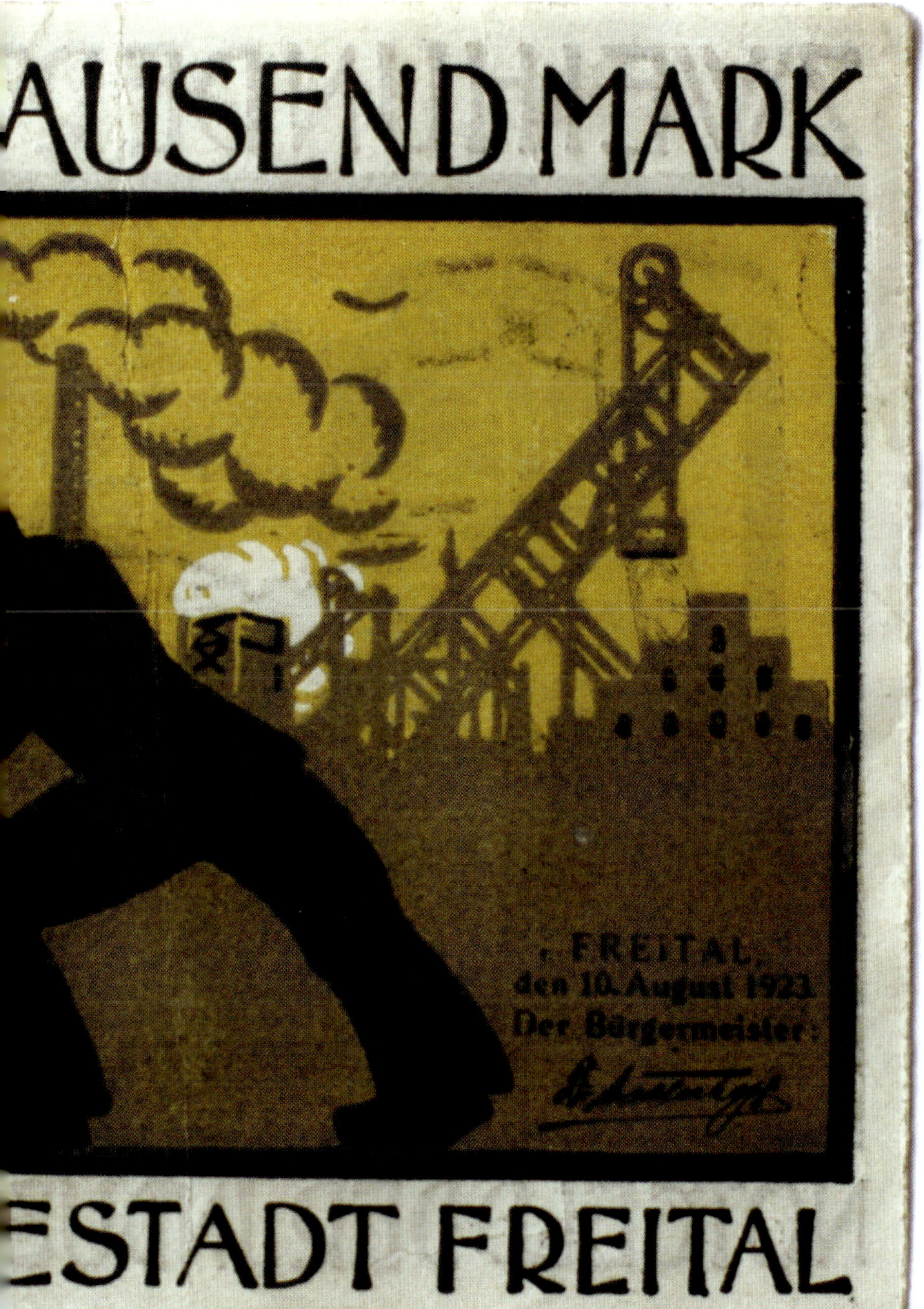
AUSEND MARK
FREITAL,
den 10. August 1923
Der Bürgermeister:
ESTADT FREITAL

labor and value that is the subtext of most such emergency money, but unlike in Grosz's image this value is not laboriously produced, nor is it, as the story accompanying Grosz's illustration makes clear, appropriated by the workers' boss.[19] Instead, value arrives pristine out of the earth, borne by the worker—whereupon it is delivered directly into the hands of the selfsame worker. Many industrialists printed money during the inflation, often in enormous quantities, and, in the absence of sufficient Reichsbank notes, this money was often used to pay employees—an expediency that also happened to accrue its issuers large profits.[20] In 1923, the famous businessman Hugo Stinnes even printed a series of million-mark notes that, instead of expiring on a certain date, became valid only *after* a certain date, by which point they had lost 95 percent of their value.[21] The workers who supposedly produced the value behind these notes were repaid with precisely these valueless pieces of paper.

As well as functioning as mystificatory idylls of value, these notes also featured slogans urging the bearer to knuckle down. These two tropes are coupled on another example from a coal-producing region, Waldenburg in Silesia. This shows a relief sculpture of miners by Constantin Meunier—a study for his *Monument to Labor*, no less, the most monumentalizing work of this pioneering monumentalizer of the laboring body—together with the words: "Work is the source of all wealth. Without work, nation and people perish."[22] The first sentence is a commonplace with socialist overtones—it was the opening line of the Gotha Program adopted by the Social Democrats in 1875—but a second sentence has been added that gives the statement a nationalist slant.[23] As Joan Campbell has pointed out, though in Germany the drive to ameliorate industrial labor was first developed by "socialists who wanted to overturn the existing order, it was quickly appropriated by defenders of that order."[24] We see that moment of appropriation on this note. Similarly nationalist formulations appear elsewhere on emergency money, as for instance in an example from Bielefeld, which bears an inscription around its border stating: "Germany's future lies in quality work! Work and save! We can work better than any other people!" (Of course, the idea that saving was of any use during the inflation was for the birds.) In his 1931 book *The Moral History of the Inflation*, Hans Ostwald went so far as to attribute the end of the inflation to the German work ethic: "The nightmare vanished. The German people resurrected itself. It created a

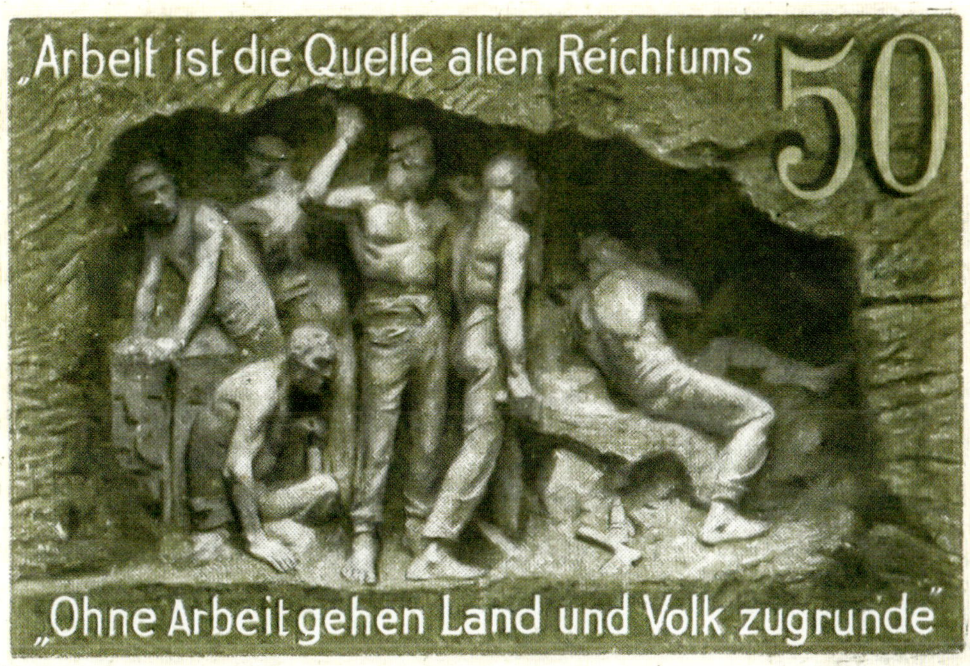

Notgeld from Waldenburg, 1920. Collection of the author.

new currency—on its own. And with that it rebuilt its economy, which was only possible because they were a people of work. Only through attention to work, only through work could it create values that became the basis for a new life." As Widdig points out in his gloss on this passage, it is, "from an economic point of view, complete nonsense."[25] Indeed, it had been confirmed as such by the denouement of the crisis, when the inflation was halted not by work but by the introduction of a new currency.

Such harangues seem doubly peculiar, given that they were made in a time of nearly full employment, a time, furthermore, when work, however diligent, barely kept the worker alive. While Notgeld proclaimed, "Wenn groß der Not, Arbeit bringt dir Brot" (When the distress is great, work brings you bread), food riots were breaking out around the country. In rhetorical terms these anachronistic notes are in fact echoes of the revolutionary moment, when, in the face of revolt and chaotic demobilization, the new government desperately tried to find work for the masses streaming into Berlin and to find workers for the mines and farms that stood desolate in the countryside. In 1918 the provisional government

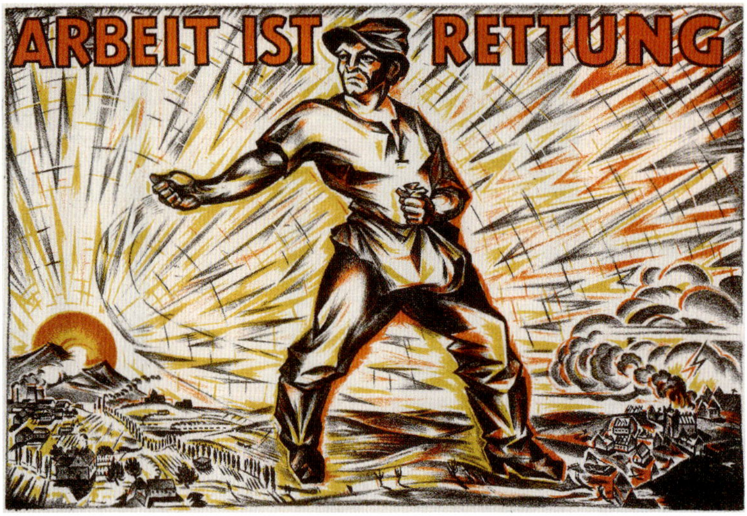

O. H. W. Hadank, *Arbeit ist Rettung*, 1919.

established the Werbedienst der deutschen sozialistischen Republik, the Publicity Office of the German Socialist Republic, to produce posters encouraging a return to order; these were partisan propaganda, aimed against the more hardline revolutionaries, especially the Spartacists.[26] Many of these graphics were made by expressionist artists such as Max Pechstein and Heinz Fuchs. As the situation became more chaotic, their tone grew shriller, threatening workers with terrible consequences if they did not go back to their jobs. One of Fuchs's designs shows a giant skeleton menacing crowds of people, with the slogan "Workers, hunger and death draw near; strike destroys, work feeds; do your duty, work." A source of some disquiet within the government, these posters did not go down well with their intended audience, either. This failure has been attributed to their unfamiliar style, but it seems unlikely that such attacks, which went so far as to assert that striking workers were digging their own children's graves, would have been appreciated by the revolutionary masses.[27]

Not all of the imagery produced by the Werbedienst was so hectoring or so avant-garde. Posters for rural audiences were more conventional in appearance, such as a more moderately expressionist 1919 example designed by O. H. W. Hadank. Beneath the slogan "Work is salvation," it shows a colossal laborer standing athwart a landscape; at one side is a ruined town, but where he casts his seed a harmonious settlement flourishes.[28] An official coin was struck by the Reichsbank the same year with the slogan *Sich regen bringt Segen* emblazoned across a sheaf of wheat. The perpetuation of these motifs and phrases into the years of "relative stabilization," 1920–1922, when the economy was booming, may seem mysterious, but they begin to make sense if we regard them as referring not to unemployment or to idleness but to labor that has been intentionally withdrawn: in other words, to strikes. There had been 5,000 of these in 1919, when it seemed a "second revolution" might be in the offing—that is, until the Social Democratic government called in the Freikorps to bloodily subdue the unrest. Industrial action continued throughout the period as workers demanded their wages keep up with inflation, and, in 1920, a general strike saved the republic from the Kapp Putsch. This was later put down when the Freikorps were once more called to act on behalf of the SDP; in the Ruhr, upward of 3,000 people were killed. Though these Notgeld images do not explicitly address the miserable conditions of work during Weimar, nor the violent social conflicts that these conditions provoked, in their relentless exhortations to work they do in fact present a clear *negative* image of labor: every diligent peasant, every heroic steelworker, is the shadowy twin of a striker on a picket line. A hint that such entreaties might have been received with something less than enthusiasm is furnished by an example from Münsterberg, which shows a downcast laborer who has set his tools aside, together with the phrase "Nur nicht verzweifeln" (Just don't despair).[29] But even here,

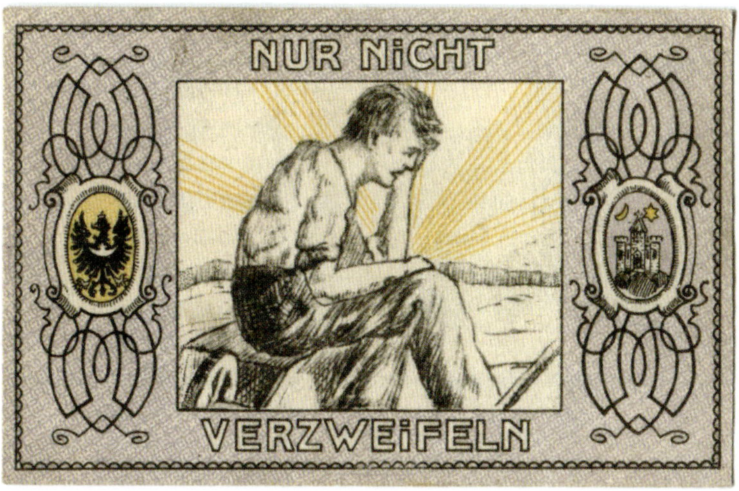

Notgeld from Münsterberg, 1921. Collection of the author.

though work has ceased, it is not in the cause of organized labor but rather through hopelessness. Nevertheless, it is the most accurate depiction of work to appear on Notgeld.

The Production of Money

Despite being invoked to support belief in these notes, the images of labor discussed so far had little to do with their value, such as it was. What value they did possess derived instead from another source: the work of artists, printers, and paper manufacturers. The printers made Notgeld in a double sense, both directly and, one might say, in an Operaist sense. Although they were vital to the physical manufacture of money in this period, they also contributed by *not* manufacturing it: when the printers of the Reichsbank and its suppliers went on strike in September 1922, the government was forced to allow the issue of Notgeld once more—having banned it only two months earlier—in order to make up the shortfall.[30]

These professions do appear on Notgeld, but their representatives are not shown in the act of making emergency money. The only figure to be depicted thus is a bureaucrat, who receives the inspiration for the new currency from a cosmic source:

> Comet-like came the idea
> To the mayor, bright and clear:
> Geldnot [money emergency]? Let's turn it about!
> Some Notgeld [emergency money] will sort it out!

As in this annunciation scene, when Notgeld's *material* origin is depicted on these notes, it issues from mystifying sources, from cornucopias and the mouths of mythical beasts. However, I would speculatively suggest that the images of workers that appear on these notes, though mystificatory if taken at face value, are in fact stand-ins for the artists who designed them. This proposal is most convincing in the context of the note from Waldenburg discussed above. The workers here are ostensibly coal miners (it was a coal-producing region), but their activity is somewhat obscure. If we consider the fact that the image is a photographic reproduction of a relief sculpture, and that the figures appear to be digging themselves out of the stone, then we see that they are at work on their

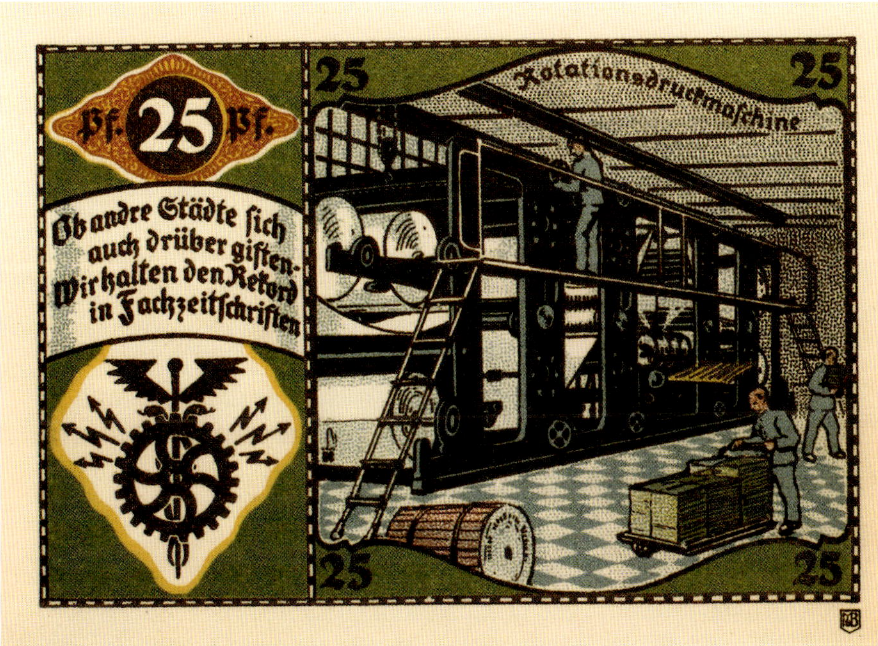

Notgeld from Pößneck, 1921. Fitzwilliam Museum, Cambridge.

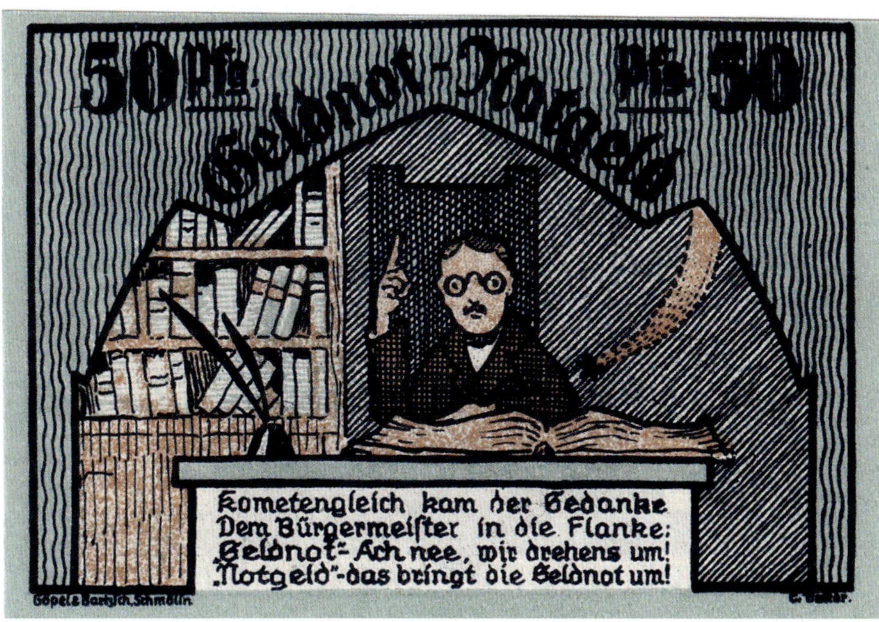

Notgeld from Schmölln, 1921. Nathaniel Butler.

own creation as a work of art. They are, in other words, artists, and what they are producing is at once artwork—and Notgeld.

Besides equating the Notgeld note with the artwork, this autopoietic image implies that, as artists work on their own creations, they are also producing themselves. These ambiguities chime with the situation at the beginning of the Weimar Republic, when the social role of the artist and the value of the artwork were both thrown into crisis. These developments had prewar roots: the Brücke group of expressionists in Dresden had been established in part to find an independent means of supporting artistic production, which was to be funded by "passive members" who received prints in return for their subscription fees. Such efforts were radicalized during the revolution, when, parallel to the workers' councils that demanded the socialization of industry, artists agitated for the socialization of art production.[31] Several groups were established with this end in mind, among them the Novembergruppe, named for the November Revolution, and the Arbeitsrat für Kunst, the Workers' Council for Art. The former was a large and disparate organization that lasted until around 1933. In its earliest phase, it called for a revolution in the institutions of art (while skirting the question of political revolution), with one of its demands being that artists be supported directly by the state. The somewhat more radical Arbeitsrat für Kunst, while equally concerned that art be socialized, wanted to avoid governmental paternalism, and so it proposed that commissions be awarded by worker's councils. The establishment of the Bauhaus in 1919 must be seen in the context of these ideas, and also as part of the older discourse regarding "joy in labor" referred to earlier. The school was, in its early years, an attempt to reform the labor of the artist by looking back to the social structures of the feudal era, specifically to the guilds that had formed in order to secure the position of the artist in the face of the development of the capitalist market. As Gropius (who was a founding member of the Arbeitsrat) put it in the school's first prospectus, "let us then create a new guild of craftsmen without the class distinctions that raise an arrogant barrier between craftsman and artist."[32] This demand was partly born of a revolutionary impulse to move closer to the workers, but it also reflected pressing material concerns. He expanded on these in a speech to the students: "we will no longer stand by the side of the crafts but be a part of them, since we have to earn money."[33]

The first, provisional government of the republic was not entirely deaf to the demands being made by artists. The establishment of the Werbedienst, the posters of which were discussed above, was one manifestation of this openness, in that it offered work to avant-garde artists at a moment when commissions were otherwise scarce. The body also published a pamphlet in 1919, titled *An alle Künstler!*, an appeal "to all artists" to support the new republic, with a pathos-laden drawing by Pechstein on its cover. It contained several essays on the future of the arts, including one by Kurt Eisner, who had briefly been president of the equally brief Bavarian Socialist Republic before he was murdered earlier that year. The text of his speech, "The Socialist State and the Artist," reproduced here, argues that the artist should be supported by the state—and also that the artwork should have no exchange value.

At the time of its publication, the latter demand was very far from corresponding to reality. Even during the last years of the war, the art market had been surprisingly buoyant, and as the inflation surged in 1919–1920, and again in 1922–1923, it boomed.[34] This expansion was driven by the so-called *Flucht in die Sachwerte*, the flight into real values, when people sought to translate their rapidly devaluing money into more stable commodities. As soon as they were paid, the poor rushed to the shops to buy food before their wages became worthless; meanwhile the rich put their profits into luxury goods, especially contemporary art. In 1920, a prominent Werkbund member, Bruno Rauecker, wrote that "art dealerships are springing up like mushrooms, the 'new' art lovers are more numerous than the old ones. Understandably: they prefer to hang on their walls, in the form of artworks, their life insurance, their stocks, their war and revolution profits."[35]

Ironically, given the presence of his drawing on the cover of the pamphlet *An alle Künstler!*, Pechstein was one of the greatest beneficiaries of this trend. Indeed, modern prints boomed especially.[36] They could be produced and distributed rapidly and cheaply, and, once purchased, required little room to store. This opportunity was not seized by expressionists alone; Grosz's vast output of works on paper in these years was partly a response to the same situation. The artist and his publisher had embarked on the kind of speculative venture that characterized much economic activity during the inflation. They were hardly alone in this. If speculation is taken to mean a financial operation that attempts to turn risk into profit, then, in a situation in which the future had become entirely uncertain, it was not only swindlers, bankers, industrialists, and currency speculators who were so engaged. So too was everybody who turned their marks into foreign currency or into goods as quickly as possible; indeed, every purchase, every hour of work advanced for a paycheck, was a speculation.[37] The sense that life itself had become a speculative venture was testified to by the contemporaneous ubiquity of the figure of the gambler, most famously in Fritz Lang's 1922 film *Dr. Mabuse the Gambler*, based on a popular 1921 novel of the same name that had been inspired in turn by postwar profiteering.

Artists also became speculators during the inflation, or perhaps it would be more accurate to say that their speculative activity intensified. Marina Vishmidt has described an apparent corollary between financial speculation and art, with the artist operating as a dealer in insubstantial and (hopefully) self-valorizing values.[38] Vishmidt identifies this kind of artistic speculation with the post-conceptual, post-Bretton Woods moment, but the apparent parallelism goes significantly further back, at least to the inflationary period following 1914—another derangement of value caused by a departure from the gold standard. In fact, artists have been producing speculatively ever since they became independent economic agents working for the market, and it remains uncertain to what extent this parallelism can be boiled down to a direct causality between particular economic conjunctures and particular developments in the history of art. Many have attempted to assert the existence of such links, nonetheless, but the connecting tissue has rarely been satisfactorily dissected. In the context under discussion here, this parallelism was first made in 1973 by Jean-Joseph Goux, who argued that the rise of abstract painting could be tied to Western Europe's departure from the gold standard at the onset of the First World War.[39] This essentially semiotic argument rests on the assertion that in both cases, the signifier is detached from the signified. Rosalind Krauss expanded this interpretation to encompass Picasso's collages, and similar attempts have been made with regard to Duchamp's readymades and to Dadaism more generally.[40] These "isomorphisms," to borrow a word beloved of Goux, are open to some obvious criticisms: Kandinsky's abstract work began around 1910, Braque and Picasso made their first collages in 1912, Duchamp produced his first readymade in 1913, and although Dadaism "officially" began in Zurich in February 1916, this was a time and place when inflation, though present, was by no means so oppressive as it would later become.[41] Goux attempts to circumvent this problem by stating that he is not concerned with "ascribing to economic *symbology* an anterior or causal role" (my emphasis); however, this threatens to leave the historiographic value of these observations hanging in the air.[42] (At the risk of attempting the kind of move that Goux abjures, we might say that, being made in the wake of the linguistic turn, when money's semiological status became preeminent over the value to which it refers, the interpretations cited above can themselves be attributed to the cultural logic of late capitalism, which followed Nixon's suspension of the gold standard in 1971.[43] The irony is that, despite being clothed in poststructuralist rhetoric, they sound rather like the vulgar Marxism from which they were trying to distinguish themselves, while returning at the same time to idealism—because where else can these mysteriously universal motivating forces gestate other than in the womb of the world spirit?) However, Goux continues: "we can only note within the historical world of sociality correspondences and contradictions between its procedures and those that govern signifying metabolisms."[44] Apart from the defeatist "only," this formulation suggests a more promising line of inquiry in which the quasi-autonomy of the art object permits the possibility of reconfiguring the economic conditions that structure it—including in the area spotlit by Goux and others, that is, the problematic relationship between the sign and value.[45] While these writers emphasized the semiotic, however, to the point of evacuating the value of money, here I have attempted to keep an eye on the latter, too.

In any case, regarding the development of Dada, other factors were certainly more influential than monetary policy, not least the war itself. But although we cannot attribute the origins of Dada or of abstraction directly to the end of the gold standard, in the context of the inflation that followed, speculation of an entirely material sort was unambiguously present in the art world. This was clear to contemporaries. Already in 1919, the critic Curt Glaser—who was a prolific collector of contemporary prints—complained in *Das Kunstblatt* about the vast number of print portfolios being made available. Tellingly, he compares these to devalued paper currency: "From every side, dozens of names are called to the poor collector, on whose desk mountains of printed paper pile up; today valuables, as certain for the artists and publishers as their own banknote press, tomorrow wastepaper, as worthless as the paper money of a fallen government."[46] And this *did* affect the artwork itself, albeit not in the sense argued by Goux, Krauss, and others. In his article, Glaser goes on to argue that speculation determines the form of the art being produced, too, with artists and publishers chasing the dead cert—with the inevitable consequence that the bubble will eventually burst.[47] He turned out to be correct about this: the decline of expressionism can to some extent be attributed to its saturation of the market, as I will discuss in the next chapter. For his part, Grosz complained of being a "banknote factory," working to satisfy the demands of the market—a statement that must to a certain extent be taken as self-critical.[48] In the 1920 text from which the above citation is taken, "Statt einer Biographie" (Instead of a Biography), Grosz goes on to argue that artists should work for the proletariat instead of for bourgeois collectors, but he was playing a double game. His own work for Malik Verlag was issued at a number of prices: as well as being available in cheap pamphlets affordable to workers, luxury signed editions were also produced.[49] Taking a more dialectical view of this situation, Paul Westheim, editor of *Das Kunstblatt*, wrote in a 1923 article titled "Kunst als Sachwert" (Art as Material Asset) that it was precisely speculation that had made the free development of art possible in those difficult times, though to admit this was "deeply unpleasant."[50] The ambiguous status of works of culture in this period, which seemed to be on the verge of being, or indeed of having become, a form of currency, was thematized in a cartoon published in a 1922 issue of the satirical magazine *Simplicissimus*. Gutenberg stands by an anthropomorphic printing press, which spews banknotes into the eager hands of a waiting crowd. Clutching his Bible, head in his hand, he moans: "That wasn't what I wanted!" Here we see the means of production of culture, the press, become the origin of what was seen in conventional *Kulturkritik* as being its nemesis: money. However, the cartoonist has also inadvertently anticipated what Marc Shell would later say about poetry and coinage—that these are twins, in fact, born at the same moment and sharing the same features, the same structures. Money was also, as Shell points out, the first mechanically reproduced work of art.[51]

In 1921, the writer Max Herrmann-Neisse had made a similar observation: "This culture now comes full circle to what was always at its basis: to capital. Money is not only time—in this culture, money is everything: love, religion, science. Art too is money

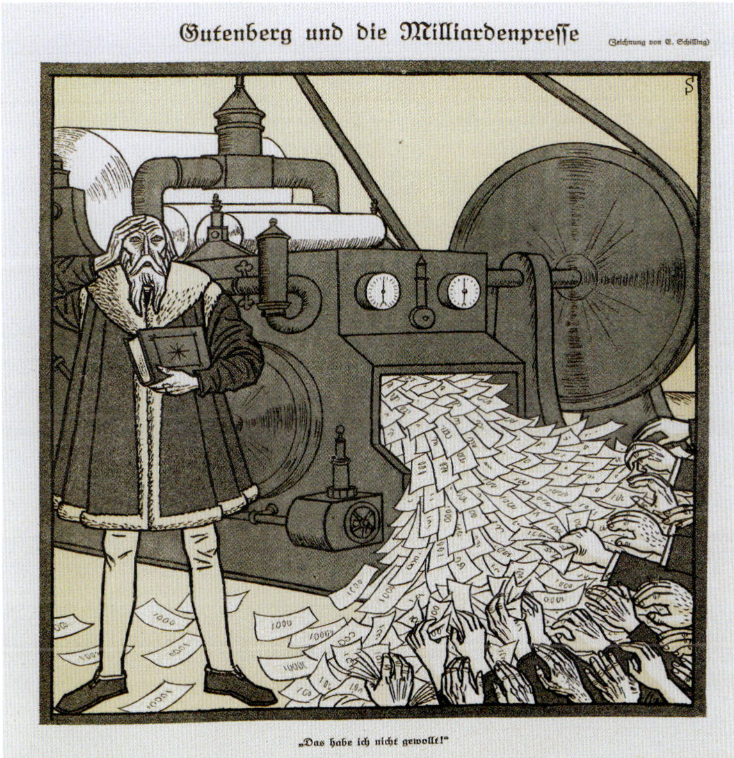

Erich Schilling, "Gutenberg und die Milliardenpresse," *Simplicissimus*, 1922. Private collection.

and, like money, is spent, exchanged, forged and—devalued."[52] But while the critic could not observe the situation without reaching for a narrative of decline, and his friend Grosz saw it with a degree of disgust, others seized on this gray area as a field of operations in which they might reconfigure both the artist and the artwork. We do not need to subscribe to deterministic models or analogical thinking in order to perceive this or to recognize the obvious fact that the inflation entered into the artwork as both content and medium. An article signed by the "Central Committee of Dadaism" in the first issue of the journal *Der Dada*, which appeared in June 1919, is titled: "Invest Your Money in Dada!" It instructs readers: "Dada is the only savings bank that pays interest in eternity."[53] This parodic invocation of the artwork's increasingly unambiguous status as store of value was a mordantly topical statement to make during the first wave of postwar inflation. Had such a claim been genuinely advanced by a bank, it would have been seized upon by desperate savers; however, given the state of the economy, it would in fact have been recognized immediately as the language of the con artist. This fraudulent posture was likewise signaled by the way the Dadaists dressed, like contemporaneous caricatures of profiteers, with flashy suits, monocles, and arrogant stances. This costume was fitting, since the deviousness of these folk-devils ran parallel to their own program; one observer noted that the success of swindlers stemmed from the fact that they "follow precisely the opposite rules to those of the solid period of development before the war."[54] The most extreme expression of this congruence was performed by Walter Serner, a central if somewhat mysterious figure in the development of Zurich Dada. Serner explicitly posed (and sometimes operated) as a swindler, even subtitling his "Last Loosening" manifesto, when it was reworked and republished in 1920, as "A Handbook for the Con Artist and Those Aspiring to Become One."[55] In the manifesto's opening paragraph he cynically compares the artwork to a pair of silk stockings; both are commodities, but the former "cannot be grasped," and hence is less valuable. But, he adds, critics "unleash rivers of money," resulting in the artwork being valued more highly, a state of affairs that he regards with regret.[56]

Though he vigorously opposed the way the Berlin Dadaists rejected art as a category (and was rejected by them in turn for maintaining bourgeois artistic ideals), Kurt Schwitters was also engaged in this period in a project of reconfiguration of both the artwork and the artist, although he took more legitimate forms of commerce as his model than Serner had. Quite literally: the term he used for his multimedia productions, Merz, was derived from a snippet of text reading *Kommerz- und Privatbank*, included in a now-lost artwork of 1919, *Merzbild 1*. In a text published in the expressionist journal *Der Sturm* the same year, the artist stated, "The word Merz denotes essentially the combination of all conceivable materials for artistic purposes, and technically the principle of equal evaluation of the individual materials."[57] In 1921, he went further: "at the end of 1918 I realized that all values only consist in their relationship to one another. ... I formed Merz from this realization."[58] As Christoph Zeller has pointed out, this attributes to Merz the same function as the universal equivalent, money, which makes all things the same. During the inflation, Zeller continues, Schwitters attempted to reorder the chaos of the commodity world, represented in his pictures via the detritus of commerce: tram, cinema, and cloakroom tickets; postage stamps, packaging, advertisements. In Zeller's words: "The play of art with the laws of economics, the economization of art as the rules of the game of life. Economic unreason could only be dealt with by 'artistic logic.'"[59] Although this may sound superficially like Serner equating paintings with silk stockings, Schwitters insists on the primacy of art, with only the artist retaining the capacity to bring order to a disordered world. This is achieved not through money, which had failed in this regard, but through an improvement on money, an aesthetic ordering principle: Merz. For Schwitters, we might say with Adorno, "Form works like a magnet that orders elements of the empirical world in such a fashion that they are estranged from their extra-aesthetic existence, and it is only as a result of this estrangement that they master the extra-aesthetic essence."[60] Schwitters thereby sought to aestheticize economics, and in doing so he turned silk stockings—among many other things—into art, while transforming art at the same time by bringing it into structural proximity with the universal equivalent.

Money itself is surprisingly scarce in Schwitters's collages, given the predominantly commercial character of the paper ephemera he assembles, but it does make some significant appearances in his work, as it does in that of several other artists in the Dadaist milieu. (I will turn to these shortly.) Notgeld is included in two consecutively numbered Merzbilder of 1920, *Mz 157: Hindenburg* and *Mz. 158: Das Kotsbild*, "The Excrement Picture." The former includes a Notgeld note from Göttingen juxtaposed with the name of the famous general and an image showing a woman's legs as she pulls up her stockings, among other elements. While the "extra-aesthetic element" being manipulated here seems to be the right-wing war hero, in *Das Kotsbild* Schwitters expands on the feminine theme, in a way that has appeared to some to be misogynistic.[61] Several images of fashionable young women are presented alongside an image of a small dog, the phrase "dog collars," and the phrase "women's professions"; the latter element is directly beneath the textual fragment KOTS, which on its own sounds like *Kotz*, puke, but in conjuncture with *Frauenberufe* it sounds like "crappy women's jobs." Alongside these apparently disparaging allusions to the changing status of women are two pieces of paper money: a Polish one-mark note, a devalued currency that had been introduced during the German occupation, and one half of a Notgeld note. Here money seems to appear as—almost worthless—payment for the working woman.[62]

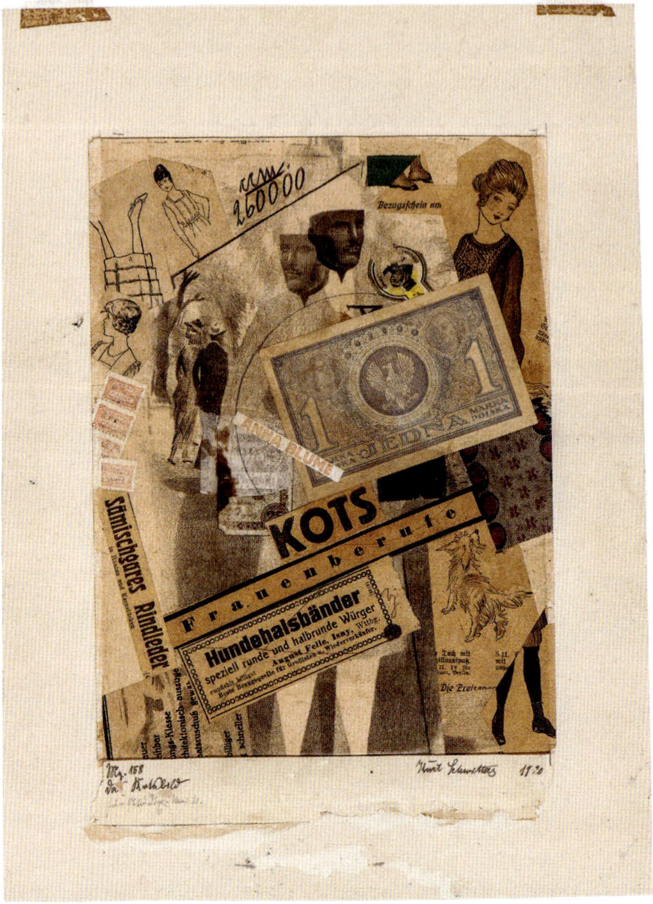

Kurt Schwitters, *Mz. 158: Das Kotsbild*, 1920, collage, 27.5 × 20.7 cm. Sprengel Museum, Hannover.

In light of this we might ask whether Schwitters, though appearing close to misogynistic narratives, is not in fact questioning the value of submitting to the harness of exploitative employment.

Schwitters's most prominent use of money appears in his lost 1922 work, *Mz 383: Der Kenner nimmt* (The Connoisseur Selects). This composition incorporates two Notgeld notes showing historical buildings; the upper of these, issued by Schleiz in 1919, represents that city's mint, with the inscription "Valuable coins were once stamped here / now 'coins' are printed on worthless paper." Schwitters also includes two illustrations of ammunition, one labeled "machine gun" and the other "dumdum bullets," as well as geometrical forms cut from colored paper, elements unusual in his oeuvre, reflecting his engagement with constructivism

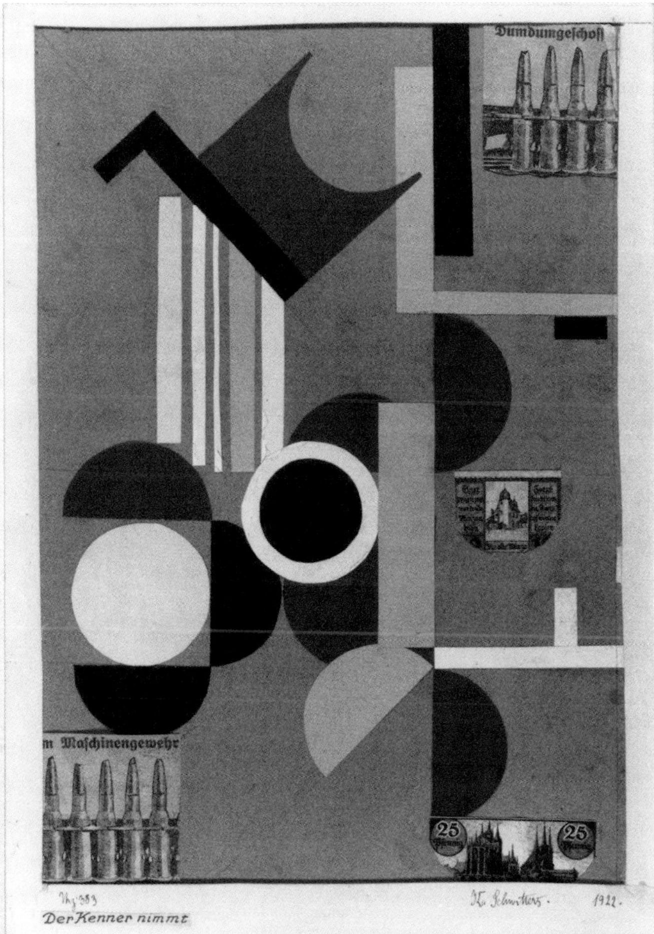

Kurt Schwitters, *Mz. 383: Der Kenner nimmt*, 1922, collage, dimensions unknown (original lost). Kurt Schwitters Archive, Sprengel Museum, Hannover.

at the time. The latter include a bull's-eye at the center of the composition, possibly the eye of the connoisseur referred to by the title, and a clawlike form at the bottom, which snaps at one of the pieces of Notgeld. The connoisseur—a Notgeld collector, perhaps, or an art lover more generally speaking—seems to be selecting the conventional representation of the conventionally valorized townscape, the "framed" image that is at once "worthless paper [money]." And the act of connoisseurial discernment takes place against a background of technological violence. This may be a critique of the market and a negative valorization of the ordering capacity of hegemonic art: the connoisseurs are mocked for their interest in worthless, kitschy representations, with the implication that better options are available. Yet there is an ambivalence at work here, and the connoisseur may in fact be the artist himself. Schwitters's collaborator Kate Steinitz later recalled him looking through waste paper in the basement of a printers' shop: "he sorted out the unfinished pages that appealed to him as carefully as a connoisseur would have examined the precious prints in a museum collection."[63] Seen in this light, this is a self-portrait of Schwitters at work, reordering the waste products of the culture industry, commoditized violence and kitsch, within his redemptive aestheticized economy, Merz.

Der Kenner nimmt is presumably one of the works, and perhaps precisely the work, referred to by Moholy-Nagy, who shared a freezing studio with Schwitters during the winter of 1922–1923: "We had no money to buy paint or canvas. So Kurt inspired me to follow his example and use the currency of the day as a material for collage."[64] The result was Moholy-Nagy's montage *25 Pleitegeier* of around 1922–1923, the title of which is a wordplay: a *Geier* is a vulture, and *Die Pleite* means bankruptcy, so this literally means bankrupt vultures, but *Pleitegeier* is also a figure of speech meaning "specter of bankruptcy." Moholy-Nagy takes this image literally: two of these animals appear in the work, figuring as more sinister versions of the German imperial eagle, as has been pointed out.[65] These are combined with segments cut from official Reichsbank notes and snippets of Notgeld. Several fragments of text have been organized to read "The city treasury office pays money without marks." Compared with Schwitters's uses of money, it is a fairly direct satire, composed as a more or less coherent image, which is perhaps unsurprising given that it was Moholy-Nagy's first attempt in the medium. Unlike in Schwitters's *Merzbilder*, there is no sense that money is being employed here for its indexical quality, its (disastrously inadequate) representation of value; rather, it is an iconographic element. In Adornian terms, the material is insufficiently estranged from its extra-aesthetic existence, so that these poles cannot be held in a productive tension, and resolve too easily into caricature.

Schwitters was not the only Dadaist working with Notgeld during the inflation. His collage *Das Kotsbild* was made as a gift to Otto Dix in 1920, and the same year Dix also incorporated money into his own work, presumably in response to Schwitters's example. In Dix's case, Notgeld notes are employed as indexical signs of

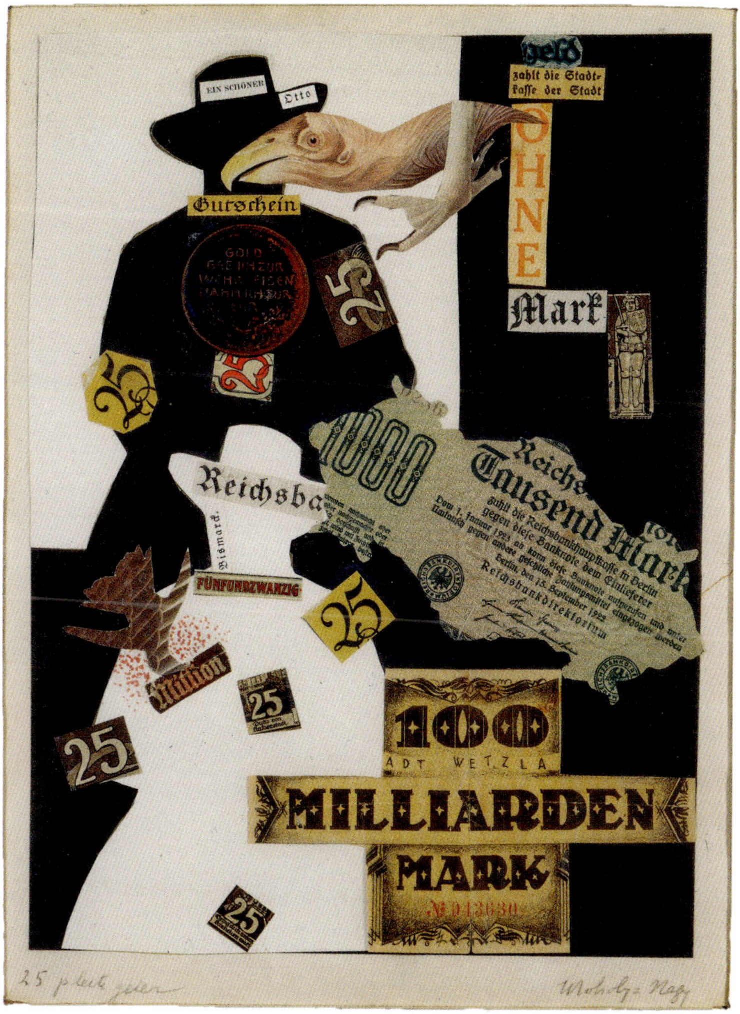

László Moholy-Nagy, *25 Pleitegeier*, 1922–1923, collage, 30 × 23 cm. The Israel Museum, Jerusalem.

abject worthlessness, but unlike in Schwitters's collages, in which worthless money is redeemed by aesthetic ordering, for Dix these objects maintain their worthlessness; indeed, their abjection infects the rest of the image, revealing the worthlessness of art itself. (This was also the year in which Scholz included money in his *Industrial Farmers*, to similar effect.)[66] Notgeld appears in two major paintings by Dix of 1920, his *Skat Players* and *Match-Seller*. In the former, notes are pasted beneath the cards on the table; in the

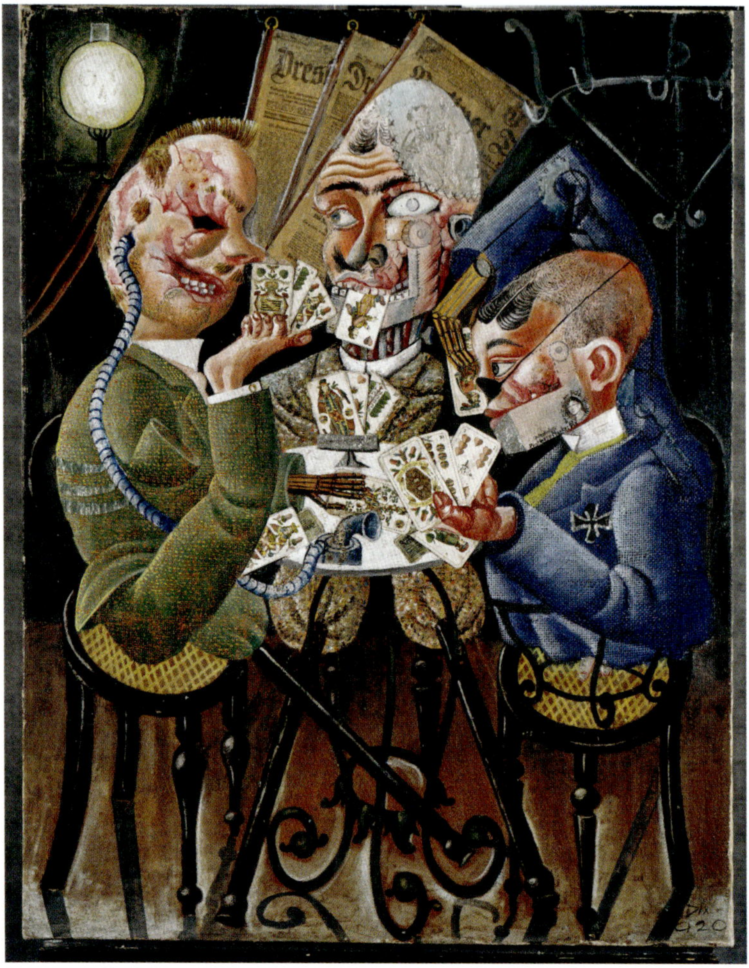

Otto Dix, *Die Skatspieler/Kartenspielende Kriegskrüppel* (The Skat Players/Card-Playing War Cripples), 1920, oil and collage on canvas, 110 × 87 cm. Neue Nationalgalerie, Berlin.

latter, they appear in the tray slung around the neck of the beggar. In both instances, they stand, paradoxically, in their "realness," for ersatzness: first, they show that the stakes these disabled veterans are playing for are valueless, just as unreal as the various prostheses bolted onto their truncated bodies, and second, they show that the concern of well-dressed passersby for the blind and disabled beggar is equally fake, since they discard worthless pseudomoney into his lap.[67] More generally, they stand, as they do in Scholz's painting of the same year, for the bankruptcy of the ironically deployed, kitschy representational strategies employed by

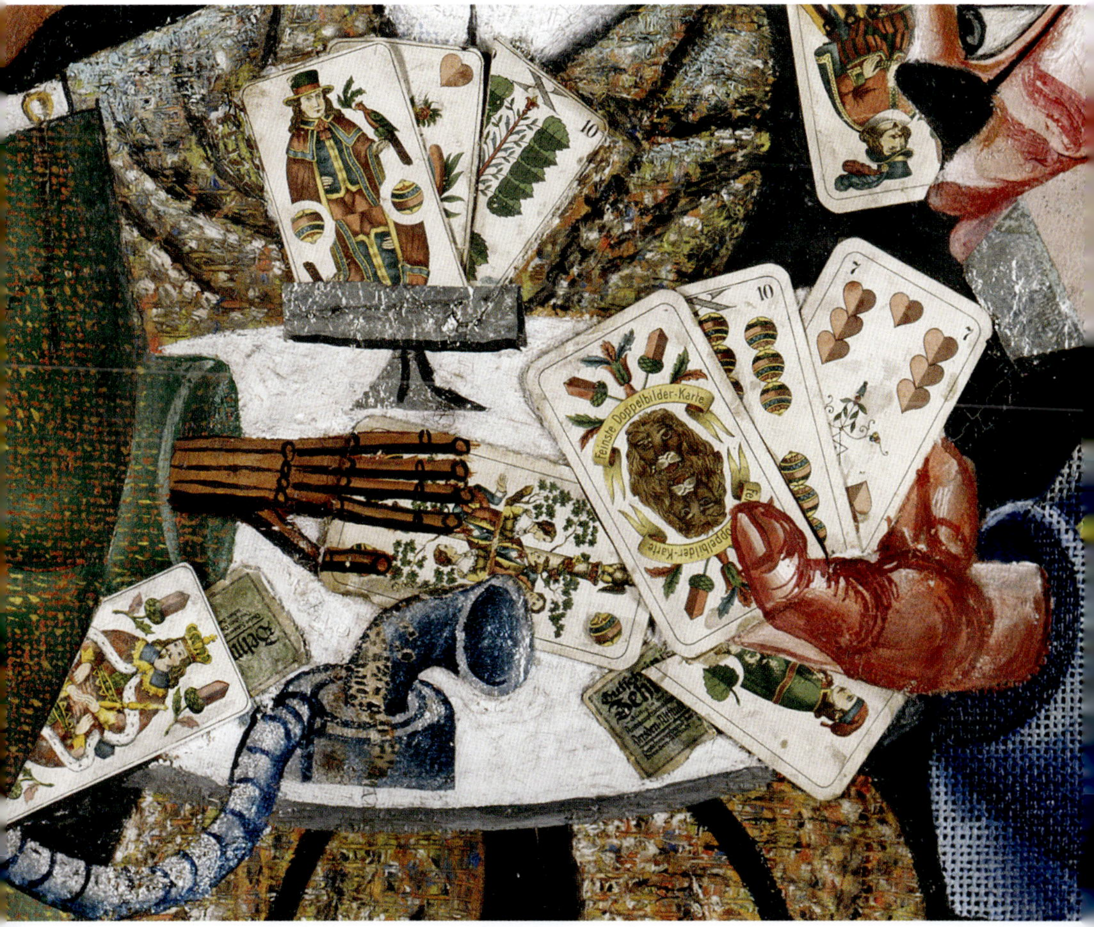

Detail of Otto Dix, *Die Skatspieler/Kartenspielende Kriegskrüppel.*

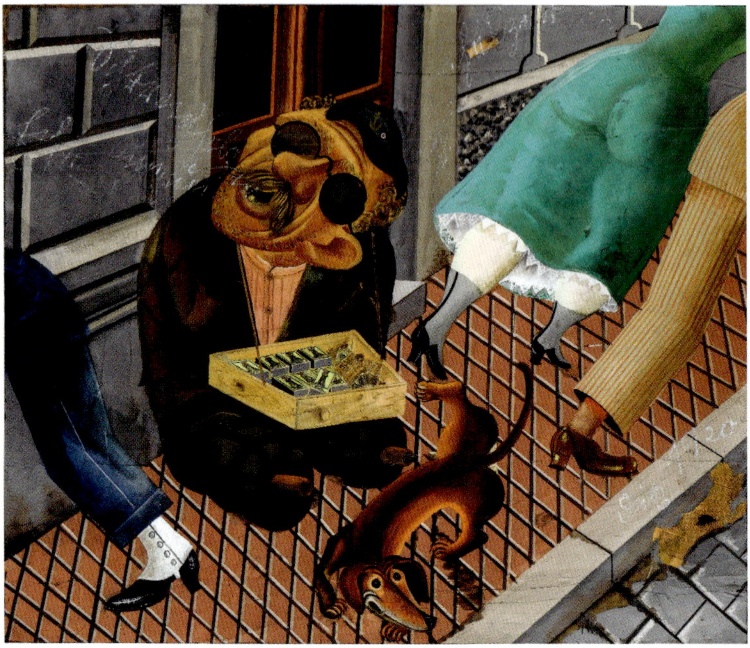

Otto Dix, *Streichholzhändler* (Match-Seller), 1920, collage and oil on canvas, 141.5 × 166 cm. Staatsgalerie Stuttgart.

these artists, bursting through the more or less carefully applied oil paint of the pictorial surface to reveal the substrate of money: the mode of representation shares the commodity form, but it is as worthless and as worn out as a Notgeld note.

This reading is reinforced in the *Match-Seller* by the presence of another collaged element, a scrap of newspaper lying in the gutter (where it soaks up some of the piss that the dachshund is spraying on the beggar's stumps). This bears an open letter from Oskar Kokoschka on the subject of an incident during the Kapp Putsch when street fighting broke out in front of the Zwinger Gallery; during the unrest 59 people died and a stray bullet struck a Rubens painting. In response, Kokoschka, who was then teaching in Dresden, wrote his letter—which was published in over 40 newspapers at the time—asking that the fighting be carried on away from museums in order to protect the art. This provoked a violent retort from Grosz and Heartfield titled "Der Kunstlump" (The Art Scab), which they published in the magazine *Der Gegner* the next month. While Brigid Doherty has intricately traced the ins and outs of this controversy in relation to Dix's painting, she does not mention his incorporation of emergency money.[68]

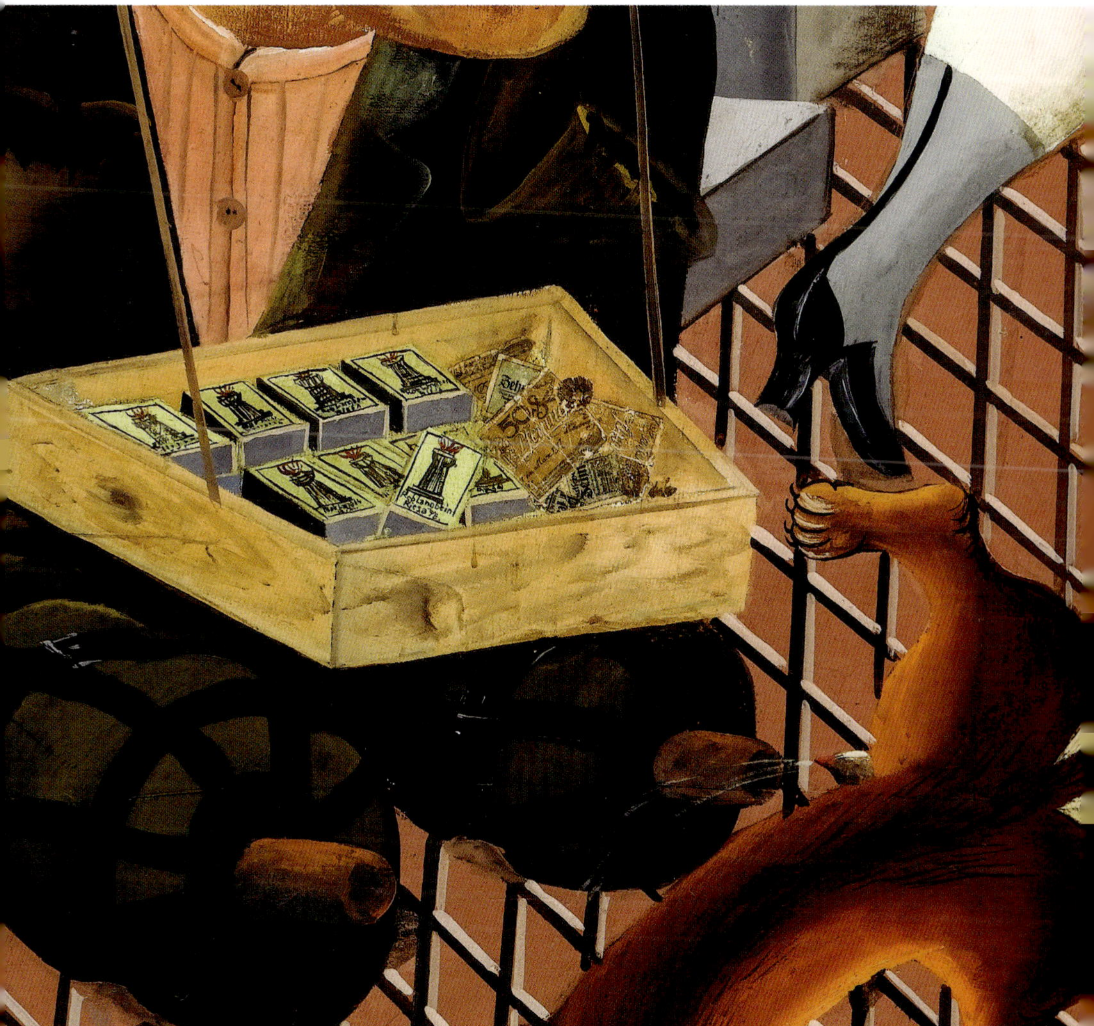

Detail of Otto Dix, *Streichholzhändler*.

Both elements are important here, however, as their simultaneous presence makes them equivalents: the pseudo-money Notgeld, and the bourgeois discourse of art, which is equally ersatz, it turns out, even in its avant-garde form. It is a kind of currency, a printed item that circulates and thereby contributes to the valorization of art (as Serner had complained in his "Last Loosening" manifesto)[69]—and yet it has no real value.[70]

The ways in which advanced artists used money as a medium during the inflation betray substantial differences, especially when we compare the work of Schwitters with that of Dix and Scholz. However, contrasted to that of other artists working with money at the time, their work attains a degree of coherence, insofar as they share a critical stance toward the problem of value and the artwork. At the other pole is Notgeld, which must likewise be seen as a part of the wider image economy of the inflation, but one that—unlike the work of the Dadaists—attempted to shore up value. Not all artists could exploit the demand for *Sachwerte* as successfully as Grosz, after all, and not all buyers were as wealthy as his patrons. His friend Georg Scholz aspired to get into the print business in this period, but lacked the necessary capital. Instead, he made money designing advertisements, as well as illustrations for novels and cigar boxes. He wrote in a letter:

> The disgusting money-making continues apace, sadly. At the moment I'm making posters for really big firms, like Kornfranck, Pils, Persil, etc. That pays the best. I need two days for each poster, my wife paints the lettering. So big business, and if potatoes, coal, wood, winter coats, etc are paid for, then I can start thinking about "Kunscht" again.[71]

(Here Scholz employs a neologism of his own devising, a mixture of *Kunst* and *Kitsch*, to describe the effect he was aiming for in works like his *Industrial Farmers*.)

While Scholz labored on advertisements and packaging, other artists turned their hands to another sort of paper ephemera: Notgeld. Sometimes these were one-off commissions, but other artists produced multiple notes, or series of notes. Some went further still, and turned Notgeld production into a cottage industry. The most prolific of Notgeld designers was the Würzburg-based sculptor Heinz Schiestl. Known for his ecclesiastical decorations in late gothic style, Schiestl designed his first emergency money for Lindenberg in 1917. This received favorable notices in the national press, and he went on to supply 57 towns with Notgeld, usually in cooperation with local printer J. A. Schwartz.[72] His designs were careful but formulaic: sturdily cellular compositions, featuring coats of arms and localizing motifs such as landmarks and historical personages. Source materials for these images were frequently presented to Schiestl in the form of postcards and other printed matter sent directly to the artist by his customers. While they hardly stand out among the welter of Notgeld imagery, these notes appealed to municipalities who wished to emulate Lindenberg's success. They also fulfilled another requirement of the time. An article published in the January 1919 issue of the graphic design magazine *Das Plakat*, titled "Artistic War Notgeld," critically surveys various examples from around the country. In general, the author patriotically prefers them to French emergency money, attributing the distinction in quality to the influence of the German design reform movement, as exemplified by the Deutsche Werkbund. Schiestl's work for Lindenberg is cited as a key moment in the development of sophisticated Notgeld design: "Schiestl knows how to wield the pen with a rare gift for the application of heraldic ornament, and has a splendid compositional facility."[73] Unsurprisingly, given the audience of the journal, the author implies that the success of Notgeld can be attributed entirely to the work of its designers; *Das Plakat* thereby reassures its readers that to design effective Notgeld is no mean task. More than this, however, the reference to the Werkbund suggests that Schiestl's success was rooted in his ability to give aesthetic form of a sort valorized in the critical discourse of the time to a disturbing economic phenomenon. Whereas Schwitters did so by insisting on the artist's role as orderer, for the Werkbund—as Frederic Schwartz puts it—"commodity production was to be redirected: from the cause of social chaos and alienation, it would function to recreate Culture as it was believed to have existed in precapitalist eras," that is, as a homogeneous and organic whole.[74] Here, however, this strategy was to be applied not just to any commodity but to that commodity which is the measure of all commodities, money itself—the most perilous link in the capitalist metabolism, which at that moment had become dangerously unhinged.

It is a piquant irony that this artist, whose medievalizing craftsmanship should (according to the design reform discourse

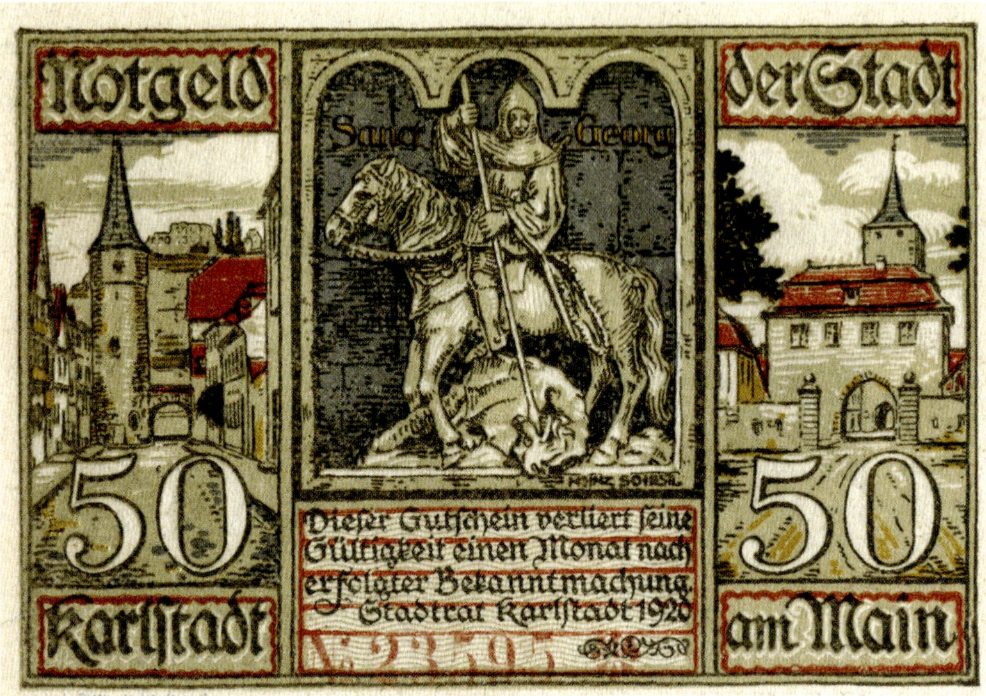

Notgeld designed by Heinz Schiestl, Karlstadt, 1920 (front and back). Collection of the author.

of the day) have neutralized the chaos of inflation, became instead a ready exploiter of the economic disaster. By forming a union with a skillfully self-promoting publisher, he hitched his labor to a lucrative venture and made a modest success. But does this mean that he was, like the expressionists in the Novembergruppe or the Dadaists, trying to reconceive the artists' role? Was his labor itself transformed? Apparently not. Schiestl had no discernible reforming ambitions, and despite what I called his "cottage industry," this cannot be held up as an instance of real subsumption in the realm of artistic production, either, since he continued to produce his drawings on a solitary craft basis (however efficiently). Indeed, we may surmise that the retention of unalienated working methods contributed to his success: corresponding as closely as he did to the image of the medieval craftsman so widely idealized during these years, he may have seemed a reassuringly premodern source for Notgeld. But although the nature of artistic labor was not transformed by the inflation, it did offer (indeed, it insisted on) new tasks for the artist.

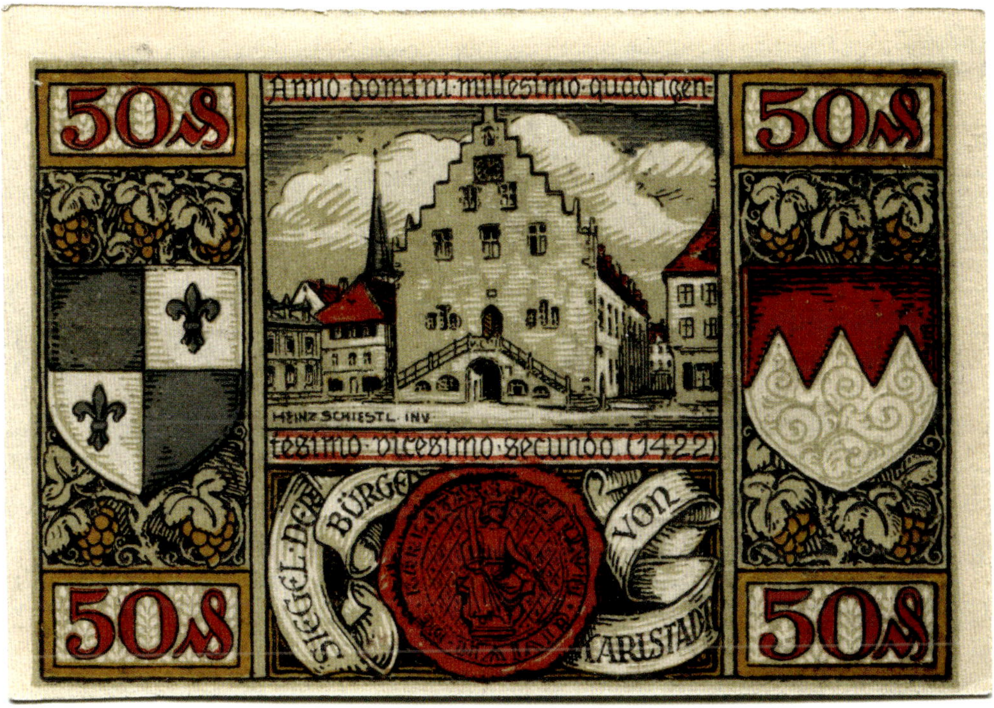

While the labor of Notgeld designers was not speculative in the same sense as that of producers of luxury print portfolios, and, for the most part, not speculative in an aesthetic sense, either, this cannot be said of the town halls that commissioned such notes, nor indeed of the people who purchased them. These notes were a speculation on both the part of their patrons and their eventual buyers; the latter, while urged on by the collector's drive to completion and order, were also motivated in part by the same *Flucht in die Sachwerte* that inspired the purchasers of more traditional tangible assets in this period. As fine art and furs were to the bourgeoisie, so was Notgeld to the less well-off: a store of value in a time of value depletion. Or at least that was the hope of some of its purchasers. In a few cases it turned out to be a good investment. Porcelain coins produced in Dresden, for instance, were soon changing hands at 30 times their face value, and years after the end of the inflation luxurious albums were being sold for significant sums—in 1929, Aby Warburg wrote to his brother Max asking for the money to purchase an album of Notgeld.[75] It was titled *Historic*

Memorial Pages from Germany's Hardest Time and Deepest Emergency, and cost 350 marks (see frontispiece).[76] However, Notgeld was generally speaking a meager and uncertain store. Its true beneficiaries were the bodies that issued it, which thereby echoed the actions of the central government in a minor key. As the latter depreciated the national currency, diminishing the national debt while destroying the assets of the middle classes, local governments saw the opportunity to extract more value from the very populace being pauperized by offering a haven for their money. In the case of Halle, the production of Notgeld raised 526,619 marks for the town hall. One numismatist has remarked that "that was an unexpected, and so even happier result!,"[77] but we should take a more skeptical view, not least because another municipality justified its own Notgeld issue by stating, with unguarded defensiveness, that it had invested the profits in nondepreciating assets.[78] However, while many issuers made a tidy profit from their Notgeld, this was not always guaranteed—it was, after all, a speculative venture. Celle, for example, commissioned sets of Notgeld from a printer-distributor; these sold more slowly than anticipated, and when the final profit of 200,000 marks was made over to the town in 1923, this sum was worth almost nothing thanks to the inflation.[79]

In the course of this tumult, Notgeld oscillated perilously between commodity and sign. A 1922 article in the collectors' magazine *Das Notgeld* uses the conventional terms of art criticism to praise the work of Josef Dominicus, referring to the designer's economy of means and unified style, the latter being, in the author's opinion, appropriate to the subject matter in hand; the writer adds that "these leaves [*Blätter*] will, thanks to their uniqueness, stand out from the mass of Notgeld."[80] The rather pretentious use of the term *Blatt* to describe this money is significant, since this word is more usually used to refer to artistic works on paper, that is, prints. The slippage between the two became a matter of serious dispute the previous year, when the editor of *Das Notgeld*, Arnold Keller, wrote to the Westfalian provincial government to complain about a series designed for the city of Münster—by none other than Josef Dominicus. "We see in the two-mark issues a sheer mockery of all Reich decrees which allow values of up to only 50 pfennigs," wrote Keller, who was a vociferous opponent of what he describes as sham or swindle notes. The mayor wrote back, defending the notes as *Kunstblätter*, artistic prints, which "have not and were not intended to be put into circulation as means of payment."[81] Here we see the status of the artwork being invoked to defend the quite transparent issue of ersatz money in order to raise funds for municipalities, which was, as Keller points out, a contravention of federal law: from the point of view of their producer, however, these objects, which are issued on the pretext of being money, are prevented from becoming too much like money on the pretext of their being artworks. This ambiguity is essential in order to maintain their utility: they must appear enough like money to attract the interest of buyers, during both the functional and aesthetic phases of their issue, but must seem sufficiently unlike money to evade circulation (which would negate the profit of their issuers and attract the censure of the federal government). It should be noted that the "moneyness" of emergency money fluctuated substantially throughout the period: at first, it was a clear ersatz, then it became more elaborate in response to the demand of collectors; at moments in which the demand for substitute media of exchange was high, it regained its similarity to conventional money. But these moments were not clear-cut, they were contested by the various actors involved, and these permutations had unintended consequences.

While Notgeld designers were issuing objects of instrumental ambiguity, incidentally undermining the categories both of the artwork and of money, other figures were at work on precisely the same territory in this period—but with an explicitly critical intent. During the inflation, the artwork and money become radically reversible (to borrow Yve-Alain Bois's term for another project of the period, Lissitzky's Prouns; a more direct comparison could be made to Duchamp's 1919 *Tzanck Check*).[82] While the expressionists had sought to reconceive themselves as socialized artists working for the new republic, and briefly did so during the revolution, they ended up supplying galleries and salons; meanwhile, the Notgeld designers actually achieved these aims, by taking commissions from municipalities. And while the Dadaists employed the ambiguity of the artwork as commodity, or as speculative financial instrument, in order to critique the bourgeois institution of art, or in Schwitters's case, in order to aestheticize economics, Notgeld designers were engaged in precisely the same operation, albeit without any critical intent. On the contrary, Notgeld designers attempted to heal money with art, with references to Goethe and peasants and compositional coherence, hoping to leave art unchanged in the process, whereas Schwitters perceived that in performing this operation art must also change, must be rescued, in fact, by becoming more like money itself. But although they did not think they were doing so, as the Notgeld artists worked on something like money, they transformed it into something like an artwork, and thereby simultaneously transformed something like the artwork into something like money. As all these "somethings" suggest, they were working with already ambiguous categories, but they deepened these ambiguities significantly—indeed, they pushed them to the point of crisis. In doing so, they were far more successful revolutionaries than the Dadaists: their artistic labor contributed to the near destruction of the German economy, and with it, the German state. Almost, but not quite, and in the stabilization that followed, the role of the artist would be reconceived once more. After a winter working together with Notgeld scraps in a freezing studio in Berlin, Moholy-Nagy arrived at the Bauhaus in 1923, dressed in engineers' overalls, and in 1924 Schwitters set himself up as a one-man advertising agency, the Merz-Werbezentrale.

3 *Spooks*

What can we do with all this spirit? It is constantly being spewed out in truly astronomical quantities on masses of paper, stone, and canvas, and just as ceaselessly consumed at a tremendous cost in nervous energy. But what becomes of it then?
Robert Musil, *The Man without Qualities*, 1930

In 1931, an alchemist named Franz Tausend was tried by a Munich court for fraud. While awaiting trial, he offered to demonstrate his mysterious process under strict observation by the director of the city mint, and spectacularly succeeded in producing a grain of pure gold. The judge dismissed the relevance of this operation, however, since Tausend was being prosecuted for fraud, not alchemy. And the people he had allegedly defrauded were very influential. After beginning his swindling career by setting up a fake buyers' cooperative at the end of the war, he began to advertise his esoteric ideas in 1922, by which point he was already claiming to have produced gold. Then, in the heady atmosphere of 1923, Tausend convinced the 21-year-old lover of an elderly countess to invest his partner's money in his alchemical project. The young man in question was a National Socialist, and through him, Tausend attracted a circle of right-wing backers, including General Ludendorff and the industrialist Alfred Mannesmann. This group expanded to form a kind of pyramid scheme, the later subscribers to which eventually became suspicious, and, in 1929, Tausend was arrested at his castle in the Tirol and extradited to Germany to stand trial.

Tausend hadn't managed to make gold in his laboratory, but, as his castle—one of several—attests, he *had* found a way of making money out of reactionaries. His theories regarding the harmonic oscillation of materials, however ludicrous, appealed to the geopolitical aspirations of his supporters. At one point he promised the "rescue of the *Mittelstand*" by manufacturing domestic gold-producing apparatuses that could be distributed to unemployed families, endowing them with a "glittering existence"; more grandiose yet was his claim that, in the words of one contemporary observer, "the hour of freedom had arrived. Soon enough gold would be produced to release Germany, indeed the world, from the chains of loaned capital."[1] In other words, Tausend seemingly offered a means of escaping from the reparations demanded under the terms of the Versailles Treaty, and more: he would destroy the global financial system itself. As his business partner put it: "We wanted to show the German Volk that the power of capitalism by which it was afflicted rested on a cold stone, gold. If gold were devalued, then something would really have been achieved."[2]

It seems clear, therefore, that Tausend's scheme, as well as the credulousness of his followers, can be traced to the inflationary moment, when value had been so deranged that its magical generation (and destruction) seemed plausible. He had even picked up some tricks from Notgeld: Tausend issued *Goldgutscheine*, gold vouchers, a form of words that sounds like the kind of phrase that appeared on later examples of emergency money. These notes were ostensibly backed by the gold that he *would one day* produce. In fact, the bizarre claims made at the trial had been yet more obfuscation. For the inner circle of his backers, the scheme was actually a means of turning gold into *paper*: it was a money-laundering operation that allowed indirect (and untaxed) donations to the Nazis, in particular Ludendorff's financing of their newspaper the *Völkischer Kurier*.

And yet Ludendorff—who subscribed to a variety of bizarre conspiracy theories, extending to the machinations of Tibetan lamas—does also seem to have believed in the alchemical front man of this operation. Such ideas were not just the province of cranks and crooks in these years, when respectable people were also seduced by the promise of alchemy. Nobel Prize winner Fritz Haber, the "father of chemical warfare" and discoverer of the process behind the chemical fertilizers that now help feed half the world, wasted much of the 1920s trying to turn seawater into gold.[3] These cases were inextricably linked to the experience of inflation, with one of the explicit motivations of both alchemists being the desire to help the nation pay off its war debts.

The figure of the alchemist makes an appearance on Notgeld, alongside a veritable grimoire of otherworldly beings. Such supernatural notes are the subject of this chapter. One of these shows the seventeenth-century duke Christian of Saxe-Eisenberg, who ran up enormous debts and spent the last years of his life in desperate alchemical study. In the image in question he works at a blazing vessel, with robed skeletons standing at either side. The inscription reads: "If Christian had gold found / we would have been from worries unbound." The other side of the note makes the connection to the present explicit: "No matter how much the debt grows, more and more Notgeld is printed." In this context, there is an insinuation that the duke's otherworldly advisers are not simply assisting him in his investigations; they have nefarious motives, since the more spurious money is produced, the higher the debts grow. In other words, they are akin to the sorcerer's apprentice—a warning to be careful what you wish for. The apparition of the supernatural has, in this as in other instances, an ambiguous quality, being at once sincere—the plaintive wish for money is genuine, as is the invocation of irrational forces, which certainly seemed ubiquitous at the time—and cynical, since the appeal to the demonic is shown to be worse than futile. This cynicism is redoubled by the fact that the note itself was base matter indeed, mere paper, which had been turned into pseudo-money in order to extract "real" money from its purchasers. In this situation, the alchemy is actually performed by the designer of the note, the artist; as discussed in the previous chapter, it is from this source that the value of the note, such as it is, originates.

The revival of alchemy was connected to the inflation by more than just a desire to pay off Germany's debts. The peculiar combination of nationalism and pseudo-scientific investigation in Haber's case, and of esoteric beliefs, cynical financial dealings, and anti-Semitic anticapitalism in that of Tausend, reflected a much-commented feature of the inflation years, when reason was subject to strange distortions. Kracauer detected a compensatory psychological motivation behind these phenomena, of which he was a keenly critical observer. He wrote in 1923 that "today more than ever, mortal tribulation and all-darkening despair awake in the masses the desire to depart our terrestrial regions and to have a look around in the realm of the spirits, who are perhaps set up more comfortably."[4] The spirit realm offered a truly bewildering variety of options at the time. Religious revivals in Christianity

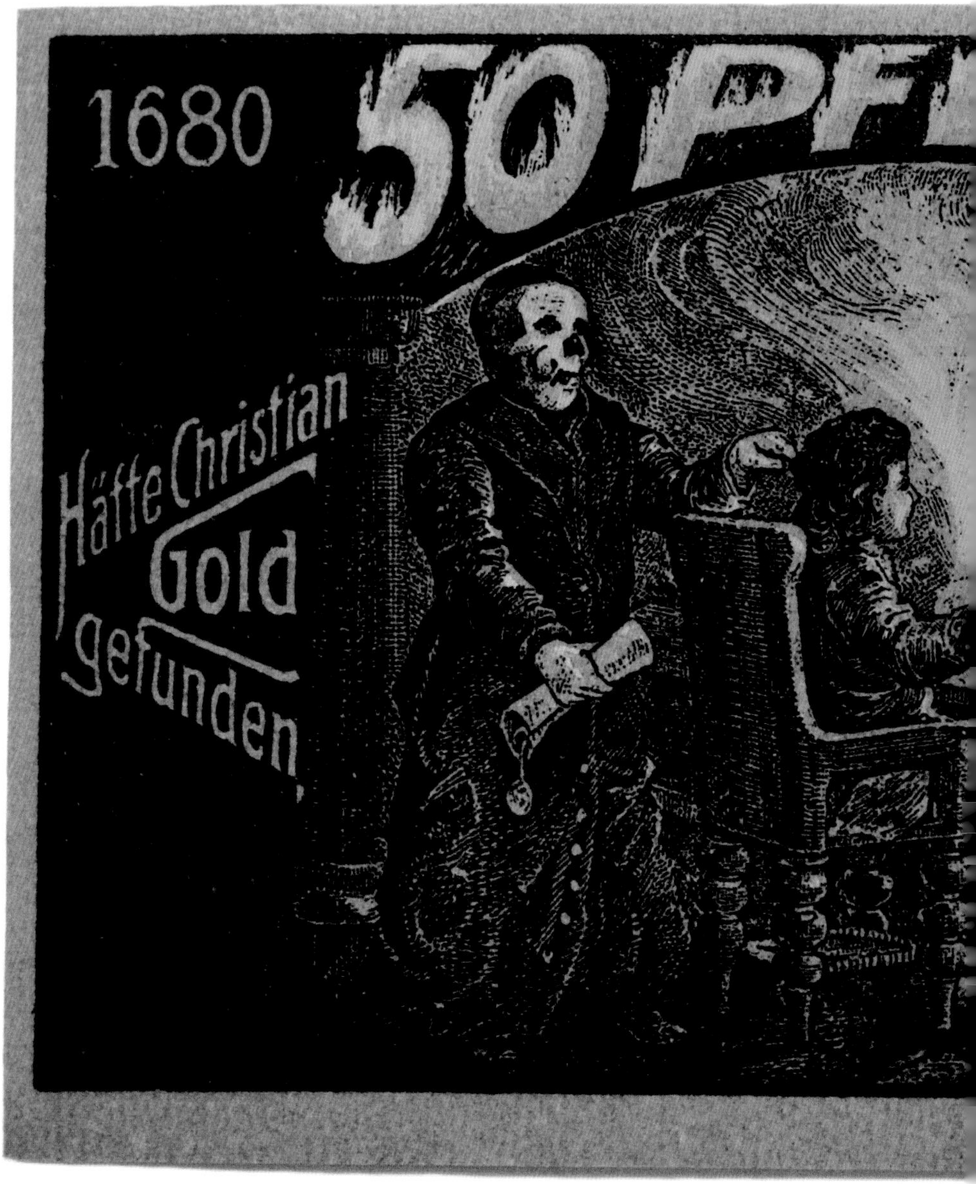

Notgeld from Eisenberg, 1921. Fitzwilliam Museum, Cambridge.

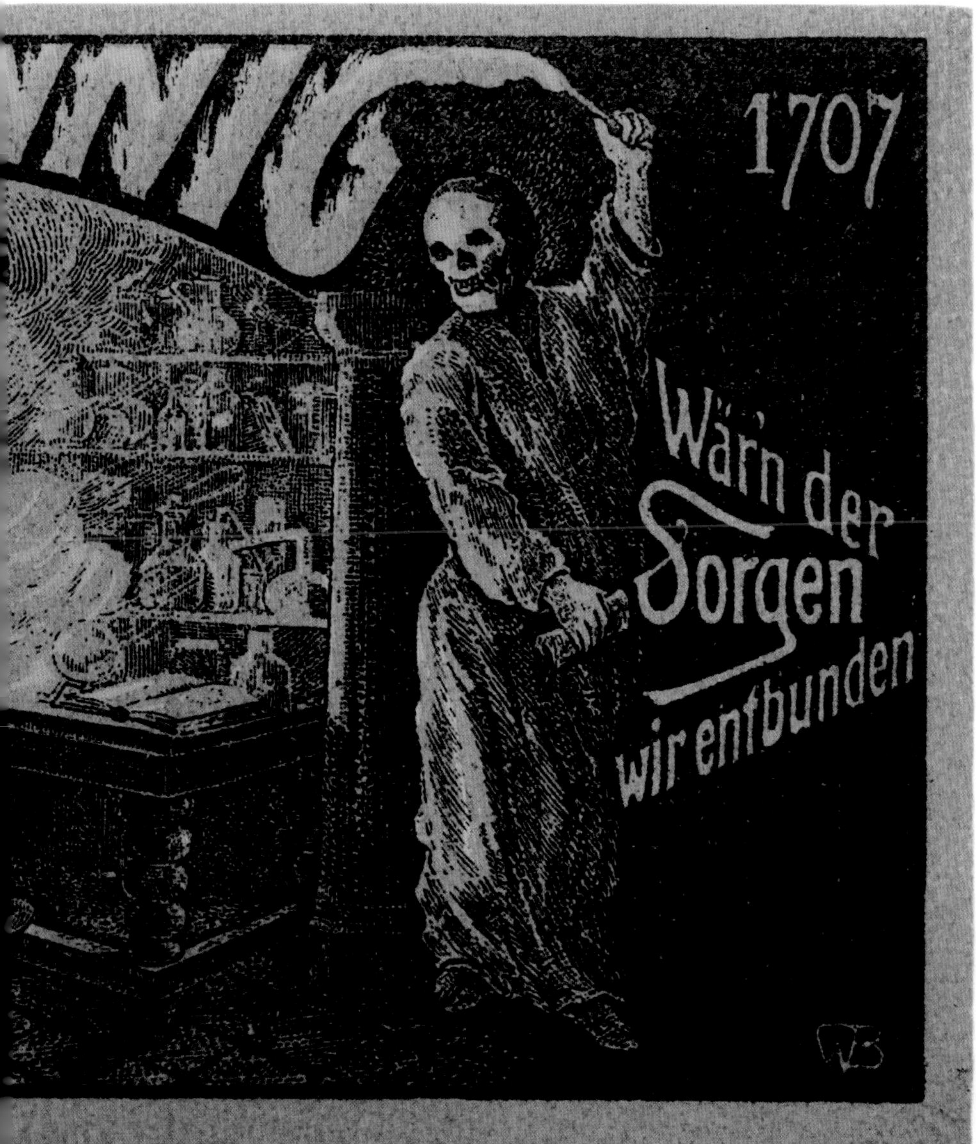
1707
Wär'n der
Sorgen
wir entbunden

and Judaism, messianic wandering preachers, luxuriant conspiracy theories, occult secret societies, racist mysticism, astrology, anthroposophy, and so on, flourished during and after the war, as did charismatic figures as varied as "Oberdada" Johannes Baader, Jewish mystic Oskar Goldberg, berobed Bauhaus teacher Johannes Itten, and Tausend, whom Ernst Bloch later referred to as "a kind of scientific Hitler."[5] As this phrase suggests, the *Führerprinzip* was much in evidence among the gimlet-eyed prophets of the era. Indeed, National Socialism also developed out of this milieu, descending as it did from the Munich-based Thule Society, and although Hitler was later to disown such associations, he was recognized as being a member of this genus at the time.[6] However, this was not solely a reactionary phenomenon, as the examples listed above attest. Bloch himself was deeply influenced by the mystical currents of these years, as was Walter Benjamin. They also registered in the realm of art, where the expressionists dreamed of crystal cathedrals.

Many of these phenomena preceded the inflation, being traceable to the *Lebensreformbewegung* (life reform movement) of the last decades of the nineteenth century. This itself was a reaction to the perceived triumph of capitalism in Germany, as has often been remarked. At a more abstract level, the analytical elaboration of this materialism, Marxism, met at the turn of the century with its own reaction, in the works of Georg Simmel and Max Weber, who counterposed an idealist genealogy of the capitalist economy.[7] Weber wrote with self-conscious paradoxicality of *The Protestant Ethic and the "Spirit" of Capitalism* (1904–1905), which in his opinion had developed out of the practices of nonconformist sects, and Simmel's equally paradoxical-sounding *Philosophy of Money* (1900) attributed the origin of value to psychological factors. They would have a powerful influence on writers associated with the Frankfurt School, who came to Marx via their ideas. The mediating figures here were Ernst Bloch and Georg Lukács, who met while studying with Simmel in Berlin, and went on to Weber's seminar in Heidelberg together. Though initially close, by the mid-1930s they had diverged to the point of acrimonious dispute, most famously on the subject of expressionism; in crude terms, Lukács saw its irrationalism as a forerunner of National Socialism, whereas Bloch insisted on its oppositional potential. Yet their approaches had evinced clear distinctions from the outset, as, in the period under consideration here, they worked through the legacy of Wilhelmine sociology while turning toward Marx. For Bloch, this journey led him through chiliastic fervor and expressionism, as demonstrated in his early works *The Spirit of Utopia*, with its final section on "Karl Marx, Death, and the Apocalypse" (1918, revised edition 1923), and his book on the Peasants' War, *Thomas Münzer as Theologian of Revolution* (1921). While Lukács is superficially soberer, his famous work from the end of the inflationary period, *History and Class Consciousness* (1923), sets out to resolve the aporias of bourgeois philosophy (including those to be found in the work of Weber, Simmel, and Bloch), particularly the division between object and subject. In this Hegelianized Marxism, matter and spirit are fused in the working classes: "His consciousness is the self-consciousness of the commodity," Lukács says of the proletarian, that is, "nothing but the contradictions of history that have become conscious."[8]

As this discourse reveals, the facet of modern society that seemed most intractable at the time was the troubled relationship between matter and spirit under capitalism. This nexus attained an explosive intensity during the course of (lost) war and (failed) revolution.[9] These crises opened up a field for the cultivation of new relationships between *Geist* and *Material*, and the inflation constituted a potent addition to this witches' brew. More than just the reaction to misery diagnosed by Kracauer, there was a structural aspect to this connection: the irrationalism that is essential to the capitalist economy became in this moment ineluctable, and this bled into irrationality in all aspects of society.

Capitalism as Religion

The supernatural aspect of capitalism had of course been an important (if elusive) facet of Marx's analysis in *Capital*, where, in the section titled "The Fetishism of the Commodity and Its Secret," he famously asserted, "A commodity appears at first sight an extremely obvious, trivial thing. But its analysis brings out that is a very strange thing, abounding in metaphysical subtleties and theological niceties." He continues: "the commodity form … is nothing but the definite social relation between men themselves that assumes here, for them, the phantasmagorical form of a relation between things. In order, therefore, to find an analogy we must take flight into the misty realm of religion."[10] Recently,

Michael Heinrich has argued that this is not a matter of "false consciousness": that commodity producers' "social relationship to one another appears as a social relationship between things is ... not at all an illusion."[11] Heinrich insists on a close reading of Marx's phraseology in the above-cited passage. The commodity *normally* seems to be quite straightforward, he says: it is naturalized. Only when it is analyzed according to *this* method is its peculiarity revealed, rendering it supernatural. During the inflation, however, one did not have to be a forensic dialectician to observe that commodities—and especially the money commodity—had started behaving strangely. In a 1923 essay titled "Attack of the Objects," Arnold Zweig wrote:

> A pair of shoes, a tie, a block of margarine, a pound of rice, ordinary plates, a cigar—these are objects today. But with what new tone! Threatening and violent they intrude on us, constantly there, always announcing themselves anew, whether as lacking, as requiring repair, as needing care, or as lost. Pushing their way into the center of attention, feeding off the strength of all, they rend the peace in which creation takes place. They have banded together, surrounded us, and, going on the offensive, they make us old and tired.[12]

In the context of this debilitating world of animated and antagonistic things, the profusion of Notgeld notes dealing with supernatural themes is understandable. However, it presents a puzzle in terms of the rhetorical and iconographic function of money as established in this book's introduction—that is, the stabilization of value. While much Notgeld attempted to achieve this with appeals to spatial fixity and to labor, as we saw in the preceding chapters, here stabilization is apparently abandoned by notes that refer more or less directly to the inflation. Otherworldly beings such as witches, devils, skeletons, and ghosts haunt these destabilizing notes, as do demonic representations of Jews.[13] These speak of the widely held perception that something uncanny was afoot during the inflationary period—that it was, in Thomas Mann's later diagnosis, a "witches sabbath."[14] This was a reiteration of contemporaneous readings, among them a 500-million-mark note issued by Vohwinkel in 1923. Here the inflation is a Goyaesque "dance of death," with sinister figures in a barren landscape reaching for money fluttering from the hands of a gigantic skeleton. The

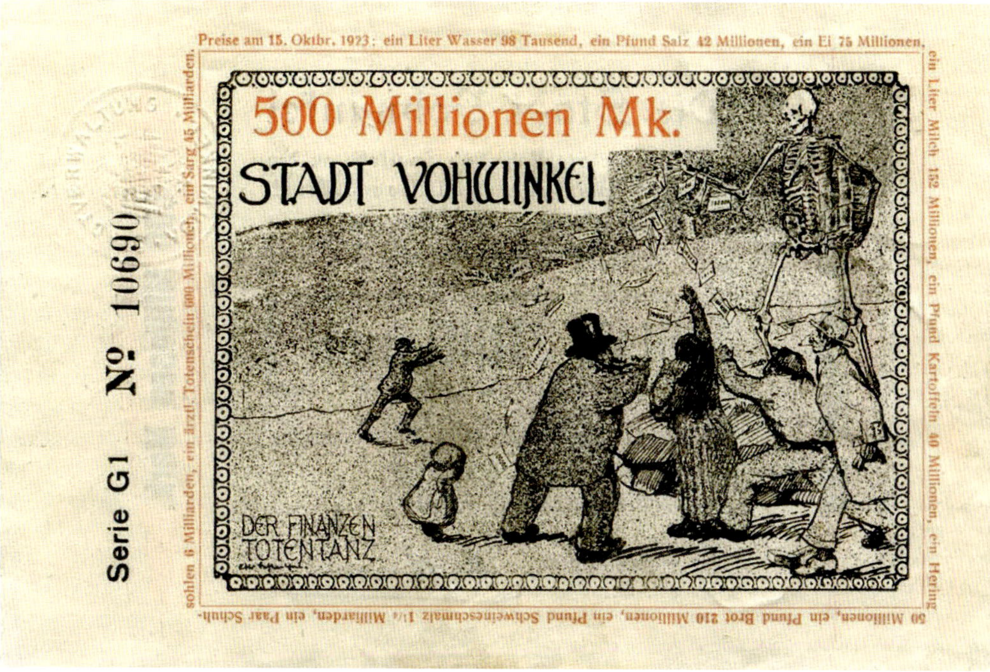

Notgeld from Vohwinkel, 1923. Hans-Ludwig Besler.

occult economic forces that govern our lives had been deranged, and they had, as a result, become visible.

Benjamin asserts something of the sort in his book *One-Way Street*, the first section of which, "Imperial Panorama: A Tour through the German Inflation," he drafted in 1923. Here he writes: "All close relationships are lit up by an almost intolerable, piercing clarity in which they are scarcely able to survive. For on the one hand, money stands ruinously at the centre of every vital interest, but, on the other, this is the very barrier before which almost all relationships halt."[15] The insurmountable difficulties presented by money's peculiar behavior at this time (in Benjamin's case, these amounted to serious financial disagreements with his parents, with whom—and from whom—he was living) brought to light the centrality to social life of money, which likewise casts an unforgiving light on the relationships it mediates. Certainly, polite indifference to financial matters could no longer be feigned by the middle classes, but in many cases this light obscured more than it illuminated. The ineluctability of money also produced monstrous misconceptions, and many of these are registered on Notgeld.

Benjamin was certainly aware of the mythological aspect of money. Elsewhere in *One-Way Street*, he writes of "the innocent cupids frolicking about numbers, the goddesses holding tablets of the law, the stalwart heroes sheathing their swords before monetary units."[16] Birger P. Priddat has discussed these strange tableaux vivants in more detail, attributing apotropaic powers to their members: "The note receives a printed, visible tutelary spirit, a reassuring figure which is deeply immersed in the fertility myths of the sophisticated middle-class spiritual treasury of antiquity."[17] These classical accoutrements helped to soothe the "shock of the modern"; Priddat reminds us that, in the nineteenth century, paper money, though no longer new, was still an object of suspicion. Would it really fulfill the promises printed on it? Could this paper have and retain any value? How could it function with only partial backing?

> Thus the "ornamentics" of banknotes is not just a legitimating sign for nascent capitalism; gold in the form of "appearance/note" [*Schein*] must itself be loaded with spirits, who are fortune, fertility, wealth, all of them young women, mother and victory goddesses, etc. Money shall be fertile, "money-breeding" [*geldheckend*], as Marx commented.[18]

These ancient gods apparently departed from Notgeld, as they did from central bank-issued notes in the twentieth century more generally. In Priddat's opinion, this was because capitalism had become familiar and no longer required supernatural prophylaxes. We might ask why the gods do not reappear on Notgeld, in that case, as capitalism grew strange and frightening once more.[19] The lesser beings, the demons, step in here instead; but sometimes the gods themselves do return, albeit in mortal guise. For instance, Priddat describes a ten-thaler note issued by the Gera bank in 1856 on which an earth goddess and a goddess of labor are united: the goddess of justice Dike holds laurel crowns over these personifications of "city and land—reconciled. Banknotes are ideational papers, which convey peculiar utopian images. Dike reconciles that which is suspected of being irreconcilable."[20] This was a common theme of nineteenth-century monetary notes, and the human offspring of these vanished gods return on the emergency money discussed in chapter 2, in which agricultural and industrial labor are invited to shake hands. Though the gods themselves have fled, one item from the classical treasury remains ubiquitous on Notgeld—the cornucopia—but this is replumbed so that it no longer spouts fruit and grain but something altogether less savory; I return to this subject in the next chapter.[21]

Priddat's essay is a response to Benjamin's enigmatic fragment "Capitalism as Religion." This brief text was written in 1921, around the time that its author was in Heidelberg, where he met Max Weber's widow Marianne and his brother Alfred. During the war, Benjamin had been in Bern, where he had become acquainted with Bloch; at the time the older man was working on his book on Anabaptist leader Thomas Münzer, which was published in the same year that Benjamin drafted "Capitalism as Religion." Benjamin reacted harshly to Bloch's text, but in "Capitalism as Religion" we find him occupying a position between the fiery messianic Marxism of Weber's former student, Bloch, and the tenders of the flame of Weber's decidedly non-Marxist and far more sober analysis of capitalism. It is in "Capitalism as Religion" that Benjamin first suggests an iconographic study of money, a "comparison between the images of saints of different religions on one side and of the banknotes of different states on the other. The spirit that speaks from the ornamentics of banknotes [Der Geist, der aus der Ornamentik der Banknoten spricht]." This spirit, Benjamin implies, derives from religion: "Methodologically, one should begin by investigating the links between myth and money throughout the course of history, to the point where money had drawn so many elements from Christianity that it could establish its own myth."[22]

So far, so Weberian, but he goes further: capitalism is "not merely, as Weber believes … a formation conditioned by religion, but … an essentially religious phenomenon."[23] Benjamin's argument rests on the double meaning of the German word *Schuld*, which can be translated as both guilt and debt: "Capitalism," he says, "is probably the first instance of a cult that creates *Schuld*, not atonement."[24] And this *Schuld* has mounted up to incredible levels: "it is the expansion of despair, until despair becomes a religious state of the world in the hope that this will lead to salvation."[25] This double meaning was of more than etymological or genealogical interest at the time: Benjamin was writing in the context of the reparations demanded from Germany by the Allies, the enormous sum of which had first been announced in January 1921, the year the text was written. This *Schuld* or debt was added to the *Schuld* or guilt already declared in the infamous "War Guilt" clause of the Treaty of 1919. Beyond parallels to contemporaneous political events, this is also Benjamin's riposte to Bloch's messianic Marxism; no charismatic preacher in the mold of Münzer will intercede here, but rather Nietzsche's superman, "who has arrived where he is without changing his ways; he is historical man who has grown up through the sky."[26] Like Weber, Benjamin does not believe the iron cage of capitalism can be escaped; instead, he suggests that this cage itself will be transformed into whatever lies beyond it, and transformed not by heroic action but by intensification, by inflation we might say—a perspective that he attributes to Marx as well as to Nietzsche. However, this transformation will occur in a decidedly non-Marxian fashion (which Benjamin nevertheless attributes to Marx), "by means of the simple and compound interest that are functions of *Schuld*."[27] Benjamin's curious immanent messianism of debt feels as much a product of the inflation as of reparations. While the sum owed to the Allies appeared unattainably high, the ever-increasing quantity of money in circulation seemed as if it could blot out this figure. In other words, there is a kinship between the logic (if not the sophistication) of Benjamin's self-canceling debt and that of the alchemical investigations described at the beginning of the chapter.

There are also supernatural notes that refer to this geopolitical aspect of the postwar polycrisis. Olaf Gulbransson, a well-known illustrator whose work frequently appeared on the pages of *Simplicissimus*, designed a series of notes for the town of Kahla, one of the most prolific issuers of Notgeld. Among these is a note showing a skeletal Michel, personification of the German everyman, fixing a poster to an advertising column, that unmistakable signifier of Parisian urban modernity. However, in a piquant combination of contemporary commercial display and ancient legend, the poster bears the fateful words that appeared in burning letters on the wall at Belshazzar's feast: "Mene, Tekel, Upharsin" (You have been weighed in the balance and found wanting). The sin being judged here is the avarice of the French—the commercial medium of the poster is intentional in this regard—and the consequences of their demand for reparations are visible in Michel's ribs. Gulbransson was a xenophobe who later supported the Nazis; his vision, or perhaps we might call it an incantation, of a German specter haunting the French capital was to be enacted 18 years after this emergency money was issued. Benjamin's speculations, on the other hand, remained confined to paper.[28]

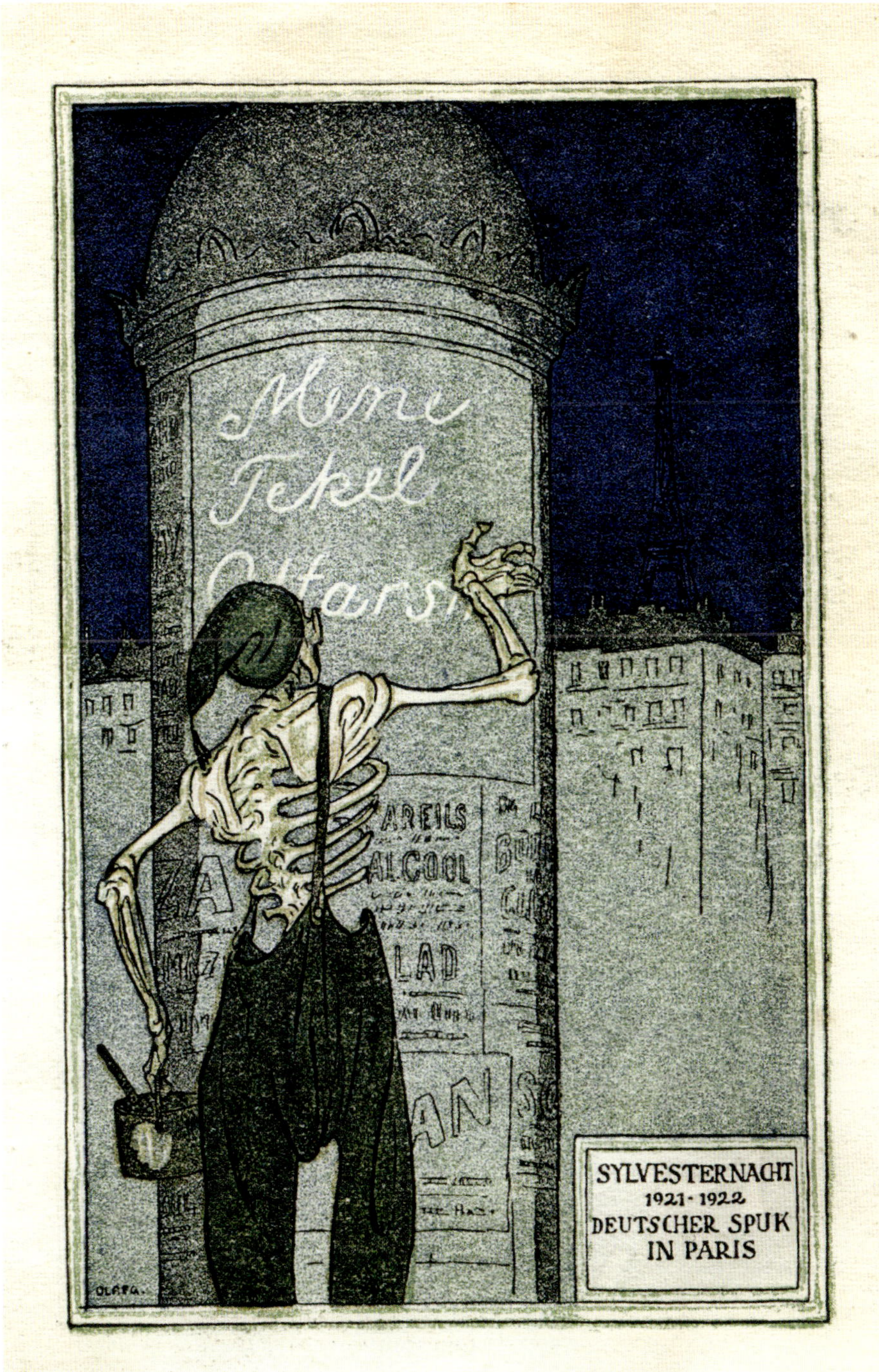

Notgeld designed by Olaf Gulbransson, Kahla, 1922. Collection of the author.

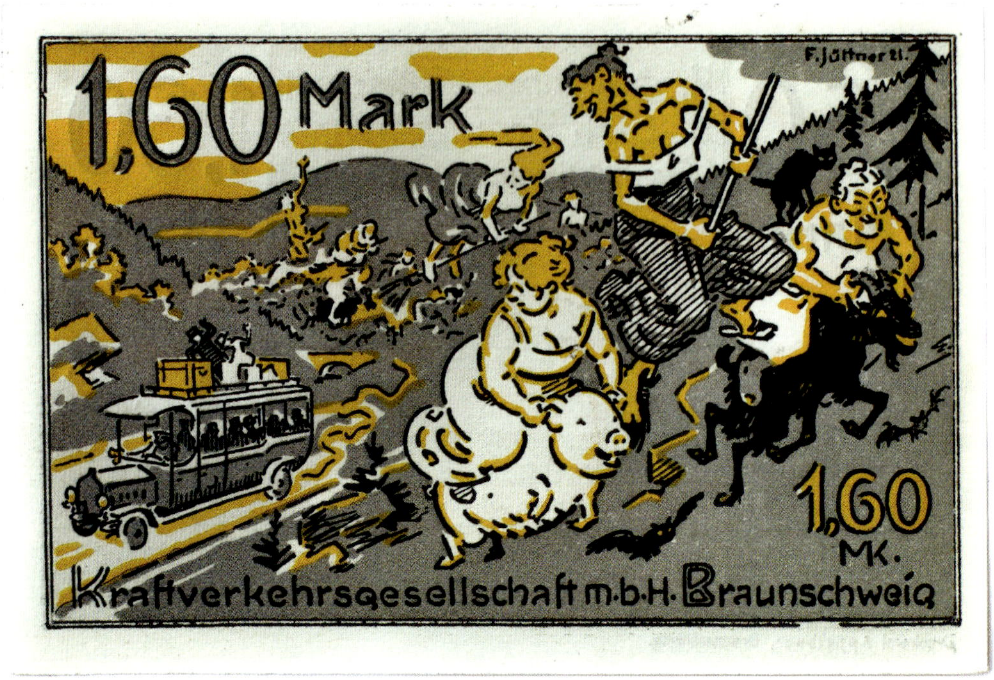

Notgeld designed by Franz Jüttner, Braunschweig, 1921. Warburg Institute, London.

Night on a Bare Mountain

More innocuous-seeming than Gulbransson's visitation—indeed, apparently entirely frivolous by comparison—is a series of notes designed for the public transport corporation of Braunschweig by Franz Jüttner (like Gulbransson, Jüttner was a regular contributor to satirical magazines, in his case *Kladderadatsch* and *Lustige Blätter*). One of these shows witches riding their legendary steeds—including a goat, a pig, and a broomstick—through the air as they wave to a passing omnibus; again, there is the curious conjunction of modern technology and supernatural beings. This image refers to legends regarding the Brocken, a mountain in the Harz range where witches supposedly gathered on Walpurgisnacht; another note shows the party's host, the devil himself, towering over the mountaintop. Jüttner designed a series with a similar theme for the village of Schierke, high up in the Harz. On these notes a naked nymph offers spring water to some fauns, who seemingly rush off to urinate after drinking it; witches ride to the sabbath, once again mounted on various improbable modes of conveyance; and they

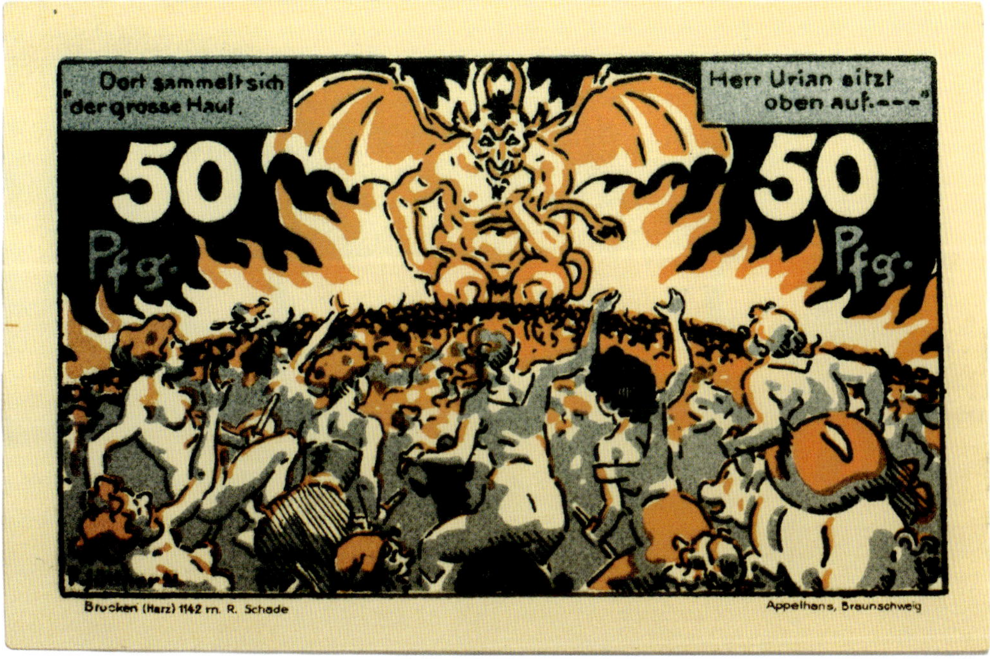

Notgeld designed by Franz Jüttner, Schierke, 1921. Fitzwilliam Museum, Cambridge.

gather before the huge figure of Satan. The crude humor and titillating nudity of these images coexists with inscriptions from *Faust*; the sabbath scene in Part I takes place in the Harz "near Schierke," and Goethe's dialogue was similarly enlivened with ribald sexual humor. The Faustian theme is developed on another note in the series that shows Faust and Mephistopheles voyeuristically peeping at naked witches in a clearing; on the other side, the two men dance with the much younger women.

Of these notes, erotic and humorous as they are, we might borrow Goethe's judgment of his own play: they are "very serious jests."[29] Freud would also have something to say about the earnestness of jokes; here, let it suffice to observe that the inflation was often depicted in plutonian colors, but, though these frequently had a Goethean levity, the subject to which they referred was clearly no laughing matter. The smile becomes a rictus in a cartoon by Thomas Theodor Heine, published in *Simplicissimus* in 1922, which shows a witches' sabbath and is simply titled "Inflation." Here the word is made grotesquely literal: naked witches dance around a stone altar, upon which lies a decomposing male

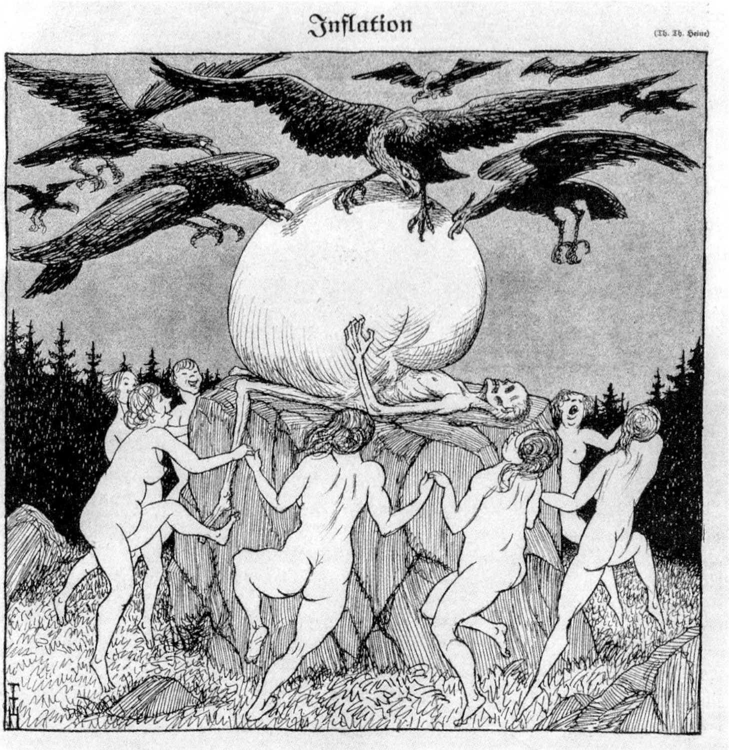

Thomas Theodor Heine, "Inflation," *Simplicissimus*, 1922. Private collection.

body, its abdomen monstrously distended in a parody of pregnancy. Vultures descend from the sky—*Pleitegeier* again, the vultures of bankruptcy—and threaten to burst the bloated corpse with their beaks.

Widdig quite rightly discusses this image and others like it in terms of misogyny. Women had acquired a new economic role during the war, when they replaced men sent to the front in factories and farms, and disquiet regarding their assumption of masculine positions, as well as the imagined proclivities of these *neuen Frauen*, elicited widespread mockery and censure.[30] Suspicions regarding their supposed dissoluteness and susceptibility to the temptations of fashion—the negative, culture-destroying aspect of capitalism—had been present since the onset of modernity, but they were heightened as the tempo of capitalism was sped up by inflation.[31] These tendencies were incorporated in the figure of the sex worker, both gaudily dressed and for sale; in Grosz's inflation-era prints, the profiteer is almost invariably accompanied by a scantily clad woman (or two). The sex worker embodies the transformative power of money at its most drastic, capable as the latter is of purchasing love; as Marx puts it, "I am ugly, but I can buy for myself the most *beautiful* of women. Therefore I am not *ugly*, for the effect of *ugliness*—its deterrent power—is nullified by money."[32] For Baudelaire and Manet the sex worker had also been the shadowy double of the flâneur-artist, a stark reminder that the body of the male is for sale under capitalism, something that Grosz likewise noted with disgust in his writings of the period. In the postwar moment, this misogynistic shudder of self-recognition from the left was mirrored by a poisonous resentment from the right, as defeated soldiers transferred their feelings of shame and emasculation into violence against the women who had remained at home.[33]

Widdig makes a number of interesting suggestions regarding the recurrence of the historic scapegoating of women as witches in the early 1920s, and draws parallels between discussions of the sabbath and the inflation. The more recent work of Silvia Federici allows us to give these parallels more precision. In her celebrated book *Caliban and the Witch: Women, the Body and Primitive Accumulation* (2004), Federici argues that the early modern witch hunt was instigated in a context of population decline and of mercantilist theories regarding the central significance of demographics for economic success, in order to discipline the female body and to eradicate female knowledge of contraceptive techniques. Women were thereby relegated to a reproductive, domestic role—creating the modern housewife, in other words, producer of the workers without which capitalism could not function. In one of the most striking observations in the book, for my purposes here, Federici points out that the demographic crisis was caused, at least in part, by financial crisis: this was a period of inflation, known as the price revolution, which had been unleashed by the first wave of globalization. As a result, the European peasantry and artisans were reduced to extreme poverty, and birth rates plummeted. Federici asserts that "the battle against magic has always accompanied the development of capitalism" and cites some compelling circumstantial evidence in support of this claim, such as the fact that the author of the first work on inflation, French political theorist Jean Bodin, was also a vigorous persecutor of witches, and wrote a tract arguing for their violent punishment.[34] However, the account presented in the present work problematizes this reading.

There was no official campaign against magic during the inflation of 1914–1923; in fact, quite the opposite, as magic seems to have flourished under the conditions of economic crisis, and was later absorbed into the official ideology of the National Socialist state.[35] These two contexts were, of course, very different, but there were some similarities: in the immediate postwar moment, German capital's biggest problem was the propensity of workers to strike—and reactions to this resistance were frequently gendered, as Klaus Theweleit's account of right-wing literature has revealed. When the figure of the witch recurs in this period, her revelries correspond to a fear of female disinclination regarding productive as well as reproductive labor. Indeed, she is accompanied by a distinct echo of the obsession with female reproductive power that suffused her origin. But I would like to suggest that this is not to be understood solely in a literal sense.

Returning to Heine's cartoon via this materialist reading of witch hunts, we see that inflation is a bodily phenomenon, in which the dead become fecund and reproduce. Unnatural birth is a common theme of witchcraft tales, but in this instance the devilry is in actuality a matter of economic forces, not occult ones. This is reminiscent of Marx's supernatural image of the dead labor that is reanimated by capital to suck the life force of living labor, or perhaps more specifically the monstrously self-reproducing interest-bearing capital, *M-M′* (money loaned and returned plus interest), "the irrational form of capital" in which "capital obtains its pure fetish form." Marx also reaches for *Faust: Part One* at this point, saying that "the money's body is now by love possessed"; this refers to a grotesquely comic scene in Goethe's play involving a poisoned rat that, though dying, races around as if in pursuit of a mate. More suggestive yet, Marx concludes his discussion of interest-bearing capital with a striking image: "The product of past labour, and past labour itself, is seen as pregnant in and of itself with a portion of present or future living surplus labour."[36] The swollen corpse—past labor itself—is disturbingly full of life, except that in Heine's cartoon, just as in the work of the classical economists criticized by Marx, the uncanny power of money is not tethered to a class but runs riot in a netherworld of dark forces. We might also see the witches on the notes depicting Walpurgisnacht in such terms: powerfully erotic figures, whose generative power—a power of money celebrated on nineteenth-century notes in the form of naked fertility goddesses—has been perverted. For during the inflation, "self-valorizing value" goes into reverse, jams, devours itself. The more that money grows and grows, the *less* it is worth; the swollen belly is a sign not of value's reproduction but of its death.

The Currency of Allegory

Other examples of supernatural Notgeld seek explanations for the inflation elsewhere in *Faust*. The second part of the play opens with an origin myth for paper money, with Faust and Mephistopheles informing the impecunious emperor that he may resolve his financial difficulties simply by printing notes backed by reserves of gold hidden beneath his kingdom. The positive consequences of this invention are depicted on a series of notes issued by Weimar. The first of these shows the notes fluttering about the marketplace, while the others illustrate the way that they are spent, enriching the various trades.

> It was impossible to catch the flying things;
> Quick as lightning they spread themselves about.
> The changers' desks are standing fast and stout:
> There each note is honoured, every one,
> With gold and silver, of course for a commission.[37]

Strikingly, the demonic origin of this form of money is not alluded to here, but it would have been clear enough to anyone familiar with Goethe's narrative—and, for that matter, with the contemporary situation.

The paper money episode has been subjected to numerous analyses, two of which I shall mention here. Heinz Schlaffer's classic commentary argues that *Faust: Part Two* is an "allegory of the nineteenth century." When Goethe's work was posthumously published, critics were bemused—if not repulsed—by the return of the long-dead allegory form, especially in the masque that separates the two parts of the paper money narrative. This apparently antiquated scene is populated by a group of personifications, such as "fear" and "hope," classical figures like the fates and the furies, as well as mere objects, including an olive branch and garlands of corn. As such, we might add, they are rather like animated and eloquent versions of the figures who assembled on banknotes of the era.

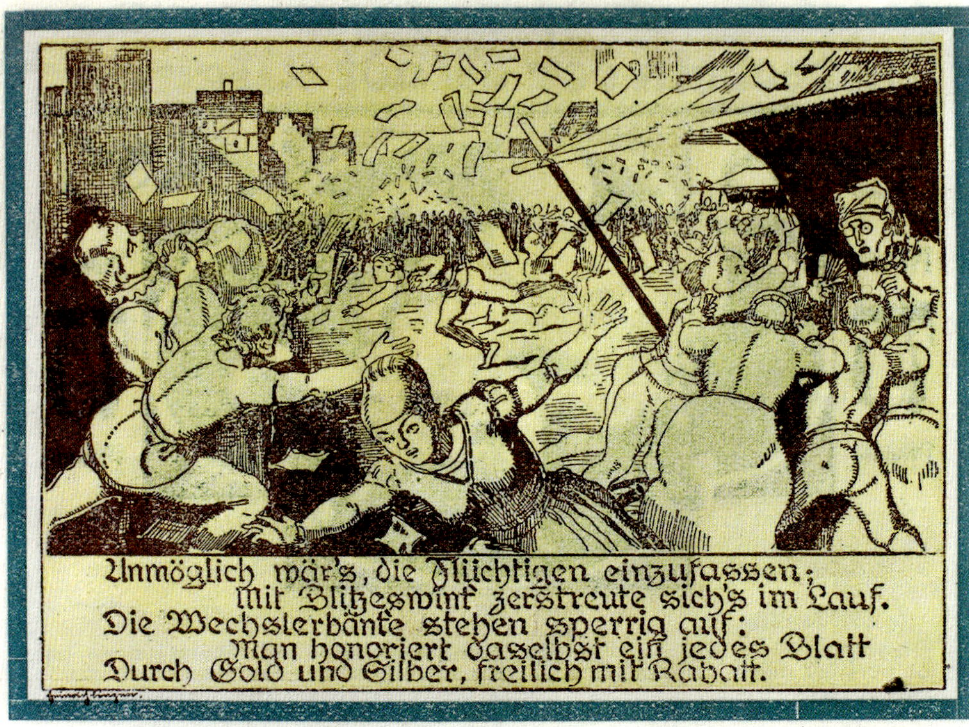

Notgeld from Weimar, 1921. Warburg Institute, London.

Indeed, they are led by Plutus—personification of wealth—in their frankly mystifying discourse. One member of the procession, the herald, remarks:

> As my office bids, I should
> Give you an interpretation
> Of these shapes; I wish I could!
> They defy all explanation ...
> To describe you I might try;
> But that's not to identify.[38]

The difficulty of identifying these figures confirms their allegorical status; symbols, by comparison, with their united form and content, are immediately comprehensible. For Schlaffer, this return of allegory corresponds to "the personification of things and the reification of people"[39] described by Marx in his analysis of the commodity world, that "phantasmagoric form of a relation between things." In the masquerade, the hollowed-out forms of feudal society are filled with the strange new life of the dawning age of capitalism, where things cavort and converse among themselves. "The mummer's dance is a passing era's dream of the one to come," Schlaffer says.[40] "The religious world and the commodity world are the two worlds, one old and one new, from which allegories, the old and the new, arise. However, a difference exists between the two analogous worlds: in the earlier one allegories were fictional, but in the modern one they are real."[41]

In the final year of the inflation, Benjamin was also sketching out his ideas on allegory, which would be published in his 1928 book *The Origin of German Tragic Drama*. In his reading, the allegorical forms of the seventeenth century are a melancholic image of "history as a petrified, primordial landscape. Everything about history that, from the very beginning, has been untimely, sorrowful, unsuccessful, is expressed in a face—or rather, a death's head." It is "the baroque, secular expression of history as the Passion of the world; its importance resides solely in the stations of its decline."[42] As has often been remarked (including by Schlaffer), Benjamin projects an essentially modernist perspective onto the seventeenth century, finding there a reflection of contemporaneous discontinuity and estrangement. While its historiographic accuracy may be questionable, the congruence between his vision and the moment in which his thesis was first developed, 1923, is quite clear. These were certainly years in which the world seemed to be treading a secular via dolorosa. And the alienation from the material world encoded in the allegorical form, in which things are no longer immediately accessible to our understanding, clearly corresponds to the occultation produced by the inflation. As Zweig's essay on the attack of the objects shows, commodities really did seem to take on an occult aspect at the time, and this estrangement suggested a hidden meaning. This gap between matter and spirit was filled, as I mentioned at the beginning of this chapter, with a variety of wild conjectures. While many of these make an appearance on Notgeld, the allegorical form itself is almost entirely absent from the surfaces of these notes. Instead, they themselves became allegorical: no longer the self-evident (if deceptive) money symbol, with its conventional identity of value and paper, they became strange objects, mere husks in fact, with the increasingly histrionic symbols that covered them attempting to compensate for the meaning that had drained away.

In a second analysis of the paper money episode in *Faust: Part Two*, the economist Hans Christoph Binswanger asserted that Goethe, himself a conservative bureaucrat who was skeptical of paper money, and a failed alchemist to boot, presents the reader with an alchemical parable. This anticipates the contemporary economy, "a continuation of alchemy by other means" in which money is seemingly miraculously produced by money.[43] That we now inhabit this Faustian world of autopoietic finance goes without saying, and for those who lived through the hyperinflation such a satanic genealogy of paper money would also have struck a chord. In a drawing of 1920, George Grosz sets the miracle of compound interest in this religious framework: be fruitful and multiply, the priest announces to a congregation of genuflecting money bags. These are labeled with endless series of zeroes. But this central tenet of the capitalist faith had, as Benjamin's "Capitalism as Religion" hinted, been flipped into reverse, and the growing numbers seemed to cancel themselves out. The more there was of it, the less it was worth, and debts vanished from bank ledgers. The beneficiary of this was not the common man but the bourgeoisie, who took the opportunity to borrow as much as possible of this magically vanishing money. To less canny contemporaries, the apparently solid ground of the gold standard had been undermined and replaced by magical techniques that produced value out of thin air—value, however, that seemed equally ready to vanish back into the ether, just like Faust's conjurations.[44] The eerie images on these notes can therefore, despite their apparently destabilizing implications, be considered a form of what Joseph Vogl has recently called "oikodicy"; just as theodicy was the attempt to explain the presence of evil in a world created by a benevolent God, oikodicy is an attempt to explain economic evil in a world supposedly governed by the hidden hand, employing (in this instance) leftover superstitions and fragments of German classicism.[45] These notes are quite literally mystifications.

The Desecration of the Host

The most dangerous of these mystifications took the form of demonizing representations of Jews. One such note, issued by a wine merchant in Schmölln in 1921, shows a hunched and hairy devil rolling a large silver coin along the ground. This monster

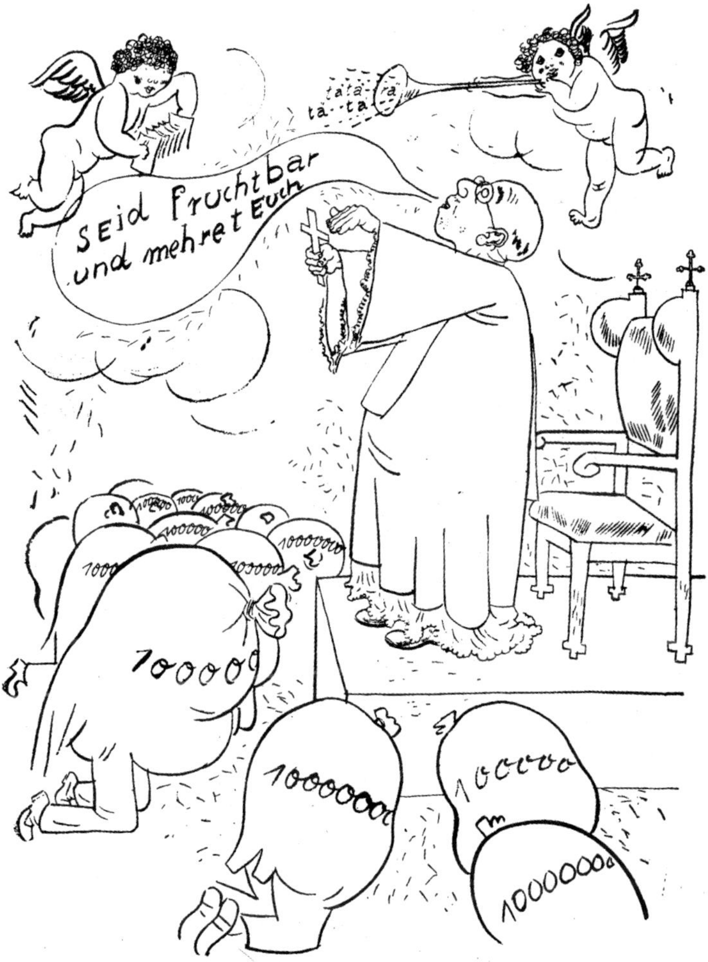

George Grosz, "Be Fruitful and Multiply," from *The Day of Reckoning*, 1923. Collection of the author.

has features that are unmistakably anti-Semitic. The reverse of the note states, "The devil strives only for silver—I have made myself paper money, and gladly exchange this note for official money [*Reichsgeld*]." This ambiguous statement seemingly attempts to shift the responsibility for this note from the businessman who issued it to the devil depicted upon it, a rather perilous operation since it makes the dubious status of the object explicit and risks identifying the true issuer with his demonic stand-in. Nevertheless, the broader message is clear, and deeply sinister in its implications: the Jews are responsible for the substitution of the

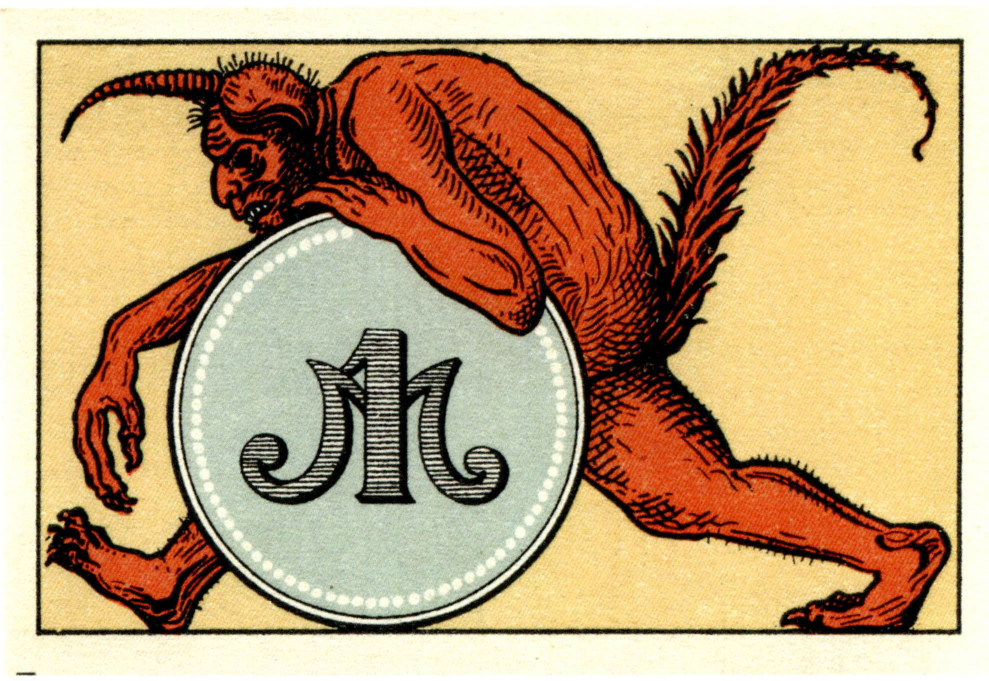

Notgeld issued by Weinhandlung Otto Seidel, Schmölln, 1921. Collection of the author.

paper in your hand for the solid coin that has been carried away. More than this, they are embodiments of the—failed or inimical—economic system itself. As Vogl puts it, following Aristotle's distinction between "good" uses of money for production and "bad" uses as self-generating wealth via interest, "there emerged a striking array of figures which, as outcast, sinful, parasitic, or simply spectral personifications, were made to embody the precarious status accorded the monetary economy."[46] Preeminent among these, from the Middle Ages onward, were Jews. Such characterizations abounded in the inflation period, especially in the literature of the far right.[47] Hitler was to write in *Mein Kampf* (which he largely composed during his imprisonment following the failed putsch of 1923) that "the personification of the devil as the symbol of all evil assumes the living shape of the Jew."[48]

The disciplining or elimination of these personifications therefore promised the reform or redemption of the economy via magical, sacrificial means. Hence other notes demanded and visually enacted violent punishments on these supposed culprits—punishments that were eventually enacted in reality. A series of notes designed by Josef Dominicus for Sternberg in 1922, for example, reaches back into the medieval past for a parable on the subject, namely, a spurious accusation that local Jews had desecrated the host. Such libels were made across Europe in the late Middle Ages, and frequently led to pogroms; according to the particular tale recounted here, a priest sold consecrated wafers to a group of Jews in Sternberg, and they stabbed the objects with needles, producing a miraculous flow of blood. On the discovery of these bloodied hosts, the priest and 27 Jews were subjected to questioning under torture, and, on being found guilty, they were burned to death. The remainder of Sternberg's Jews were expelled from the town.

As depicted on Dominicus's notes, the first episode of this narrative shows the priest proffering the hosts to the Jews, one of whom holds out some coins in exchange for the sacred comestibles. The mirrored gesture of the hand filled with small round objects, only some of which glow with the radiation of sanctity, makes the central issue clear: simony, the exchange of the sacred, the very body of Christ, for the utterly profane, money. Exchange produces equivalence, but here such equivalence is blasphemous, despite the external similarity of these objects. This similarity has been explored by Jochen Hörisch, who writes that communion and monetary exchange are two historical "ontosemiological" paradigms that have successively organized relationships between being and meaning. "The stamped Host will be inherited by the stamped coin. Those two, the Host and the coin, resemble each other, not coincidentally, in their design; both must be issued by an authority, both have two sides; both raise the Faustian question of whether the thing is sacred or profane."[49] I might add that the host is both bread *and* body of Christ, the sign that is the referent; or at least it was until the Reformation, when it was supplanted by the "real abstraction" of money, another sign (supposedly) identical with that to which it refers. We do not have to subscribe to Hörisch's elaboration of this analogy in order to perceive the root of the problem here: money threatens and indeed supplants the preceding paradigm of value (not just of semiology, I might add). The perpetrators of this travesty must be punished, since money itself cannot be made to pay, and on another note the Jews are duly shown being burned at the stake. The significance of this episode during the inflation is their exchange of a false sign for a true one, false money for real. But in using the host as a metaphor or stand-in for the true money of present-day Germany, the artist commits the very crime he attributes to his subjects.

Less explicitly violent, but equally disturbing in its implications, is a note issued in support of a "German Day" planned for the city of Bremen in 1921, on which a group of dinner-jacketed men with aquiline noses whisper over documents. The caption, "Die Weisen von Zion," refers to the notorious forged tract, *The Protocols of the Elders of Zion*, which had first been published in German translation in 1920. The other side of the note bears the inscription: "The current profiteer economy belongs on the *Schandesel*"; literally a "shame donkey," this was a form of pillory on which criminals were forced to parade in the Middle Ages. In fact, the man responsible for this note ended up being subjected to legal penalty himself, albeit briefly. Richard Rüthnick was a Bremen schoolteacher and founder of an anti-Semitic organization called the Schutzbund, which was behind the German Day advertised on the note. He was also a member of a right-wing group named Organisation Consul, which was responsible for the murder of finance minister Matthias Erzberger in August 1921; Erzberger had been a signatory of the Treaty of Versailles and had authored a high-tax economic program introduced in 1919, and

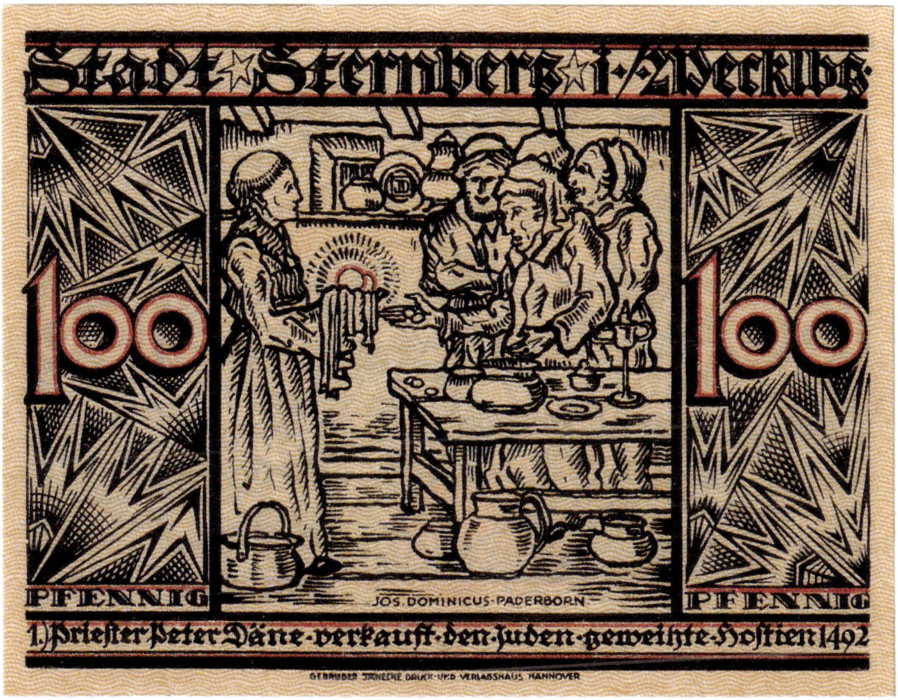

Notgeld designed by Josef Dominicus, Sternberg, 1922. Nathaniel Butler.

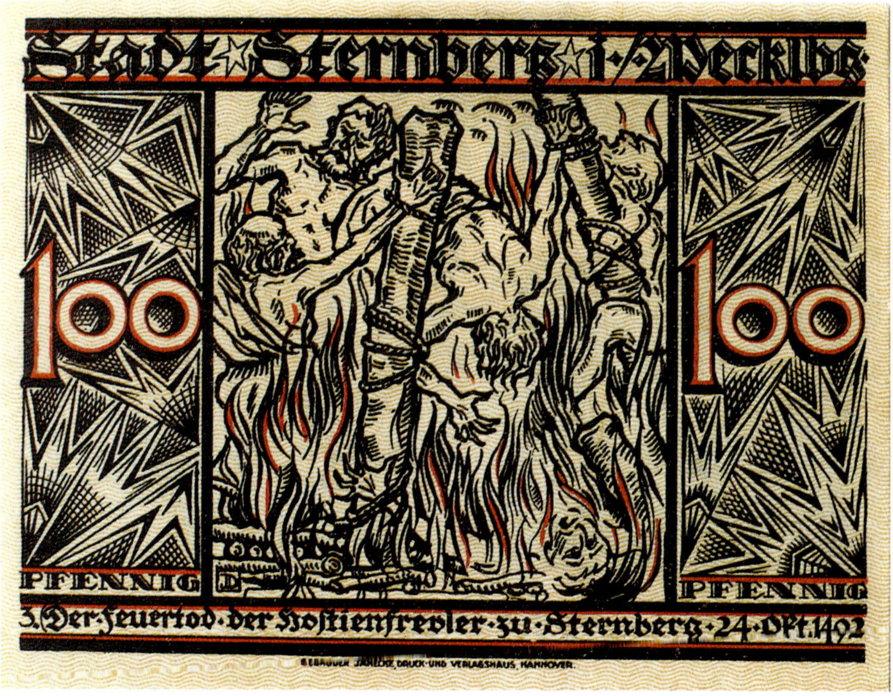

Notgeld designed by Josef Dominicus, Sternberg, 1922. Warburg Institute, London.

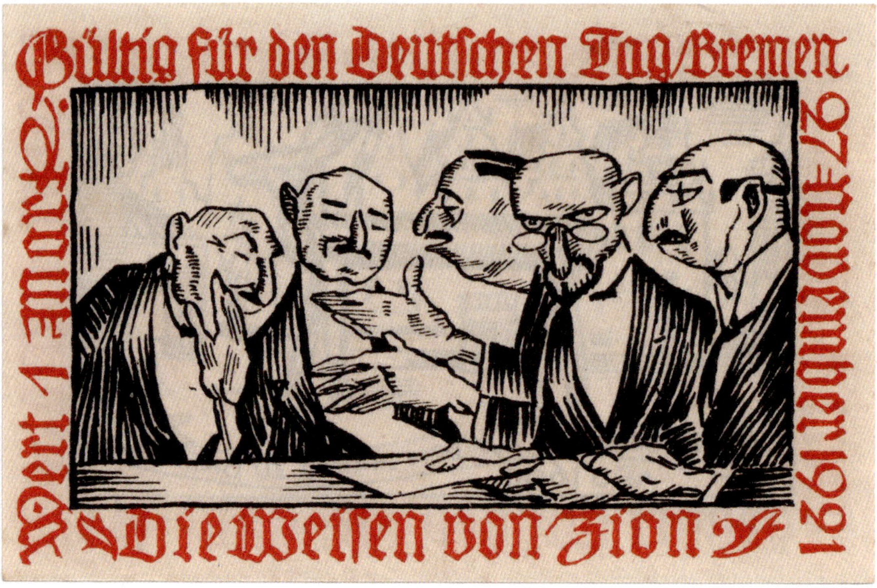

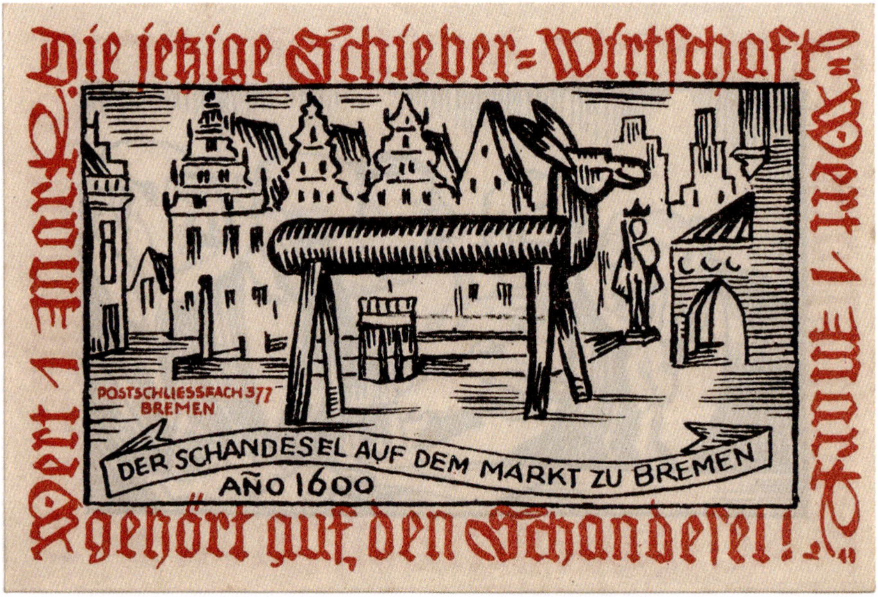

Notgeld issued in support of Deutschen Tag (German Day), Bremen, 1921 (front and back). Nathaniel Butler.

was consequently hated by the right. Rüthnick was arrested in November that year under suspicion of involvement in his killing, but he was released after a few days—not without missing the German Day advertised on this note, however. The next year, members of Organisation Consul assassinated foreign minister Walther Rathenau, who was Jewish.[50]

The most brutal of these notes was issued by the town of Tostedt in 1921. It shows two figures, clearly anti-Semitic caricatures, hanging from a tree. The Plattdeutsch inscription reads: "This is what must happen to all profiteers / then Germany could be in a better position." The iconography of the note was later reiterated as propaganda for right-wing political parties. In the run-up to the 1924 Reichstag election, agitators printed anti-Semitic messages onto the blank reverse sides of Reichsbank notes; both the image and slogan from the Tostedt note were redeployed in support of the Völkisch-Sozialer electoral block, which included the Deutsche Arbeiterpartei, precursor of the National Socialists. In some cases, a swastika appears above the hanging tree. Other such notes incorporated rhymes that attribute magical powers of devaluation to these demonic figures: "The Jews take our silver, gold and bacon, and leave us with this papery muck." In 1923, pogroms broke out around the country.

Formal Spookiness

The supernatural notes in this chapter do not apparently seek to stabilize the belief on which money as a whole depends; rather, they upend such "positive" acts of faith by invoking creepy superstitions and destructive occult forces. Nevertheless, they do have something in common with the emergency money, described earlier, which asserted that its value derived from either labor or land: all of these were mystifications of money, its value, and its behavior during this period. In the hands of some Notgeld designers, mystification went beyond the invocation of demonic beings to attain a unity of form and content, using motifs and formal gestures that had become, since the war, conventional symbols of the realm of *Geist*: expressionistic tropes such as rough or agitated lines (often emulating if not derived directly from woodcuts), collapsed perspective, dynamic angles, garish and unnatural colors, crystalline forms, and medievalizing religiosity.

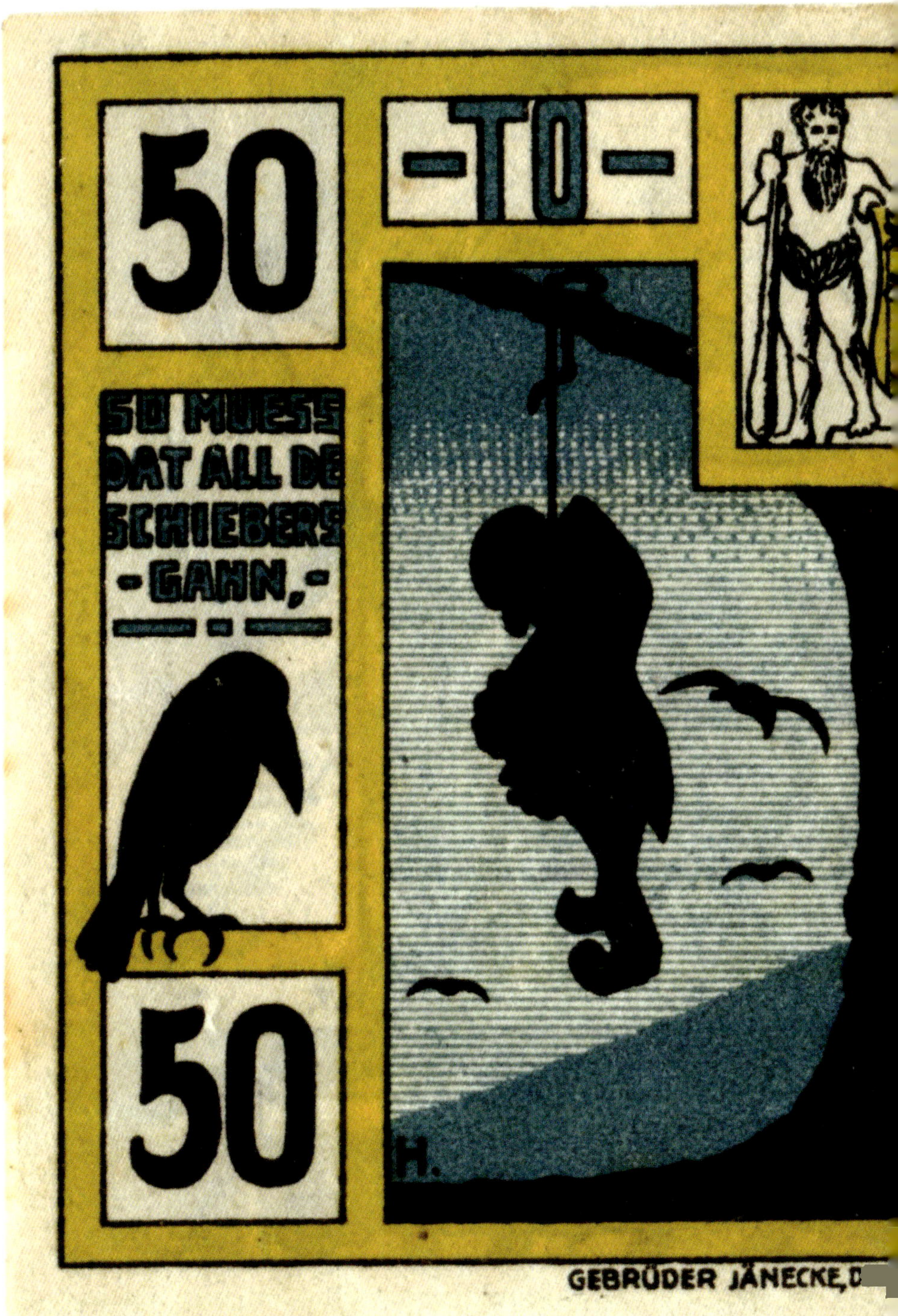

Notgeld from Tostedt, 1921. Collection of the author.

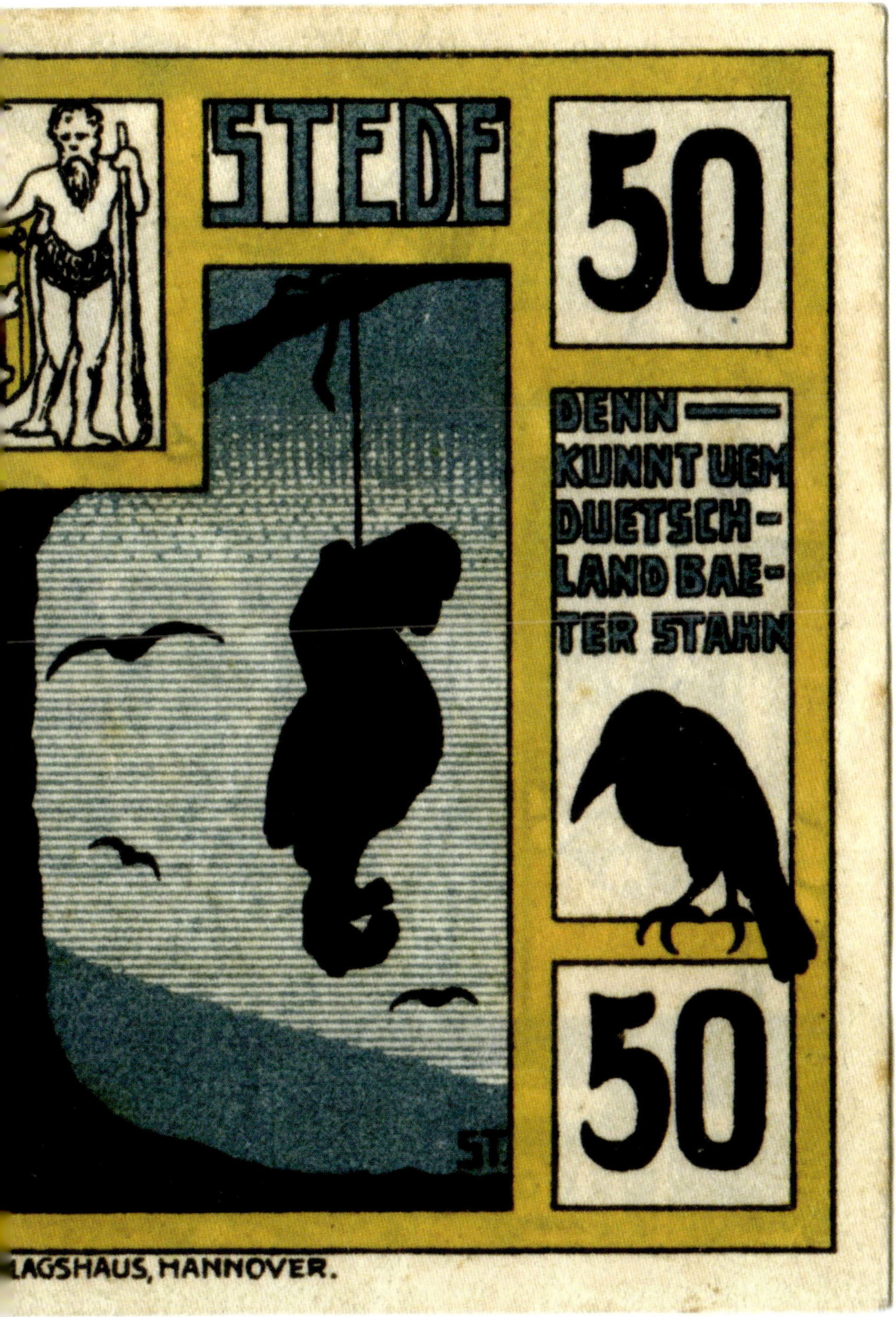
STEDE
50
DENN—
KUNNT UEM
DUETSCH-
LAND BAE-
TER STAHN
50
LAGSHAUS, HANNOVER.

A striking example employing several of the formal strategies enumerated above was issued by a Frankfurt tobacconist in 1921. Here, the fractured, multiperspectival picture plane reveals a folkloric episode of medieval origin of the sort irresistible to expressionist artists, the story of the golem. The legendary creature depicted on the note is also a reference to the film on the same subject directed by Paul Wegener and Carl Boese that had been released the previous year, the modishness of the allusion being employed in this instance to advertise a shop. Expressionism is a marketing device for the note itself, a means of distinction in a crowded field. The suitability of the style for this purpose becomes especially clear when such notes are compared with the rather staid Notgeld designed by Heinz Schiestl, for instance, which were so prized by municipalities and critics. This can be seen in a series issued in 1922 by the women's section of the Deutsche Kolonialgesellschaft in Bremerhaven to raise money for the German school in Okahandja, Namibia. The notes employ expressionistic forms to depict scenes from erstwhile German colonies.[51] On these notes, agitated line primitivizes the images yet further—a formal strategy ironically derived from European woodcut printing, which nevertheless successfully distinguishes the notes from other irredentist examples discussed in the first chapter. One final example: in 1921, the town of Roda issued a series of notes designed by the artist Georg Kötschau that show the story of Faust, as derived from the original *Faustbuch*. Here a sequence of magical and terrible episodes—including Faust's invocation of the devil, his visit to hell, his encounter with Helen of Troy, and his violent end—are depicted in shimmering, brightly colored pen strokes; these suggest the supernatural forces at work behind these events, while effectively catching the eye of the prospective buyer.

Advertisements for tobacconists were far from the only commercial examples of expressionism in these years. In February 1920, the journal *Kunst und Künstler* reported:

> There is feverish activity on the art market. Works are being bought virtually without being seen, and everywhere there is a shortage of goods. What to do with paper money? . . . Then one remembers that paintings, books, and antiques are objects of value. ... In the studio, the artist can hardly keep the customers at bay. In the exhibitions, every third

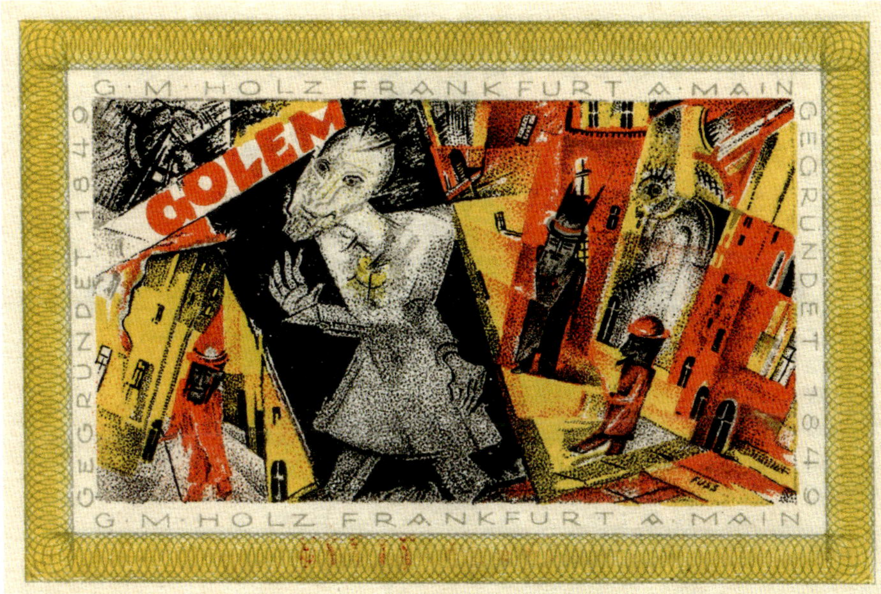

Notgeld issued by G. M. Holz, Frankfurt, 1921. Collection of the author.

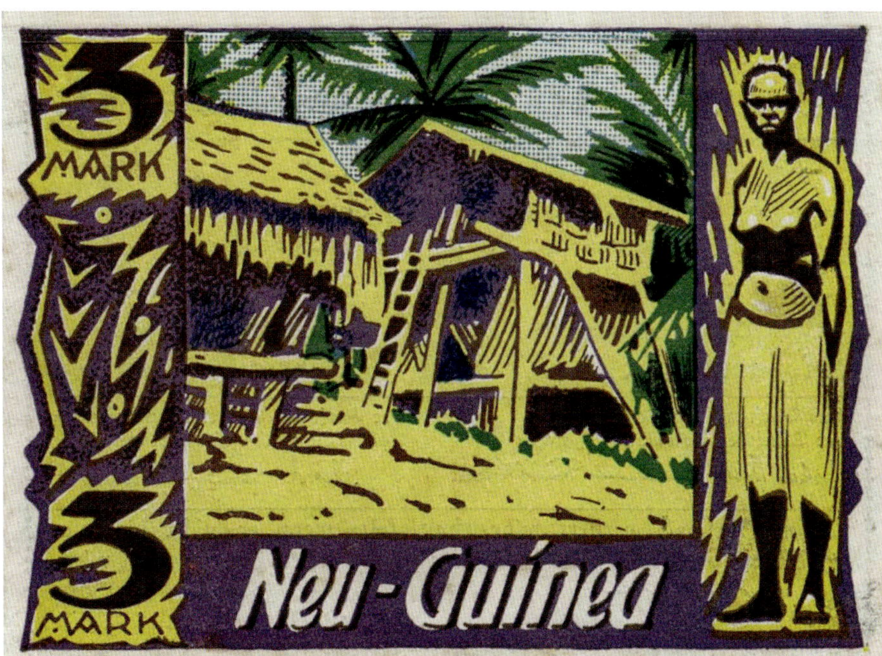

Notgeld issued by the Deutsche Kolonialgesellschaft, 1922. Hans-Ludwig Besler.

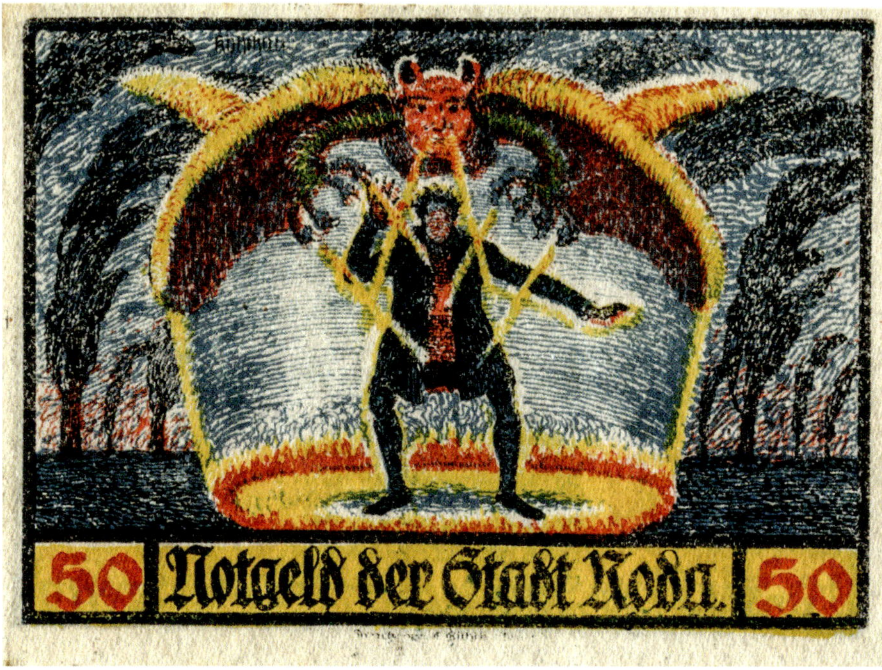

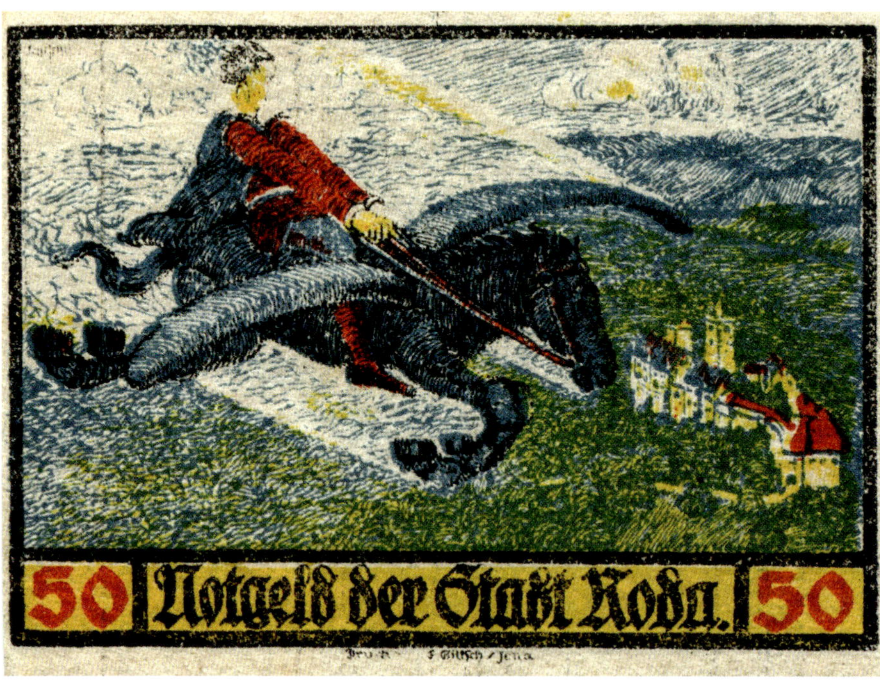

Here and following pages: Notgeld designed by Georg Kötschau, Roda, 1921. Collection of the author.

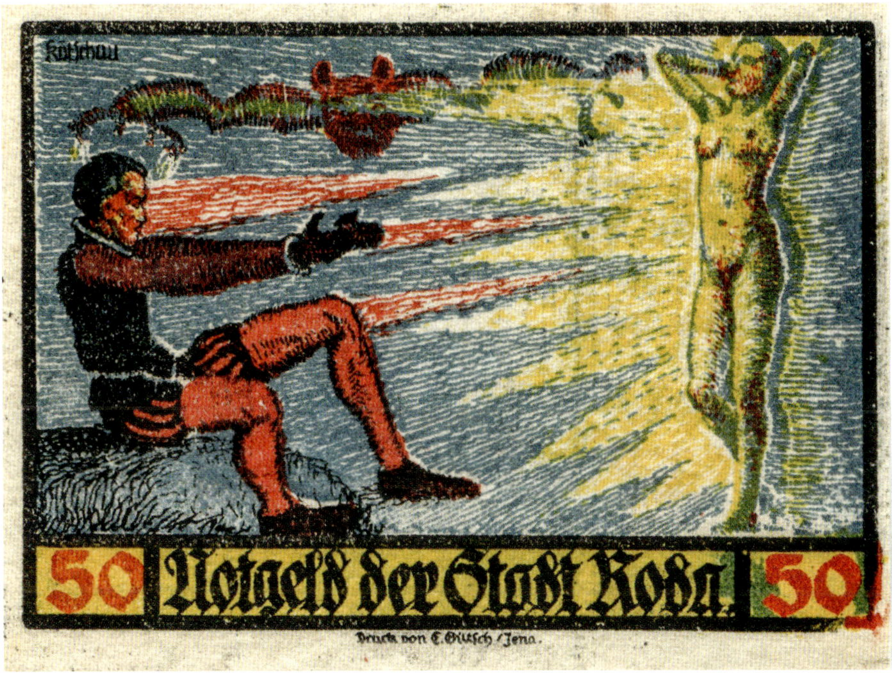
50
Notgeld der Stadt Roda.
50
Druck von C. Giltsch / Jena.

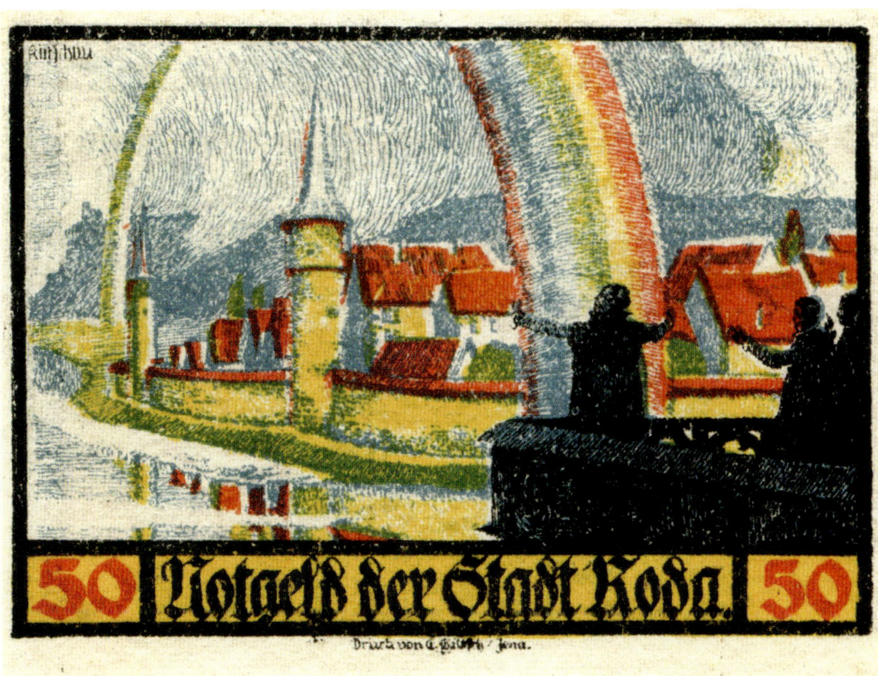
50
Notgeld der Stadt Roda.
50

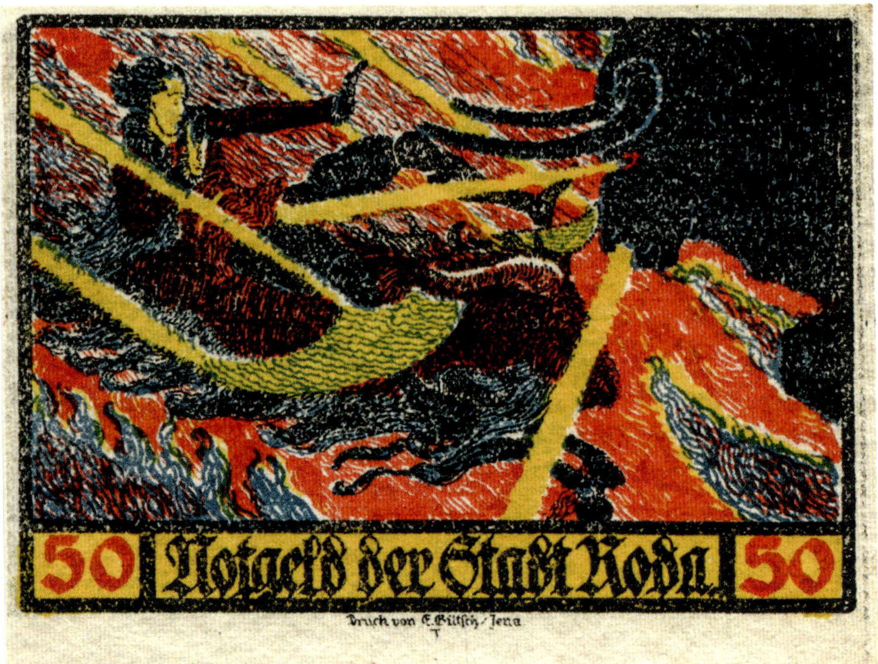
50
Notgeld der Stadt Roda
50
Druck von E. Gütsch / Jena

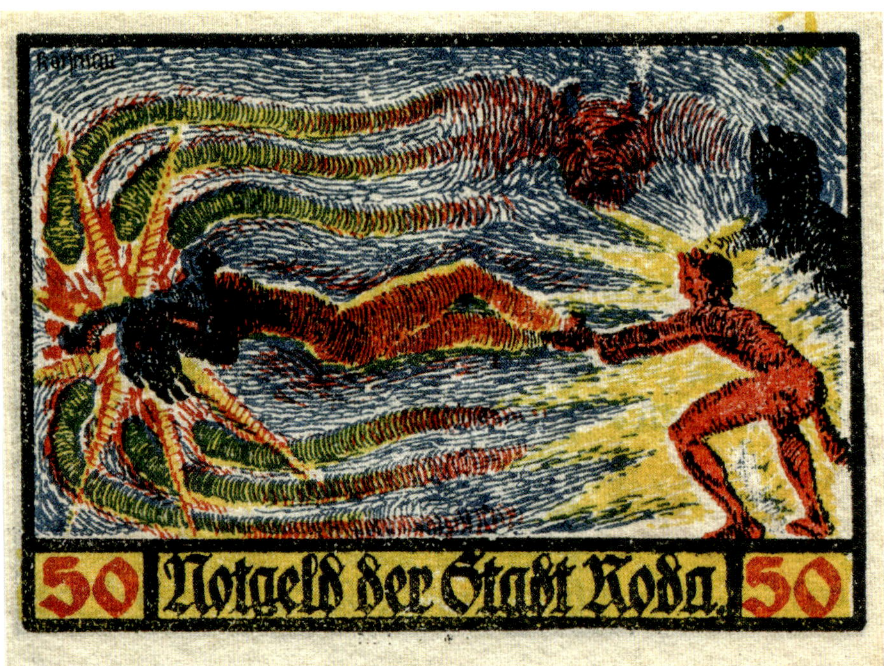
50
Notgeld der Stadt Roda
50

> painting boasts a "sold" tag. And since there is no longer a reactionary art, since everyone paints and draws modern, the Expressionist who was laughed at yesterday has overnight become a capitalist who caters to the public.[52]

In other words, the style had become a beneficiary of the booming art market, part of the "flight into real values" by which people sought to congeal their liquid assets. It was this accommodation of expressionism to the market that provoked its Dadaist critics—but, as we have already seen, these critics did not abjure the money pouring into the sector, either. Given the desperation of the circumstances, this was hardly surprising.

Yet the case of expressionism—and especially of expressionistic Notgeld—is particularly provocative because, if anything can be said to unite the various forms of artistic production commonly lumped together under the name, it is a drive to reenchantment. This was a reaction to the situation famously described by Max Weber in 1917: "The world is disenchanted. One need no longer have recourse to magical means in order to master or implore the spirits, as did the savage, for whom such mysterious powers existed. Technical means and calculations perform the service."[53] It was in this context that Wassily Kandinsky concerned himself with the spiritual in art, and that Franz Marc wrote: "Today we seek beneath the veil of appearances the hidden things in nature."[54] Furthermore, these artists had at least pretended to be implacably opposed to the commercial exploitation of their work.[55] From this perspective, the commercial diffusion of expressionism after the war struck several of its erstwhile partisans as a corruption of its initial aims.[56] In 1920, the left-wing critic and former advocate of the style Wilhelm Hausenstein wrote: "No cigarette poster, no nightclub manages without Expressionism. It is loathsome ... Expressionism is dead."[57] This and similar contemporaneous reactions suggest that the belated appearance of signifiers of reenchantment on money amounted to nothing more than the decay of a burned-out idealism as it returned to earth, cynical and depleted, and collided with reality.

Not all expressionistic Notgeld was so transparently mercenary, however, nor was the style always so lightly adopted. Sometimes the designers in question were noted, or at least committed, adherents of the approach. We have already encountered one such note, the example with which this book began: Wenzel Hablik's

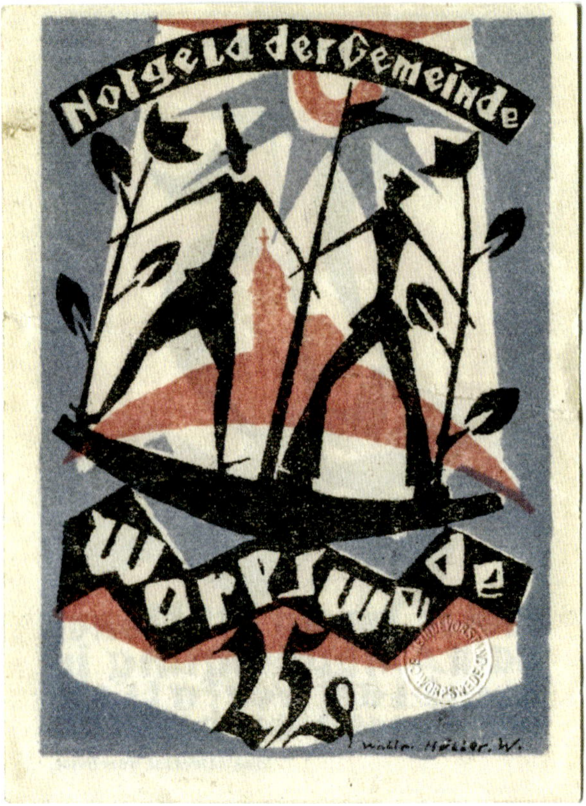

Notgeld designed by Walter Müller, Worpswede, no date. Collection of the author.

depiction of a shitting man, one of several pieces of emergency money he designed for Itzehoe. Hablik was a member of the correspondence network inititated by Bruno Taut known as the Crystal Chain, and as such he participated in the discursive core of the expressionist movement. Likewise, Walter Müller—though less prominent a figure than Hablik—was an active member of the artists' colony at Worpswede, a significant expressionist center; he produced Notgeld that was probably intended to raise funds for the community.

In Erfurt, Alfred Hanf—founder of a local group of expressionist artists, Jung-Erfurt—designed a large number of Notgeld notes. The first set of these was commissioned by Edwin Redslob, an important supporter of modern art who until recently had been the curator of the local museum (in 1919 Redslob had also been appointed Reichskunstwart, National Art Intendant, and

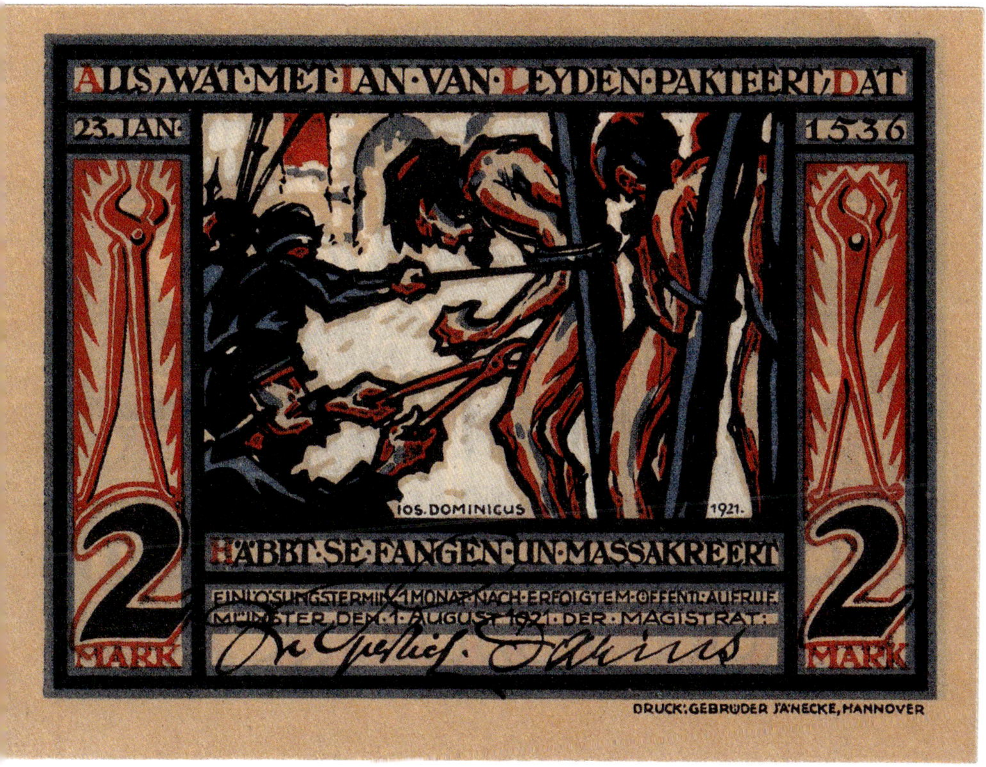

Notgeld designed by Josef Dominicus, Münster, 1921. Nathaniel Butler.

as such he was responsible for the visual identity of the new state, including its banknotes).[58] The series depicted a selection of episodes from the life of Luther, a ubiquitous presence during and after the war, when he was celebrated as a representative of German culture. (Critics such as Bloch and Hugo Ball opposed this fashion—which extended from Aby Warburg to the "driveling Pan-German speechmakers and scribblers" decried by Ball—by adopting in his stead Anabaptist leader Thomas Münzer, Luther's antagonist, whom they painted as a proto-revolutionary. However, when Münzer appears on Notgeld he is shown as a rabble-rouser, while his comrades are tortured to death for sedition.) Hanf also produced a set of notes showing picturesque views of Erfurt; like his Luther Notgeld, this is a familiar theme, but he gives both series an expressionist spin that in the latter case attains an almost psychedelic intensity. The series attracted the attention of *Das Notgeld*, if not its approval: the magazine described the notes as "übermodern."[59]

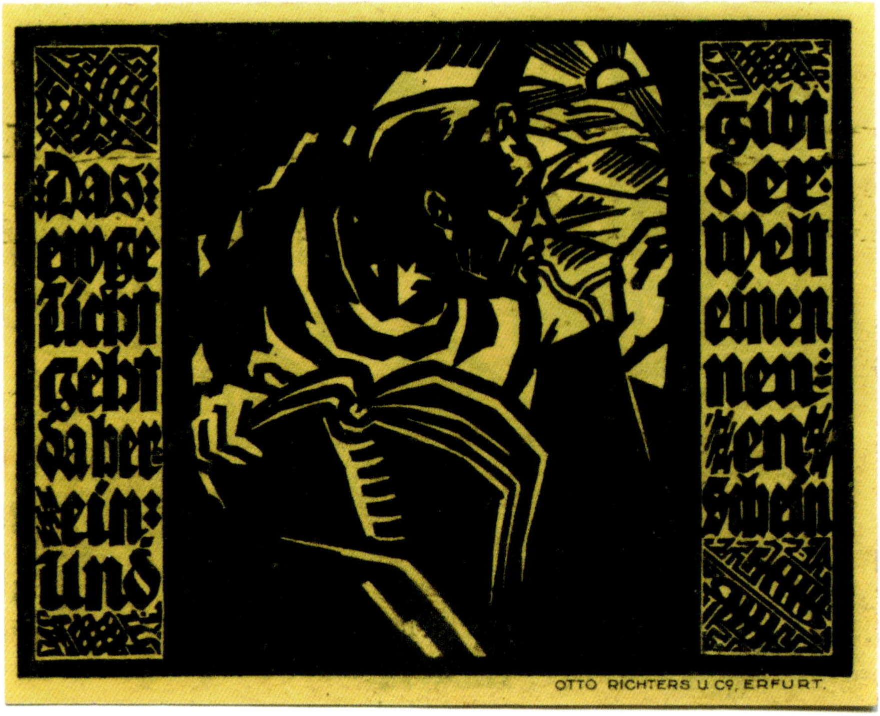

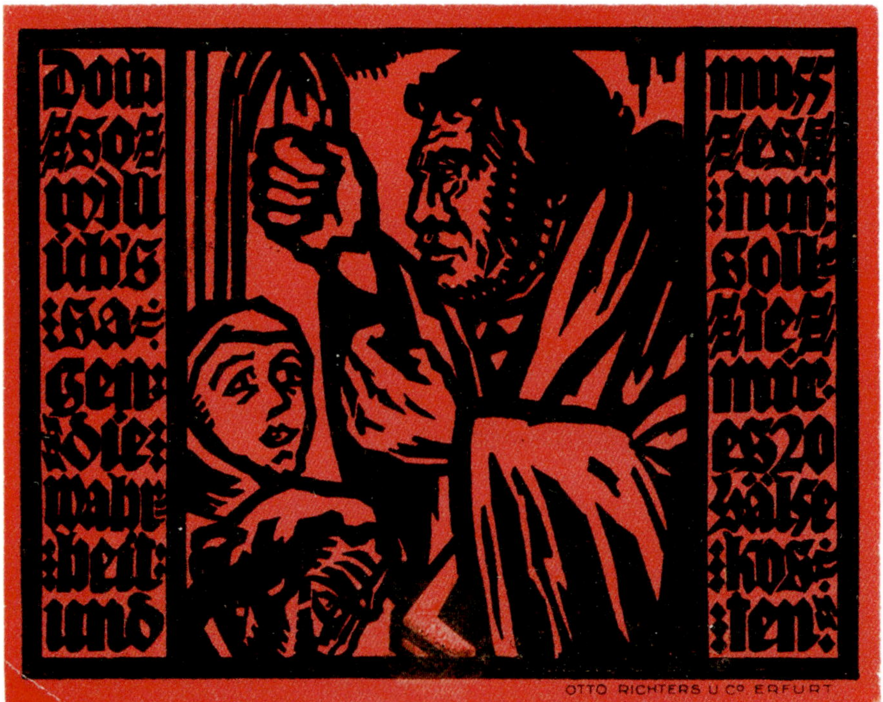

Here and following pages: Notgeld designed by Alfred Hanf, Erfurt, 1921. Collection of the author.

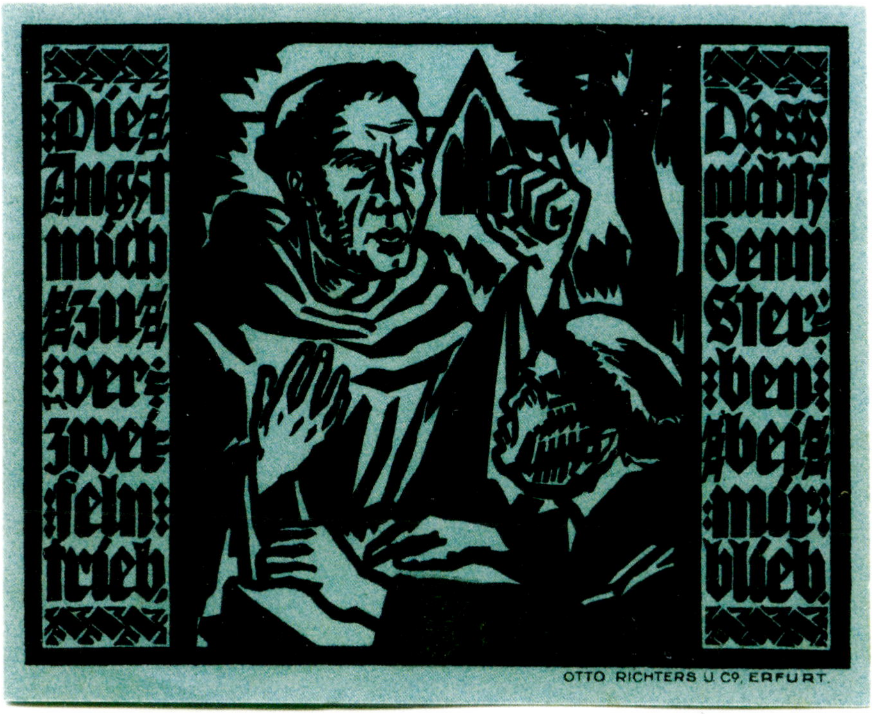
Die Angst mich zu verzweifeln trieb,
Dass nicht denn Sterben bei mir blieb.
OTTO RICHTERS U. C°. ERFURT.

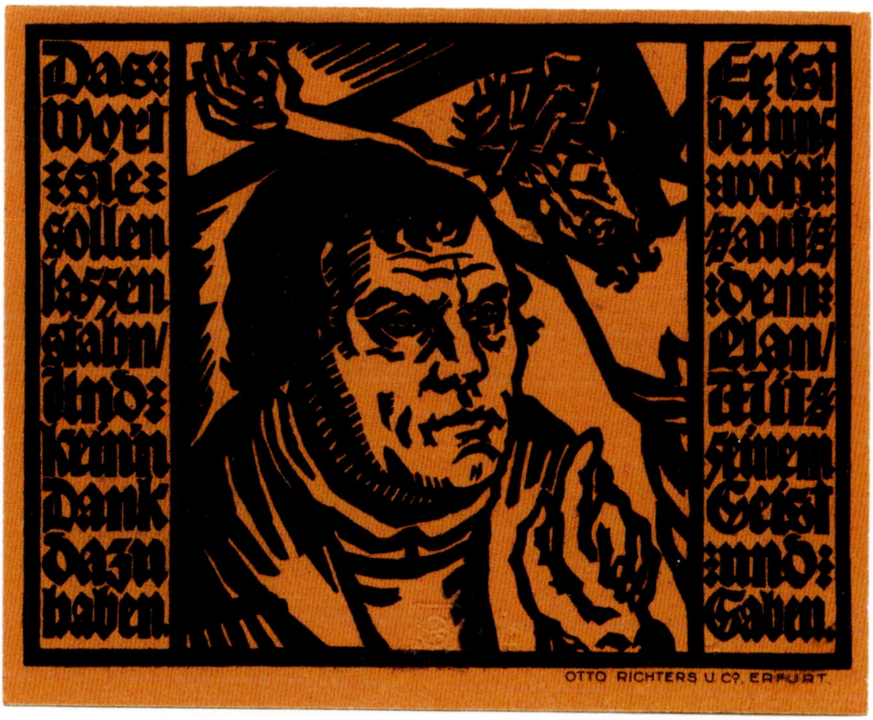
Das Wort sie sollen lassen stahn/ und kein'n Dank dazu haben.
Er ist bei uns wohl auf dem Plan/ mit seinem Geist und Gaben.
OTTO RICHTERS U. C°. ERFURT.

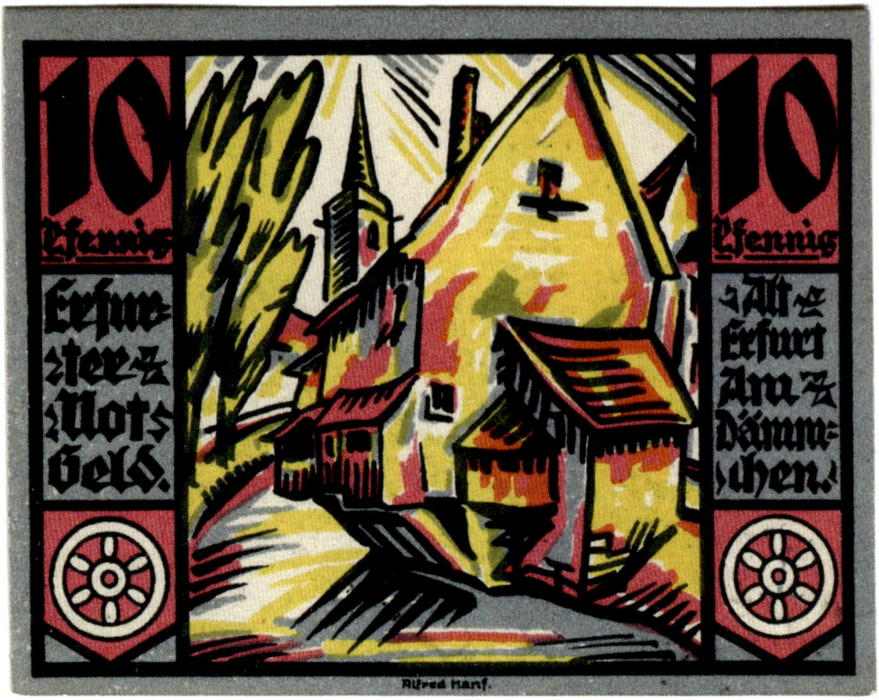
10
Pfennig
Erfurter Not Geld.
10
Pfennig
Alt Erfurt Am Dämmchen.
Alfred Hanf.

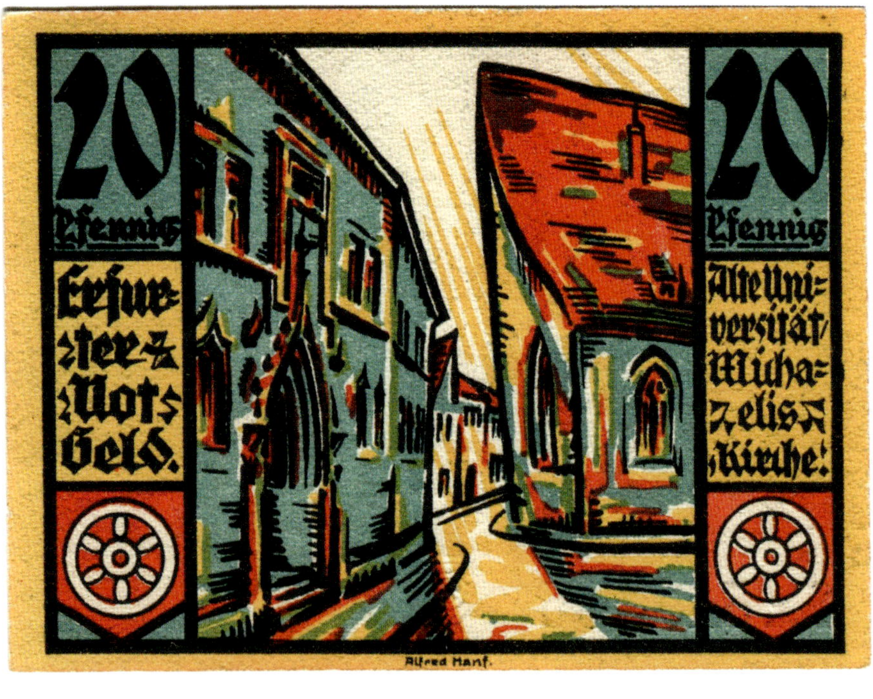
20
Pfennig
Erfurter Not Geld.
20
Pfennig
Alte Universität Michaelis Kirche!
Alfred Hanf.

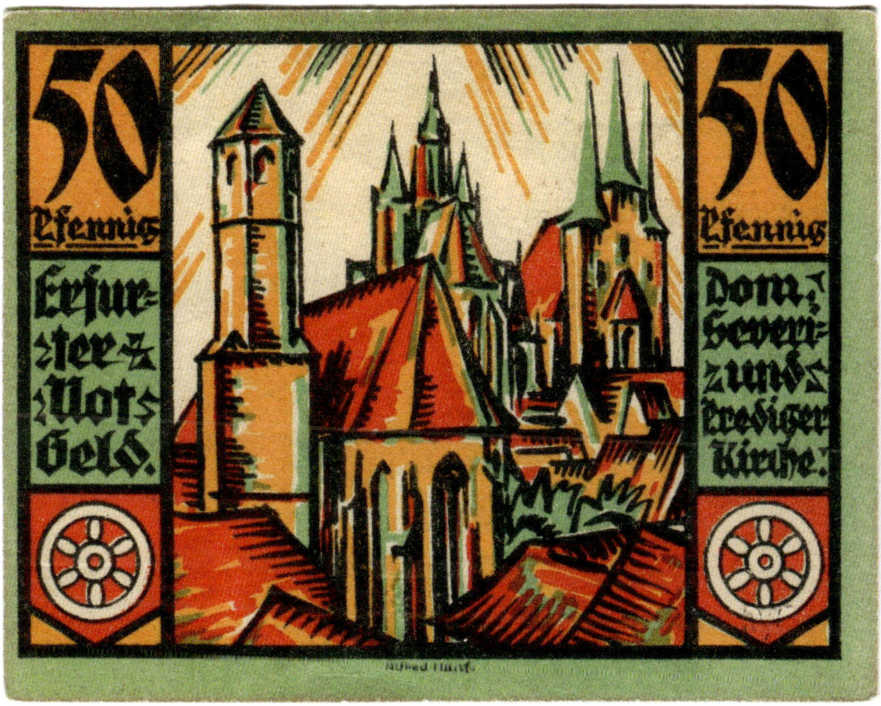
50
Pfennig
Erfurter Not Geld.
50
Pfennig
Dom, Severi und Prediger Kirche.

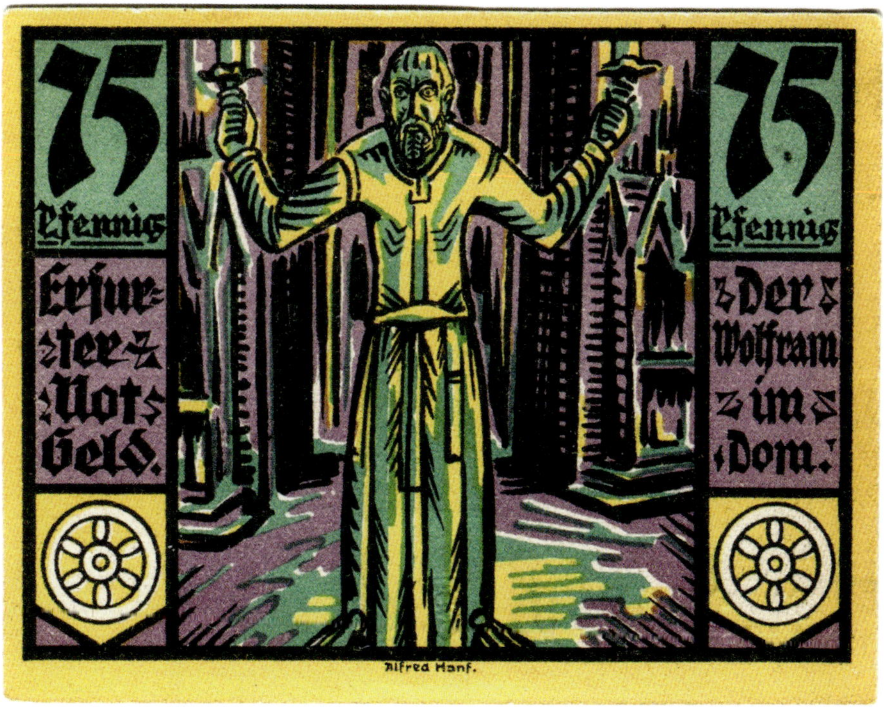
75
Pfennig
Erfurter Not Geld.
75
Pfennig
Der Wolfram im Dom.
Alfred Hanf.

To mention one final "legitimate" expressionist note, in 1921 a professor at Magdeburg's art school named Kurt Tuch produced a design celebrating the work of Bruno Taut, who had lately become the city architect.[60] It shows a vision of the future in which strange flying machines fill the sky and a large crystalline structure, reminiscent of Taut's Glass Pavilion, rises above the harbor. "One day in untrammeled creativity, New Magdeburg will be the world's most beautiful city"—so says the inscription, although Taut never got very far with his plans. Nevertheless, these examples suggest that, although there is merit in the arguments regarding the debasement of the style, these could be countered by an immanent critique of expressionistic emergency money. Understood in the movement's own terms, the application of these tropes to Notgeld might be seen as a sincere attempt to reenchant the modern world, precisely at the point of its most debased materiality. Kandinsky wrote of "the incubus of materialism"—on expressionist Notgeld this nightmare is countered with the wistful dream of metaphysics.[61]

Even the more questionable examples cited earlier could be said to at least have a striking congruence with the situation. The revival of the old Jewish legend of the golem during and after the war, when it was the subject of a successful novel by Gustav Meyrink and no fewer than three films by Paul Wegener, indicates its appeal for contemporaneous audiences. In the 1920 film (the only one that survives), the monstrous clay figure is brought to life by the insertion into its body of a piece of paper inscribed with a magical word. Although Meyrink's psychological horror (Bloch described his writing as "mercenary spookiness")[62] has little in common with the medieval tale, the eerie life he bestows on the objects and houses of the Prague ghetto suggests a common concern with animation. In one passage, the narrator explicitly discusses this phenomenon, recalling the sight of some newspapers moving in an unfelt breeze, and asks, "What if, after all, we living beings were nothing more than such scraps of paper?"[63] Spyros Papapetros has located the origin of this concern with the "animation of the inorganic" in fin-de-siècle discourses of empathy, which, he claims, were sublated in modernist design.[64] Among Papapetros's subjects are the film *Nosferatu*, which was released in 1922, two years after *The Golem*; it is striking that the era of so-called expressionist film and the birth of cinematic horror—both of which were so often concerned with the intrinsic characteristic of the medium, the bringing of dead matter to life—should

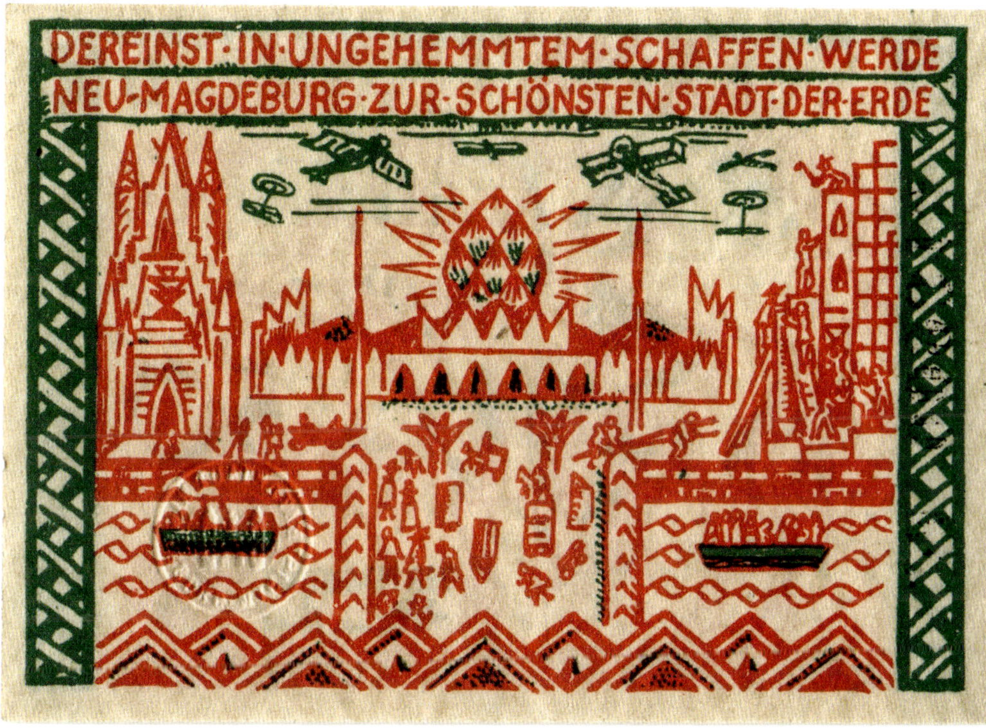

Notgeld designed by Kurt Tuch, Magdeburg, 1921. Collection of the author.

have coincided with the inflation years, when, to return once more to Zweig's 1923 essay "Attack of the Objects," inanimate objects, the world of commodities, became "threatening and violent."

Seen in this light, the appearance of the golem on Notgeld, though "merely" an advertisement, is more than fitting, since these sinister pieces of paper also seemed to have a life of their own. The golem, as the iconic representative of living matter—matter moved by paper, no less—stands for the animating power of money. It stands, in other words, for commodity fetishism. (As Adorno would later note, "The occultist draws the ultimate conclusion from the fetish character of commodities: menacingly objectified labour assails him on all sides from demonically grimacing objects.")[65] This is made particularly clear in Meyrink's novel, where the uncanniness of the narrative lies not just in the sense that the external world of objects has become possessed by ill-intentioned life; the narrator starts to suspect that he might actually be the golem himself, a mere object, brought to life by unseen forces. So it is precisely on this note, this debased example of expressionism advertising a shop, that we find its kernel of truth. While it comes to the fore here, it should be noted that this is in fact characteristic of all expressionistic money—and all Notgeld besides. For although money in this period has shed the chorus line of allegorical personifications that crowded banknotes of preceding eras, it has not lost that quality of opacity that Benjamin identifies as being essential to the allegorical mode. Instead, money itself has become allegorical: a sign (of value) that is no longer transparent. It is still a sign, but what it points to is uncertain. Expressionist Notgeld attempts to tether this disturbing numinousness by bringing it to expression—not iconographically, as allegory had, but formally, through its shivering lines (it is worth noting that Benjamin relates baroque allegory to expressionism in the prologue to his *Trauerspiel* book). Whether sincere or mercenary, the designers of expressionist Notgeld were essentially striving to endow this money with *value*—by formal aesthetic means, just as Schiestl had, albeit in another mode, with his sturdy, orderly compositions. Expressionistic money therefore attempts a kind of alchemy, through which the most debased material was to be transformed into the most elevated via the catalysis of form. At the same time, this form was transformed into value—monetary value. However, among these expressionist notes there is one exception to this mutual adequation, or at least one example that puts up some resistance: the notes designed by Wenzel Hablik for Itzehoe. I return to them in the next chapter.

In his retrospective account of the Weimar period, *Heritage of These Times*, Bloch clings to the possibilities that may inhere in these occult modes of thought: "theosophy, by burrowing in the mud and in formerly religious rubble, possibly also cuts through temple passageways which honest excavation fails to see."[66] Yet, in the end, it may appear that all that was cut through here were necks. Adorno's own look back on the Weimar years, which, unlike Bloch's, was written after the Nazi Götterdämmerung, takes a dimmer view:

> The power of occultism, as of Fascism, to which it is connected by thought-patterns of the ilk of anti-semitism, is not only pathic. Rather it lies in the fact that in the lesser panaceas, as in superimposed pictures, consciousness

famished for truth imagines it is grasping a dimly present knowledge diligently denied to it by official progress in all its forms. It is the knowledge that society, by virtually excluding the possibility of spontaneous change, is gravitating towards total catastrophe.[67]

Sobering Up

During the inflation, these occult forces began to be confronted by a countervailing impulse, which also made itself felt within the realm of Notgeld. In 1921, the city of Weimar commissioned a series of notes from the Bauhaus, and Herbert Bayer, then a student at the school, designed a set characteristic of what would later become known as the New Typography.[68] It is worth comparing such emergency money with the state's official banknotes. At the same time that town halls around the country were commissioning local artists to produce Notgeld, a debate was being conducted over the design of the Reichsbank's own notes in the pages of the national press. In a 1921 article in the *Vossische Zeitung*, the National Art Intendent Edwin Redslob defended the first set of notes to be issued by the republican government. Although the Reichskunstwart was nominally responsible for the appearance of banknotes, the autonomy of the Reichsbank meant that he was not always involved in their design. This was especially the case during the inflation, when speed was of the essence, and so his contribution was limited to the proposal of famous figures for depiction. Nevertheless, he was publicly criticized for the perceived shortcomings of the hastily prepared notes.[69] In response, he argued that a new state required time to develop a "style"—indeed, his article was titled "Banknote Style"—which should be characterized by the *Sachlichkeit*, or sobriety, appropriate to these objects. As such, these notes should supersede the "*Gründerzeit*'s demand for opulence and finery," which had resulted in its banknotes being "so filled with representational motifs that instead of being 'commercial papers' [*Wertpapiere*] they were nothing other than little pictures in pocket format."[70] Here we see Redslob trying to pull the banknote back from the precipice of ambiguity toward which the Notgeld designers had been pushing it; according to his anonymous and rather more plain-speaking interlocutor, the notes of the *Kaiserzeit* had "set a record in tastelessness."[71] What both participants in the discussion agreed on was the importance that should be accorded to the aesthetic dimension of banknotes, which ought to evince a unity of conception and design, and which should further stabilize the value referent by employing complex antiforgery devices—a technique intended as much to reassure the bearer of the note's authenticity as to confound the malfeasant intent on illicit reproduction. This exchange evinces a widespread anxiety regarding the search for a style adequate to the conditions of modernity, which crystallized in Germany in the well-known debates carried out in the Werkbund's journal *Die Form*. As Frederic Schwartz has argued, the project of the Werkbund was to spiritualize the commodity by making it a bearer of culture (in this chapter, we have already seen the expressionists doing the same, albeit in a different register).[72] However, in the context of money itself, a complication is added to this program, which was always intended as a tonic to the more chaotic elements of capitalism. How could these be tamed at the very site and moment of their wildest efflorescence?

While Redslob was frustrated in his attempts to reform the national currency, Bayer's note was shortly to fulfill the Reichskunstwart's demands for aesthetic coherence and *Sachlichkeit*. We have seen that Heinz Schiestl's notes were praised for similar reasons. However, these were rare instances among the designers of Notgeld, who competed to attract attention with images more frequently garish and outrageous. By contrast, both the Bauhaus and the government, in the form of its in-house avant-gardist, Redslob, were looking for a form for money that would have a stylistic unity—that is, that would visually, coherently, and in the timeliest way possible paper over the cracks in the currency that was then falling apart. While for Schiestl this had meant arranging local references in sturdy compositions, in Bayer's hands it meant clearing a space on the note in which ever-growing ranks of zeroes could accumulate in an orderly fashion.[73] His design responds with apparent rationality to a situation of enormous irrationality, attempting to set up a visual framework in which the latter could be reduced to the former. Other notes, as an example from Bamberg demonstrates (see p. 173), exhibited anxious, morbid humor with regard to the fear that "zeroes now control our lives," an anxiety that formally manifests itself as a kind of logorrhea; words (which still mean something) crowd out the hated zero, the endlessly reiterated sign for the abyss of meaning into which the republic had plummeted. For Bayer, by contrast, the zeroes are welcomed into the equally blank space of the note. That this stabilization technique is also a kind of mystification is clear enough, and seemed so to observers at the time, as Bloch's critical remarks make explicit. For him, such objectivity was "nothing but sheer façade; behind the in-built rationalities the total anarchy of the profit economy remains."[74]

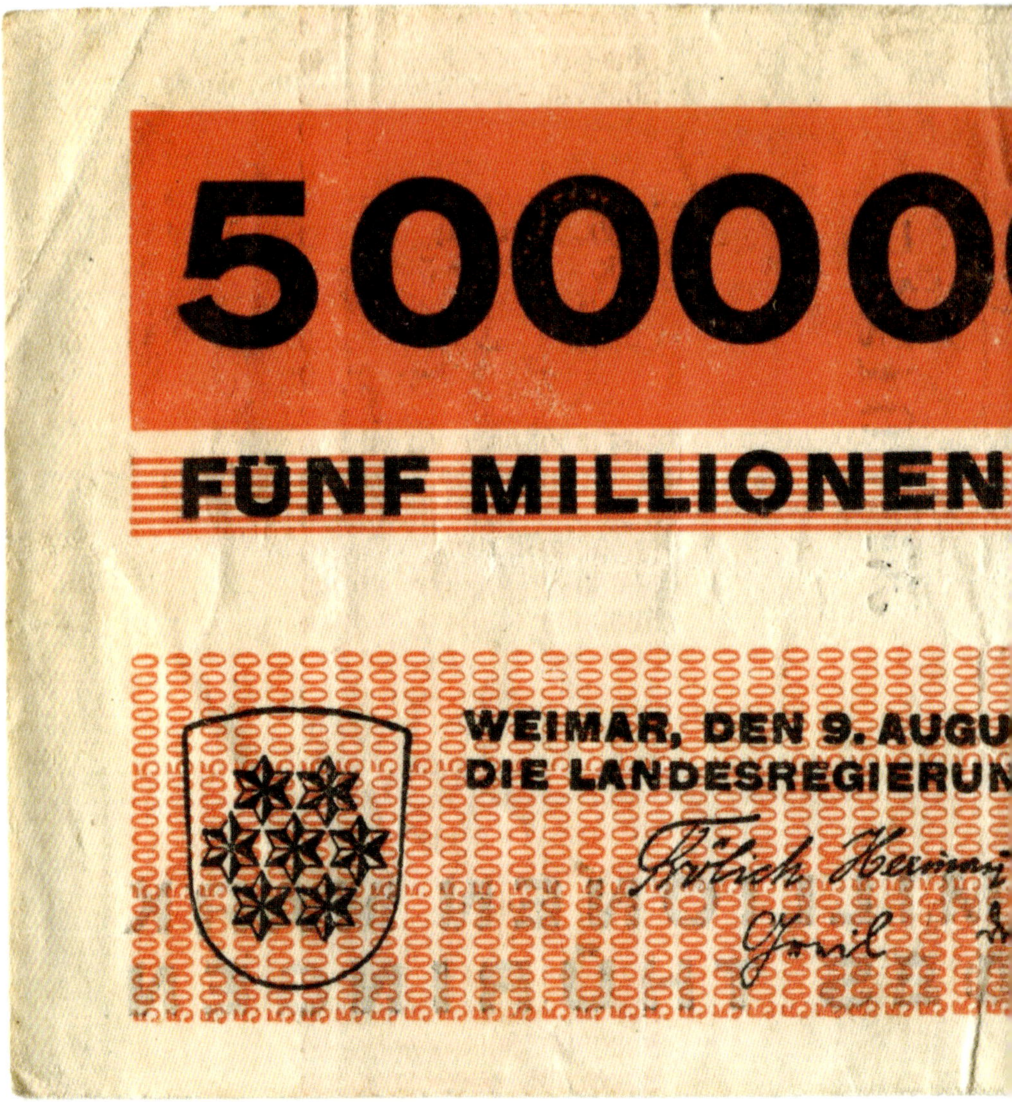

Notgeld designed by Herbert Bayer, Weimar, 1923. Collection of the author.

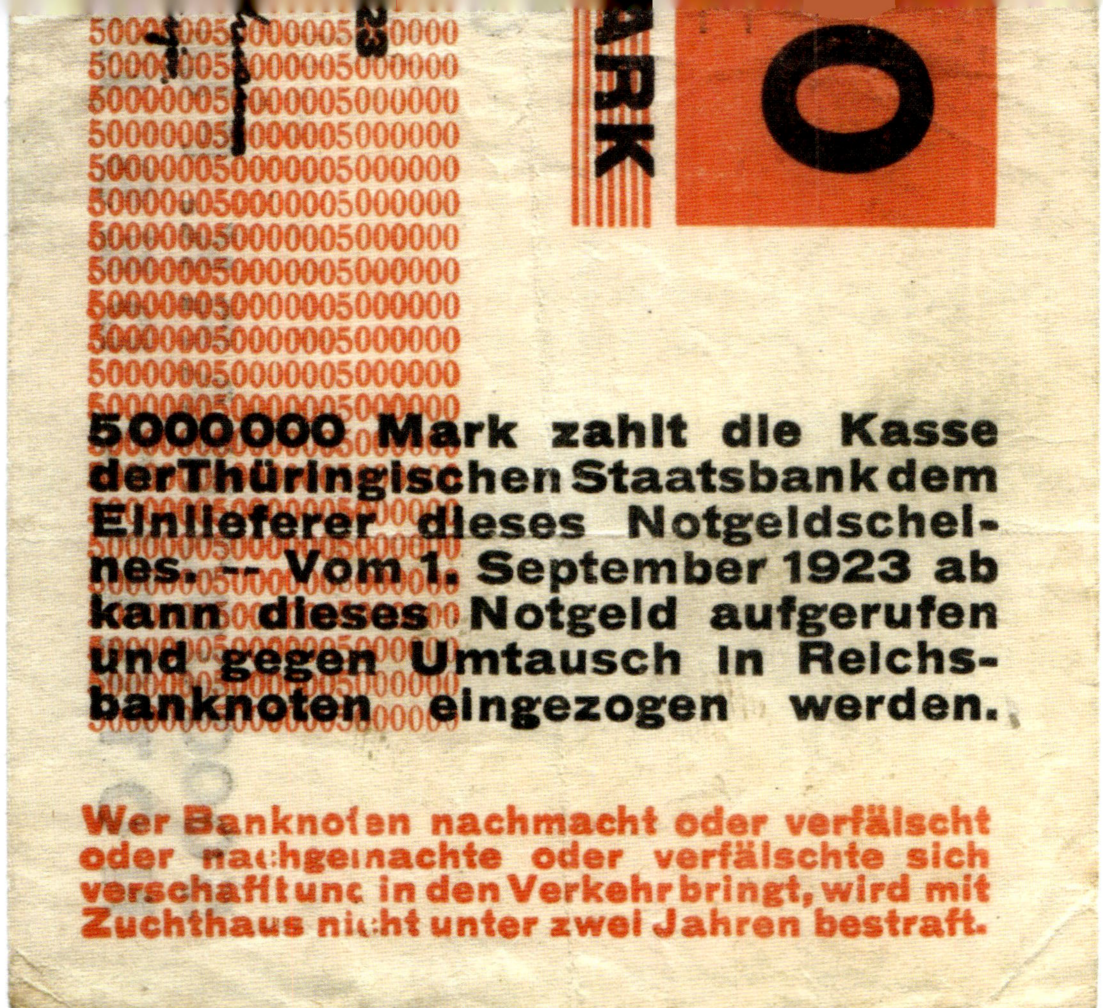
ARK
5000000 Mark zahlt die Kasse der Thüringischen Staatsbank dem Einlieferer dieses Notgeldscheines. -- Vom 1. September 1923 ab kann dieses Notgeld aufgerufen und gegen Umtausch in Reichsbanknoten eingezogen werden.
Wer Banknoten nachmacht oder verfälscht oder nachgemachte oder verfälschte sich verschafft und in den Verkehr bringt, wird mit Zuchthaus nicht unter zwei Jahren bestraft.

4 *Crisis*

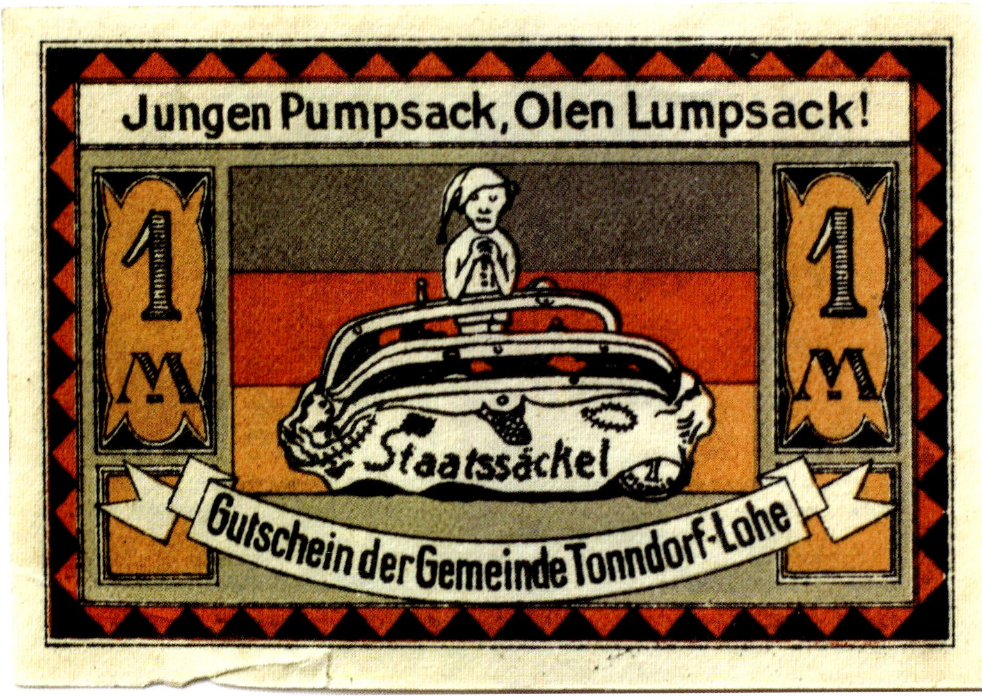

Notgeld from Tonndorf-Lohe, 1921. Warburg Institute, London.

The Germans suffer from a humiliating alternation between constipation and diarrhoea.
Raoul Hausmann, "Return to Objectivity in Art," 1920

A pathetic figure prays forlornly by an empty purse; profiteers dance around a moneybag on a pedestal; an invalid crawls through a ruined landscape strewn with animal corpses; and a graph traces the rising number of infant mortalities. In addition to the supernatural notes discussed in the previous chapter, there is a further category of destabilizing Notgeld, the design of which seems intended to *accelerate* the double crisis of value and the sign. Such notes refer to the inflation in more or less explicit terms, with humorous, cynical, tragic, or sober affect. These critical notes could be called *Gegengeld*, or anti-money, since they appear to reverse the conventional technical apparatus of the medium-as-stabilizer: instead of supporting belief in their value, these notes undermine it.[1]

Sometimes *Gegengeld* is humorous, albeit often bitterly so. In the first instance mentioned above, a tiny figure, identifiable by his nightcap as Michel, personification of the German everyman, prays or perhaps begs before a ragged and empty "public purse," as the label on the object informs us. The Plattdeutsch phrase above this scene reads something like: "Young freeloader [specifically, someone who is always borrowing money], old raggedy bugger [literally, ragged bag]!" Other such notes are vituperative, like the second example. The money worshipers here, who include a seminude sex worker and an anti-Semitic caricature, are captioned "Nothing is sacred anymore, and all vices reign freely." The note comes from a series designed by Max Eschle in 1921 for the far-right organization Liga zum Schutze der Deutschen Kultur (League for the Protection of German Culture); the other notes in the series show scenes of civil strife, a felled German oak, and a mother grieving over a dead child in a ruined landscape.[2] A similar scene of ruination appears on the third note mentioned above; issued in 1923, it takes a more tragic perspective. In this case, furthermore, the connection to the inflation is made explicit. The inscription, a typical piece of Notgeld doggerel, reads as follows:

> Thousands have we long transcended,
> Millions also quickly ended,
> Billions too were made to dash:
> Today trillions are our cash.
> Zeros now control our lives,
> Yet we Germans keenly strive,
> To rouse the Reich, nearly undone,
> From the nothing it's become.

However, the image does not lend credence to the rather desperate optimism of the poem's closing lines. Once again we see Michel, but in this case he is ailing, and reaches for a medicine bottle labeled "Goldmark," referring to the idyll of a gold-backed currency.

The final, statistical, example mentioned above is equally stark, although it takes a very different visual tack. In fact it has more in common with the note by Herbert Bayer discussed in the previous chapter, insofar as it adopts a sober, objective affect, employing that most sober and objective of representational modes, the graph. It is part of a series issued by the town of Kahla, a prolific producer of emergency money; other notes in the set show the contribution of Upper Silesia to the German economy in 1913 (i.e., before the region was partly lost to Poland following the 1921 plebiscite); the composition of the reparations demanded under the terms of the Versailles Treaty; the value of the mark on the international currency markets; German exports by sector; the number of applicants for each position advertised; the cost of living; the relative value of foreign currencies in Germany; the reduced extent of the nation following the Versailles Treaty; and the price

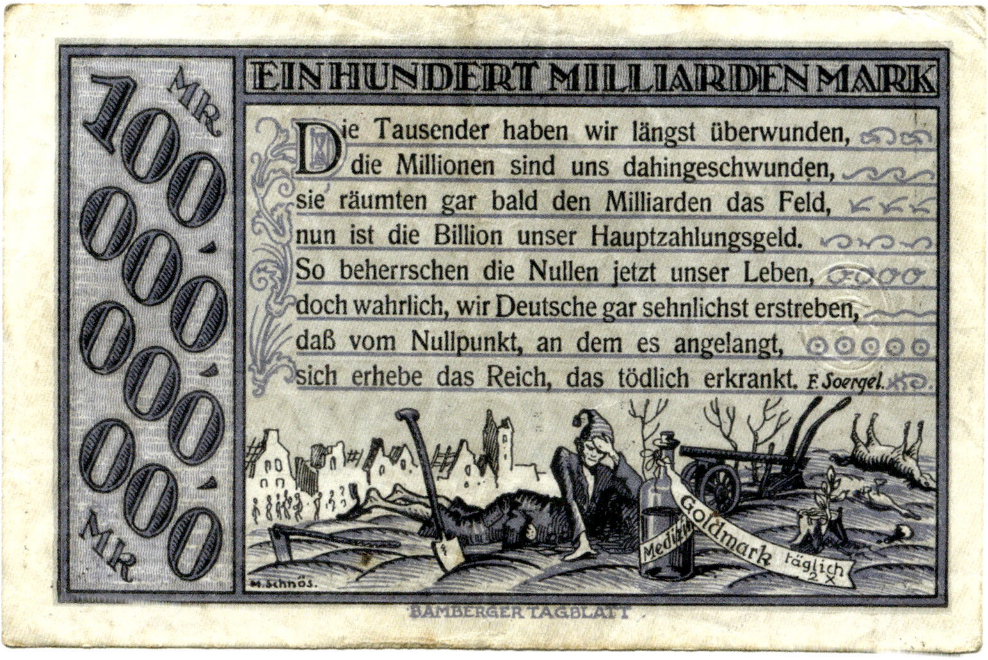

Notgeld from Bamberg, 1923. Collection of the author.

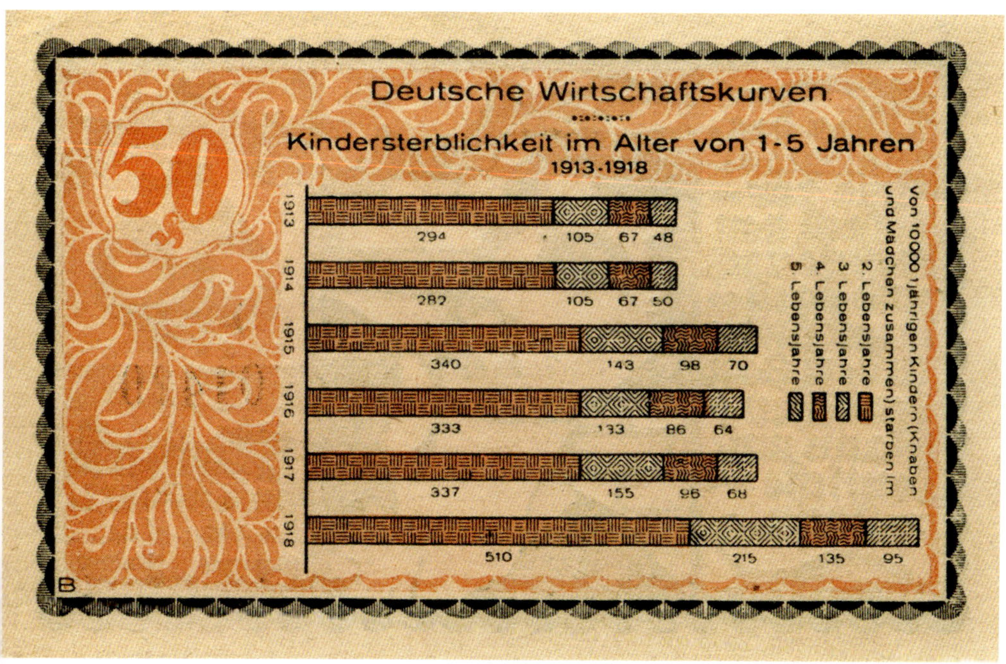

Notgeld from Kahla, 1921. Collection of the author.

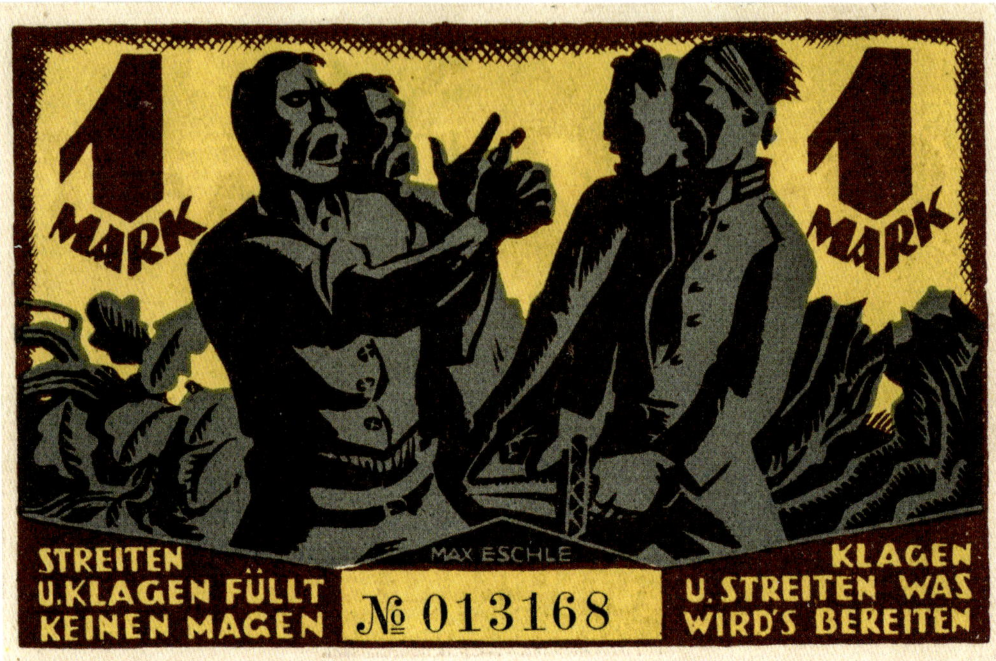

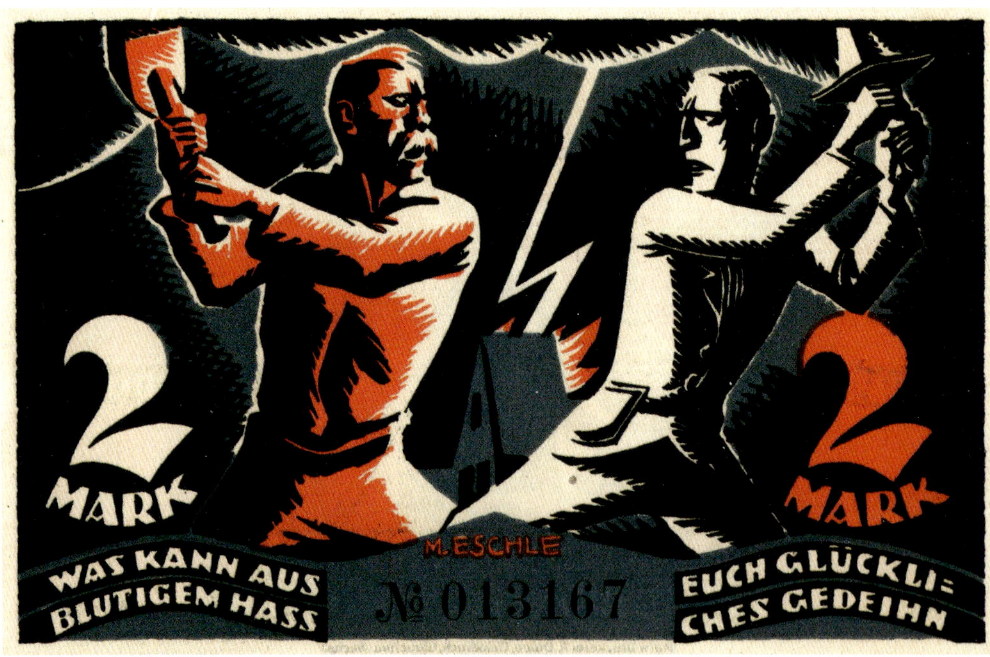

Here and facing page: Notgeld designed by Max Eschle for the Liga zum Schutz der Deutschen Kultur, 1921. Collection of the author.

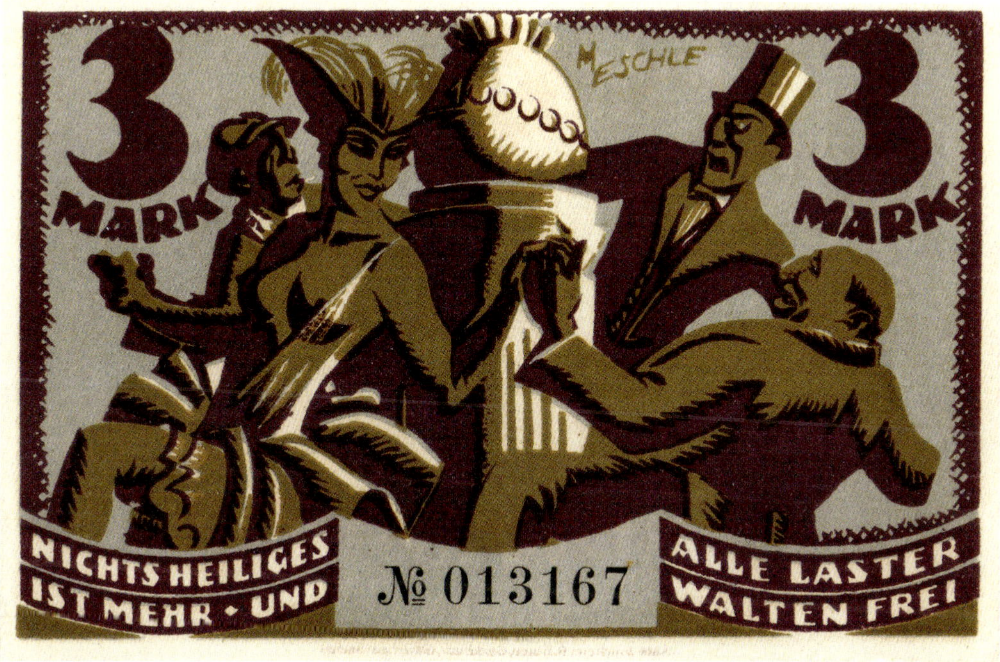
MESCHLE
3 MARK
3 MARK
NICHTS HEILIGES IST MEHR • UND
№ 013167
ALLE LASTER WALTEN FREI

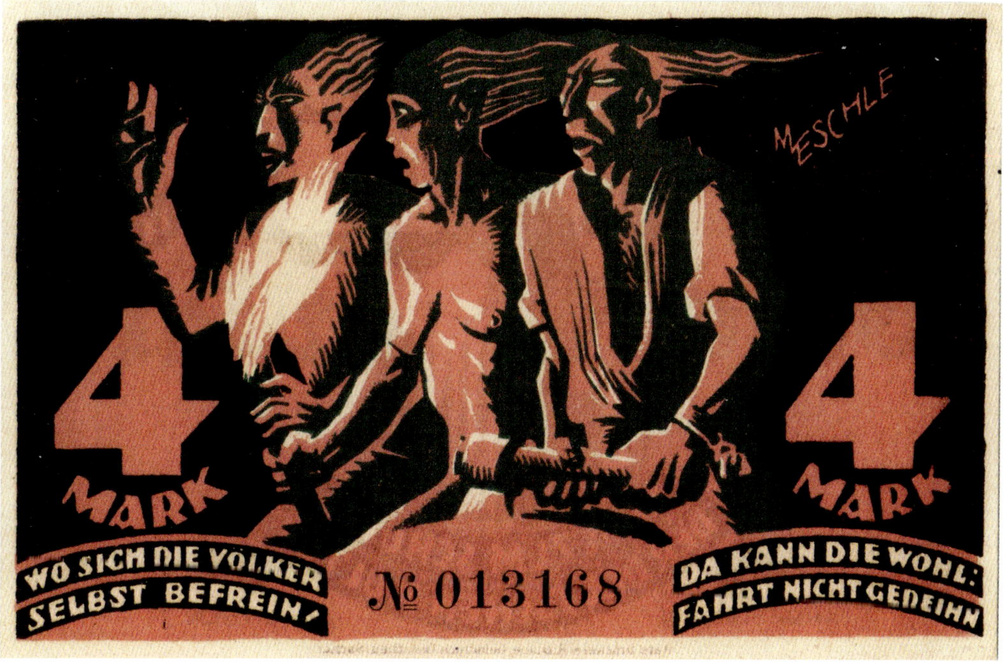
MESCHLE
4 MARK
4 MARK
WO SICH DIE VÖLKER SELBST BEFREIN/
№ 013168
DA KANN DIE WOHL: FAHRT NICHT GEDEIHN

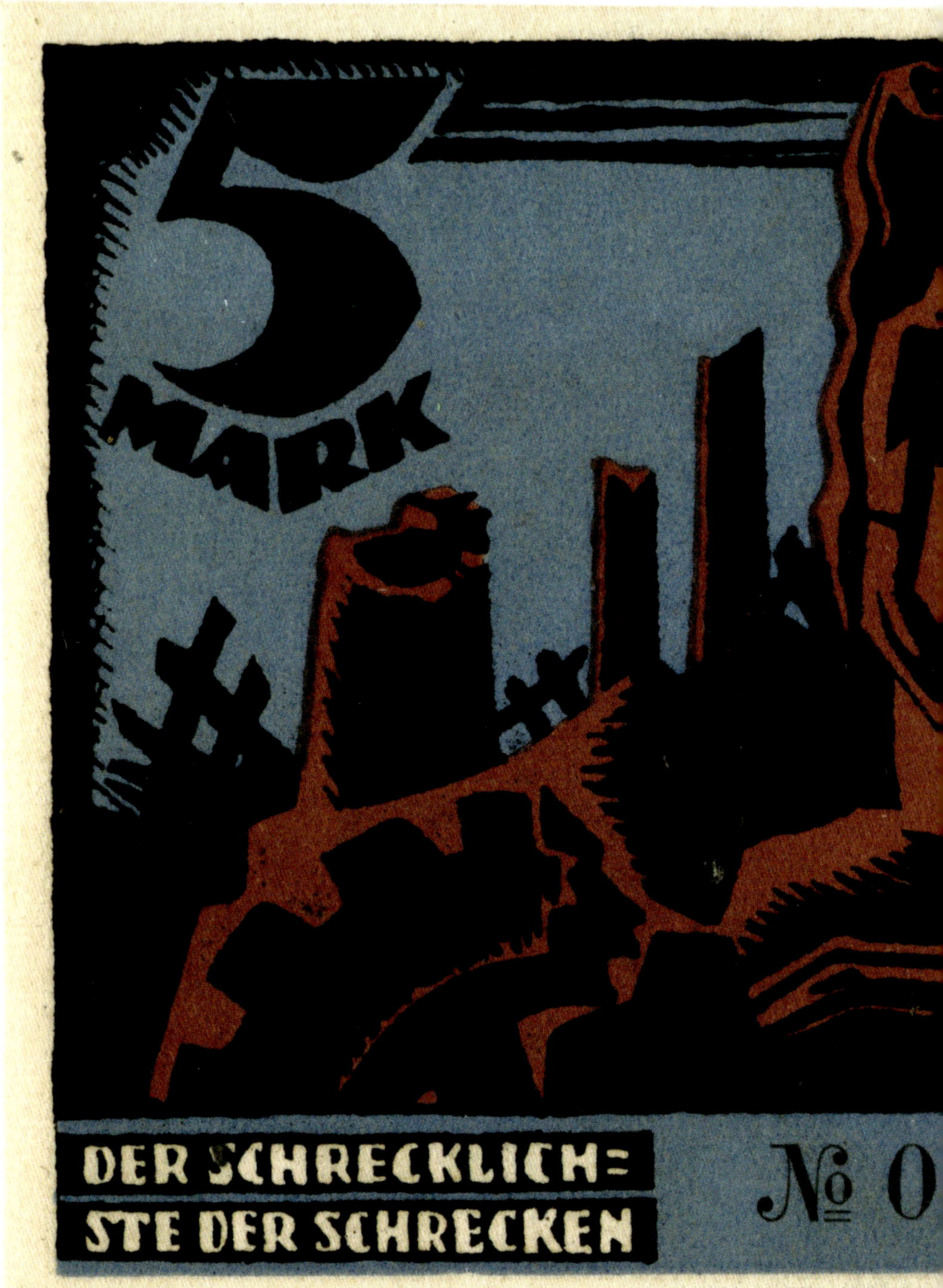

Notgeld designed by Max Eschle for the Liga zum Schutz der Deutschen Kultur, 1921. Collection of the author.

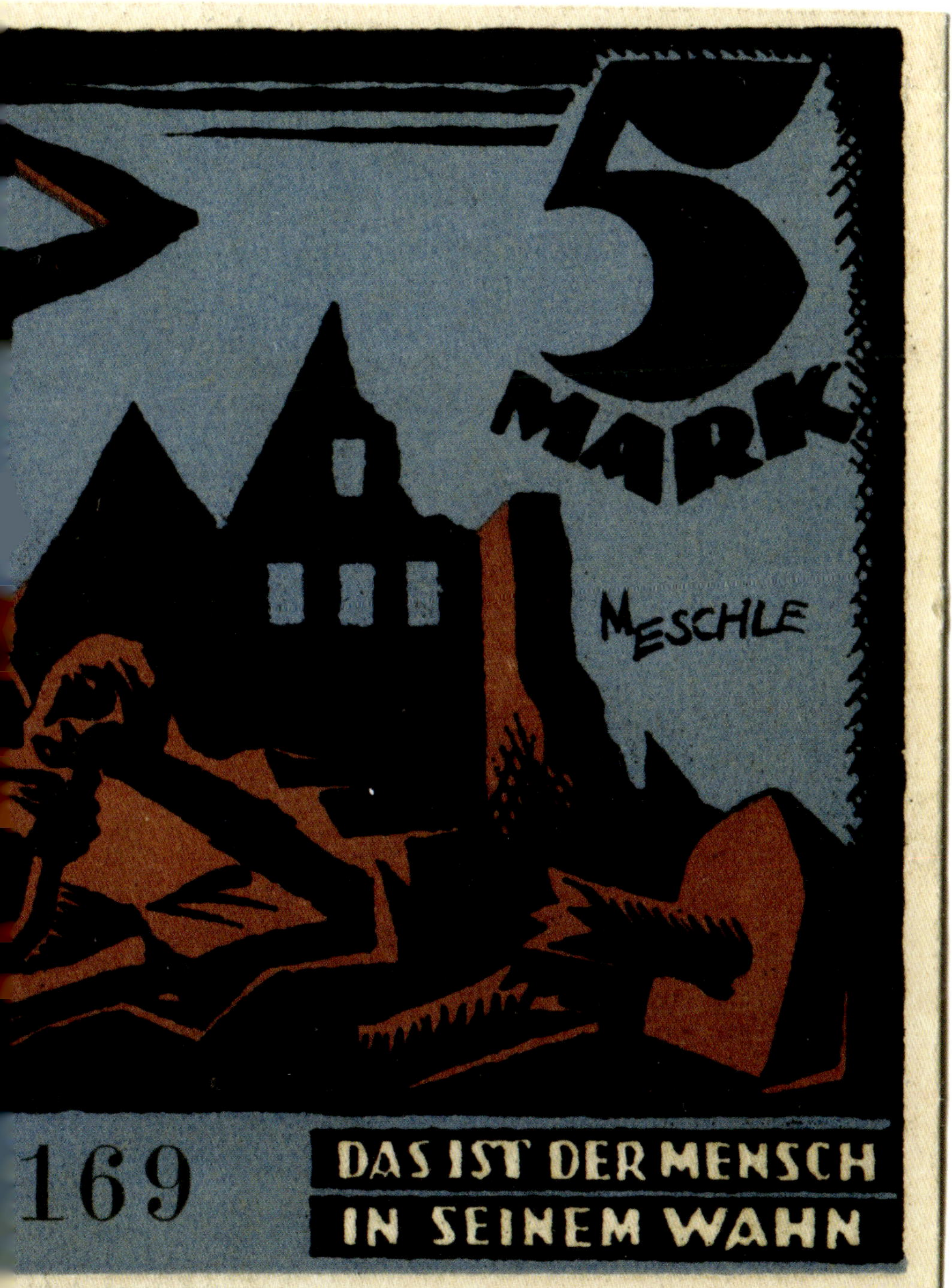
5
MARK
MESCHLE
169
DAS IST DER MENSCH
IN SEINEM WAHN

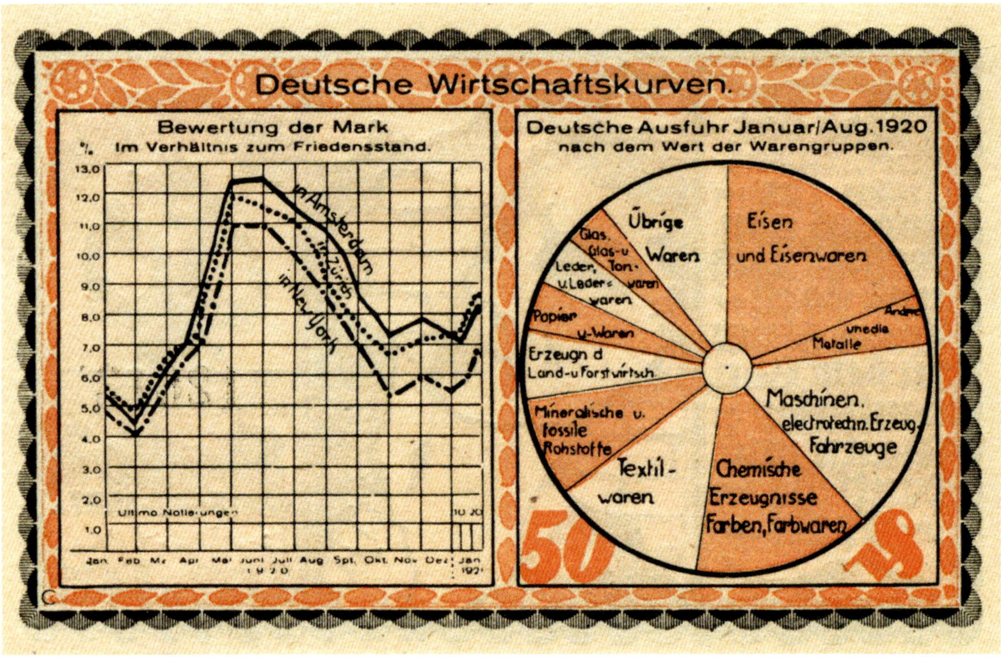

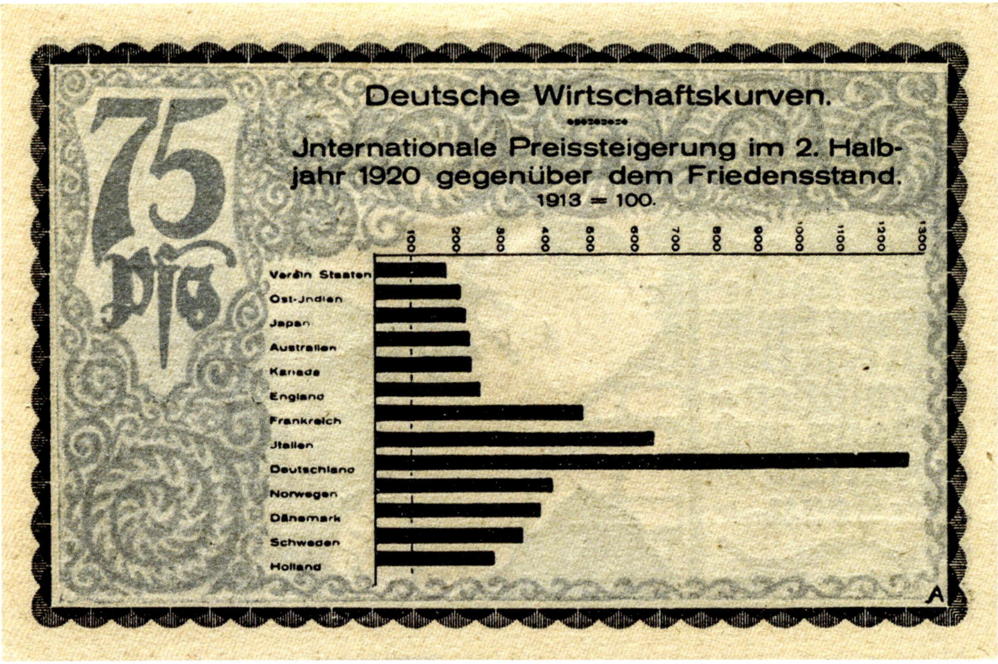

Here and facing page: Notgeld from Kahla, 1921. Collection of the author.

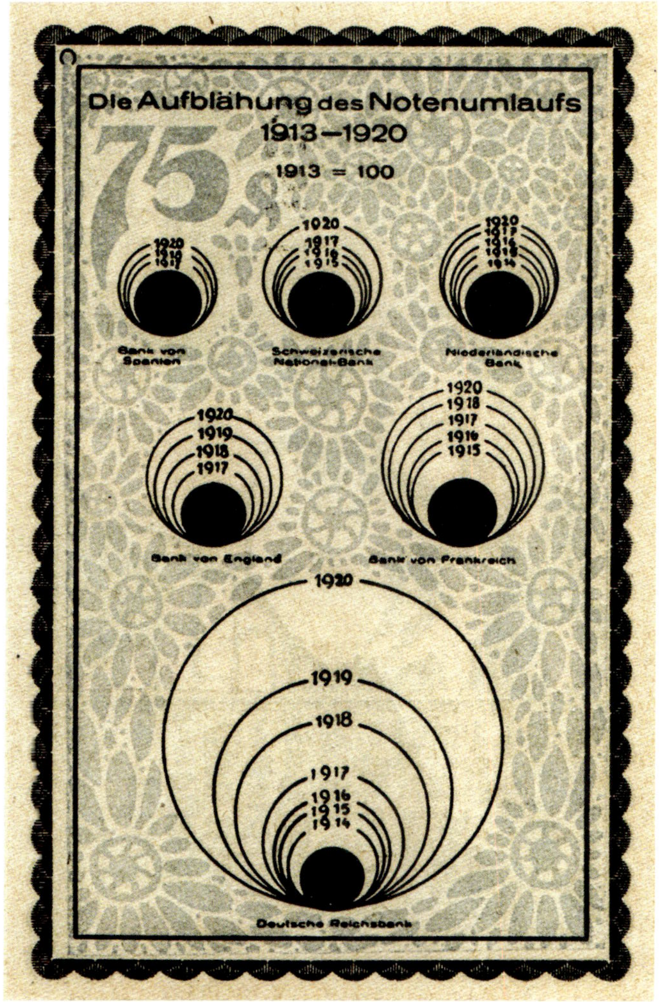
Die Aufblähung des Notenumlaufs
1913–1920
1913 = 100
75
1920
1919
1917
Bank von Spanien
1920
1917
1916
1915
Schweizerische National-Bank
1920
1917
1916
1915
1914
Niederländische Bank
1920
1919
1918
1917
Bank von England
1920
1918
1917
1916
1915
Bank von Frankreich
1920
1919
1918
1917
1916
1915
1914
Deutsche Reichsbank

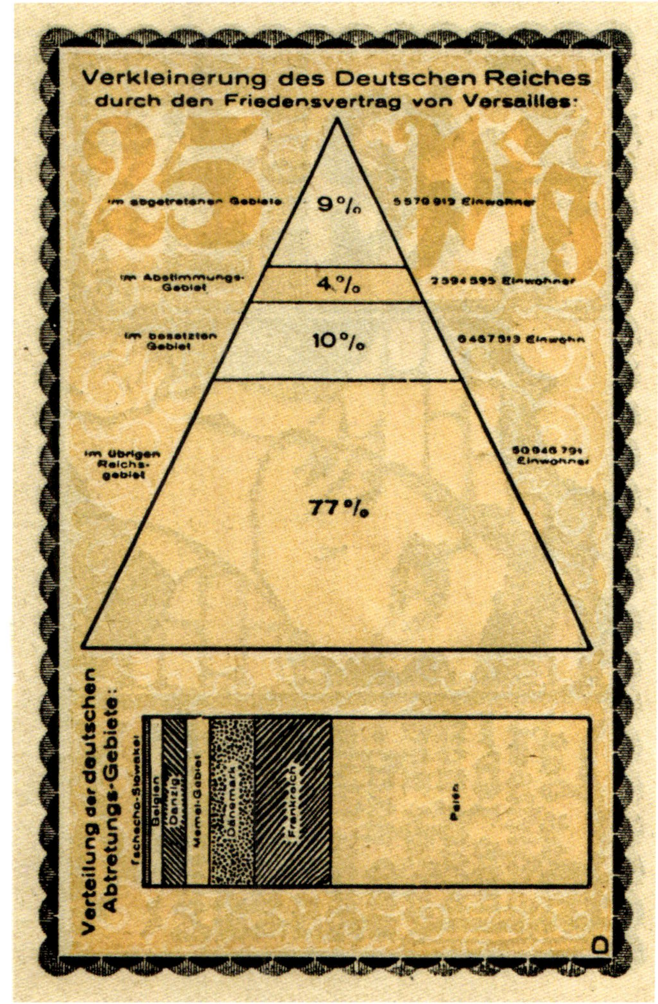
Verkleinerung des Deutschen Reiches
durch den Friedensvertrag von Versailles:
25
im abgetretenen Gebiete
9%
im Abstimmungs-Gebiet
4%
2 394 595 Einwohner
im besetzten Gebiet
10%
im übrigen Reichsgebiet
77%
50 946 791 Einwohner
Verteilung der deutschen Abtretungs-Gebiete:
Tschecho-Slowakei
Belgien
Danzig
Memel-Gebiet
Dänemark
Frankreich

of essential foodstuffs—eggs, milk, and butter—in various German cities. (The latter information was, in fact, a common feature of Notgeld; however, on other such examples the present cost of items would usually be compared with prewar prices.) These statistical notes take up many of the same issues referred to by the notes discussed in previous chapters, but they communicate them with relative sobriety—quite the opposite of the pathos of more histrionic notes, or the numinousness of expressionistic examples. Nevertheless, the presentation of negative economic data on currency is a strikingly bizarre approach, and this objectivity consequently has an affective charge of its own, especially when it comes to the subject of child mortality. All of these images, in other words, powerfully convey the catastrophic state of the German economy, and the valuelessness—or worse—of the notes on which they are printed.

Shit/Money

Among these destabilizing notes can be included the example discussed in the introduction to this book, Wenzel Hablik's figure of a man shitting money. Extraordinary though this image may appear, it is not alone in its theme. Several other notes allude to the act of defecation, the majority of them equating money and excrement; these will be the focus of the remainder of this chapter, in which I will discuss the significance of this motif, and on this basis develop a speculative media theory of money informed by the Bataillean

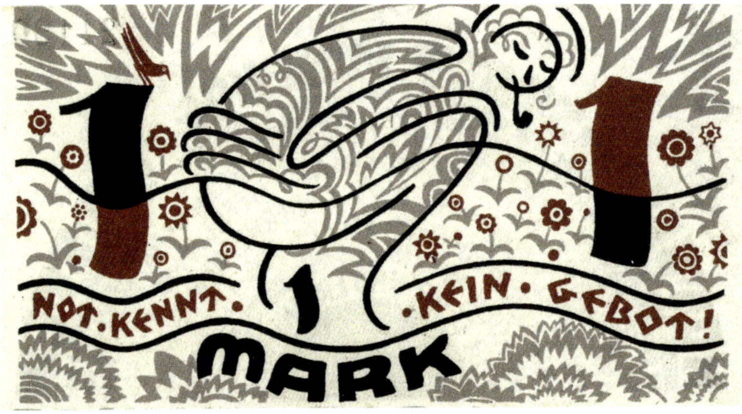

Notgeld designed by Wenzel Hablik, Itzehoe, 1921. Collection of the author.

conceit of base materiality. On a superficial level, the message of this comparison between shit and gold is of course simple: money is now worthless; indeed, it is akin to the most worthless matter of all. Far from being unusual, in Germany this image is a common figure of speech: one might still say, for instance, to a demanding child, "Ich habe kein Geldscheißer" (I'm not made of money—literally, I don't have a moneyshitter). As might already be clear, the idea is not quite so simple after all: money is like excrement, worthless, but the moneyshitter is also a wish-image that money could be produced as easily as excrement. Money-shit is therefore as desirable as it is disgusting.

This ambiguous idea has roots much deeper than the inflation. Hegel enthusiastically noted:

> It is a stroke of genius, the way people in Germany disparage money. The Germans attribute an origin to it that could not be more despicable. It is represented by figures that are called money-sh-ers [*Geldsch-r*]. This is supposed to have a mythological basis. It is hard to imagine associating a sausage or whatever one might think of with a more lowly mode of origin.[3]

The sculpted moneyshitters that Hegel mentions, often euphemistically referred to as *Dukatenmännchen* (little ducat men), go back to the early modern period in Germany. The most famous surviving example can be seen on the facade of a guild hall in Goslar—the building dates from 1494—where it forms the irreverent pendant to a classicizing figure of abundance. While she balances on a pedestal holding aloft a horn of plenty, the little man beneath her pulls apart his arse cheeks and shits golden coins. This doubling and its location is revealing: on this edifice, which represents the power of the cloth workers at the dawn of capitalism, the classical deity and her cornucopia in the upper realm bring forth goods—use values—whereas the homunculus in the lower expels money—exchange value—which is mingled with his shit. The hierarchy of values is clear, but nevertheless the pairing suggests an equivalence:

$$\frac{\text{Use value}}{\text{Exchange value}}$$

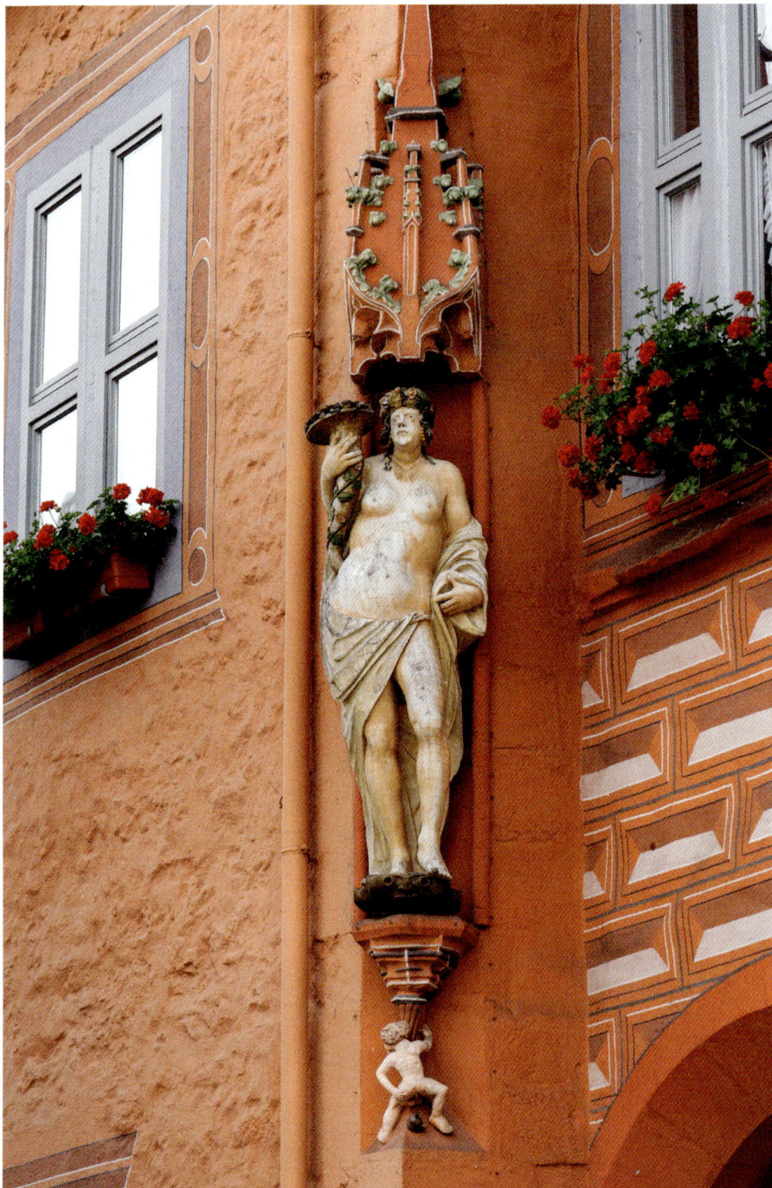

Abundantia and Dukatenmännchen, Kaiserworth, Goslar, c. 1494.

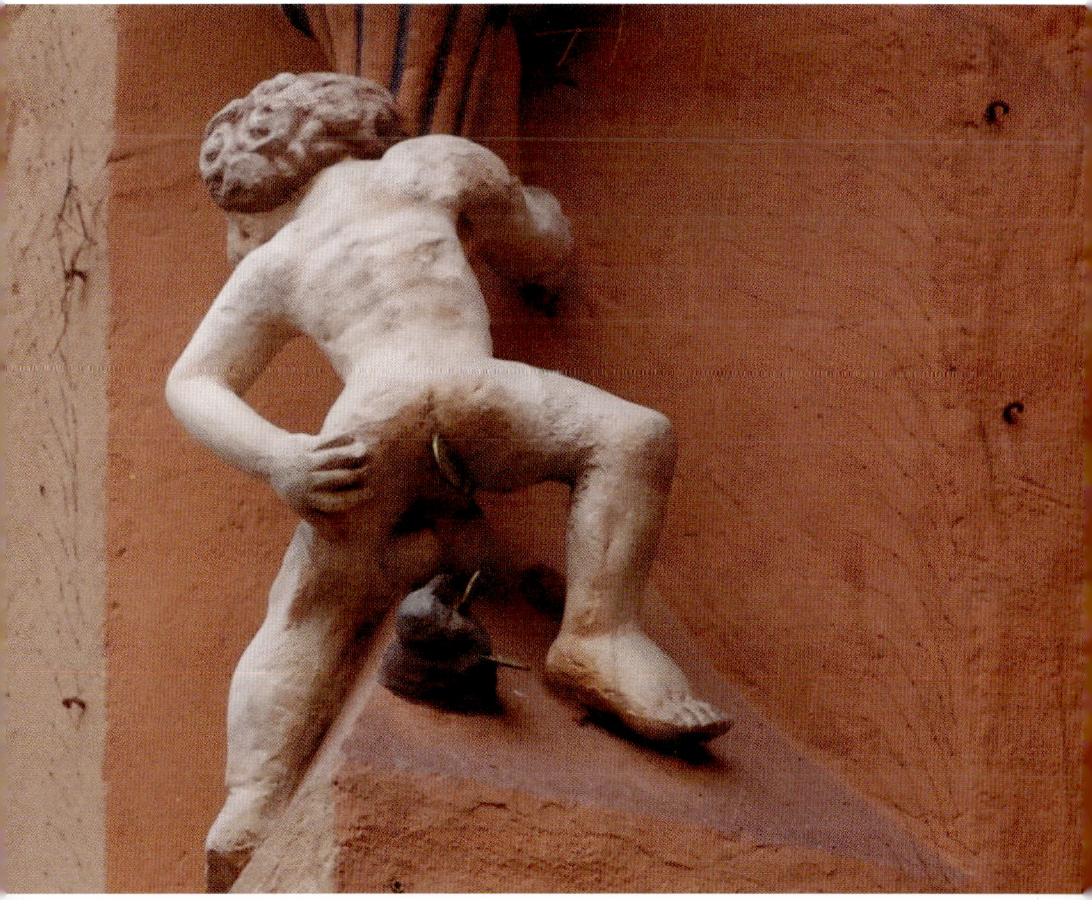

Detail of figure: Dukatenmännchen, Kaiserworth, Goslar, c. 1494.

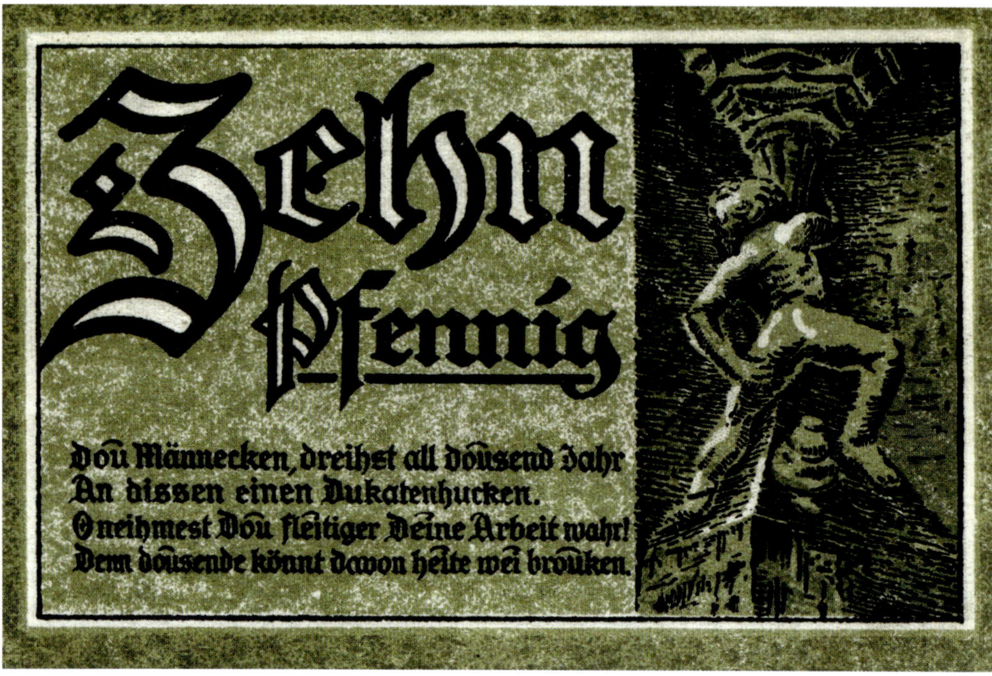

Notgeld from Goslar, 1920. Collection of the author.

This famous moneyshitter appears on a piece of emergency money issued by Goslar, but tellingly, his partner is now absent.

At around the same time that this sculpture was erected, a corpus of stories was developing involving the folk figure Till Eulenspiegel, a trickster who plays practical jokes and undermines figures of authority. Many of his tricks are of a scatological nature. Even on his deathbed, Eulenspiegel convinces a priest to bury his arms in a jug of coins, which turns out to be only a glittering crust covering a mound of his own feces.[4] Although the earliest extant Eulenspiegel anthology, which dates from 1515, is full of such escapades, by the nineteenth century the stories had been thoroughly sanitized. This is also the case with Notgeld, where Eulenspiegel is featured several times, but only in two instances does he return to his dirty tricks. The episode these images illustrate occurs early in the Eulenspiegel narrative: while riding as a child behind his father he exposed his backside to the townspeople. But Eulenspiegel's trickster spirit, though not depicted unreservedly, is nevertheless present as a motivating force behind some more critically self-aware—or one might say cynical—notes. In all the cases in which

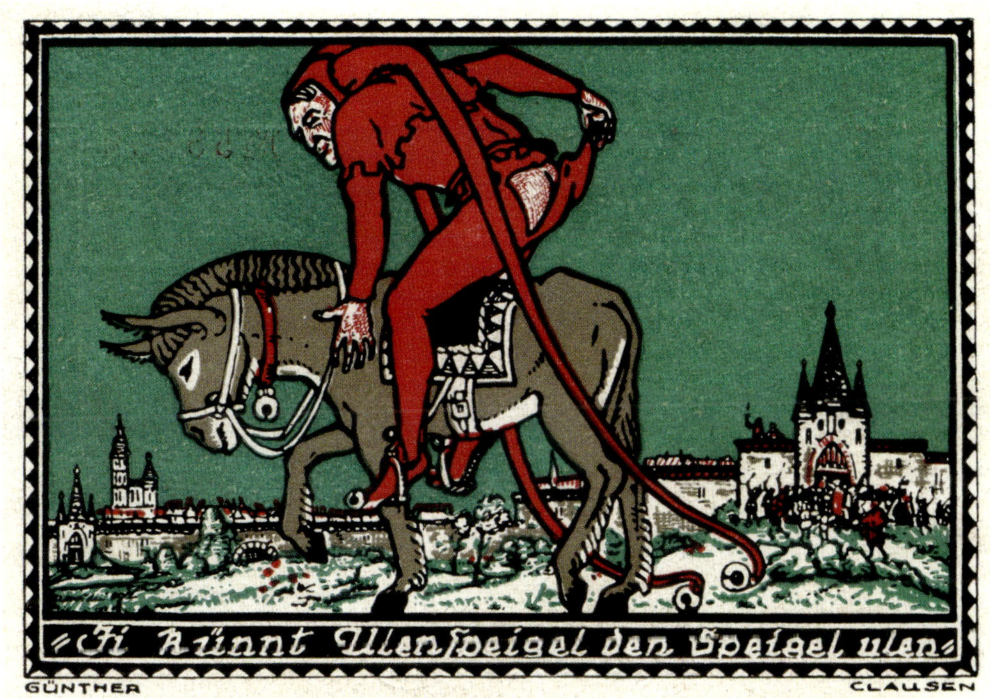

Notgeld designed by Günther Clausen, Kneitlingen, 1921. Collection of the author.

the worthlessness of Notgeld is made manifest, the artist is a kind of Eulenspiegel, a trickster bringing people into unsought proximity with excremental matter.

Other examples of excremental Notgeld are unsparing in their assertion of the currency's scatological status. A silk note issued by Bielefeld in 1922 refers to the Grimm Brothers' fairytale "Tischlein, deck dich!," which tells the story of a magical donkey, the Dukatenesel, that excretes golden ducats. (The subject was in the air: the previous year, Wilhelm Prager had directed a feature-length adaptation of the tale for Ufa, *Tischlein deck dich, Eselein streck dich, Knüppel aus dem Sack*.) On this note, the Dukatenesel is labeled "Deutschland" and is beaten by French soldiers until it produces money, a comment on reparations. Another note combines Dukatenesel and Eulenspiegel, with the latter riding on the former. The animal exudes money from both ends, from which sources it is collected by an unkempt man in a tailcoat, presumably a profiteer, and a young woman, whose Phrygian cap reveals her to be Marianne, personification of France. In lifting her skirt to

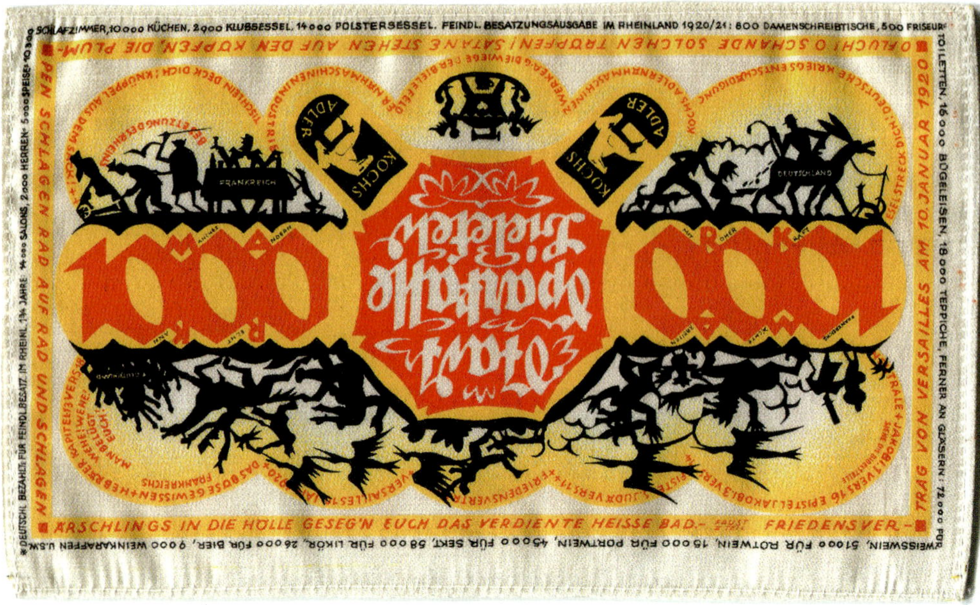

Notgeld from Bielefeld, 1922. Collection of the author.

catch the money Marianne exposes her underwear to the viewer, to whom she directs a coquettish glance. The reverse of the note shows a parallel scene of contrasting propriety: instead of a magical donkey, a sturdy horse is accompanied by a group of modestly attired agricultural laborers, led by German Michel. In the former case, money is conjured from shit, a critique of financial sleight-of-hand; in the latter, it is extracted with honest toil from the earth.

This strategy of employing both sides of the note to contrast destabilizing vice with a wish-image of stabilization may perhaps have been derived from an earlier example issued by Niederlahnstein in 1918. Here the donkey becomes a white charger mounted by a puny figure armed with a quill. This is a conventional depiction of the satirical character St. Bürokratius, patron saint of bureaucrats, who had appeared in a similar guise in the drawings of Julius Diez for the magazine *Jugend*. As in Diez's images, the animal drinks from an inkpot, but in this case it also produces scraps of paper from its other end. Meanwhile, to the right of the note a hamster carries a sack, presumably full of money, to a strong room. The image is laden with visual puns: a *Hamster* is in German a hoarder, whose behavior was subject to official opprobrium at the time. The white horse also has a double meaning: in German

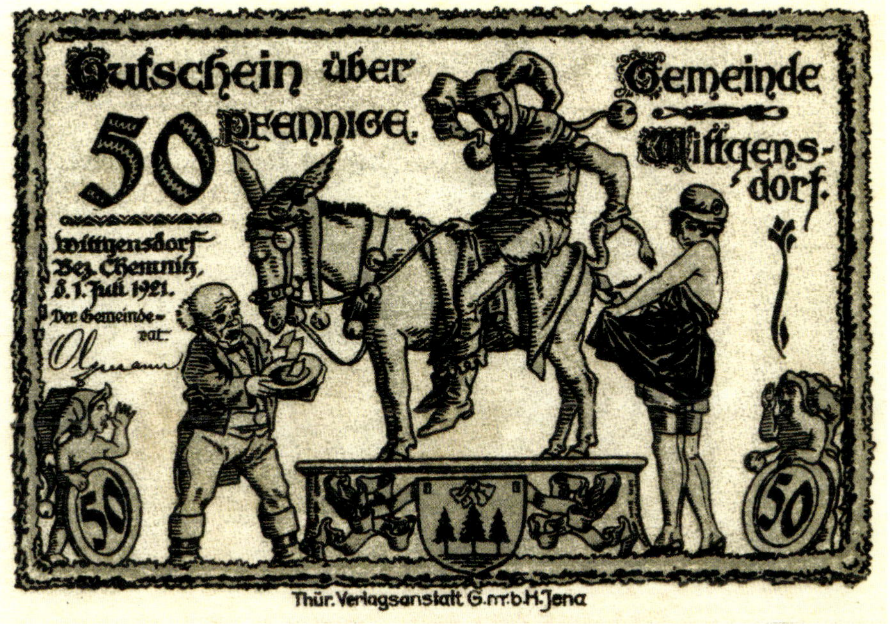

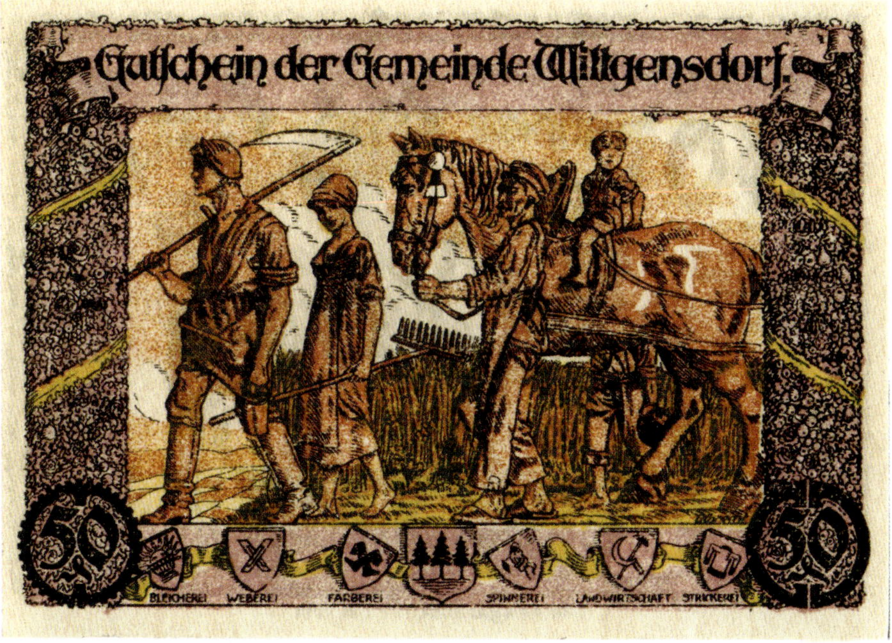

Notgeld from Wittgensdorf, 1921 (front and back). Collection of the author.

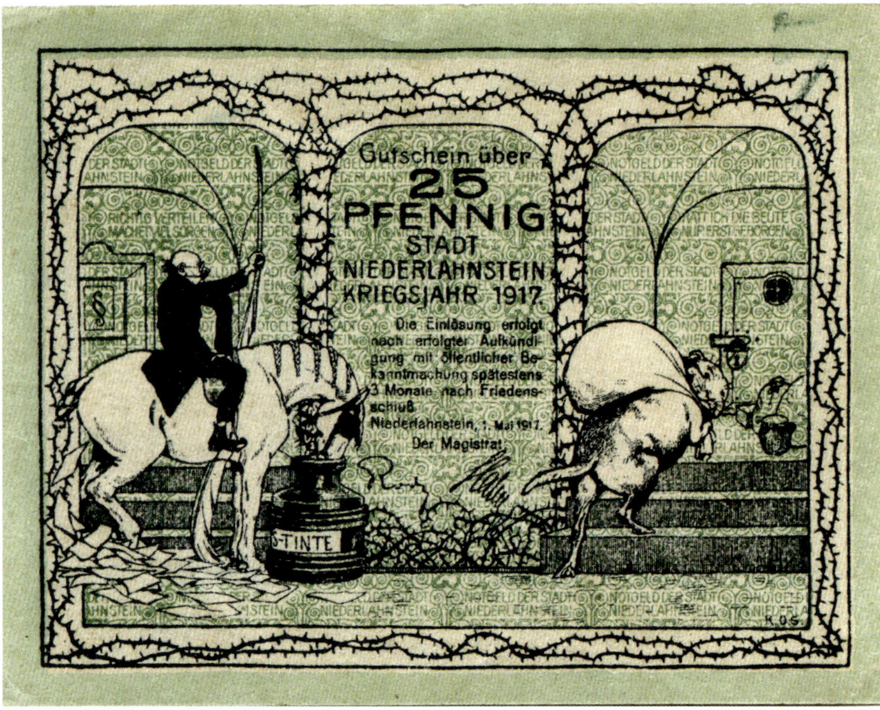

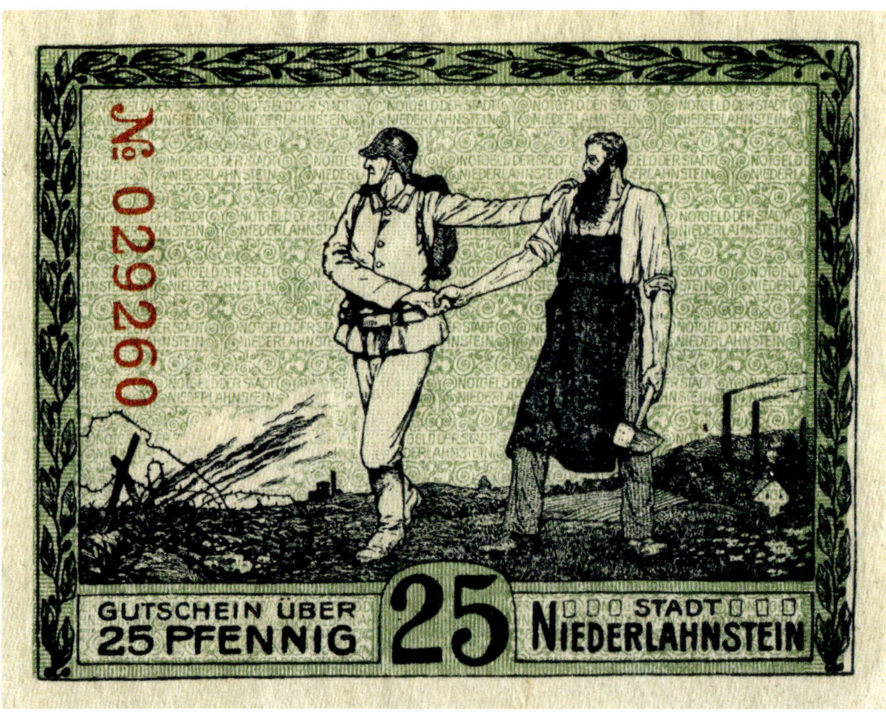

Notgeld from Niederlahnstein, 1917 (front and back). Collection of the author.

it is a *Schimmel*, while *Amtsschimmel* means "red tape." This punning figure therefore suggests that the excremental papers produced by the animal are official regulations, an interpretation confirmed by the framed paragraph sign in the background. But these fluttering scraps could also be read as Notgeld, which is being produced at the command of the bureaucrat in response to the *Hamsterei* occurring in the other half of the scene.

Excursus: Zettelkasten

Scraps of paper (*Zettel*) are a recurring motif on emergency money, where they figure as a *mise-en-abyme* depicting the most salient characteristic of Notgeld considered as a whole: it is an enormous mass of worthless objects, an abundance of base matter that remains valueless no matter how much one has of it. Indeed, the more there is of it, the less it is worth, mocking the accumulatory logic of capitalism. On Notgeld, *Zettel* are shown falling from the sky like snow, they are vomited from the mouths of dragons, and—more promisingly—they bury the skulls of Germany's enemies. A series of notes issued by Gera, the other parts of which show the illustrious history of the town and its erstwhile prosperity, culminates with a scene of *Zettel* drifting across a barren field behind a ragged, starving family. The caption reads, "Poor again now, and only a seeming life"—a pun, common at the time, on the word *Schein*, which means both banknote and appearance.

A common source for *Zettel* in these images is the cornucopia, the sole survivor of nineteenth-century banknotes' allegorical waxwork museum.[5] While goddesses and cupids fled the scene, the horn of plenty remained and continued spouting—but instead of fruit and corn, it now spouts paper, worthless paper. The sculptural ensemble in Goslar with the Dukatenmännchen squatting beneath Abundantia, his anus mirroring the horn above, suggests that there is something excremental about this gushing matter being showered over Germany. This is made explicit in Fallada's novel *Wolf among Wolves*:

> Somewhere in this town there was a machine ... which vomited paper day and night over the city and the people. "Money" they called it: they printed figures on it, beautiful neat figures with many noughts, which became increasingly

rounder. And when you had worked and sweated to put by a little for your old age, it all became worthless paper, paper muck.[6]

In earlier times, paper had quite a different value. It was the medium with which Germany had become the land of *Dichter und Denker*, after all; it was how Gutenberg and Dürer had transformed European culture in the fifteenth century. The disturbing devaluation of this substance during the inflation was the subject of the *Simplicissimus* cartoon discussed in chapter 2, where Gutenberg's press is repurposed to dispense banknotes. This transformation is also depicted on a Notgeld note designed by Olaf Gulbransson for the city of Kahla, on which German Michel sweeps up a pile of crumpled *Zettel*. A closer look reveals that these are the detritus of German culture: truisms, proverbs, and commandments such as "Pray and work," "Do right and fear nobody," "Thou shalt not steal," and "Be united, united, united" (the latter is a quotation from Schiller, which also appeared on postage stamps at the time).

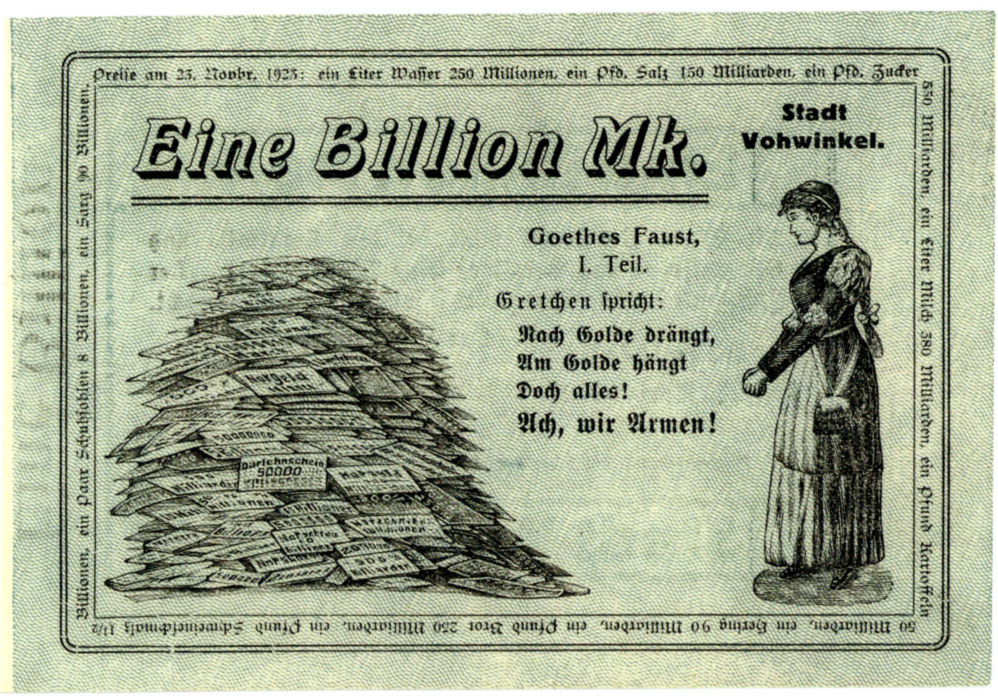

Notgeld from Vohwinkel, 1923. Giesecke+Devrient Geldscheinsammlung, Munich.

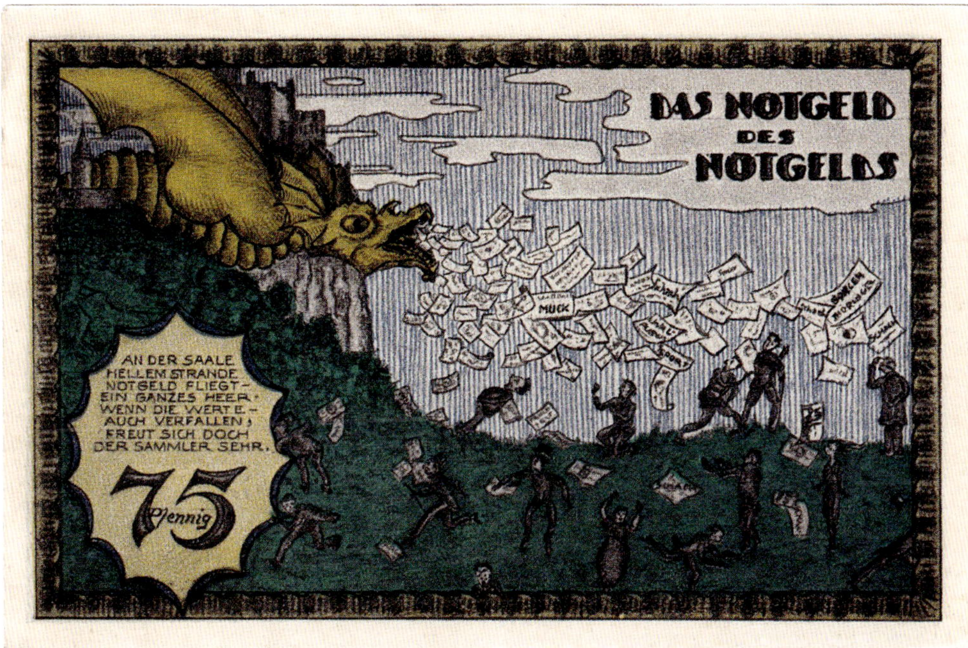

Notgeld from Kahla, 1921. Nathaniel Butler.

Among these scraps can be seen a book with a cross on its cover; as another anti-Semite, Hugo Ball, said at the time: "even the Bible is a pile of paper."[7]

The mutations of paper are described by Yvan Goll in his 1929 novel *Sodom Berlin*, where he points out that it had already begun its creeping spread in 1914:

> In retribution for her overweening pride, Germany was now suffering a similar fate [to that of Midas]: everything she touched was turning to paper—and then to ashes. Some said that the country had slipped back from the age of steel to the stone age. In actuality it had regressed to the age of paper. The paper epidemic had already made itself felt during the War. As raw materials became scarcer, paper was what replaced them. Men were spotted wearing paper collars and paper coats, women paper blouses, and children paper shoes. Towels, tablecloths and bed sheets were all made of paper. An inventor was on the point of manufacturing paper bicycles when the War ended—and the dominion of paper, seemingly, along with it. But not so fast!

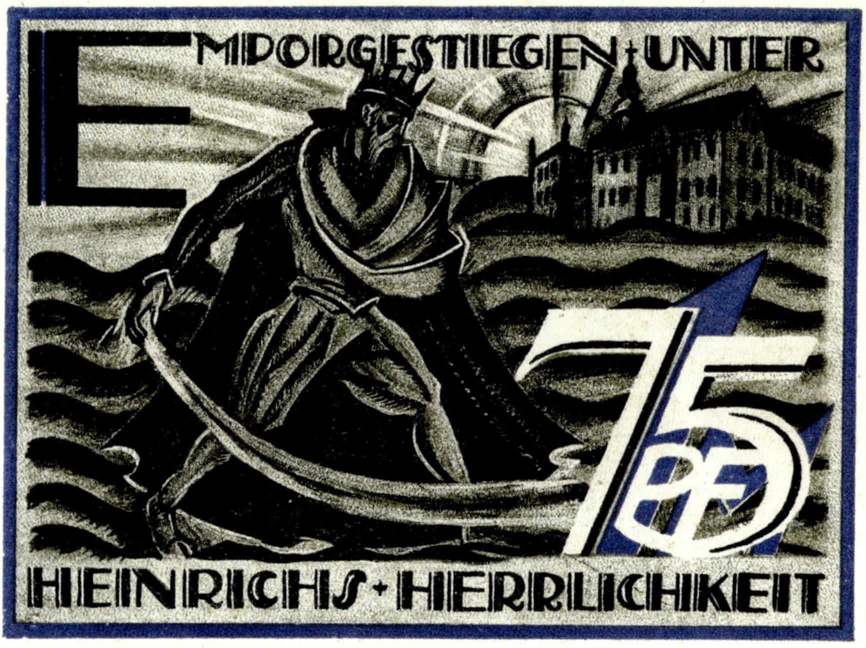

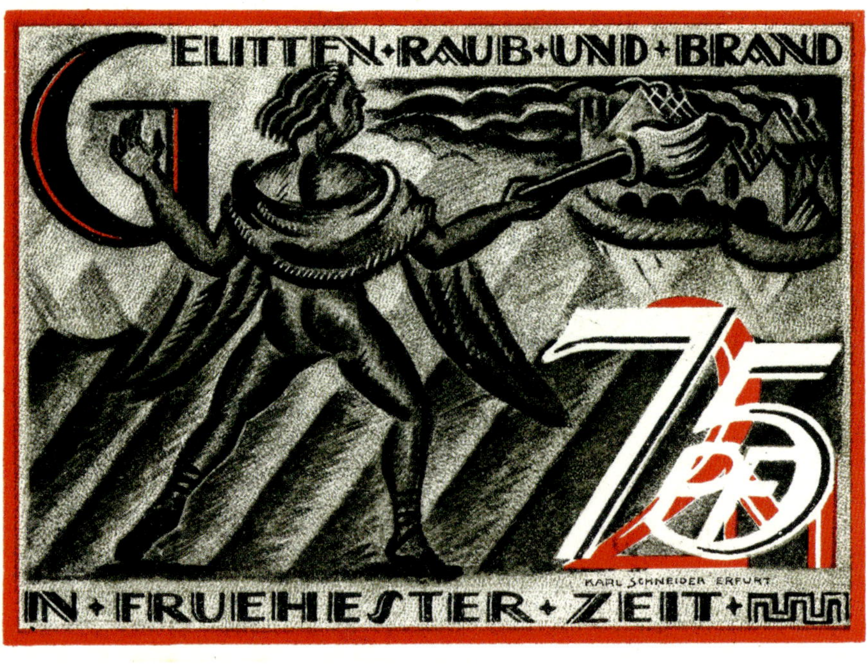

Here and facing page: Notgeld designed by Karl Schneider, Gera, 1921. Collection of the author.

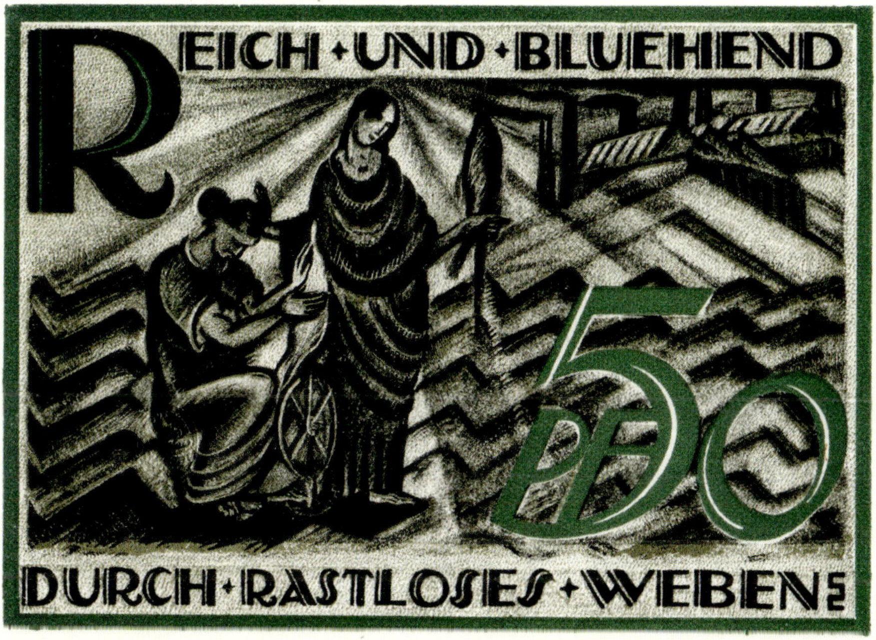
REICH + UND + BLUEHEND
50 PF
DURCH + RASTLOSES + WEBEN

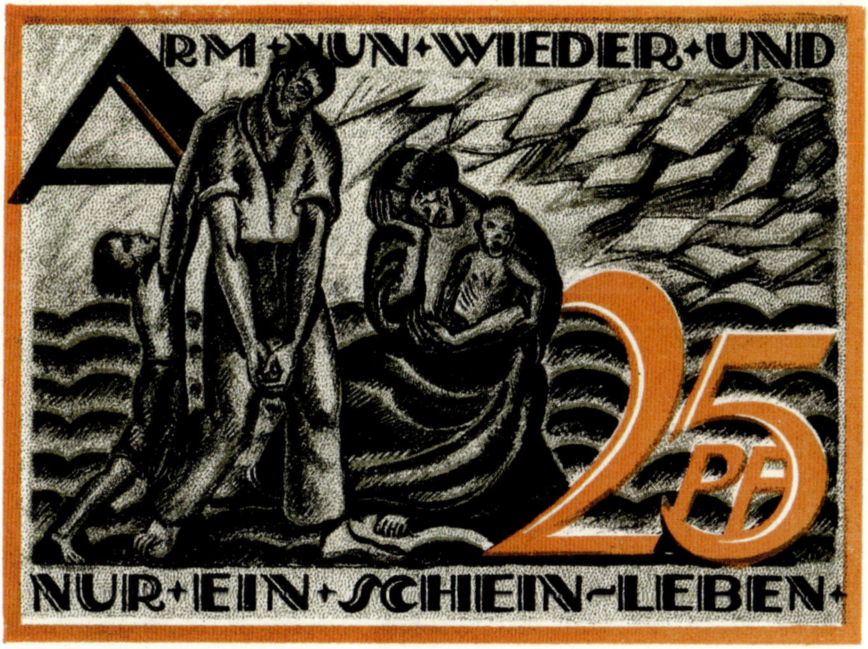
ARM + NUN + WIEDER + UND
25 PF
NUR + EIN + SCHEIN - LEBEN +

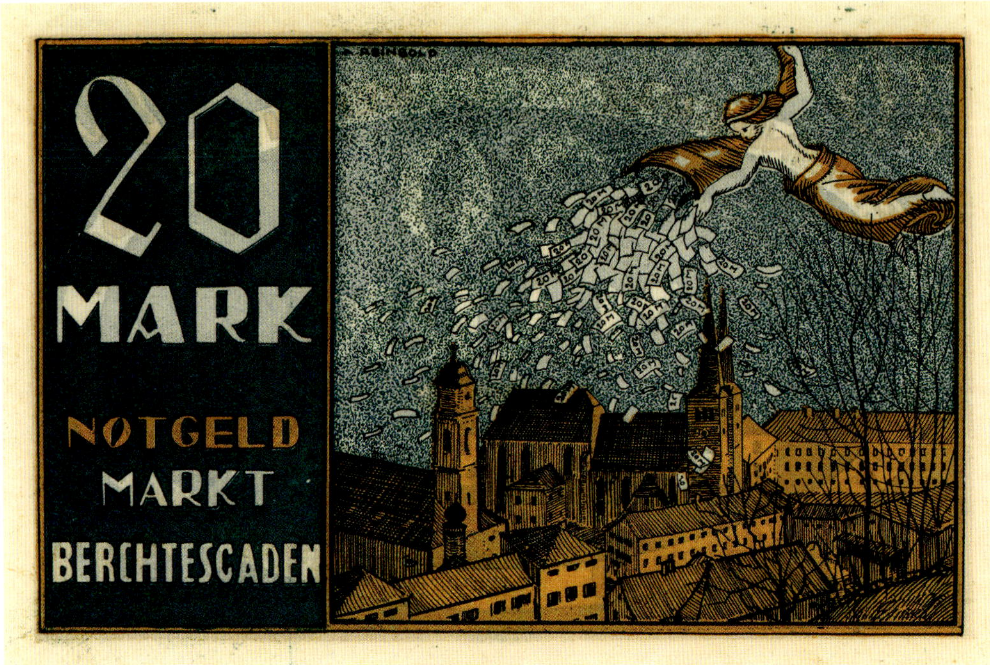

Notgeld from Berchtesgaden, 1922. Giesecke+Devrient Geldscheinsammlung, Munich.

> This was the very moment when the spectral presence of paper became universal. Banknotes expanded extravagantly. Like millefeuille pastry, a one-mark note multiplied under the influence of a mysterious force that changed it into a thousand-note wad of currency. ... All Germany was now an empire of mere paper. Public buildings, bridges, factories—paper, nothing but paper! This frightening development deranged the populace. How indeed could it have failed to drive people mad?[8]

To make matters worse, it wasn't clear whether there was too much of it or too little. Perhaps it would be more accurate to say that it was, like the money it pretended to be, inadequately distributed. Indeed, there were severe paper shortages during the inflation. In 1919, an article in *Das Plakat* complained that this was caused by the profusion of political posters and pamphlets, speaking of a *Papierkrankheit*, a paper sickness. "The election for the National Assembly has allowed the flood of paper to grow so deep that one believes one could literally drown in it," the author

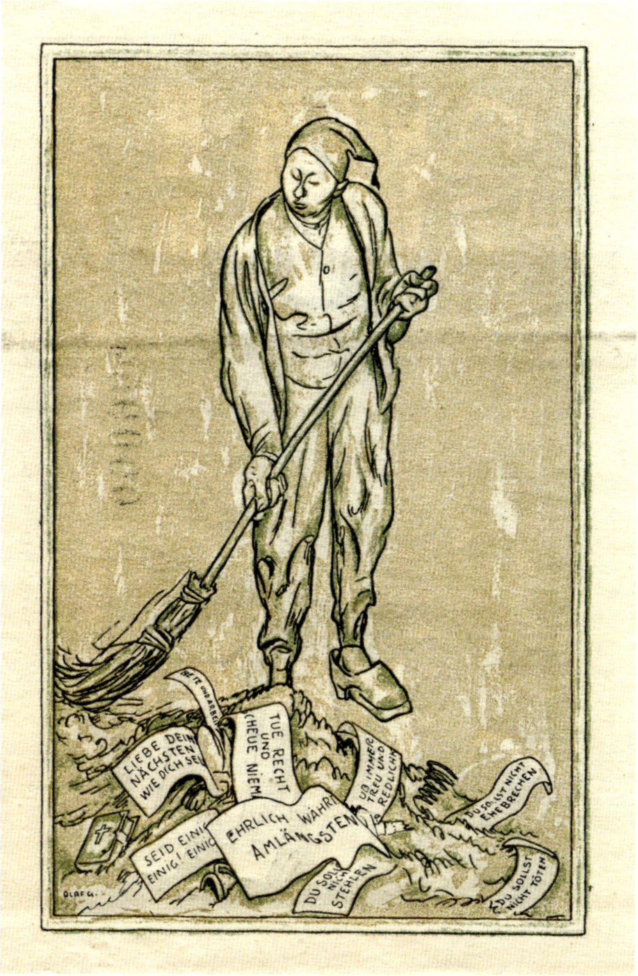

Notgeld designed by Olaf Gulbransson, Kahla, 1922. Collection of the author.

says, and predicts that this discursive inflation will lead to a devaluation, the impossibility of taking all these words in. The piece concludes: "clearly we have both: a lack and a surfeit of paper [*Papiernot und Papierüberfluß*]."[9]

As this sheaf of citations makes clear, the abundance of paper was seen as problematic by contemporaries. What was to be done with it all? It was in this context that Schwitters roamed the streets collecting his scraps, with the intention of revaluing them aesthetically, as I discussed in chapter 2. His collaborator Kate Steinitz recalled a visit to one of his favorite hunting grounds, a printers' shop in Hannover. This establishment

> had a basement room for all the rubbish and wastepaper. All the proofs and misprints from the lithography department were broomed twice a day toward a chute that dumped them down into the cellar. This cellar was a treasure trove for Kurt. ... One day the chute suddenly opened and a mountain of paper came down. Standing safely at the door with the children, I watched as the avalanche hit Kurt Schwitters, threatening to bury him alive. He stood bent over, defending himself against the onslaught. Then, raising his head, he stood up in the midst of this rubbish, a new Gargantua, twisting and dancing in the whirl of papers. In both arms he held paper, paper, paper. Around his feet lumps, scraps and buckets of wastepaper swirled. Kurt Schwitters groaned and laughed. Finally he emerged—alive.[10]

While for Schwitters the storm of *Zettel* was a source of material, and even of joy, for the majority of his compatriots it was more disturbing. Aby Warburg collected it in *Zettelkästen*, card files, where he compiled a huge number of clippings on the subject of the war—90,747 of them, to be precise. Tortured by the conflict and the anti-Semitism it had unleashed, these fragments he shored against his ruins, to paraphrase Eliot; nonetheless, he ended up in a sanitorium. Another approach was to attempt to deflect this matter. If we return to the note from Niederlahnstein that prompted these reflections and turn to its other side, we see that the destabilizing, excremental *Zettel* produced by the union of the bureaucrat and the hamster are countered on the reverse of the note by a stabilizing scene of labor, land—and war (see p. 188). While low dealings are taking place on the home front, the warrior and the laborer are united, hand in hand, in the defense of the fatherland, which blends indistinguishably from battlefield to wheat field. This rich little object thereby encapsulates a conservative worldview on its two sides, which taken together form the stab-in-the-back legend that would prove so inimical to the as-yet-unborn republic. To the stabilizing devices of land and labor analyzed earlier in this book it adds the figure of the soldier, which, as Klaus Theweleit's account of conservative writing of the period demonstrates, adopted its ironclad demeanor in defense against filth. This posttraumatic and deeply misogynistic reaction against the mud and corpses of the trenches was transferred to the "traitors" at home, with Freikorps member and novelist Thor Goote, for example, writing of "the so-called Germans who, after squatting behind the lines like cowards, are now trying to do their sticky business with profits from the collapse of the nation." As Theweleit observes, for the enemies of the republic, "The whole world has turned sticky."[11] Martial figures like the one featured on this note are avatars of reterritorialization and of the antipathy toward flows—flows of filth and of filthy finance. Here stabilization, figured in opposition to the destabilizing gush of excremental money, takes a pathological turn.

Second Circuit

My final examples of scatological Notgeld lead us back out of these steely shells, suggesting that filthy flows need not be resisted with armor since they are in fact reversible, and that what I have been calling destabilizing techniques may actually have a stabilizing function—in more than a discursive or iconographic sense. A ten-pfennig note designed by the right-wing satirist A. Paul Weber identifies an excreting creature with the nation once again. Here, however, the animal is no donkey but an imperial eagle, which seems to eat notes and shit coins, while the latter are gathered by a man with a large purse slung round his neck. The rhyme gives a clue as to what is going on:

> It's not all bad.
> Hopefully it pays off!
> Don't cash me in,
> Then it might come off.

A second note cleaves more closely to the equation of money and shit in the story of the Dukatenesel, even in this case denying the possibility of alchemical transmutation: this shit remains stubbornly shitty. The cynical rhyme makes the message even clearer, pointing to another kind of revaluation of base matter:

> We do not have in Paderborn
> A ducat-shitting donkey,
> But there are ample donkeys born
> To buy our paper money.

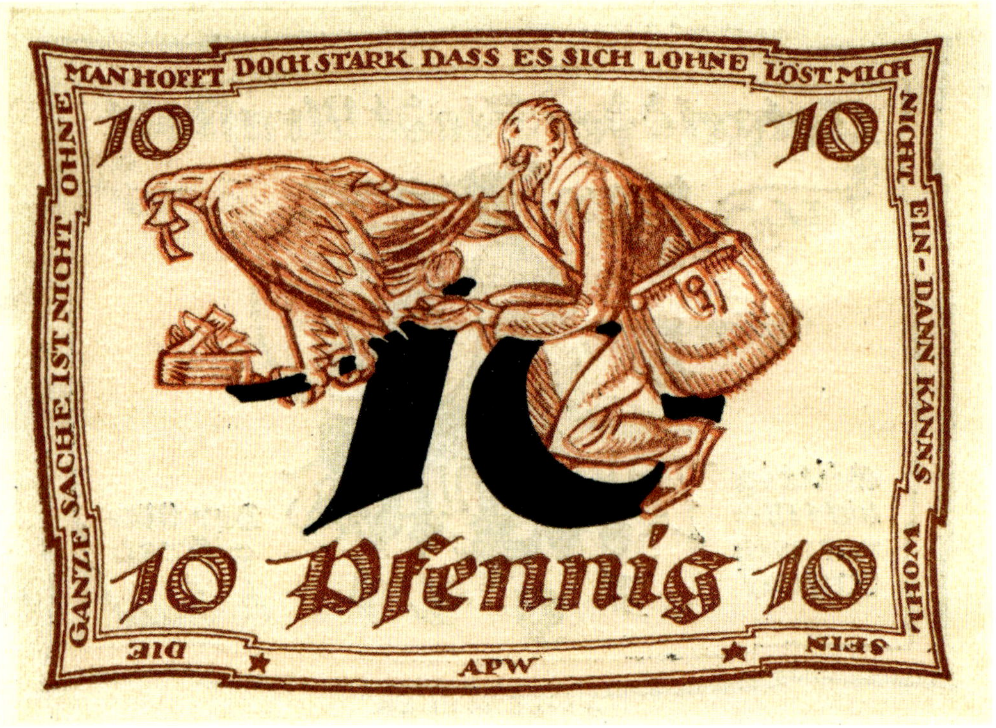

Notgeld designed by Paul Weber, Arnstadt, 1921. Collection of the author.

The final couplet alludes to the fact that, by 1921 when this note was issued, a large appetite had developed for emergency money among collectors. An extensive network of dealers was established, several periodicals were devoted to the subject (one estimate suggests that there were as many as 20 of these magazines), and Notgeld fairs regularly took place around the nation.[12] In response to this growing demand, around 1918, town halls and other Notgeld issuers began to print notes aimed directly at this market. In order to compete for the attention of buyers, they ramped up the intensity of the images and inscriptions, with bolder colors, more dynamic designs, and grotesque iconography, leading to a kind of rhetorical and aesthetic inflation. Many of the examples reproduced in this book can be understood in these terms, with depictions of violence, bizarre and supernatural creatures, and obscene anti-Semitism and scatology functioning as unique selling points in this crowded marketplace of images. As well as their visual exceptionalism, some of these notes were also given unusual denominations—75-pfennig notes are common—and others were

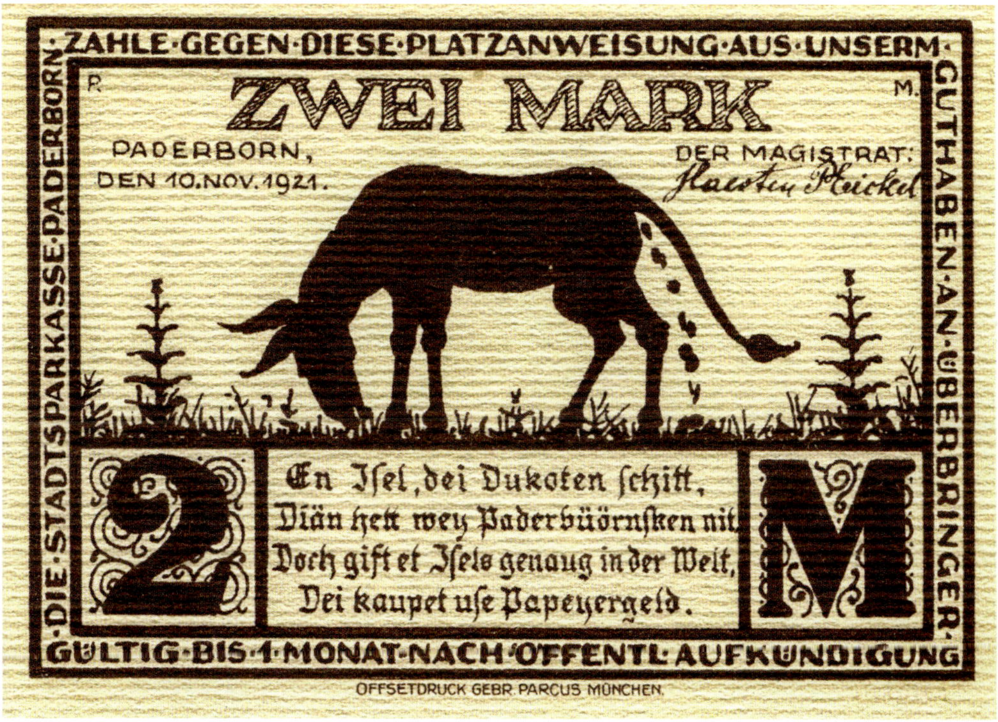

Notgeld from Paderborn, 1921. Collection of the author.

marked with an expiration date that actually preceded their date of issue. Some, indeed, backdated their Notgeld to before 1918. This was an attempt to circumvent the growing resistance of collectors to such *Serienscheine*, by suggesting instead that a specimen originated from the period of "true" Notgeld.[13] These notes were often sold for significantly higher sums than their face values (the justification for this being "administrative fees"), and in many cases were issued by publishing houses or printers on behalf of local authorities as a speculative venture.[14] Such notes were regarded with suspicion by collectors, who called them "sham" and "swindle money"; early Notgeld expert Arnold Keller said they derived from "vile speculation."[15] The central government outlawed the further production of Notgeld on July 17, 1922, partly in response to such abuses. Their status has remained dubious. During the course of researching this book, one curator disparagingly remarked to me: "They're not *real* money."

"As soon as such materials reveal their practical, aesthetic or other value they are withdrawn from circulation and are no longer money."[16] So wrote Simmel. However, although it may have strayed very far from money as it is conventionally understood, Notgeld does in fact function as a store of value, and in some cases a more efficient one than so-called real money in this period. The very inflation of the images and rhetoric of such notes was a technique intended to make this money *sticky*, to return to Marx's language of viscosity.[17] By virtue of its exceptional appearance, it was meant to cease its circulation as a medium of exchange and remain in the hands of its possessor, never returning to its source to be redeemed. This motivation is expressed with cynical frankness on one Austrian note (Austria experienced a comparable inflation following the war):

> Off you go across the land
> Be lucky on your way
> End in a collector's hand
> And don't come back this way!

In fulfilling this demand, Notgeld escaped the circuit through which money conventionally travels, but it did not come to rest. Instead, it switched onto a secondary circuit of dealers, fairs, and collector's albums and continued to travel between these points. This was intended to discipline and canalize the flows of Notgeld, but it was not without incident. The system grinds in peristaltic fits and starts. There are flows and refluxes, bursts and floods; sometimes it seems that all will be washed away. At other times the flow backs up, it dwindles to a trickle. Behind the blockage a pool accumulates, causing on the one side drought, on the other inundation. The operations of the German image economy circa 1920 are pictured here in their several modes. According to one idealized representation from Hamburg, the system functions smoothly. Images are conveyed via the rail network to be disgorged at nodes, from which they will be absorbed by sumps; the implication is that they will eventually leach from these to continue their circulation once more. In other depictions the system breaks down and torrents of images pour from the sky, threatening to submerge the frantic onlookers. Elsewhere we see systemic failure of an opposite sort: the flow has ceased, its customary reservoirs run dry.

The two circuits, it becomes clear, are not entirely separate, and they share some of the same characteristics and functions. The secondary circuit or image economy is certainly motivated

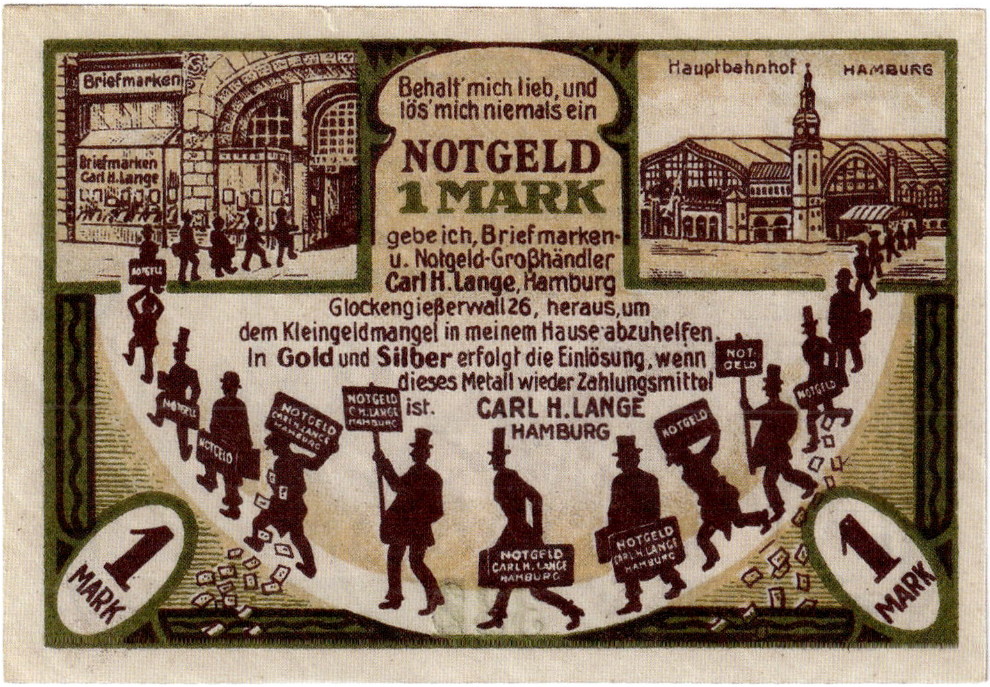

Notgeld for Carl H. Lange, Hamburg, no date. Nathaniel Butler.

by the collecting impulse, born out of aesthetic pleasure and the desire for order and completion. But, as I have mentioned before, it was also an escape valve for the *Flucht in die Sachwerte*, the "flight into real values" that characterized the inflationary period, when people sought to coagulate their liquid assets as quickly as possible by transferring their rapidly devaluing cash into commodities that retained their value more effectively. As described in the second chapter, this led to a sustained boom in the art market that stimulated the production of works on paper in particular. Among the products of this situation can be counted the works of Dix and Grosz, whose violent and scatological imagery functioned much like the more rhetorically inflated examples of Notgeld described above, that is, as a means of product differentiation. The strategies of the avant-garde were shared by the designers of Notgeld, and the extremity of affect that resulted can be considered as being an effect of the inflation on the image economy across the board. But although the apparently value-destabilizing techniques of *Gegengeld* were in fact intended as recuperative by the municipalities that employed them, they nevertheless had, on the macro level, a devastatingly destabilizing effect. The huge profusion of notes and their cynical deployment to raise funds could not help further undermining the effectiveness of value reference *tout court*. The agents of these techniques—the alchemists of the image—were the artists who designed these inflated notes, turning gold into shit and then back into gold. And the question of stabilization or destabilization of the value referent is therefore exposed, thanks to the material labor of these artists and the material rewards for their patrons—as well as the very material disaster that was exacerbated by these actions—as a question that points beyond iconography or discourse. The medium does not simply transmit, store, or process information; rather, it congeals and deliquesces value.

Cloacal Economy

Hablik's image of the excretion of money, like the other scatological notes discussed above, visualizes a radical grounding of the medium. Where others depict the earth in order to tether their flimsy scraps to value, here such references become instead a Bataillean insistence on the baseness of this matter, the sticky nature of its congealment. This also makes a stark contrast to the spookification attempted by most expressionistic notes. Despookification, as we may call this opposing tendency, was not confined to emergency money in this period. A commemorative medal of 1923 and a postcard, presumably made around the same time, also show the figure of the *Dukatenscheißer*, the ducat-shitter.[18] Like Hablik's image, these figures speak of the desire that money could be produced as easily and as abundantly as excrement, but there is an ambiguity to this wish-image, since it simultaneously implies that shit and money might share some obscure equality. The equivalence is also asserted in a different register by Schwitters's 1920 collage *Kotsbild*, in which a Polish banknote abuts a scrap of paper printed with the word *Kot*, "feces."[19] Indeed, Schwitters gave his works in this medium the collective title *Merzbilder*, a pun on both *Kommerz* and *merde*. They can therefore be considered as falling in their totality under the double sign of the monetary and the scatological—despite the fact that he carefully washed his material before gluing it together.[20]

The long-standing association between money and excrement was investigated by Freud in his 1908 essay "Character and

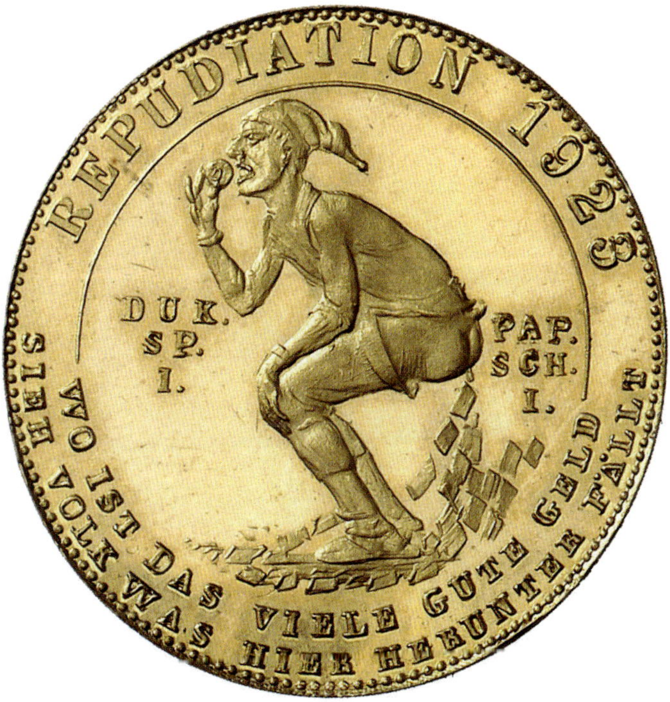

Dukatenscheißer medal, c. 1923. Deutsche Bundesbank, Frankfurt.

Anal Eroticism," and psychoanalytic literature has continued to develop the theme.[21] For Freud, the origin of this nexus lies in early childhood, where any derailment of toilet training—a process whereby we learn when it is socially acceptable to expend or to withhold—can create characters that are "exceptionally orderly, parsimonious and obstinate," a complex popularly known as anal retentiveness.[22] For the purposes of this chapter, however, I want to take up Deleuze and Guattari's criticism that "the Marx-Freud parallelism between the two remains utterly sterile and insignificant as long as it is expressed in terms that make them introjections or projections of each other without ceasing to be utterly alien to each other, as in the famous equation money = shit."[23] But rather than following Deleuze and Guattari, via the door opened by Pierre Klossowski, into the world of libidinal economy, I want to return to their shared Bataillean source, and indeed to remain with Bataille at the level of base materialism, developing instead what I will call a *cloacal economy*.[24] This entails thinking of this nexus as being mediated not via mere analogy, nor even by the

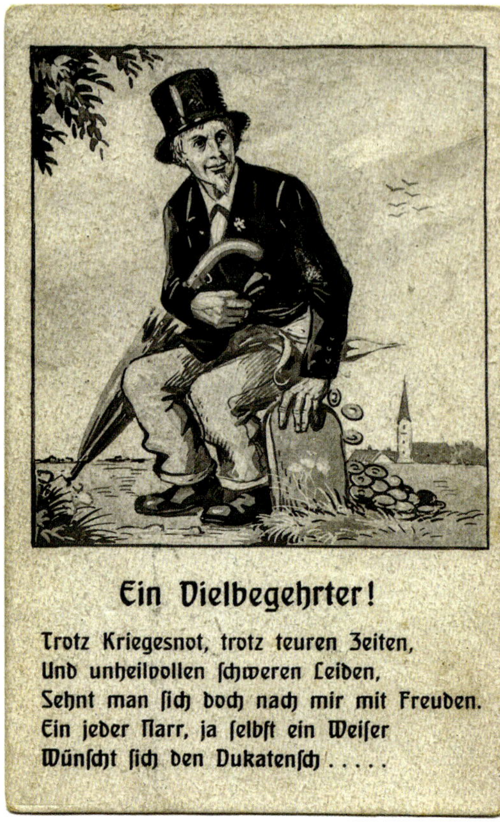

Dukatenscheißer postcard, c. 1923. Collection of the author.

productive labor of the subconscious, but rather by the laboring body and the discipline thereof.[25] The ultimate beneficiary of the infant learning to follow commands and exert bodily control is, after all, none other than capital. Capital exploits this skill in workplaces where physical impulses are suppressed in exchange for money—despite often discomfiting or even crippling results. But discipline can never be total. In their 1981 book *History and Obstinacy*, Oskar Negt and Alexander Kluge describe the involuntary acts of compensation necessary to maintain this bodily obedience. The central figure in their account of compensatory labor is a woman welder working on an assembly line who intermittently stretches her arms back "in a winglike fashion" to relieve the physical tension that results from her repetitive labor.[26] While such acts help maintain our physical utility for capital, Negt and Kluge imply that within such an unstable locus also lurks a potential site of resistance, as compensation cannot be maintained eternally and involuntary motions can have unexpected outcomes.

This turn to the unthought resources of the body is a reaction to post-Fordist capital's invasion of the psyche as the final frontier of primitive accumulation, and as such, it is something of a counsel of despair. Yet there is indeed one last zone, beyond—or beneath—that of affect, and beyond even our twitching, money-making limbs, that remains unexploited by capital: the excremental.[27] Hablik's note shows a form of cloacal resistance hinging on this locus. It reads *Not kennt kein gebot* (Necessity knows no command), and the figure drops his pants accordingly. This intervention from the bowels brings labor to a halt, at least for a moment. Importantly, this occurs at a moment of *Not*, or emergency, and perhaps can take place only then. It thereby forms a bottom-up counter to Carl Schmitt's employment of the emergency as a sphere of self-defining action for the sovereign: no commands are known here.[28] Perhaps Negt and Kluge would nevertheless call this a form of infantile disorder, since it fails to gather up the obsolete and fragmentary characteristics that lie unexploited and neglected by capital beneath the conscious level of the psyche in order to unite them as a coherent revolutionary subject. They remain instead at the level of mere dumb protest. Returning to their text, however, there are some passages in the book that give their intimation of compensatory derangement a base inflection. The authors hint at a form of cloacal resistance when they recount the story of an American bomber pilot flying over "Far Eastern territories" who, just at the moment he is about to drop his payload on a wedding, inadvertently shits in his "hermetically sealed flight suit," and pulls away in confusion, missing his target.[29] If this close shave sounds too serendipitous, that the cloacal is an enduring site of political oppression, and hence of potential resistance, is revealed by recent reports regarding the elimination of toilet breaks in so-called fulfillment centers and other workplaces, with employees in American poultry factories resorting to the use of diapers.[30] Indeed, the toilet—and in its absence, the necessity of open defecation—presents a site of potential struggle on a global scale.[31] One can easily imagine a corresponding form of protest, something along the lines advocated by the Defecator, a prophetic character in Juan Goytisolo's 1995 novel *State of Siege*: "Yes, I'm shitting! take a good look at all this shit! it's mine and nobody else's! nobody can keep me from shitting! it's the one right I have left!"[32]

Nevertheless, the cloacal remains thus far relatively untested as a site of resistance, and on the rare historical occasions that it has been tried its success has been questionable, most notably in the case of the dirty protests of Irish republicans in the Maze prison.[33] However, there is more to Hablik's image. It not only visualizes an act of resistance, and the scatological emergency not only brings the laboring body to a halt; it also and at the same time sets the earth in motion. This makes quite a contrast to the stabilizing image of the earth as depicted in other examples of Notgeld. Here the earth is not a reified, unchanging landscape, nor the mere subject of human productive labor. It is a field filled with flowers, soil that is both fertile and fed: a living process rather than a thing. And though the body has involuntarily, and despite all commands to the contrary, come to rest and ceased its labors, this body is not inactive. It labors too on this natural process, which is a shared productive process. The labor of this body produces a substance that, though excluded from society by the taboo against filth and excreta, is actually very valuable indeed, though its use value has been denied for a century or more.[34] Its potential can be seen immediately: the field flourishes, plants sprout, and to either side of the figure two gigantic number-turds thrust up into the sky. A contemporaneous illustration made for the popularizer of science Fritz Kahn explains what it at stake: this image makes visible the *metabolic* relationship between humans and the earth.

In recent years, this relationship has received considerable attention as the locus of Marx's engagement with ecological crisis, a problematic that has lately gained in topicality for obvious reasons. In order to defend Marx against critics who claim that he espoused development at any cost, John Bellamy Foster has turned to his remarks on soil depletion.[35] In the nineteenth century, intensive cultivation led to the exhaustion of nutrients in agricultural land, and eventually to innovations in crop rotation and the introduction of guano and chemical fertilizers. For Marx, both the crisis and its solutions were symptoms of a problem in social relations. As people were forced from their communal land and into conurbations, they ceased to return the nutrients they had absorbed from the soil directly to their source. As well as depleting the soil, this created a concomitant problem of pollution in cities. This did not just take place locally, either; via colonial expansion, the

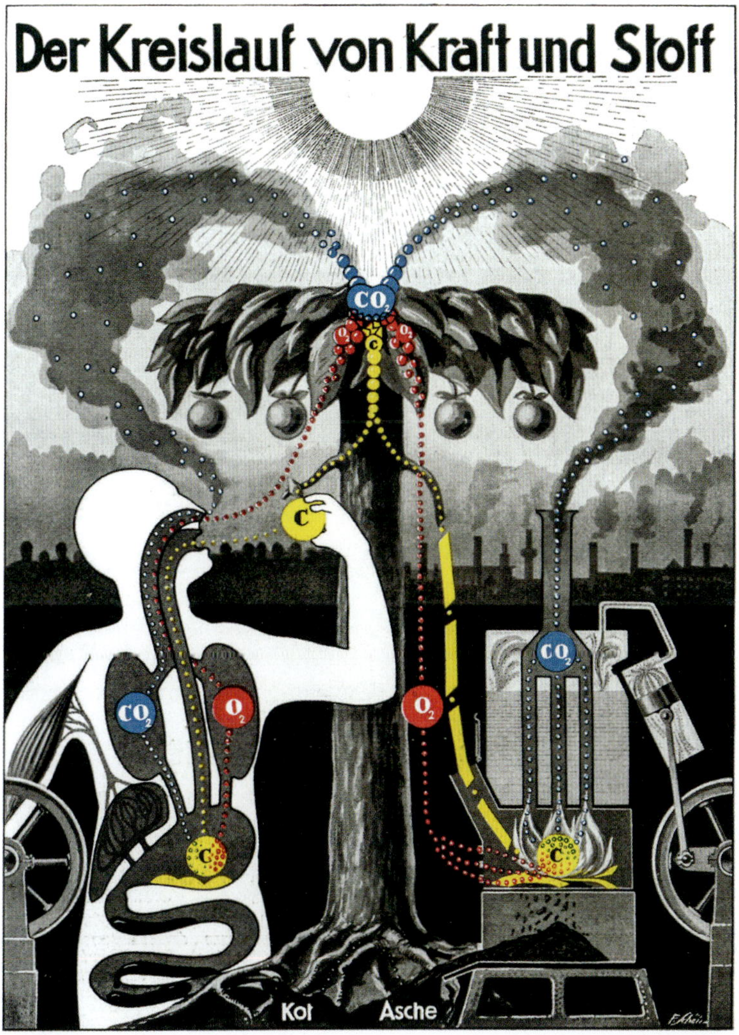

"The Circulation of Energy and Matter," from Fritz Kahn, *Das Leben von Menschen*, vol. 3, 1926.

entire world was swept into this vortex of displacements and disruptions. Foster describes this situation with the phrase *metabolic rift*, under which the delicate interrelation of humans and nature is ripped apart by the development of capital.

The inflation years were not without schemes intended to rectify this cleavage, of varying degrees of practicality. Influenced by Raoul Francé's ideas regarding soil metabolism and Kropotkin's politics of self-sufficiency, prominent landscape designer

Leberecht Migge developed something of an obsession with the use of human feces as fertilizer. He first published on the subject in 1918, in a popular pamphlet on allotments titled *Everyman Self-Sufficient!* One year later, he wrote:

> The city may not only take from the land,
> The city must also give to the land ...
> All city waste to the land. Unify city and land.
> We should create our own "earth."[36]

He experimented with his ideas at Worpswede, where, attracted by Vogeler's commune, he bought a house and set about creating his own earth alongside his wife and children, who were all subject to his grueling insistence on metabolic self-sufficiency. However, his real interest lay in the possibility of reestablishing a link between the recently urbanized masses and the land by installing circulating waste systems on the new modernist housing estates that were then being planned. While his collaborations with Bruno Taut were never fully realized, in 1926, together with a student of Adolf Loos named Leopold Fischer, Migge built a *Siedlung* for a housing cooperative at Ziebigk, outside Dessau. The residents were each allocated a "metroklo," a toilet of a Migge's own design that collected their waste for use on their vegetable gardens. The residents complained of flies and rats, and the dry toilets were soon replaced with flushing ones. Sanitary engineers were skeptical, too, mocking the "fairy-tale-like calculation of sums of gold" that Migge projected could be derived from human waste.[37] Taking a more metaphysical approach, in 1924 Rudolf Steiner, founder of anthroposophy ("mystery-mongering as a large-scale enterprise," in Bloch's view), delivered a series of lectures that would lay the foundation for biodynamic farming.[38] This pseudo-scientific agricultural method was to some extent a reaction to the chemical fertilizers that had been developed before the war by Fritz Haber, whose alchemical experiments I discussed in the previous chapter. Instead of nitrates, biodynamics turns to the mystical properties of shit:

> The cosmic influences which are effective in a plant rise upward from the interior of the Earth. They are led upward. Suppose a plant is especially rich in such cosmic influences. The animal which eats the plant will in its turn provide manure, out of its whole organism, on the basis of this

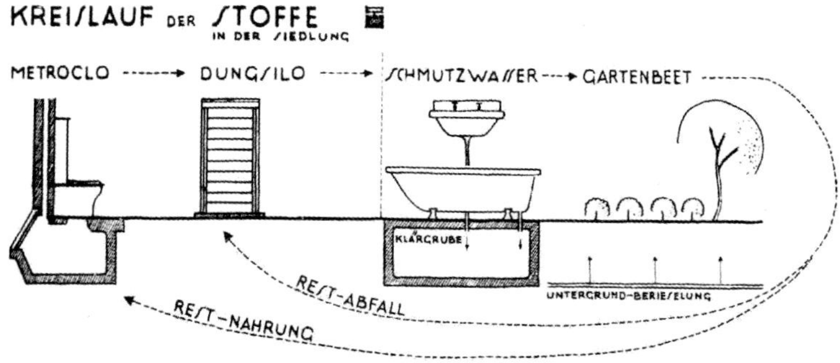

Leberecht Migge, "Circulation of Matter in the Siedlung." David Haney.

> fodder. Thereby it will provide the very manure which is most suited for the soil on which the plant is growing.[39]

However, unlike Migge—who may have inspired his ideas, and who violently rejected biodynamics in return—Steiner was not interested in human feces. Many of the "preparations" stipulated by the anthroposophist are peculiar potions involving animal dung, such as "preparation 500," which requires a cow's horn to be filled with excrement and buried for a certain period of time before its contents are spread across fields (his followers continue to employ this technique today). Both Migge himself and Steiner's biodynamic disciples ended up supporting the Nazis, but during the Weimar period Migge's ideas, at least, were not easily squared with *Blut und Boden* ideology: the reconnection he envisaged between humans and the soil was not racially determined.[40]

In the context of these utopias of shit, the apparent cynicism of Hablik's image comes into question, even though this affective label certainly fits the rest of the series he made for Itzehoe. The smallest-denomination note, worth 25 pfennigs, shows a pair of hands grasping desperately from choppy waters for a straw, which bends but remains tantalizingly out of reach. The next note shows an aerial view of Itzehoe's center, a semi-island encircled by a loop of the river Stör. The only words on the note indicate the denomination, 50 pfennigs, and *Ebbe*, "ebb," the latter pointing in the direction of the river's flow. This might also be read as a hopeful reference to the incontinent flow of finance around the relatively steadfast city. However, despite this intimation of solidity, the submersion of the texts in the river's water recalls the drowning figure of the previous note and hence gives a more sinister edge to

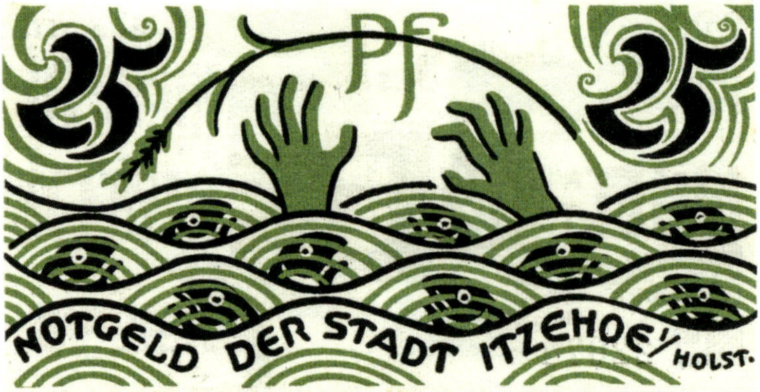

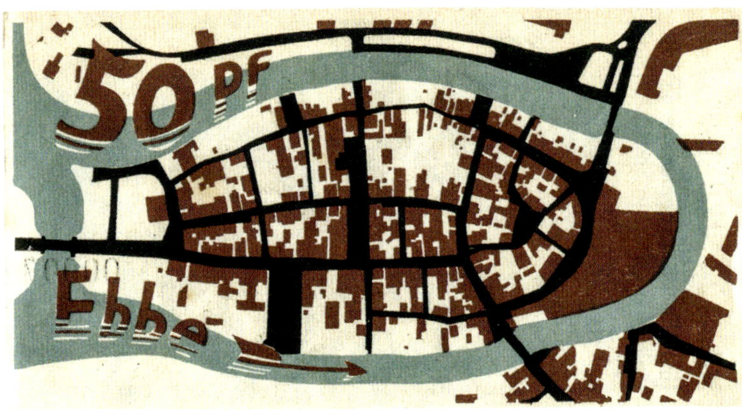

Here and facing page: Notgeld designed by Wenzel Hablik, Itzehoe, 1921. Collection of the author.

this otherwise innocent-seeming image. The next in the series, the 75-pfennig note, shows a chicken laying an egg. The inscription is written in the local Plattdeutsch dialect and can be translated as "Que será, será—it's not gold, but it's still money!" Together with the illustration, this paradoxical phrase suggests the story of the goose that laid the golden egg. However, on closer inspection this chicken, with its pronounced wattle, comb, and spurs, turns out to be a rooster, making its production of monetary value even more miraculous, more unnatural, and more improbable.

Taken as a whole, Hablik's 1921 series reveals a concern with flows and refluxes, with natural processes of production, and with the creation of base and precious materials. These notes also constitute a kind of critical commentary on what had become the

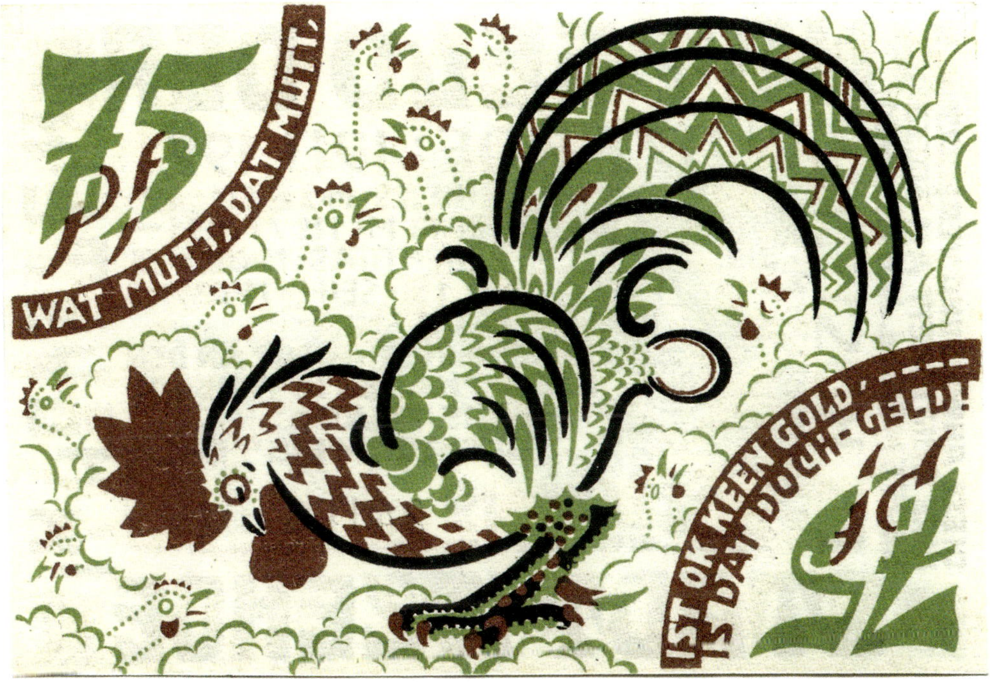

conventions of Notgeld design (we might also read them against Nolde's more pathos-filled Schleswig-Holstein landscapes of the time). The natural landscape is transformed into a site of desperate, accidental death, in which the ear of corn—formerly a symbol of fecundity—fails to save; the cityscape is deprived of picturesque pathos and is instead rendered "objectively" from above, as a collection of dwelling units through which flows move (of water, traffic, and money); and the farmer at his plow is replaced by a figure using a field as a toilet. These notes may also, despite their expressionistic qualities, be considered ambiguous objects in formal terms, somewhere on the way to what is conventionally designated as Neue Sachlichkeit in their uneasy mix of formal intensity and cool iconographic cynicism.

Whither, then, the utopianism that characterizes Hablik's other work, even during this period of crisis? It is salient to note in this context that he was commissioned to make a final pair of high-value notes in 1923, which evince an even greater sense of alarm—one of them shows a gang of tiny figures desperately rowing beneath the phrase "It's hard to keep your head on a burning boat." However,

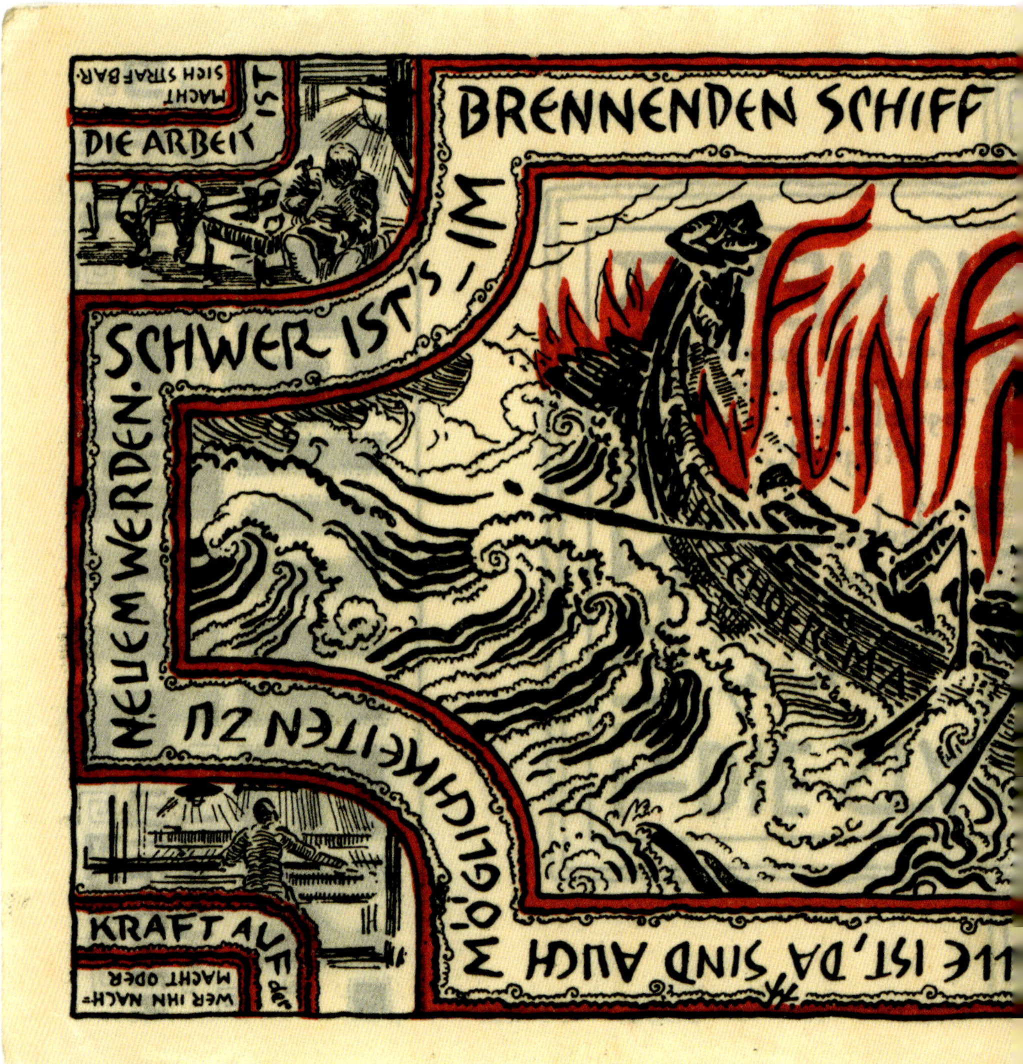

Notgeld designed by Wenzel Hablik, Itzehoe, 1923. Giesecke+Devrient Geldscheinsammlung, Munich.

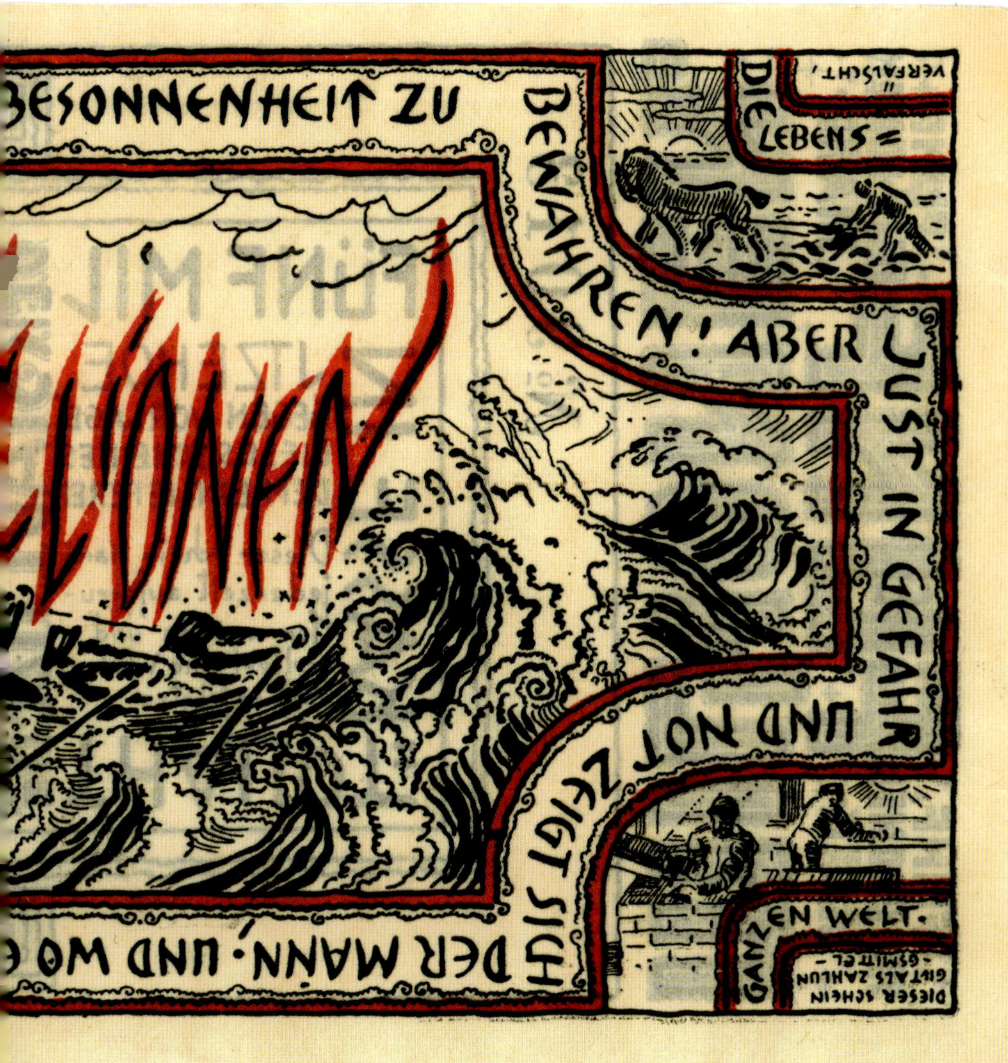

BESONNENHEIT ZU
BEWAHREN! ABER
JUST IN GEFAHR
UND NOT ZEIGT SICH
DER MANN. UND WO
DIE LEBENS=
VERFÄLSCHT,
GANZEN WELT.
DIESER SCHEIN GILT ALS ZAHLUN-GSMITTEL

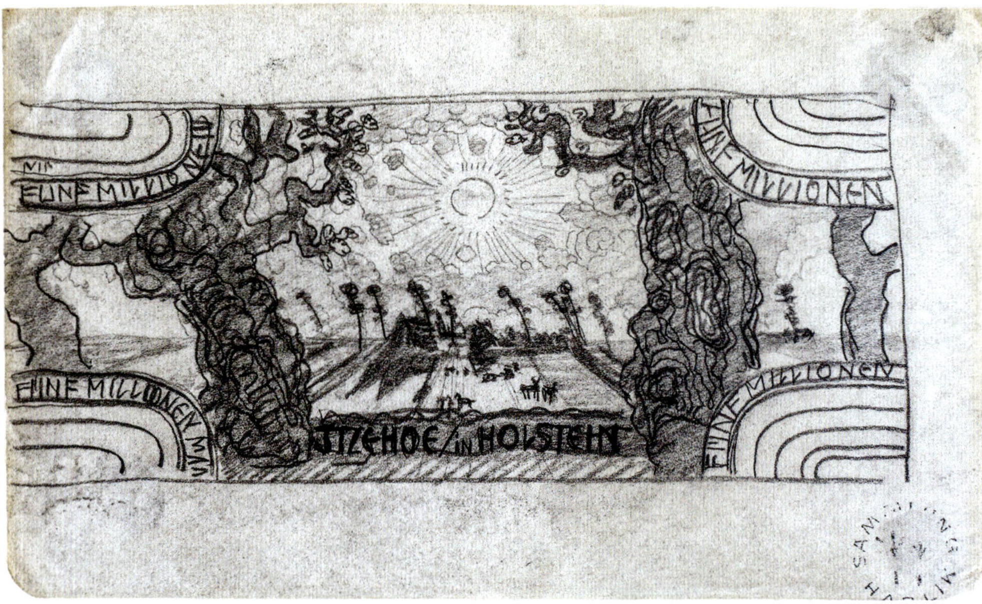

Notgeld sketch by Wenzel Hablik, Itzehoe, 1923. Wenzel Hablik Museum, Itzehoe.

an unused design for a 5-million-mark note made at the same time conveys an entirely different impression, showing a view between gnarled trees of a sunset over a peaceful landscape. Why this utopian image, which, with its sunburst and sinuous forms, is comparable to the large-scale cosmic paintings executed by Hablik at this time, was rejected in favor of scenes of death and disaster cannot, in the absence of documentary evidence, be conclusively answered. Instead, I propose that this paradisiacal landscape is not in fact so distant from the images that *were* distributed, especially in the case I have been focusing on here. Hablik was capable of thinking both states simultaneously, to the extent that the question of how he got from the crystal to the turd should be met with a reversal of its terms: *the turd is the crystal.*[41] By visualizing the closure of the metabolic rift, Hablik depicts a utopian resolution of the severance of human and nature. This encompasses both aspects of the design discussed above: alienated labor ceases, and instead we return to a productive relationship with the earth.

The excremental may not be a feature of Hablik's usual image-making practice, but it is not an aberration in the context of his thought. In his contributions to the Crystal Chain correspondence network, Hablik evinces a preference for scatological turns of phrase, which he employs to convey an unusually earthy utopianism. Although in one undated note he expresses the conventionally exuberant expressionist aspiration "Soon we shall also be able to fly! We can live in the air!," on another occasion he was to write that "even if we could cast off our terrestrial shackles—we would still be tied to earth ad infinitum. There are no two ways about it—we are earth."[42] Elsewhere he affirms his future orientation in paleo-scatological terms: "Should we look back even for the duration of a spark of life in order to criticise the coprolites of fossilised reptiles, or even pass our own excrement over the scales of the 'ego'?"[43] And in another, undated draft, Hablik asked an unknown correspondent:

> With what right are you alarmed about "natural forms," or "artistic forms in nature"? Even if you protest strongly against these forms, how do you propose to eliminate them? Ridiculous! "Everything is in flux"—very true, but as a current of endless, penetrating energy for which we, if you like, can be good conductors. ... Perhaps, in the attempt to resolve the mystery of life, some of us might act as the fixed point needed to conduct the energy streams that flow over the earth.[44]

With this final comment, Hablik suggests a relation to the earth that is fixed but not essentialized according to race or nation. This view is also expressed by his Notgeld that shows a figure anchored to the earth by an energy stream of organic matter. With his utopia of shit, Hablik imagines a possible alternative to the more dangerous relation with the earth posited by conservative voices at this time. As a means of relating to place, Hablik offers a potential universalism grounded in shared participation in global metabolic systems, which reacts against the displacements of modernity without turning to blood and soil.[45]

Alchemy in Reverse

Hablik's utopian closure of the metabolic rift imagines a harmonious reintegration of humans and their habitats. However, despite the Edenic setting, a jarring ambiguity remains at the heart of this image. The excremental lightning bolt that connects this figure to the soil is not just organic matter. It is also a numeral, the denomination of the note. Or rather, it oscillates between these two positions: at once abject, organic matter and the ultimate figure of ratio. What are we to make of this binary status? To a certain extent, it echoes that of Notgeld itself, which, as both commodity and general equivalent, has more in common with gold than it does with token money. But in the context of Hablik's image, it is worth noting John Bellamy Foster and Brett Clark's observation that "Marx's critique of the capitalist political economy rested in large part on the contradiction between metabolic interchange and the economic value form of commodities." However, for Marx "human metabolism with nature under capitalism was mediated by value."[46] Does the denominatory excrement reflect the impossibility of escape from this relation with the earth under capital? Without a change in social relations, is it inevitable that the utopian turd will be transmuted, not into expressionistic crystal but into what Marx calls the "money crystal"?[47]

I believe that a further probing of the image reveals that Hablik anticipates this problem, and offers a solution: an intimation that it may be possible to escape this frozen metabolism by introducing a third term to our reading of the note. For this excremental figure is not just a turd and a number; it is also simultaneously a brushstroke, the indexical trace of the artist. It is therefore possible to see this image as a self-portrait, and not just because Hablik was a heavy smoker. The labor, after all, that produces the value behind these notes is that of the designer. It is perhaps more than an irony of history that Heinz Schiestl, the most prolific designer of Notgeld, also carved at least two Dukatenmännchen, including one for the Ratskeller in Würzburg. On its base is inscribed:

> That which our dear old city
> Needs above all—I am he.
> Each nobody and each big-hitter
> All require the ducat-sh ...

This figure called upon by the town and its people, no matter their rank (the original German has "beggar, townsman, pope and Kaiser"), can be read as a self-portrait of the artist, who, ten years earlier, had been run ragged by demands upon his own money-producing powers.

Without the colorful and eye-catching designs that adorn these objects, they would simply be worthless scraps of paper, of

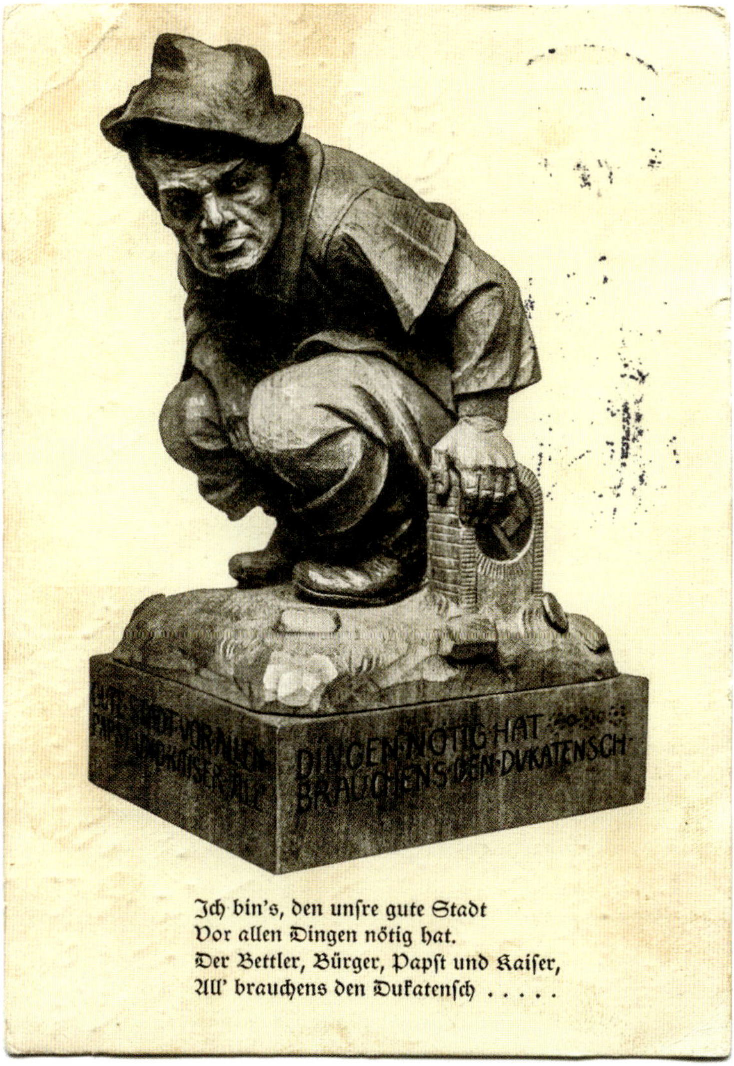

Heinz Schiestl, Dukatenmännchen, Ratskeller, Würzburg, c. 1934. Collection of the author.

no interest to anyone but the ragpicker. Seen in this light, the figure that comes to rest on this note is not breaking off his labor at all: he is in fact hard at work *producing money*. But this is a different kind of labor from that of the plowman or the miner seen on other notes: it is neither waged nor alienated. That the labor of the artist remains, like the act of defecation, a direct and "natural" one is the contention of Dave Beech, who in his recent book *Art and Value* claims that "art has been commodified without being commodified"—that is, although its products are undoubtedly commodities, its mode of production remains at the precapitalistic stage of independent handicraft.[48] Within the trinity of number-turd-brushstroke, then, lies an affirmation that the possibilities of a new world are already at hand. Such possibilities evidently seemed (to some) particularly close under the conditions of economic emergency; and yet the very fact of Hablik's engagement with this ephemeral material, as with that of other artists working on Notgeld, is testimony to the real desperation that they felt. And seen from our current perspective, in which the glamorous image of creative labor has been deployed to sweeten the bitter pill of precarity, this utopia may seem a hollow one.[49]

Furthermore, however insistent Hablik was regarding the base materiality of his work and the naturalness of his labor, the medium of his utopia—like the turd in the image—continued to turn away, again and again, from the good soil toward the money crystal. To recapitulate my argument: this oscillation of Notgeld, between commodity and general equivalent, was instrumentalized by its producers to raise funds. Its twin status, which superficially resembles that of the money commodity, that is, gold, was at first accidental. These stopgap tokens were intended as a circulating medium. It was only their spontaneous absorption into collections that alerted issuers to their other possibilities, which were then developed via the employment of artists. However, it was necessary to at least imply the enduring monetary status of these objects, and so this ambiguity was cultivated. Seen from one angle these remained currency, but from another, only commodities. They should not be sufficiently monetary to smooth the path to further circulation, nor should they be inadequately so to invite the contempt and rejection of collectors. This abject matter had to retain its denomination, however fictitious.

The consequence of this metabolic process was not the ripening of blossoms in a delightful garden; quite the opposite. One contributor to the conservative local paper the *Itzehoer Nachrichtung* complained about such currency in strikingly excremental—and racist—terms:

> These municipal war emergency notes are nothing but token money [*Zeichengeld*], which primitive people also use, and if porcelain money is produced in such quantities that it clatters in our pockets, we are no more advanced than the savages who

drag their weapon money and feather money to market. Even Togo negroes, weighing their dark, filthy rubber balls in their hands, would be justified in regarding these as more valuable than our notes, since rubber presently has a considerable market value, which cannot always be said of our Notgeld.

The author's focus on dark and filthy matter is, I think, a reference to a very specific example of Notgeld that had been issued in the same city and around the same time that the article was published: Hablik's one-mark note. For the anonymous writer, Hablik's image is too obscene for explicit mention; instead, we have to approach it through the lens of the exotic, the other, the primitive—to which this excremental money joins us. We are no better than the savage, and in fact even worse, since Notgeld has no real value. It is a mere token. "There is no longer any connection," the author continues, "between the material used for money and its value."[50] These confused fulminations—all paper money is, after all, token money—are another example of how Notgeld was seen to undermine economic and also cultural norms, leading to a negative transvaluation of all values: a universal shittification.

Toward a Base-Materialist Theory of the Money Medium

In their work on metabolic rift, Foster and Clark observe that Marx derived his concept of metabolism, *Stoffwechsel*, which is so crucial to his theory, from the work of agrochemist Justus Liebig. The relation of Marx's economics to his embryonic ecology is not merely articulated via chemical metaphor, however; rather, this connection illuminates the core of his critique of political economy. By bursting through the cordon with which classical liberal political economy had bound itself, Marx looked beyond questions of supply and demand, turning instead to the earth, "source of all value" as he put it in his critique of the Gotha program. From this worm's-eye perspective it is therefore possible to assert that Bataille, for all his other deviations, adheres quite closely to this project with his notion of general economy, albeit striking out beyond the confines of the earth to engage with cosmic forces.

Turning back from the cosmos to the sphere from which Marx (and Bataille after him) endeavored to escape, what are the implications of these excursions for our understanding of money and

Notgeld? Perhaps now is the time to tease out some loose ends. Firstly, this expanded view allows us to resolve—or perhaps to sidestep—the question of causality. Rather than puzzling over which came first, we can say that image and economy are (like ecology) both part of the general economy, which is nevertheless a material rather than an ideal realm. Secondly, there is the question of money's medium status. What exactly did Marx mean when he said that banknotes "symbolize" money? Marx states that this deputization can only succeed if enforced by state power, but this does not answer the question of how precisely this symbolization works—in other words, how money functions as a medium. More recent authors, such as Gottfried Gabriel and Jens Schröter, have begun to investigate the rhetorical and visual means by which these objects support the belief in their value. Schröter moves beyond this discursive realm into the question of the material constitution of money, with reference to the work of Kittler and the media archaeology he inaugurated. However, Kittler may not be the friend Schröter seeks, since his arsenal is not equipped with the means to tackle questions of political economy and he tends to return us, despite all his protestations, to the realm of discourse.

Instead, I have turned repeatedly over the course of this chapter to Bataille, whose notion of base materialism seems peculiarly apposite to this subject, and not just because so many examples of emergency money feature images of defecation. The excremental recurs in Bataille's writings as an antidote to what he perceived as the inexorable slide of materialism into idealism. In Denis Hollier's gloss, "scatology does not propose an idea, even a new one, of matter, but produces matter as something eluding the idea."[51] It is for this reason that I have looked to Bataille in the hope of countering the idealist tendencies of much recent media theory, radicalizing (or congealing) Kittler's turn toward the matter of the medium and thereby promising to depart the realm of discourse—at last. And yet it does not cross over into that land of object-agents in which so many dwell today, since this particular thing is the mediating term in the human-nature metabolic relation: the turd, to put it bluntly, does not shit itself.[52] This paper was made by somebody. Or numerous bodies, in view of the ever-growing mass of paper circulating in Germany: in 1868, 242 mills produced 80,000 tons of paper; in 1873, 423 mills were producing 180,000 tons, and by 1914 some 2 million tons of paper were produced by 940 mills.[53] This vast increase inevitably sucked in thousands of workers, and while the growth in demand for paper stimulated by the inflation was certainly not as exorbitant, it was by no means negligible. Indeed, one prominent industrialist complained in 1923 that the printing of notes was "the one productive activity of the government."[54] And behind the printing presses stood a sequence of paper mills, sawmills, and acres of timber, with an attendant army of labor at each stage.

We can envisage a base-materialist media theory that expands to encompass this hinterland—that constructs a sewer beneath the medium, we might say, paraphrasing Simmel's claim to "construct a new story beneath historical materialism" in his *Philosophy of Money*—although it is beyond the scope of the current work to do more than nod in its direction.[55] Such an approach could do worse than taking as its starting point a short story published by Herman Melville in 1855, "The Paradise of Batchelors and the Tartarus of Maids." In this bifurcated tale Melville juxtaposes two vignettes: on one side a lavish dinner hosted near Fleet Street in London by a group of publishers and lawyers, those two paper-based trades, and on the other a satanic paper mill in New England worked by young women, "where the air swam with the fine, poisonous particles, which from all sides darted, subtilely as motes in sunbeams, into the lungs."[56] By giving equal weight to these exploited workers—workers whose labor produces the medium by which the author is communicating, and whose very bodies are invaded by the medium they produce—the usually invisible base matter of the medium is brought to light, like motes illuminated by sunbeams. It is also hinted at by the swarming clouds of *Zettel* or scraps of paper that appear on numerous examples of Notgeld, reminding us of this matter's materiality; it is more directly invoked by the squatting figure on Hablik's note, producing money out of his own body. Citing Vespasian's famous defense of his tax on the collection of urine from public lavatories, *Pecunia non olet* (Money does not smell), Marx wrote that "since every commodity disappears when it becomes money it is impossible to tell from the money itself how it got into the hands of its possessor, or what article has been changed into it. *Non olet*, from whatever source it may come."[57] Excremental Notgeld bucks this deodorizing tendency, reminding us that the medium comes dripping from head to toe, from every pore, with blood and dirt.[58]

Epilogue: Necrometabolism

Count yourselves lucky that you're lying there,
While banknotes and bullets just fly through the air.
Of your heroic actions such tales will be told!
While you're soaked in blood we're just swimming in gold.

Karl Kraus, *The Last Days of Mankind*, 1922

Notgeld designs generally evince a conservative view of money, and however wildly they excoriate the situation, no matter how hygienically they discipline its flows, they dream of a restoration of the status quo ante—with Hablik being an exceptional case. However, there were others among the avant-garde who also emphasized the materiality of this substance in quite a different way, by turning it into an artistic medium. By cutting it, rearranging it, and pasting it, they deprived it finally of whatever currency it had once had. In doing so they echo the behavior of the collector, who withdraws money from circulation and thereby, as Simmel noted, transforms it into an object of aesthetic appreciation. But although the note may theoretically be released from the collector's album to continue its circulation, it will never escape the gluey trap of the collage, as in Schwitters's *Kotsbild*. Here the note is reduced to an object, indeed to the most abject object, *Kot* (feces), its magical powers drained away—although they make their ironic return thanks to the commodity status of the artwork of which the note forms a part. Hablik's ambiguous turd, though valorizing artistic labor as utopian when seen from one angle, also described this ineluctable tendency.

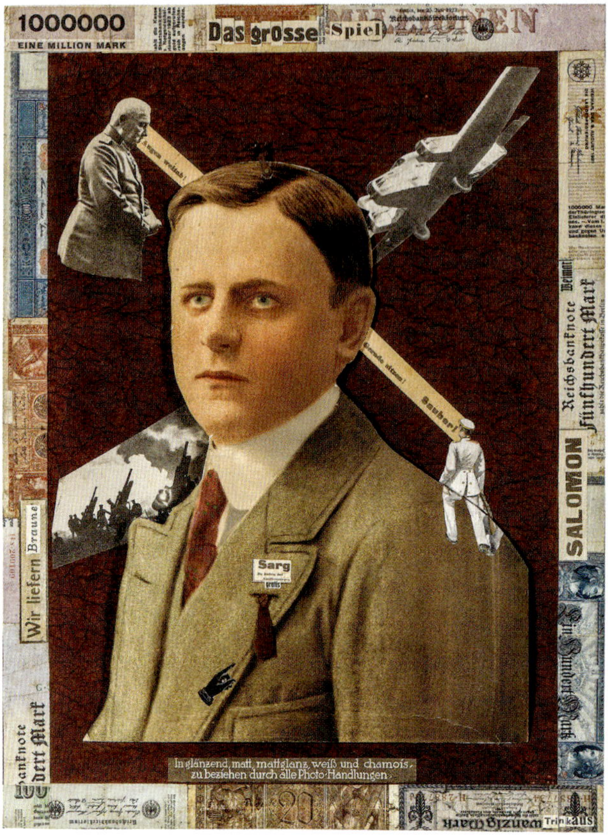

Karl Hermann Trinkaus, *Das große Spiel* (The Great Game), 1933, collage, 53 × 39.5 cm. Private collection.

A decade later, another artist would return to the same material, looking from this new vantage point beyond its slippery position within the matrix of artwork-currency-value. In the early 1930s, Karl Hermann Trinkaus, who had studied at the Bauhaus, produced a series of highly worked photomontages, several of which convey a critical view regarding the final years of the Weimar Republic and the Nazi seizure of power.[1] Two of these works incorporate pieces cut from high-denomination Notgeld and inflationary notes issued by the Reichsbank, which are arranged as a border around portraits of young men. In both cases, a small figure of Hindenburg takes a commanding position above the young men's heads, asking in one instance, "Is your heart heavy?" (to which the response is a repeated "Yes!"), and in the other barking orders: "Eyes open! Sit straight! Clean!" The central figure in both

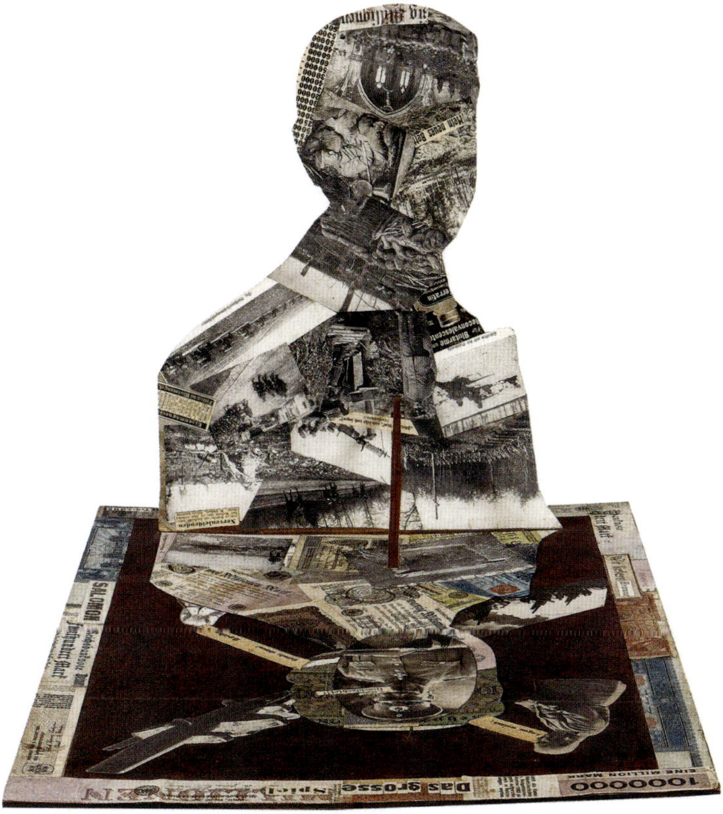

Interior view of Karl Hermann Trinkaus, *Das große Spiel* (The Great Game), 1933, collage, 53 × 39.5 cm. Private collection.

images can be lifted from its backing by a tab. Doing so reveals in one instance Hitler's glowing head floating above a vast crowd with saluting figures and lines of marching soldiers, and, beneath this triumphant scene, a now-famous photograph of two figures measuring the nose of another man with a pair of calipers. Echoing the latter image, and perhaps foretelling the fate of the blue-eyed boy on the recto of the montage, is another face photographed in the course of reconstructive plastic surgery, presumably treating an injury incurred during the previous war. In the case of the other montage, lifting the hinged element reveals Hindenburg again, this time intoning the word "slaughtered" with a sinister smile. Around him are a series of battle scenes, including a soldier curled up, possibly dead, in a foxhole, juxtaposed with an image of a graveyard. The latter pair of images is labeled with the words "My new bed."

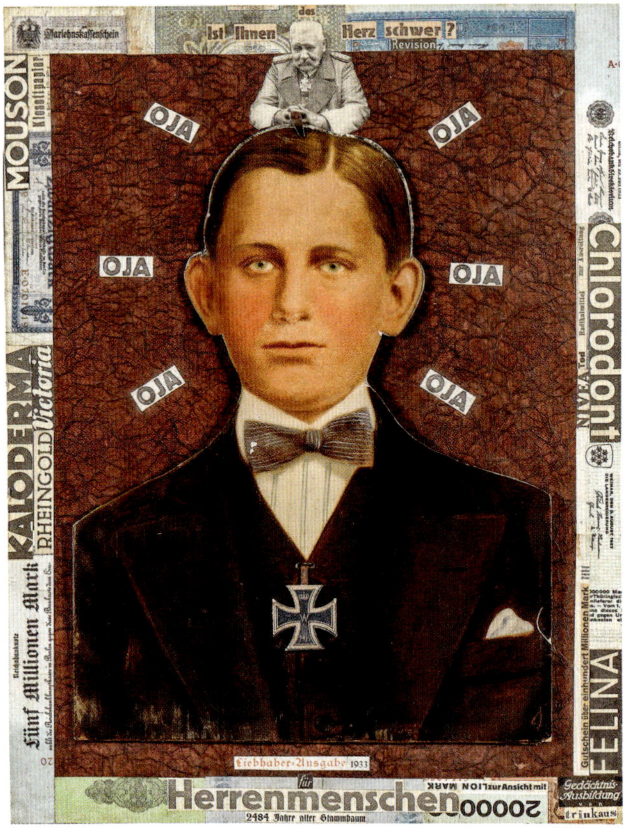

Karl Hermann Trinkaus, *Ist Ihnen das Herz schwer?* (Is Your Heart Heavy?), 1933, collage, 53 × 40 cm. Private collection.

How do the Notgeld borders around these montages relate to the scenes they frame—scenes of militaristic exploitation of youthful ennui, culminating in racism, demagoguery, mutilation, and death? The degree to which the inflation contributed to the rise of the Nazis is a matter of long-standing historiographic dispute. Gerald Feldman began his monumental work on the subject of the inflation, *The Great Disorder*, by stating that the resolution of the question lies beyond the scope of historiography, while citing several less cautious affirmative voices.[2] In any case, it is clear from looking at these images that the connection was not absent from the minds of contemporary observers. Trinkaus does not go so far as Thomas Mann, who made the counterintuitive claim that the German people had voted for the Nazis precisely because the inflationary period had given them a taste for chaos.[3] His argument

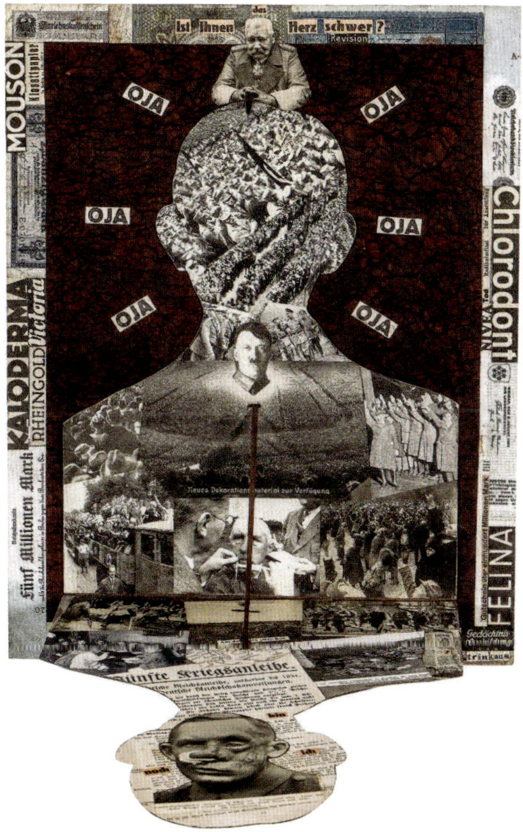

Interior view of Karl Hermann Trinkaus, *Ist Ihnen das Herz schwer?* (Is Your Heart Heavy?), 1933, collage, 53 × 40 cm. Private collection.

is more materialist. Notgeld is not the only substance making up these borders, for a start—there are also brand names and advertising copy (including the word "toilet paper"). This combination of elements, and its location around the edge of the image, suggests a milieu of economic chaos and commercial sloganeering in which meaning has been emptied away. The repeated zeroes are, like the words "Chlorodont" and "Nivea," meaningless signs divorced from reality. Within this structural framework of intentional derangement of signification—including, crucially, value signification —slogans shouted by revered political figures can also be severed from reality and their inevitable consequences (which transpire behind the heads of the central figures), to the extent that the resulting distance permits unthinking assent: "Oja! Oja! Oja!"

I think that, in this context, one final observation ought to be made regarding Trinkaus's montages. Although they depart from the utopian materialism of Hablik to confront the violence unleashed by the decay of value signification, Trinkaus is still concerned to some extent with the questions that Hablik had raised in his designs for money, not least those regarding the role of the artist. For among the snippets of cash there is included, in both cases and in one case very prominently, a fragment cut from the Notgeld that Herbert Bayer had designed while studying at the Bauhaus ten years earlier. Trinkaus's own years of study at that institution, which spanned 1927–1928, coincided with the last two years that Bayer worked there as the master of the typography and advertising workshop, a class that Trinkaus himself attended. As is well known, Bayer would later go on to work for agencies of the National Socialist government, producing promotional material for the exhibitions *Deutsches Volk, deutsche Arbeit* (German People, German Work) in 1934, *Das Wunder des Lebens* (The Wonder of Life) in 1935, and *Deutschland* in 1936. Whether Trinkaus could have had Bayer's accommodation to the regime in mind when he produced these collages is uncertain. The inclusion of a propagandistic photomontage in one of them suggests that this may be the case; however, their presumed date, 1933, precedes Bayer's work for organizations such as the Deutsche Arbeitsfront by one year. On the other hand, Bayer's continued prominence after the seizure of power—he designed numerous covers for the nation's leading illustrated lifestyle magazine, *die neue linie*, while other Bauhäusler were fleeing the country—may have been enough for the politically active Trinkaus.[4] In any case, whether or not Bayer had already stooped to explicit collaboration, Trinkaus is certainly concerned with questioning the equation of good design to social good that had been associated with the school and the modernist project *tout court*.[5] In this bitterly critical assemblage, the "rationalizing" works of the Bauhaus merge into a background of capitalist chaos, from which emerges a monstrous vision of the future: the soil as a "new bed," and the human body in a metabolic relation with the earth quite unlike that depicted by Hablik.

This vision would shortly be realized. Under the new regime, the massive chemical conglomerate I.G. Farben had its own work camp adjacent to Auschwitz in which it "reduced slave labor to a consumable raw material, a human ore from which the mineral of life was systematically extracted. When no usable energy remained, the living dross was shipped to the gassing chambers and cremation furnaces ... where the S. S. recycled it into the German war economy—gold teeth for the Reichsbank."[6] Although the circumstances are very different, a comparable process continues today, when the cobalt used to power the devices with which we make and view much of our media—including this book—are dredged from filth by child laborers whose working conditions are little better than those of slaves.[7]

Acknowledgments

I am particularly grateful to my parents and sisters for their support; without them, this book (and much else besides) would not have been possible. The research on which this book is based was largely conducted during a Leverhulme Early Career Fellowship, and I thank the Leverhulme Foundation for the freedom engendered by its generosity. I undertook this fellowship at the Warburg Institute in London, a wonderful place to work; I especially wish to mention Michelle O'Malley, Bill Sherman, Claudia Wedepohl, and Nessa Malone, whose warm welcomes made me feel at home there, likewise John Tresch and Johannes von Müller, who also offered helpful comments on earlier versions of this project. The three anonymous reviewers also made numerous suggestions that have much improved this text. I am deeply indebted to Frederic Schwartz, without whose inspiration and encouragement, now stretching back over many years, I could not have got here; his influence is present throughout this book. Birkbeck provided additional support during the completion of the manuscript, and my colleagues there were good comrades in these difficult times for the academy, during which it has sometimes felt that we are heading the same way as the *geistige Arbeiter* of the 1920s. I thank my students, too, for helping to generate ideas collaboratively—in this context, I must especially mention Beatrice Speelmans and Michelle Zhu. I have also been fortunate in my contacts at archives, namely Elke Bannicke and the staff of the Münzkabinett of the Bode Museum; Birgit Staack at the Altonaer Museum; Katharina Graeber and Janina Willems at the Wenzel Hablik Museum; Hadwig Goez at the Kunstmuseum in Stuttgart; Iain Birkett at the British Museum; Richard Kelleher at the Fitzwilliam Museum; Katharina Depner and Leonard Königer at the Giesecke+Devrient Geldscheinsammlung; and Jennifer Gloede at the Smithsonian. At the MIT Press, Thomas Weaver has been a convivial collaborator, and I am grateful for Gabriela Bueno Gibbs's patient assistance with the publication process, as well as that of the book's production and copy editors, Jay Martsi, Matthew Abbate, and Stephanie Sakson. I would also like to thank the support staff of the institutions at which I have been employed over the years that I was working on this project, which includes the Courtauld Institute as well as the Warburg and Birkbeck; Robin Schuldenfrei, who organized the symposium at which the idea for this book first germinated; Hans-Ludwig Besler and Nathaniel Butler, who kindly supplied reproductions of notes from their collections; Philipp Ekardt, for advice and letter-writing; Bianca Grizhar, for her friendship (and help with Plattdeutsch); Christian Kustermann, likewise for his assistance with translations; Isabel Wilkinson, for cleaning up the images; and Joy Ahoulou, from whom I learned so much.

Notes

Introduction: Full Pockets, Empty Signs

1. On Hablik, see Katrin Maibaum and Katharina Gräber, *Wenzel Hablik—expressionistische Utopien: Malerei, Zeichnung, Architektur* (Munich: Prestel, 2017).

2. The most detailed account of the inflation and debates over its interpretation remains Gerald D. Feldman, *The Great Disorder: Politics, Inflation, and Society in the German Inflation, 1914–1924* (New York: Oxford University Press, 1997).

3. However, it should be noted that orthodox monetarists have until recently been pursuing a similar policy under the euphemistic name of quantitative easing, which has produced rocketing asset price inflation and, among other things, a global housing crisis. Radhika Desai, "Vectors of Inflation," *New Left Review*, 2022, https://newleftreview.org/sidecar/posts/vectors-of-inflation (accessed October 7, 2022).

4. Georges Bataille, *Visions of Excess: Selected Writings, 1927–1939*, trans. Allan Stoekl (Minneapolis: University of Minnesota Press, 1985), 117.

5. Bernd Widdig, *Culture and Inflation in Weimar Germany* (Berkeley: University of California Press, 2001).

6. Anton Kaes, "Die ökonomische Dimension der Literatur: Zum Strukturwandel der Institution Literatur in der Inflationszeit (1918–1923)," in *Konsequenzen der Inflation*, ed. Gerald D. Feldman (Berlin: Kolloqium Verlag, 1989), 322.

7. Feldman, *The Great Disorder*, 785.

8. Walter Benjamin, *Selected Writings*, vol. 1: *1913–1926*, ed. Michael W. Jennings and Marcus Bullock (Cambridge, MA: Belknap Press of Harvard University Press, 2004), 481.

9. Birger P. Priddat, "'Geist der Ornamentik,' Ideogrammatik des Geldes: Allegorien bürgerlicher Zivilreligion auf Banknoten des 19. und 20. Jahrhunderts," in *Kapitalismus als Religion*, ed. Dirk Baecker (Berlin: Kulturverlag Kadmos, 2009), 19–34.

10. William Clare Roberts, *Marx's Inferno: The Political Theory of Capital* (Princeton, NJ: Princeton University Press, 2016).

11. See, for instance, Marc Shell, "The Issue of Representation," in *The New Economic Criticism*, ed. Martha Woodmansee and Mark Osteen (London: Routledge, 1999), 44–64. Shell's work on the economic dimension of literature is very convincing; his work on visual matter, less so.

12. Marc Shell, *The Economy of Literature* (Baltimore: Johns Hopkins University Press, 1993), 86–87.

13. The words "image economy" have previously been used to describe stock photography services by Matthias Bruhn, in his book *Bildwirtschaft: Verwaltung und Verwertung der Sichtbarkeit* (Weimar: VDG, 2003). Peter Szendy has also combined the two spheres with his use of the word "iconomy," which he derives from Marie-José Mondzain, in his book *The Supermarket of the Visible: Toward a General Economy of Images*, trans. Jan Plug (New York: Fordham University Press, 2019). The Bataillean allusion in Szendy's subtitle is unfulfilled by his text: here my argument will be substantially informed by Bataille's work. In any case, my use of the term is differently motivated: it is to some degree an attempt to put into productive tension the Warburgian and historical-materialist traditions, identified as antagonistic in O. K. Werckmeister's essay "The Turn from Marx to Warburg in West German Art History, 1968–1990," in *Marxism and Art History: From William Morris to the New Left* (London: Pluto Press, 2006), 213–220.

14. Michael Baxandall was, at least in the early 1970s, the obvious exception to the idealism of the iconographic tradition, but its more recent exponents have returned to the clouds. See, for example, Bredekamp's article on *Bildwissenschaft*, which tellingly flattens the difference between Benjamin and Panofsky. Horst Bredekamp, "A Neglected Tradition? Art History as Bildwissenschaft," *Critical Inquiry* 29, no. 3 (2003), 418–428.

15. In the period under consideration here, Warburg is of course the key example, although his approach bracketed questions of economics. Frederic J. Schwartz, "Aby Warburg and the Spirit of Capitalism," in *Renew Marxist Art History*,

ed. Warren Carter, Barnaby Haran, and Frederic J. Schwartz (London: Art/Books, 2013), 117–137.

16. On art's present status as a commodity, see David Joselit, *After Art* (Princeton, NJ: Princeton University Press, 2013), and Hito Steyerl, *Duty Free Art: Art in the Age of Planetary Civil War* (London: Verso, 2017); on NFTS, see Beatrice Speelmans, "Anomic Speculation: The Cultural Logic of Tokenisation. An Investigation of Notgeld, Complimentary Local Currencies and Non-Fungible Tokens" (MA thesis, Courtauld Institute, 2021).

17. Erin Sullivan Maynes, "Making Money: Notgeld and the Material Experience of Inflation in Weimar Germany," *Art History* 42, no. 4 (2019), 678–701; Christine Künzel, "'[D]ie dunkle Schlange des lügnerischen Papiergelds': Anmerkungen zur Ästhetik und Rhetorik von Papiernoten in der großen Inflation (1918–1923)," in *Bild Medium Geld: Bildkulturen und Medienreflexionen des Monetären*, ed. Judith Ellenbürger and Felix Gregor (Paderborn: Wilhelm Fink, 2019), 79–94. Since the 1920s, extensive research has been conducted on Notgeld by numismatists and local historians, who have unearthed a wealth of invaluable archival detail; however, they have rarely strayed into visual analysis. The aesthetics of money more widely speaking has however been the subject of growing interest in recent years. In addition to the volume cited above, see, for instance, *Der schöne Schein: Symbolik und Ästhetik von Banknoten*, ed. Stefan Hartmann and Christian Thiel (Regenstauf: Gietl Verlag, 2016).

18. Künzel, "'[D]ie dunkle Schlange des lügnerischen Papiergelds,'" 82.

19. This is demonstrated by Nigel Dodd's survey on the topic, *The Social Life of Money* (Princeton, NJ: Princeton University Press, 2014).

20. Goux's essay "Numismatiques" was first published in *Tel Quel* in 1968–1969. Jean-Joseph Goux, *Symbolic Economies: After Marx and Freud*, trans. Jennifer Curtiss Gage (Ithaca, NY: Cornell University Press, 1990), 13.

21. Jean Baudrillard, *For a Critique of the Political Economy of the Sign*, trans. Charles Levin (St. Louis: Telos Press, 1981), 143.

22. Frederic J. Schwartz, *The Werkbund: Design Theory and Mass Culture before the First World War* (New Haven: Yale University Press, 1996).

23. Baudrillard, *For a Critique of the Political Economy of the Sign*, 146.

24. "All the repressive and reductive strategies of power systems are *already present* in the internal logic of the sign, as well as those of exchange value and political economy" (my emphasis). Baudrillard, *For a Critique of the Political Economy of the Sign*, 163.

25. Jens Schröter, "Das Geld und die Medientheorie," *Zeitschrift für Medienwissenschaft* 10, no. 18 (2018), 59–72.

26. Gottfried Gabriel, *Ästhetik und Rhetorik des Geldes* (Stuttgart: Frommann-Holzboog, 2002).

27. As Schwartz put it, "Even as the circulation of signs ... simultaneously borrows from, pushes on, and exceeds the circulation of exchange values, the material base of that system of society remains." Schwartz, *The Werkbund*, 8.

28. "Base matter is external and foreign to ideal human aspirations, and it refuses to allow itself to be reduced to the great ontological machines resulting from these aspirations." Georges Bataille, *The Accursed Share: An Essay on General Economy*, 3 vols., trans. Robert Hurley (New York: Zone, 1991), 1:51. Bataille worked as a numismatist at the Bibliothèque Nationale and two of his articles for the journal *Documents* concern money and medals: "Base Materialism and Gnosticism," from which the preceding quotation is derived, and "The Academic Horse." In the latter he argues, on the basis of representations of horses on coins minted by the Gauls, that "the fantastic horses imagined by various groups revealed not so much a technical fault as a positive extravagance. ... The absurdities of barbarous peoples are out of step with scientific arrogance, nightmares with geometrical traces, and the horse-monsters imagined in Gaul with the academic horse [of Hellenistic coinage]. ... Alterations of plastic forms often represent the principal symptom of great reversals: thus it might seem today that nothing collapses, if the negation of all principles of regular harmony did not bear witness to the necessity for change." *Undercover Surrealism: Georges Bataille and Documents*,

ed. Dawn Ades, Simon Baker, and Fiona Bradley (London: Haywood Gallery, 2006), 236–239.

29. Karl Marx, *Capital*, vol. 1, trans. Ben Fowkes (London: Penguin, 1976), 225–226.

30. Bataille, *The Accursed Share*.

Chapter 1: Land

1. Wolfgang Kemp, *Wir haben ja alle Deutschland nicht gekannt: Das Deutschlandbild der Deutschen in der Zeit der Weimarer Republik* (Heidelberg: Heidelberg University Press, 2016), 17.

2. Kurt Biging, *Geldscheine in Halle an der Saale 1916–1992* (Halle: Mitteldeutscher Verlag, 2003), 82.

3. Siegfried Kracauer, "Notgeld und Kleingeld," in *Siegfried Kracauer Werke*, ed. Inka Mülder-Bach, vol. 5.1 (Berlin: Suhrkamp, 2011), 709.

4. On the subject of regionalism in the Weimar period and a brief discussion of Notgeld in this context, see Kemp, *Wir haben ja alle Deutschland nicht gekannt*, 297–306.

5. The perspective itself is obsolete, since, following changes in warfare inaugurated with the Revolutionary Wars "an overall view of battle was no longer possible." Martin Warnke, *Political Landscape: The Art History of Nature* (London: Reaktion Books, 1994), 60.

6. Jochen Hörisch, *Heads or Tails: The Poetics of Money*, trans. Amy Horning Marschall (Detroit: Wayne State University Press, 2000), 15.

7. In 1929 Ernst Bloch observed that "even in the town the soil has triumphed over motion"; this had been anticipated on Notgeld. Ernst Bloch, *Heritage of Our Times*, trans. Stephen Plaice and Neville Plaice (Oxford: Polity Press, 1991), 52.

8. "Romanticism always confuses the shamefulness of *huckstering the land* with the perfectly rational consequence, inevitable and desirable within the realm of private property, of *huckstering of private property* in land. In the first place, feudal landed property is already by its very nature huckstered land." Karl Marx, *Economic and Philosophic Manuscripts of 1844*, trans. Martin Milligan (Mineola, NY: Dover, 2007), 61. The social history of landscape began with John Barrell, *The Dark Side of the Landscape: The Rural Poor in English Painting 1730–1840* (Cambridge: Cambridge University Press, 1983). This approach has not to my knowledge been applied to the German landscape tradition.

9. Oswald Spengler, *The Decline of the West. Complete in One Volume*, trans. Charles Francis Atkinson (London: George Allen & Unwin, 1934), 505. Spengler's thought is an example of what Jeffrey Herf termed "reactionary modernism." Jeffrey Herf, *Reactionary Modernism: Technology, Culture, and Politics in Weimar and the Third Reich* (Cambridge: Cambridge University Press, 1984), 49–69.

10. Feldman, *The Great Disorder*, 604–606.

11. Ernst Jünger, *The Worker: Dominion and Form*, trans. Laurence Paul Hemming and Bogdan Costea (Evanston, IL: Northwestern University Press, 2017), 128.

12. Shell, *The Economy of Literature*, 64.

13. Manfred Wenzel, "Der Ilmenauer Bergbau und sein Einfluß auf Goethe als Dichter und Naturforscher," *Medizinhistorisches Journal* 22, no. 1 (1987), 3.

14. Kurt Tucholsky, "Berlin and the Provinces," in *The Weimar Republic Sourcebook*, ed. Anton Kaes, Martin Jay, and Edward Dimendberg (Berkeley: University of California Press, 1994), 418.

15. In Bavaria, to give one example, Marieluise Fleißer wrote a number of Heimat-themed plays that were later banned by the Nazis. On her work, see Elizabeth Boa and Rachel Palfreyman, *Heimat: A German Dream. Regional Loyalties and National Identity in German Culture, 1890–1990* (Oxford: Oxford University Press, 2000), 74–85.

16. Lion Feuchtwanger, *Success: Three Years in the Life of a Province*, trans. Willa and Edwin Muir (London: Martin Secker, 1930), 55.

17. Feuchtwanger, *Success*, 473.

18. The novel found favor with Goebbels; its skepticism regarding the republic can be regarded as opportunism on the part of an author whose own politics inclined toward the SDP.

19. Hans Fallada, *Wolf among Wolves*, trans. Philip Owens (New York: Melville House, 2010), 395.

20. Fallada, *Wolf among Wolves*, 461.

21. Feldman, *The Great Disorder*, 701.

22. As the prominent critic Paul Westheim put it, "Landscape painters in the sense of Constable,

Claude, or van der Meer; the exclusive landscape painter as a species, characteristic manifestation of Impressionism, the Fontainebleau School or the Netherlandish artists of the seventeenth century, no longer exists among the bearers of the new artistic attitude." Paul Westheim, "Die Landschaft," *Das Kunstblatt* 4 (1920), 4. Though he discounts the expressionists as not being "pure" landscape painters, there were some notable exceptions who continued making landscapes into the 1920s, especially Nolde. Schwitters also continued to paint landscapes in a post-impressionist style throughout his career, and even exhibited two of these in his retrospective *Große Merzausstellung* of 1927.

23. On one of the most popular *Heimatbücher*, see Matthew Jefferies, "Die Schöne Heimat? Depictions of Germany in a Popular Photobook from the Second Empire to the Federal Republic," *New German Critique* 46, no. 2 (2019), 35–63.

24. Anton Kaes, "Die ökonomische Dimension der Literatur: Zum Strukturwandel der Institution Literatur in der Inflationszeit (1918–1923)," in *Konsequenzen der Inflation*, ed. Gerald D. Feldman (Berlin: Kolloqium Verlag, 1989), 327.

25. A section of Ostwald's *Moral History of the Inflation*, titled "Paradise of Foreigners," is devoted to this fear. Hans Ostwald, *Sittengeschichte der Inflation* (Berlin: Neufeld & Henius, 1931), 99–108.

26. In case the identity of this creature remains obscure, it should be noted that reactionary ideologues of the period often described "international capital" as a vampire; this will be discussed further in the third chapter. See, for instance, the influential 1919 text by Gottfried Feder, "Das Manifest zur Brechung der Zinsknechtschaft," *Wikisource*, https://de.wikisource.org/wiki/Das_Manifest_zur_Brechung_der_Zinsknechtschaft (accessed July 21, 2022).

27. This reading is informed by (but ultimately diametrically opposed to) that of Spyros Papapetros, in "Malicious Houses: Animation, Animism, Animosity in German Architecture and Film—From Mies to Murnau," *Grey Room* 20 (2005), 6–37. Papapetros argues that the houses are mimicked by the vampire in his final gesture, and have been irretrievably corrupted by this association.

28. The conservative tenor of the script can be attributed in part to the contributions of Thea von Harbou, a writer and national conservative who produced many screenplays for her partner Fritz Lang, including for his film *Metropolis*. Earlier in her career she had published nationalistic novels, including *Der unsterbliche Acker: Ein Kriegsroman* (The immortal soil: a war novel) in 1915. She later became a Nazi.

29. Kemp, *Wir haben ja alle Deutschland nicht gekannt*, 298.

30. Spengler, *The Decline of the West*, 485.

31. Spengler, *The Decline of the West*, 506.

32. Marx and Engels, "Manifesto of the Communist Party," in *The Marx-Engels Reader*, ed. Robert C. Tucker (New York: W. W. Norton, 1978), 476. Georg Simmel, *The Philosophy of Money*, trans. Tom Bottomore, David Frisby, and Kaethe Mengelberg (Abingdon, UK: Routledge, 2011), 179.

33. Feuchtwanger, *Success*, 473.

34. They are identified as such by Xiaojue Michelle Zhu, "A Re-Examination of the City-Country Dichotomy in Weimar Germany: Georg Scholz's Industrial Farmers (1920)," *Immediations* 18 (2021), https://courtauld.ac.uk/research/research-resources/publications/immeditations-postgraduate-journal/immediations-online/immediations-no-18-2021/a-re-examination-of-the-city-country-dichotomy-in-weimar-germany-georg-scholzs-industrial-farmers-1920/ (accessed April 4, 2022).

35. The artist was hardly alone in struggling with the representation of an entirely new type of warfare: debates raged in the United Kingdom, for example, regarding the appropriate means for memorializing the Great War in its immediate aftermath. One particularly heated skirmish concerned the equestrian statue of Earl Haig on Whitehall, the winning design for which critics felt was too idealized, resulting in an uneasy and widely disliked compromise.

36. "Ostpreußens Notgeld," *Berliner Börsen-Zeitung*, Morgen Ausgabe, February 16, 1929, 3.

37. Kemp, *Wir haben ja alle Deutschland nicht gekannt*, 11.

38. Kracauer, "Notgeld und Kleingeld," 709–711, first published in the *Frankfurter Zeitung*, October 12, 1923.

39. Feldman, *The Great Disorder*, 731.

40. Gilles Deleuze and Félix Guattari, *A Thousand Plateaus: Capitalism and Schizophrenia*, trans. Brian Massumi (Minneapolis: University of Minnesota Press, 1987), 88.

41. Deleuze and Guattari, *A Thousand Plateaus*, 82.

42. Deleuze and Guattari, *A Thousand Plateaus*, 88.

43. Nolde's racism was partly directed against what he perceived to be the slights of the art establishment, although he was in fact increasingly successful in these years, receiving the rare tribute, for a contemporary artist, of a room dedicated to his work at the Kronprinzenpalais in Berlin.

44. Ulrich Gerster, "Kontinuität und Bruch. Georg Schrimpf zwischen Räterepublik und NS-Herrschaft," *Zeitschrift für Kunstgeschichte* 63, no. 4 (2000), 532–557.

45. Bloch, *Heritage of Our Times*, 48.

Chapter 2: Work

1. The other notes in the series make the designer's rejection of the republic clear. In 1919, Freikorps groups had been enlisted to help fight the Red Army back from the Baltic; they then ran amok and attempted to seize control of Latvia. When the government disbanded the Freikorps in 1920—a decision that precipitated the Kapp Putsch—some of their former members settled, ostensibly as civilian communities, in places like Lockstedt. These rural settlements were often used to hide armaments in preparation for insurrection—one such cache was discovered in Lockstedt in 1920—so the implication that swords have been beaten into plowshares on this note is almost certainly sarcastic. "Lockstedter Lager. Eine Notgeld-Moritat," *DENK MAL!*, https://www.denk-mal-gegen-krieg.de/assets/Uploads/Lockstedter-Lager-eine-Notgeld-Moritat-uberarbeitete-Fassung.pdf (accessed July 9, 2022). The trope of the sower working against a setting sun recurs frequently on Notgeld; it has a long history, explored by Susen Krüger Saß in "Propaganda," in *Handbuch der politischen Ikonographie*, ed. Uwe Fleckner, Martin Warnke, and Hendrik Ziegler (Munich: Beck, 2011), 266–272.

2. Alex Potts, "Labour," in *Kunst und Politik: Jahrbuch der Guernica-Gesellschaft. Schwerpunkt: Keywords for Marxist Art History Today* (Göttingen: Vandenhoeck & Ruprecht, 2019), 73.

3. Fritz Ringer, *The Decline of the German Mandarins: The German Academic Community, 1890–1933* (Cambridge, MA: Harvard University Press, 1969), 64.

4. Benjamin wrote the first text that would become his book *One-Way Street*, "Imperial Panorama," during the hyperinflation year, 1923: "Stable conditions need by no means be pleasant conditions, and even before the war there were strata for whom stabilized conditions were stabilized wretchedness." Benjamin, *Selected Writings*, 1:451.

5. Siegfried Kracauer, *Die Angestellten* (1930); translated as *The Salaried Masses*, but more literally "the employees." By the time Kracauer had written the reports on which the book was based, in 1929, the inflation was a thing of the past for this class; however, the crash was just around the corner.

6. The history of this discourse is traced in Joan Campbell, *Joy in Work, German Work: The National Debate, 1800–1945* (Princeton, NJ: Princeton University Press, 1989).

7. Horst Gies, *Richard Walther Darré: Der "Reichsbauernführer," Die nationalsozialistische "Blut und Boden"-Ideologie und Hitlers Machteroberung* (Vienna: Böhlau Verlag, 2019), 118–126.

8. The iconography of work is relatively unremarked in literature on the art of the Weimar Republic. Widdig's book contains a chapter titled "Visions of Work," but as is the case with his analysis as a whole, this is more concerned with texts than with visual sources. It also focuses on the industrialist Hugo Stinnes, rather than on workers themselves. Widdig, *Culture and Inflation in Weimar Germany*, 134–165. The question is discussed in more depth in W. L. Guttsmann, *Art for the Workers: Ideology and the Visual Arts in Weimar Germany* (Manchester: Manchester University Press, 1997).

9. Guttsmann refers to such figures as the "giant proletariat" and speculates that they derived from Daumier. Guttsmann, *Art for the Workers*, 46.

10. In Guttsmann's view, "radicalism in political and economic thinking goes hand in hand with conservative aesthetics." Here he is referring specifically to the readers of prewar socialist publications, but he asserts that this situation continued throughout the republic. Guttsmann, *Art for the Workers*, 33. Elsewhere he discusses the SDP's agitational imagery of the late nineteenth century, asking why "the portrayal of the workers in the 1 May broadsheets should so frequently present an antiquated picture of the social character of the working class," focusing on artisanal rather than industrial labor. He suggests that these anachronistic images may have confirmed "the value of virtues often associated with artisans, namely honesty, sobriety, pride in workmanship and the pursuit of knowledge," adding, "it is likely that many of the bourgeois artists who drew for the socialist press saw the organized working class in that light" (39–40).

11. Paul Brandt, *Schaffende Arbeit und bildende Kunst. Vom Mittelalter bis zur Gegenwart*, 2 vols. (Leipzig: Alfred Kröner, 1928), 2:14.

12. Bloch, *Heritage of Our Times*, 102.

13. Archiv für Bildende Kunst, *Conrad Felixmüller: Werke und Dokumente* (Nürnberg: Germanisches Nationalmuseum, 1981), 79.

14. The comment appears in Einstein's pioneering 1926 survey of modern art, *Kunst des 20. Jahrhunderts*; cited in Charles W. Haxthausen, "Bloody Serious: Two Texts by Carl Einstein," *October* 105 (2003), 115.

15. These have recently been discussed by Michael Powers in "Red Fairy Tales and Non-Anthropocentric Solidarity: Hermynia zur Mühlen, Ernst Bloch, and Siegfried Kracauer," *German Quarterly* 94, no. 2 (2021), 208–218.

16. Hermynia zur Mühlen and George Grosz, *Was Peterchens Freunde Erzählen: Märchen* (Berlin: Malik Verlag, 1921), 3–7.

17. Brandt adds: "In their place the bold ingenuity of engineers triumphed." Brandt, *Schaffende Arbeit und bildende Kunst*, 2:332. Brandt's two-volume study grew out of a 1913 pamphlet on the history of representations of work, which had presumably been published in response to the Krupp exhibition.

18. Brecht, "Der Dreigroschenprozess," cited in Carl Gelderloos, "Simply Reproducing Reality—: Brecht, Benjamin, and Renger-Patzsch on Photography," *German Studies Review* 37, no. 3 (2014), 554.

19. The same image was reprinted in *Das Gesicht der herrschenden Klasse*, where it is paired with a drawing of reveling bourgeois. Their captions respectively read "Where the dividends come from" and "Where they go."

20. A Krupp internal memo from 1923 remarks: "That the production of emergency money as a consequence of the inflation brought the firm a not inconsequential profit should not be ignored." Feldman, *The Great Disorder*, 786.

21. Eric Rowley, *Hyperinflation in Germany: Perceptions of a Process* (Aldershot, UK: Scolar Press, 1994), 128–129.

22. "Meunier's idealized coal miner and his realism dovetail with a bourgeois ideology that dealt with the then still visible proletariat by certifying that it too was beautiful humanity and noble nature." Theodor W. Adorno, *Aesthetic Theory*, trans. Robert Hullot-Kentor (London: Continuum, 2004), 301.

23. The notion that labor is the source of wealth was not without its detractors, even on the left. Marx's "Critique of the Gotha Programme" begins by rejecting the opening line of that document: "Labour is not the source of all wealth. Nature is just as much the source of use values (and it is surely of such that material wealth consists!)." Karl Marx and Friedrich Engels, *Selected Works*, vol. 3 (Moscow: Progress Publishers, 1970), 13.

24. The Nazis eventually soldered this connection by making "Joy in Work a national objective, thereby completing the identification between Arbeitsfreude and Deutsche Arbeit." Campbell, *Joy in Work, German Work*, 4–5.

25. Widdig, *Culture and Inflation in Weimar Germany*, 142.

26. Joan Weinstein, *The End of Expressionism: Art and the November Revolution in Germany, 1918–19* (Chicago: University of Chicago Press, 1989), 32.

27. Ida Katherine Rigby, "German Expressionist Political Posters 1918–1919: Art and Politics, a Failed Alliance," *Art Journal* 44, no. 1 (1984), 38.

28. Hadank would design an official 100-mark note for the Reichsbank in 1920; however, this featured not workers but the famous Bamberger Reiter, a sculpture of a knight from Bamberg Cathedral. The sculpture was a touchstone of nationalist art history.

29. This is probably a reference to the hammer-wielding mascot of popular publisher Langewiesche, which bore the slogan *Arbeiten und nicht verzweifeln* (Work and don't doubt). It is a loose translation of a line from Thomas Carlyle, whose encomiums of labor deeply influenced German ideas on the subject in the nineteenth century. The phrase is redeployed with satirical vim by Grosz on the cover of the fourth issue of *Der blutige Ernst* from 1919, where it is used to caption an image of profiteer, the subject of the issue, together with a sex worker; these paragons of idleness (according to Grosz's moralizing iconography) are surrounded by collaged advertisements for bars, casinos, and cabarets.

30. "Nr. 378. Sitzung des Reichsbankkuratoriums: Wirtschaftliche und finanzielle Lage des Reiches," Bundesarchiv (Historische Kommission bei der Bayerischen Akademie der Wissenschaften und das Bundesarchiv, 1922), https://www.bundesarchiv.de/aktenreichskanzlei/1919-1933/0000/wir/wir2p/kap1_1/kap2_143/para3_1.html (accessed July 15, 2022).

31. The most radical contemporaneous theoretical attempt in this direction—if almost totally lacking in influence—was made by Lu Märten. Rejecting the SPD's conservative cultural politics (which argued for the continued relevance of the bourgeois canon), she attempted to reconceive artistic labor as another form of work: "art was not the most accomplished manifestation of form; rather, it belonged to a 'form-giving potentiality' (which she called 'work') that had once been socially comprehensive but had atrophied under conditions of industrial capitalism. Art thus constituted merely a degraded state of form, and the contemporary artist a 'leftover worker of form.' … 'There is no such thing as proletarian art,' because once artistic labor is disentangled from its bourgeois cultivation, the need to produce art will cease to exist and its categorical distinction from proletarian labor, and the proletariat's isolation as unfree laborer, will no longer be tenable." Jenny Nachtigall and Kerstin Stakemeier, "Lu Märten: An Introduction to Four Texts," *October* 178 (2021), 3–14.

32. Walter Gropius, "Program of the Staatliches Bauhaus in Weimar," *The Weimar Republic Sourcebook*, ed. Anton Kaes, Martin Jay, and Edward Dimendberg (Berkeley: University of California Press, 1994), 435.

33. Walter Gropius, "Address to the Students of the Staatliche Bauhaus, Held on the Occasion of the Yearly Exhibition of Student Work in 1919," in Hans Wingler, *The Bauhaus: Weimar, Dessau, Berlin, Chicago* (Cambridge, MA: MIT Press, 1978), 36.

34. This situation has been described by Dennis Crockett in *German Post-Expressionism: The Art of the Great Disorder, 1918–1924* (University Park: Pennsylvania State University Press, 1999), 25–33.

35. The author makes this comment in the context of a book on the distress of the intellectuals, observing that artists were to some degree exempt from the immiseration of this class. Bruno Rauecker, *Die Proletarisierung der geistigen Arbeiter* (Munich, 1920), cited in O. K. Werckmeister, *The Making of Paul Klee's Career, 1914–1920* (Chicago: University of Chicago Press, 1989), 226.

36. For an overview of the expressionists' print production and the vagaries of the art market, see Starr Figura, "German Expressionism: The Graphic Impulse," in *German Expressionism: The Graphic Impulse*, ed. Libby Hruska (New York: Museum of Modern Art, 2011), 10–35.

37. Benjamin attempted to make money in 1922–1923 by buying and selling rare books, with some limited success; one book that he had purchased in Heidelberg for 35 marks was resold in Berlin for 600. Howard Eiland and Michael W. Jennings, *Walter Benjamin: A Critical Life* (Cambridge, MA: Belknap Press of Harvard University Press, 2014), 173.

38. Marina Vishmidt, *Speculation as a Mode of Production: Forms of Value Subjectivity in Art and Capital* (Leiden: Brill, 2019).

39. Goux, *Symbolic Economies*, 113.

40. Rosalind E. Krauss, *The Picasso Papers* (New York: Farrar, Straus and Giroux, 1998); George Baker, *The Artwork Caught by the Tail: Francis Picabia and Dada in Paris* (Cambridge, MA: MIT Press, 2007). More historiographically scrupulous investigations of this question have been made by Christoph Zeller, "Aus Müll Gold Gesponnen: Kurt Schwitters' Merzkunst und die Inflation," *German Studies Review* 31, no. 2 (2008), 345–367; Arndt Niebisch, "Excess-Zero: Dada and the Logic of Inflation," *Rheinsprung 11: Zeitschrift für Bildkritik*, 2013, https://rheinsprung11.unibas.ch/ausgabe-05/thema/excess-zero-dada-and-the-logic-of-inflation/ (accessed January 7, 2020); and Kurt Beals, "Dada Futures: Inflation, Speculation, and Uncertainty in Der Dada," *Transit* 10, no. 2 (2016).

41. Hugo Ball was of course a keen observer of political events, but even Arndt Niebisch admits that "a comparison between Dada and the time of inflation thus faces the problem that Dada preceded the hyperinflation and was not a product of it." However, he goes on to speak of "structural identities" with regard to meaninglessness; this raises the same problem vis-à-vis the nature of this identity and, I would argue, is by no means adequate to encompass the various ways in which the Dadaists employed the crisis of value as a field of activity. Niebisch, "Excess-Zero."

42. Goux, *Symbolic Economies,* 113.

43. This observation is not novel: see, for instance, Fredric Jameson, *The Prison House of Language: A Critical Account of Structuralism and Russian Formalism* (Princeton, NJ: Princeton University Press, 1972), 180–185. In 1972—the year after the "Nixon shock"—Baudrillard published *For a Critique of the Political Economy of the Sign*, in which he argues that the commodity and the sign share the same structure. It is a central tenet of neoliberal economics that money is a language: "We must look at the price system as such a mechanism for communicating information if we want to understand its real function." F. A. Hayek, "The Use of Knowledge in Society," *American Economic Review* 35, no. 4 (1945), 526.

44. Goux, *Symbolic Economies*, 113.

45. This is a paraphrase of T. J. Clark's well-known definition of the social history of art from the introduction to his book *Image of the People: Gustave Courbet and the 1848 Revolution* (London: Thames and Hudson, 1973), 13.

46. Curt Glaser, "Vom Graphik-Sammeln," *Das Kunstblatt* 3 (1919), 328–330.

47. The magazine *Kunstchronik und Kunstmarkt* was, unsurprisingly, relaxed about this turn of events. In a 1923 article on print collecting, the journal's editor, art historian Alfred Kuhn, remarked that "one may find it deplorable that today the artwork is treated like a share, that large numbers of people put their money into it, we can say calmly, for speculative reasons. But one must accept this fact, it is fruitless to wrap oneself in Cato's cloak and preach morality." Alfred Kuhn, "Über das Sammeln von Graphik," *Kunstchronik und Kunstmarkt* 30 (1923), 594.

48. George Grosz, "Statt einer Biographie," *Der Gegner* 1, no. 3 (1920), 68.

49. An advertisement in a 1921 issue of *Das Kunstblatt* lists his portfolio *Das Gesicht der Herrshenden Klasse* as costing six marks as a pamphlet, and 150 marks in a numbered and signed edition of 50. As well as appealing to the bourgeois collector, Grosz was directly supported by millionaire Felix Weill, who also funded Malik Verlag and the Institute for Social Research in Frankfurt. Rolf Wiggershaus, *The Frankfurt School: Its History, Theories and Political Significance*, trans. Michael Robertson (Cambridge: Polity Press, 1993), 13.

50. Paul Westheim, "Kunst als Sachwert," *Das Kunstblatt* 7, 1923, 231.

51. Shell, *The Economy of Literature*, 86–87.

52. Max Herrmann-Neisse, "Berliner Theaterwirtschaft," *Die Neue Schaubühne* 3, no. 4 (1921), 75; cited in Anton Kaes, "Die ökonomische Dimension der Literatur: Zum Strukturwandel der Institution Literatur in der Inflationszeit (1918–1923)," in *Konsequenzen der Inflation*, ed. Gerald D. Feldman (Berlin: Kolloqium Verlag, 1989), 321.

53. Metaphysical claims continue throughout the piece: "The Chinese have their Tao and the Indians their

Brama. Dada is more than Tao and Brama. Dada doubles your income." This mixture of religious and financial terminology anticipates the theme of Benjamin's unpublished fragment, "Capitalism as Religion," which I discuss in the third chapter. Zentralamt der Dadaismus, "Legen Sie Ihr Geld in dada an!," *Der Dada* 1 (1919), 7.

54. F. Pinner, *Deutsche Wirtschaftsführer* (Charlottenberg, 1924), 225, cited in Martin H. Geyer, *Verkehrte Welt. Revolution, Inflation und Moderne: München 1914–1924* (Göttingen: Vandenhoeck & Ruprecht, 1998), 245.

55. Serner had plagiarized the majority of his doctoral thesis, and later used his ill-gotten qualification to falsify a medical letter exempting Franz Jung from military service. He fled to Switzerland to escape prosecution for this fraud.

56. Walter Serner, "Last Loosening Manifesto," in *Blago Bung Blago Bung Bosso Bataka!: First Texts of German Dada by Hugo Ball, Richard Huelsenbeck, Walter Serner*, trans. Malcolm Green (London: Atlas, 1995), 153.

57. Kurt Schwitters, "Die Merzmalerei," *Der Sturm* 10, no. 4 (July 1919), 61; cited in *Dada: Zurich, Berlin, Hannover, Cologne, New York, Paris*, ed. Leah Dickerman (Washington, DC: National Gallery of Art, 2005), 161.

58. Biographical notice in *Sturm Bilderbuch*, no. 4 (1921), cited in Zeller, "Aus Müll Gold gesponnen," 345–367.

59. Zeller, "Aus Müll Gold gesponnen," 358. He cites here from Schwitters's "Open Letter to Mr Martin Frehsee" (1919), Kurt Schwitters, *Das literarische Werk*, ed. Friedrich Lach, 5 vols. (Cologne: DuMont Buchverlag, 1981), 5:47–48.

60. Adorno, *Aesthetic Theory*, 297.

61. Dorothea Dietrich, *The Collages of Kurt Schwitters: Tradition and Innovation* (Cambridge: Cambridge University Press, 1993), 142–144. Dietrich translates the title as "Vomit Picture."

62. One other Merzbild incorporating money has not been discussed here. The elaborate collage *Plan of Love*, which Schwitters reworked between 1919 and 1923, includes a *Dahrlehnkassenscheine* at the top of the image, alongside the details for a doctor specializing in venereal disease. This is a jaded view of romance, for which a dubious financial instrument sets the tone.

63. Kate Steinitz, *Kurt Schwitters: A Portrait from Life* (Berkeley: University of California Press, 1968), 38–39.

64. Cited in Maynes, "Making Money," 696. Maynes does not mention *Der Kenner nimmt* in her discussion, focusing instead on a later work by Schwitters.

65. Elizabeth Otto, "A 'Schooling of the Senses': Post-Dada Visual Experiments in the Bauhaus Photomontages of Laszlo Moholy-Nagy and Marianne Brandt," *New German Critique* 36 (2009), 94.

66. Raoul Hausmann also made two works around 1920 that incorporate money: *The Art Critic* and *ABCD*. In the former, a shard cut from a Notgeld note is embedded in the eponymous critic's neck, as if he had been stabbed in the back by his own love of money. By contrast, *ABCD* shows a photograph of the artist, open-mouthed and surrounded by collaged elements. These include a reiterated penetration motif, the most explicit of these being a gynecological diagram showing fingers being inserted into a uterus. Above this, a phallus penetrates a giant zero, symbol of the inflation; between the two lies a Czech banknote, which does not seem to be standing in the way of this union. This conjunction is echoed once more by a piece of paper covered with dots, somewhat resembling a galaxy, which threatens to penetrate Hausmann's mouth; however, he grips the letters ABCD between his teeth, the alphabet—poetry, in the mouth of the poet—acting as a prophylactic against the cosmic. The photograph of Hausmann's open mouth was reproduced in the July 1923 edition of *Die Pleite*, retitled "Arbeiter heraus mit Euren Devisen!" (Workers, out with your maxims/banknotes!). This makes explicit the image's equation of language, specifically, the empty slogans of the republic, and money, both being rendered as nonsensical here.

67. On *Ersatzkultur* and Schwitters's work, see Maria Makela, "Making Lemonade out of Lemons: Merz and Material Poverty," *Art History* 42, no. 4 (2019), 652–677.

68. Brigid Doherty, "The Work of Art and the Problem of Politics in Berlin Dada," *October* 105 (2003), 73–92.

69. This viewpoint has recently been elaborated as the source of art's value: "The high prices of art derive from the high status of the work within the discourse of art." Dave Beech, *Art and Value: Art's Economic Exceptionalism in Classical, Neoclassical and Marxist Economics* (Chicago: Haymarket, 2015), 312.

70. In a riposte to a critical review by Curt Glaser in the *Berliner Börsen-Kurier*, Kurt Schwitters wrote that he would incorporate both underwear and the critic's words into an artwork: "The artist creates through selection, distribution, and deformation of the material. (Including petticoats.) If, for example, I used as material Mr Kurt Glaser, a pair of lady's underpants and a Berliner Börsenkurier ... I would dissect and deform the old man and the lady's underpants and distribute them across the picture surface according to the laws of artistic logic. I would therefore use Mr Kurt Glaser as beautiful and expressive form." "Berliner BörsenKukukunst" (1920), in Schwitters, *Das literarische Werk*, 5:50–51.

71. Georg Scholz, *Schriften, Briefe, Dokumente*, ed. Karl-Ludwig Hofmann and Ursula Merkel (Karlsruhe: Info Verlag, 2018), 134.

72. In 1921, Schiestl wrote in response to an inquiry from a potential customer, "I am snowed under with Notgeld orders." He informed the same customer that he charged 600 marks for a two-sided note, and for more elaborate designs, 500 marks per side. As well as a direct fee from the customer, Schiestl also received 0.3 percent of the printer's earnings, and 3.3 percent of the issuing body's earnings. Hans-Joachim Wirthmann, *Notgeldscheine von Heinz Schiestl* (Lohr am Main: Geschichts- und Museumsverein Lohr am Main, 2007), 31–32.

73. Hermine C. Schuetzinger, "Künstlerisches Kriegsnotgeld," *Das Plakat* 10, no. 1 (1919), 61.

74. Schwartz, *The Werkbund*, 17.

75. "Das verschwundene Porzellangeld," *Glückstadter Fortuna* 182, no. 15 (January 19, 1921), 2.

76. Warburg Institute Archive, WIA GC/24861. Warburg wrote to his brother Max to ask for money for the album; when he demurred, he turned to Carl Melchior instead, arguing that it was "not only a document of the history of paper money, but also of German graphic art." Warburg Institute Archive, WIA GC/31101.

77. Kurt Biging, *Geldscheine in Halle an der Saale 1916–1992* (Halle: Mitteldeutscher Verlag, 2003), 42.

78. "The financial resources obtained via Notgeld issues were partly used to purchase supplies related to the city works, and thereby maintained their value." From a 1930 review of the inflationary period conducted by Itzehoe's municipal government, cited in Wolfgang Reschke, "Notgeld in Kreis Steinburg von 1914 bis 1923," in *Steinburger Jahrbuch 1986: Geldgeschichte, Wirtschaft und Sparkassenwesen*, ed. Alexander Ritter and Peter Fischer (Itzehoe: Heimatverbandes für den Kreis Steinberg, 1985), 33.

79. Kai Lindman, *Celler Notgeld. Notgeldscheine des 20. Jahrhunderts in Stadt und Kreis Celle* (Celle: Shriftenreihe des Stadtarchivs Celle und des Bomann-Museums, 1992), 45.

80. Uebe, "Das neue Notgeld der Stadt Osterfeld," *Das Notgeld* 4, nos. 9–10 (1922), 204.

81. Uwe Bronnert, "Kein Notgeld, sondern Kunstblätter!," *Geldscheine-Online*, 2020, https://www.geldscheine-online.com/post/kein-notgeld-sondern-kunstblätter (accessed June 27, 2022).

82. "They were no longer paintings, but documents." Yve-Alain Bois, "El Lissitzky: Radical Reversibility," *Art in America* 76 (1988), 174.

Chapter 3: Spooks

1. Cited in Franz Wegener, *Der Alchemist Franz Tausend: Alchemie und Nationalsozialismus* (Gladbeck: Kulturfoerderverein Ruhrgebiet, 2013), 69, 50.

2. Cited in Wegener, *Der Alchemist Franz Tausend*, 88.

3. Dietrich Stoltzenberg, *Fritz Haber: Chemist, Nobel Laureate, German, Jew* (Philadelphia: Chemical Heritage Press, 2004), 241–248.

4. Siegfried Kracauer, "Wiederkehr der Toten?," in *Werke*, vol. 5.1: *Essays, Feuilletons, Rezensionen. 1906–1923* (Berlin: Suhrkamp, 2011), 691.

5. Bloch, *Heritage of Our Times*, 173.

6. The extent of Nazi esotericism is a matter of long-standing debate. For a recent overview, see Eric Kurlander, "Hitler's Monsters: The Occult Roots of Nazism and the Emergence of the Nazi 'Supernatural Imaginary,'" *German History* 30, no. 4 (2012), 528–549. On Hitler as a "wandering preacher," see Ulrich Linse, *Barfüssige Propheten: Erlöser der zwanziger Jahre* (Berlin: Siedler, 1983), 38–43.

7. "From now on it was absolutely imperative to come to intellectual terms with the origin, character and perspective of capitalism. … The attitude to Marxism now changed as well. … A coarsely apodictic rejection of it appeared behind the times, not least because of the constantly growing might of the labour movement. A 'subtler' way of 'refuting' Marxism was called for. This went hand in hand with the equally necessary receptiveness to those of its elements which—in a distorted form, to be sure—seemed acceptable to bourgeois ideology." Georg Lukács, *The Destruction of Reason*, trans. Peter Palmer (London: Merlin Press, 1980), 602–603. Adorno described Lukács's broad-strokes teleology in withering terms: "It was doubtless his book *The Destruction of Reason* which revealed most clearly the destruction of Lukács's own. … He blithely ignores the fact that, unlike academic idealism, these schools were struggling against the very same reification in both thought and life of which Lukács too was a dedicated opponent." Theodor Adorno, "Reconciliation under Duress," in Georg Lukács et al., *Aesthetics and Politics* (London: Verso, 2006), 152. Nevertheless, in its outline of the consequences of Wilhelmine adoptions of the category of reification while jettisoning class analysis, Lukács's account remains (on this point) largely accurate. He had in any case already made very similar comments in his 1923 essay "Reification and the Consciousness of the Proletariat": "bourgeois attempts to comprehend the ideological phenomenon of reification … remain on the surface. … Indeed, they divorce these empty manifestations from their real capitalist foundation and make them independent and permanent by regarding them as the timeless model of human relations in general" Georg Lukács, *History and Class Consciousness: Studies in Marxist Dialectics*, trans. Rodney Livingstone (Cambridge, MA: MIT Press, 1971), 94–95.

8. Lukács, *History and Class Consciousness*, 168, 178.

9. On the prevalence of superstition during the war, see *Kasten 117. Aby Warburg und der Aberglaube im Ersten Weltkrieg*, ed. Gottfried Korff (Tübingen: Tübinger Vereiningung für Volkskunde, 2007).

10. Marx, *Capital*, 1:163, 165. As Gillian Rose points out, Fowkes translates *die phantasmagorische Form* as "the fantastic form"; however, phantasmagoria has the specific (and significant) meaning of a collection of phantom personifications. I have amended this citation accordingly. Gillian Rose, *The Melancholy Science: An Introduction to the Thought of Theodor W. Adorno* (London: Verso, 2014), 40.

11. Michael Heinrich, *An Introduction to the Three Volumes of Karl Marx's Capital*, trans. Alexander Loscasio (New York: Monthly Review Press, 2012), 71–72.

12. Arnold Zweig, "Der Angriff der Gegenstände," in *Essays. Zweiter Band. Krieg und Frieden* (Frankfurt: Fischer, 1987), 58.

13. On anti-Semitic Notgeld, see Liliane Weissberg, "Notenverkehr: Antisemitische Motive und Texte auf dem Notgeld der 20er Jahre," in *Abgestempelt! Antisemitische Bildpostkarten 1885–1945*, ed. Fritz Backhaus (Heidelberg: Umschau/Braus, 1999), 276–283, and *Der Jude nahm uns Silber, Gold und Speck …": Für politische Zwecke und antisemitische Propaganda genutzte Geldscheine in der Zeit der Weimarer Republik und des Dritten Reichs*, ed. Hans-Ludwig Grabowski and Wolfgang Haney (Regenstauf: Battenberg Gietl Verlag, 2015).

14. Thomas Mann, "Inflation: The Witches Sabbath: Germany 1923," *Encounter* 44, no. 2 (1974), 60–64.

15. Benjamin, *Selected Writings*, 1:451–452.

16. Benjamin, *Selected Writings*, 1:481.

17. Priddat, "'Geist der Ornamentik,'" 19–20.

18. Priddat, "'Geist der Ornamentik,'" 19.

19. We might find an answer in Adorno's rejection of Benjamin's "return of the archaic" as ahistorical. Theodor W. Adorno, "The

Idea of Natural-History," in Robert Hullot-Kentor, *Things beyond Resemblance: Collected Essays on Theodor W. Adorno* (New York: Columbia University Press, 2006), 266–267.

20. Priddat, "'Geist der Ornamentik,'" 27–28.

21. Priddat, "'Geist der Ornamentik,'" 30.

22. Benjamin, *Selected Writings*, 1:290.

23. Benjamin, *Selected Writings*, 1:288.

24. Benjamin, *Selected Writings*, 1:288.

25. Benjamin, *Selected Writings*, 1:289.

26. Benjamin, *Selected Writings*, 1:289.

27. Benjamin, *Selected Writings*, 1:289.

28. Gulbransson illustrated the first cover for *Simplicissimus* after it was *gleichgeschaltet*; the image was a racist one, but this was hardly unprecedented for the magazine, which had been filled with anti-Semitic and anti-Black images long before 1933.

29. Johann Wolfgang von Goethe, *Faust: Part One*, trans. David Luke (Oxford: Oxford University Press, 2008), xxviii.

30. Widdig, *Culture and Inflation in Weimar Germany*, 203–204.

31. On the contemporaneous discourse regarding fashion, see Schwartz, *The Werkbund*, 26–43.

32. Karl Marx, *Economic and Philosophic Manuscripts of 1844*, trans. Martin Milligan (Mineola, NY: Dover, 2007), 138.

33. This is the territory explored by Klaus Theweleit, *Male Fantasies*, vol. 1: *Women, Floods, Bodies, History*, trans. Chris Turner, Erica Carter, and Stephen Conway (Minneapolis: Minnesota University Press, 1987).

34. Silvia Federici, *Caliban and the Witch: Women, the Body and Primitive Accumulation* (London: Penguin, 2021), 188.

35. "In their preoccupation with witchcraft trials ... Himmler and other SS researches repeatedly lamented the medieval church's barbaric murder of women for expressing an alternative worldview, grounded in nature and folk traditions" (Kurlander, "Hitler's Monsters," 547).

36. Karl Marx, *Capital*, vol. 3, trans. David Fernbach (London: Penguin, 1991), 516–517, 517, 524.

37. Johann Wolfgang von Goethe, *Faust: Erster und zweiter Teil* (Munich: Deutsche Taschenbuch Verlag, 1997), 178.

38. Johann Wolfgang von Goethe, *Faust: Part Two*, trans. David Luke (Oxford: Oxford University Press, 1994), 29–30.

39. Heinz Schlaffer, *Faust zweiter Teil: Die Allegorie des 19. Jahrhunderts* (Stuttgart: Metzler, 1981), 51.

40. Schlaffer, *Faust zweiter Teil*, 80.

41. Schlaffer, *Faust zweiter Teil*, 60–61.

42. Walter Benjamin, *The Origin of German Tragic Drama*, trans. John Osborne (London: Verso, 2009), 166.

43. Hans Christoph Binswanger, *Money and Magic: A Critique of the Modern Economy in the Light of Goethe's Faust*, trans. J. E. Harrison (Chicago: University of Chicago Press, 1994), 33.

44. It has been suggested that the disappearing money conjured by witches in magical tales of the early modern period may reflect contemporaneous experiences of inflation. Federici, *Caliban and the Witch*, 186.

45. Joseph Vogl, *The Specter of Capital*, trans. Joachim Redner and Robert Savage (Stanford, CA: Stanford University Press, 2015).

46. Vogl, *The Specter of Capital*, 91. For a discussion of the more recent history of this identification, see Michele Battini, *Socialism of Fools: Capitalism and Modern Anti-Semitism*, trans. Noor Mazhar and Isabella Vergnano (New York: Columbia University Press, 2016).

47. "This frequent use of 'monstrous' supernatural imagery was atypical of mainstream Weimar parties, but quite common in Nazi political discourse." Kurlander, "Hitler's Monsters," 538.

48. Adolf Hitler, *Mein Kampf*, trans. Ralph Mannheim (Boston, 1943), 324; cited in Kurlander, "Hitler's Monsters," 537–538.

49. Hörisch, *Heads or Tails*, 27.

50. According to the article from which this information on Rüthnick is derived, his story had a surprising sequel. He turned against the National Socialists before the war, giving a speech in 1936 in which he praised Freud and Adler, and was dismissed from his position as a result. He later associated with the Bremen cell of the resistance group the Sozialistische Arbeiterpartei Deutschlands. Frank Hethey, "Ein Oberlehrer als Geheimbündler," *WK Geschichte*, 2021, https://wkge schichte.weser-kurier.de/ein

-oberlehrer-als-geheimbuend ler/ (accessed August 25, 2022).

51. The connections between expressionism and colonialism are political and material, as well as stylistic. Before the war two of the most prominent expressionist painters, Ernst Ludwig Kirchner and Emil Nolde, had separately traveled to the German colonies in order to make art. They were both there in a semiofficial capacity, in Nolde's case to produce ethnographic studies of the population for the use of the administration. *Kirchner and Nolde: Expressionism. Colonialism*, ed. Dorthe Aagesen, Anna Vestergaard Jørgensen, and Beatrice von Bormann (Munich: Hirmer, 2021).

52. Cited in Crockett, *German Post-Expressionism*, 28–29.

53. Max Weber, "Science as a Vocation," in *From Max Weber: Essays in Sociology*, ed. and trans. H. H. Gerth and C. Wright Mills (London: Routledge, 2009), 139.

54. Franz Marc, "Die neue Malerei," *Pan* 2, no. 16 (1912), 469.

55. "An important but little recognised topos of early expressionism—the anxious denial of any link between art and commerce." Sherwin Simmons, "Advertising Seizes Control of Life: Berlin Dada and the Power of Advertising," *Oxford Art Journal* 22, no. 1 (1999), 124.

56. On this subject, see Sherwin Simmons, "Kitsch oder Kunst? Kokoschka's *Der Sturm* and Commerce in Art," *Print Collector's Newsletter* 23, no. 5 (1992), 161–167.

57. Joan Weinstein, *The End of Expressionism: Art and the November Revolution in Germany, 1918–19* (Chicago: University of Chicago Press, 1989), 231.

58. Hanf later recalled that for his week of work he received a sum that, though nominally a good wage, was so devalued by the time he was paid that he could only rush to the tobacconist by the town hall and buy a dozen cigars with it; the town hall, meanwhile, made a profit of 1 million marks. *Alfred Hanf: Ein Erfurter Künstlerleben*, ed. Hans-Peter Brachmanski (Bad Langensalza: Verlag Rockstuhl, 2010), 18, 26.

59. *Das Notgeld* 4, no. 12 (June 15, 1922), 245.

60. Taut had commissioned the notes himself. He was shortly to force Tuch from his position when he reorganized the art school. Annegret Nippa, *Bruno Taut: Eine Dokumentation. Projekte—Texte—Mitarbeiter* (Magdeburg: Landeshauptstadt Magdeburg, 1995).

61. Wassily Kandinsky, *Über das Geistige in der Kunst* (Bern: Benteli Verlag, 2009), 26.

62. Bloch, *Heritage of Our Times*, 172.

63. Gustav Meyrink, *The Golem*, trans. Mike Mitchell (Sawtry: Dedalus, 1995), 55.

64. Spyros Papapetros, *On the Animation of the Inorganic: Art, Architecture, and the Extension of Life* (Chicago: University of Chicago Press, 2012).

65. Theodor W. Adorno, *Minima Moralia: Reflections on a Damaged Life*, trans. Edmund Jephcott (London: Verso, 2006), 239.

66. Bloch, *Heritage of Our Times*, 175. On Bloch's nonsimultaneity, see Frederic J. Schwartz, *Blind Spots: Critical Theory and the History of Art in Twentieth-Century Germany* (New Haven: Yale University Press, 2005), 103–105.

67. Adorno, *Minima Moralia*, 240–241.

68. Nele Heise, "Das Bauhaus in allen Taschen: Notgeldscheine als vorboten der neuen Typografie," in *Bauhaus-Kommunikation: Innovative Strategien im Umgang mit Medien, interner und externer Öffentlichkeit*, ed. Patrick Rössler (Berlin: Gebr. Mann Verlag, 2008), 265–280.

69. Gisbert Laube, *Der Reichskunstwart: Geschichte einer Kulturbehörde 1919–1933* (Frankfurt: Peter Lang, 1997), 87–97.

70. Edwin Redslob, "Banknoten-Stil," *Vossische Zeitung* (Berlin, March 4, 1921), 2.

71. "Das neue Papiergeld: Reichsbanknote und Geschmack," *Vossische Zeitung* (Berlin, February 12, 1921), Erste Beilage, 5–6.

72. Schwartz, *The Werkbund*, 17.

73. On the significance of the figure zero during the inflation, see Widdig, *Culture and Inflation in Weimar Germany*, 97–100.

74. Bloch, *Heritage of Our Times*, 199.

Chapter 4: Crisis

1. I am grateful to Johannes von Müller for proposing this term.

2. Eschle was a successful designer who went on to attain national prominence under the

National Socialists, when he designed propaganda posters and postage stamps commemorating the 1936 Olympic games.

3. Cited in Jochen Hörisch, *Heads or Tails*, 19.

4. *A Pleasant Vintage of Till Eulenspiegel*, trans. Paul Oppenheimer (Middletown, CT: Wesleyan University Press, 1972), 228–229.

5. In Priddat's view, the cornucopia symbolizes the idyll of trade depicted on nineteenth-century notes, where there is no action and certainly no industrial labor, with all of the social transformation the latter threatens; instead, there is "fortune from payout," in other words, self-producing capital. Priddat, "'Geist der Ornamentik,'" 30.

6. Fallada, *Wolf among Wolves*, 60.

7. Hugo Ball, *Critique of the German Intelligentsia*, trans. Brian L. Harris (New York: Columbia University Press, 1993), 31.

8. Ivan Goll, "Extracts from Ivan Goll, Sodom and Berlin (1929)," trans. Donald Nicholson-Smith, *The Brooklyn Rail*, 2006, https://brooklynrail.org/2006/02/fiction/extracts-from-ivan-goll-sodom-and-berlin-1929 (accessed March 10, 2022).

9. Erich Lauenburger, "Papiernot—Papierverschwendung," *Das Plakat* 10, no. 1 (1919), 90.

10. Steinitz, *Kurt Schwitters*, 38–39.

11. Klaus Theweleit, *Male Fantasies*, vol. 1: *Women, Floods, Bodies, History*, trans. Chris Turner, Erica Carter, and Stephen Conway (Minneapolis: Minnesota University Press, 1987), 398.

12. Manfred Mehl, *Deutsche Serienscheine von 1918–1922* (Regenstauf: Gietl Verlag, 1998), 11.

13. Mehl, *Deutsche Serienscheine von 1918–1922*, 11.

14. Mehl, *Deutsche Serienscheine von 1918–1922*, 12.

15. Kurt Biging, *Geldscheine in Halle an der Saale 1916–1992* (Halle: Mitteldeutscher Verlag, 2003), 11.

16. Simmel, *The Philosophy of Money*, 162.

17. Marx, *Capital*, 1:208.

18. The text on the postcard reads:

> Highly sought-after!
> Despite war and dereliction,
> Despite calamitous affliction,
> I'm sought with joyful predilection.
> Both sages and the ones that witter
> Dream about the Ducat sh ...

19. For a reading of other collages made by Schwitters and Moholy-Nagy that incorporate Notgeld, see Maynes, "Making Money," 696–698.

20. Anke te Heesen, *The Newspaper Clipping: A Modern Paper Object*, trans. Lori Lantz (Manchester: Manchester University Press, 2014), 126. For te Heesen, "The pieces of paper that recur in his work are examples of paper in motion: newspaper, transit passes, letters, envelopes, theatre and cinema tickets—in other words, paper that circulates. ... At the beginning of the twentieth century, paper itself had ... grown impatient and abandoned any claim to value for the ages" (173–174). Although she does not include money in her list of valueless paper, Schwitters's collage practice cannot be seen outside the context of its crisis.

21. Not without criticism. See, for instance, Otto Fenichel, "The Drive to Amass Wealth," *Psychoanalytic Quarterly* 7 (1938), 74.

22. Sigmund Freud, "Character and Anal Eroticism," in *Collected Papers*, vol. 2, trans. Joan Riviere (London: Hogarth, 1946), 45.

23. Gilles Deleuze and Félix Guattari, *Anti-Oedipus: Capitalism and Schizophrenia*, trans. Robert Hurley, Mark Seem, and Helen R. Lane (London: Athlone Press, 1984), 28–29.

24. "You introduce the category of production into desire: this seems to me of immense importance; for it is the only means to get out of the sterile parallelism Marx-Freud, Money-Excrement." So wrote Deleuze to Klossowski on reading the latter's book *Living Currency* in 1971; cited in Daniel W. Smith's introduction to Pierre Klossowski, *Living Currency*, trans. Nicolae Morar et al. (London: Bloomsbury Academic, 2017), 3.

25. "Marx ... begins in the bowels of the earth, as in the materialist bowels of proletarians." Bataille, *The Accursed Share*, 1:35.

26. Oskar Negt and Alexander Kluge, *History and Obstinacy*, trans. Richard Langston and others (New York: Zone Books, 2014), 134. Negt and Kluge had hinted, in fact, at the significance of toilet training for "the inculcation of

work discipline" in their earlier book, *Public Sphere and Experience: Toward an Analysis of the Bourgeois and Proletarian Public Sphere*, trans. Assenka Oksiloff, Jamie Owen Daniel, and Peter Labanyi (Minneapolis: University of Minnesota Press, 1993), 20.

27. In Derrida's account this is the aesthetic category of the *disgusting*, which, thanks to its unrepresentability, explodes the double structure of art-economy, both of which rely on representation. However, I want to move beyond the discursive arena to the body and base matter. Jacques Derrida, "Economimesis," trans. R. Klein, *Diacritics*, 11, no. 2 (1981), 2–25.

28. Schmitt introduced his concept of the state of emergency in his essay "On Dictatorship," which was published in the same year as Hablik's note: 1921.

29. Negt and Kluge, *History and Obstinacy*, 204–205. I am also reminded of an exchange I had with Kluge in 2014, in the course of which he suggested that the drowning of publisher Robert Maxwell was an act of suicide and thus a demonstration of the subversive power of the conscience. However, this was more likely an involuntary revenge of the cloacal, since, according to former employees, Maxwell was given to urinating from the roof of the *Mirror* building in London onto the heads of passers-by below. This propensity gives credence to the supposition that he fell off his yacht while urinating over the side, and also fits better with Kluge's own story regarding what we might call ethics and incontinence, of somatic revenge at the moment of danger.

30. Shannon Liao, "Amazon Warehouse Workers Skip Bathroom Breaks to Keep Their Jobs, Says Report," *The Verge*, 2018, https://www.theverge.com/2018/4/16/17242926/amazon-warehouse-jobs-worker-conditions-bathroom-breaks (accessed October 8, 2019); *No Relief: Denial of Bathroom Breaks in the Poultry Industry* (Oxfam America, 2016), https://www.oxfamamerica.org/static/media/files/No_Relief_Embargo.pdf.

31. Barbara Penner, *Bathroom* (London: Reaktion Books, 2013), 239–273.

32. Juan Goytisolo, *State of Siege*, trans. Helen Lane (London: Serpent's Tail, 2003), 28, 37.

33. On the dubious ambivalence of base materialist politics, see Benjamin Noys, "Georges Bataille's Base Materialism," *Cultural Values* 2, no. 4 (1998), 499–517.

34. "Paris pours twenty-four million francs a year into the water. That is no metaphor. She does so by day and by night, thoughtlessly and to no purpose. She does so through her entrails, that is to say, her sewers." Victor Hugo, *Les misérables*, trans. Norman Denny (London: Penguin, 1982), 1061.

35. John Bellamy Foster, "Marx's Theory of Metabolic Rift: Classical Foundations for Environmental Sociology," *American Journal of Sociology* 105, no. 2 (1999), 366–405.

36. Migge, "Das grüne Manifest," *Die Tat* 10, no. 2 (1918/1919), 915–916; cited in David H. Haney, *When Modern Was Green: Life and Work of Landscape Architect Leberecht Migge* (London: Routledge, 2010), 124–125.

37. Haney, *When Modern Was Green*, 144.

38. Bloch, *Heritage of Our Times*, 174.

39. Rudolf Steiner, "Agriculture Course, Lecture II," trans. George Adams, *Rudolf Steiner Archive*, 1924, https://rsarchive.org/Lectures/GA327/English/BDA1958/19240610p01.html (accessed September 15, 2022).

40. Benjamin also refers obliquely to the problem at the conclusion of the "Imperial Panorama" section of *One-Way Street*: "we are unable to make Mother Earth any gift of our own ... the earth will be impoverished and the land will yield bad harvests." Benjamin, *Selected Writings*, 1:455.

41. In his sole contribution to Taut's journal, Hablik speculates that, in the future, people will make "glass from earth! Producible at every level of transparency and brilliance via a new smelting process, producible in every color!" Wenzel Hablik, "Die freitragende Kuppel," *Frühlicht* 3 (1921/1922), 175.

42. *The Crystal Chain Letters: Architectural Fantasies by Bruno Taut and His Circle*, ed. and trans. Iain Boyd Whyte (Cambridge, MA: MIT Press, 1985), 28, 133.

43. Whyte, *The Crystal Chain Letters*, 138.

44. Whyte, *The Crystal Chain Letters*, 51.

45. As such, it recalls Marx's vision of communism: "association reestablishes, now on a rational basis, no longer mediated by serfdom, overlordship and the silly mysticism of property, the intimate ties of man with the earth." But there is a crucial difference: Hablik's is a solitary shitter. Karl Marx, *Economic and Philosophic Manuscripts of 1844*, trans. Martin Milligan (Mineola, NY: Dover, 2007), 64.

46. John Bellamy Foster and Brett Clark, "The Robbery of Nature," *Monthly Review*, July 1, 2018, https://monthlyreview.org/2018/07/01/the-robbery-of-nature/ (accessed August 28, 2019).

47. Marx, *Capital*, 1:229. Seen in this light, and in view of the metabolic closure described above, Hablik's scatology is in fact far from being Bataillean, since for Bataille base matter was intended to prevent this reversion to the ideal, and, furthermore, his notion of nonproductive expenditure was fundamentally opposed to the conservation of energy.

48. Dave Beech, *Art and Value: Art's Economic Exceptionalism in Classical, Neoclassical and Marxist Economics* (Chicago: Haymarket, 2015), 12.

49. Martha Rosler, "Culture Class: Art, Creativity, Urbanism, Part II," *e-Flux*, March 2011, https://www.e-flux.com/journal/23/67813/culture-class-art-creativity-urbanism-part-ii/ (accessed October 29, 2019).

50. "Verschiedenes Geld," *Itzehoer Nachrichtung*, April 21, 1921, 2.

51. Denis Hollier, *Against Architecture: The Writings of Georges Bataille*, trans. Betsy Wing (Cambridge, MA: MIT Press, 1989), 114.

52. For a concise critique of this position in the realm of media theory, see Ben Kafka, "Review: Jussi Parikka's *Geology of Media*," *Artforum*, November 2015. On art historical new materialisms as a revival of fin-de-siècle vitalism, see Jenny Nachtigall, "Life," in *Kunst und Politik: Jahrbuch der Guernica-Gesellschaft, 21. Keywords for Marxist Art History Today* (Göttingen: Vandenhoeck & Ruprecht, 2019), 77–86. For a more general refutation of "object-oriented ontology," see Andrew Cole, "Those Obscure Objects of Desire," *Artforum* 53, no. 318 (2015), 318–323.

53. Alexander Friebel, "Ohne Papier keine Zeitung: Die Erfindung des Holzschliffpapiers als Meilenstein in der Entwicklung des Deutschen Pressewesens," *Jahrbuch für Kommunikationsgeschichte* 3 (2001), 144–145.

54. Feldman, *The Great Disorder*, 719.

55. Simmel, *The Philosophy of Money*, 56.

56. Herman Melville, *Billy Budd, Sailor and Selected Tales* (Oxford: Oxford University Press, 2009), 90.

57. Marx, *Capital*, 1:205.

58. This is especially important today, as the media dissolve into supposed immateriality—while we view them on devices made from materials dredged from toxic sludge by children.

Epilogue: Necrometabolism

1. On Trinkaus, see *Karl Hermann Trinkaus: Bauhaus—Der neue Mensch*, ed. Alfred Weidinger, Marcus Andrew Hurttig, and Fabian Müller (Vienna: Verlag für moderne Kunst, 2019).

2. Feldman, *The Great Disorder*, 4.

3. Mann, "Inflation."

4. On Bayer's work for the regime, see Patrick Rössler, *Herbert Bayer: Die Berliner Jahre—Werbegrafik 1928–1938* (Berlin: Vergangenheitsverlag, 2013), 44–62.

5. This was hardly a unique criticism of the Bauhaus at the time. For an overview, see Michael Müller, "The Dictate of Coldness: Critique from the Left, 1919–1933," in *Bauhaus Conflicts, 1919–2009: Controversies and Counterparts*, ed. Philipp Oswalt (Ostfildern: Hatje Cantz, 2009), 50–65.

6. Joseph Borkin, *The Crime and Punishment of I.G. Farben* (London: Andre Deutsch, 1979), 126.

7. International Labour Organisation, "Child Labour in Mining and Global Supply Chains" (2019), https://www.ilo.org/wcmsp5/groups/public/---asia/---ro-bangkok/---ilo-manila/documents/publication/wcms_720743.pdf (accessed July 21, 2023).

Bibliography

Aagesen, Dorthe, Anna Vestergaard Jørgensen, and Beatrice von Bormann, eds. *Kirchner and Nolde: Expressionism. Colonialism.* Munich: Hirmer, 2021.

Ades, Dawn, Simon Baker, and Fiona Bradley, eds. *Undercover Surrealism: Georges Bataille and Documents*. London: Haywood Gallery, 2006.

Adorno, Theodor W. *Aesthetic Theory*. Trans. Robert Hullot-Kentor. London: Continuum, 2004.

Adorno, Theodor W. "The Idea of Natural-History." In Robert Hullot-Kentor, *Things beyond Resemblance: Collected Essays on Theodor W. Adorno*, 252–270. New York: Columbia University Press, 2006.

Adorno, Theodor W. *Minima Moralia: Reflections on a Damaged Life*. Trans. Edmund Jephcott. London: Verso, 2006.

Archiv für Bildende Kunst. *Conrad Felixmüller: Werke und Dokumente*. Nuremberg: Germanisches Nationalmuseum, 1981.

Baker, George. *The Artwork Caught by the Tail: Francis Picabia and Dada in Paris*. Cambridge, MA: MIT, 2007.

Ball, Hugo. *Critique of the German Intelligentsia*. Trans. Brian L. Harris. New York: Columbia University Press, 1993.

Barrell, John. *The Dark Side of the Landscape: The Rural Poor in English Painting 1730–1840*. Cambridge: Cambridge University Press, 1983.

Bataille, Georges. *The Accursed Share: An Essay on General Economy*. 3 vols. Trans. Robert Hurley. New York: Zone, 1989.

Bataille, Georges. *Visions of Excess: Selected Writings, 1927–1939*. Trans. Allan Stoekl. Minneapolis: University of Minnesota Press, 1985.

Battini, Michele. *Socialism of Fools: Capitalism and Modern Anti-Semitism*. Trans. Noor Mazhar and Isabella Vergnano. New York: Columbia University Press, 2016.

Baudrillard, Jean. *For a Critique of the Political Economy of the Sign*. Trans. Charles Levin. St. Louis: Telos Press, 1981.

Beals, Kurt. "Dada Futures: Inflation, Speculation, and Uncertainty in Der Dada." *Transit* 10, no. 2 (2016), 14.

Beech, Dave. *Art and Value: Art's Economic Exceptionalism in Classical, Neoclassical and Marxist Economics*. Chicago: Haymarket, 2015.

Benjamin, Walter. *The Origin of German Tragic Drama*. Trans. John Osborne. London: Verso, 2009.

Benjamin, Walter. *Selected Writings*. Vol. 1: *1913–1926*, ed. Michael W. Jennings and Marcus Bullock. Cambridge, MA: Belknap Press of Harvard University Press, 2004.

Biging, Kurt. *Geldscheine in Halle an der Saale 1916–1992*. Halle: Mitteldeutscher Verlag, 2003.

Binswanger, Hans Christoph. *Money and Magic: A Critique of the Modern Economy in the Light of Goethe's Faust*. Trans. J. E. Harrison. Chicago: University of Chicago Press, 1994.

Bloch, Ernst. *Heritage of Our Times*. Trans. Stephen Plaice and Neville Plaice. Oxford: Polity Press, 1991.

Boa, Elizabeth, and Rachel Palfreyman. *Heimat: A German Dream. Regional Loyalties and National Identity in German Culture, 1890–1990*. Oxford: University Press, 2000.

Bois, Yve-Alain. "El Lissitzky: Radical Reversibility." *Art in America* 76 (1988), 160–181.

Borkin, Joseph. *The Crime and Punishment of I.G. Farben*. London: Andre Deutsch, 1979.

Brachmanski, Hans-Peter, ed. *Alfred Hanf. Ein Erfurter Künstlerleben*. Bad Langensalza: Verlag Rockstuhl, 2010.

Brandt, Paul. *Schaffende Arbeit und bildende Kunst. Vom Mittelalter bis zur Gegenwart*. 2 vols. Leipzig: Alfred Kröner, 1928.

Bredekamp, Horst. "A Neglected Tradition? Art History as Bildwissenschaft." *Critical Inquiry* 29, no. 3 (2003), 418–428.

Bronnert, Uwe. "Kein Notgeld, sondern Kunstblätter!" *Geldscheine-Online*, 2020, https://www.geldscheine-online.com/post/kein-notgeld-sondern-kunstblätter (accessed June 27, 2022).

Bruhn, Matthias. *Bildwirtschaft: Verwaltung und Verwertung der Sichtbarkeit*. Visual intelligence. Weimar: VDG, 2003.

Campbell, Joan. *Joy in Work, German Work: The National Debate, 1800–1945*. Princeton, NJ: Princeton University Press, 1989.

Clark, T. J. *Image of the People: Gustave Courbet and the 1848 Revolution*. London: Thames and Hudson, 1973.

Cole, Andrew. "Those Obscure Objects of Desire." *Artforum* 53, no. 318 (2015), 318–323.

Crockett, Dennis. *German Post-Expressionism: The Art of the Great Disorder, 1918–1924*. University Park: Pennsylvania State University Press, 1999.

"Das neue Papiergeld: Reichsbanknote und Geschmack." *Vossische Zeitung* (Berlin), February 12, 1921, section Erste Beilage, pp. 5–6.

"Das verschwundene Porzellangeld." *Glückstadter Fortuna* 182, no. 15 (January 19, 2021), 2.

Deleuze, Gilles, and Félix Guattari. *Anti-Oedipus: Capitalism and Schizophrenia*. Trans. Robert Hurley, Mark Seem, and Helen R. Lane. London: Athlone Press, 1984.

Desai, Radhika. "Vectors of Inflation." *New Left Review*, 2022, https://newleftreview.org/sidecar/posts/vectors-of-inflation (accessed October 7, 2022).

Dickerman, Leah, ed. *Dada: Zurich, Berlin, Hannover, Cologne, New York, Paris*. Washington, DC: National Gallery of Art, 2005.

Dietrich, Dorothea. *The Collages of Kurt Schwitters: Tradition and Innovation*. Cambridge: Cambridge University Press, 1993.

Doherty, Brigid. "The Work of Art and the Problem of Politics in Berlin Dada." *October* 105 (2003), 73–92.

Eiland, Howard, and Michael W. Jennings. *Walter Benjamin: A Critical Life*. Cambridge, MA: Belknap Press of Harvard University Press, 2014.

Ellenbürger, Judith, and Felix Gregor, eds. *Bild Medium Geld: Bildkulturen und Medienreflexionen des Monetären*. Paderborn: Wilhelm Fink, 2019.

Fallada, Hans. *Wolf among Wolves*. Trans. Philip Owens. New York: Melville House, 2010.

Feder, Gottfried. "Das Manifest zur Brechung der Zinsknechtschaft." *Wikisource*, 1919, https://de.wikisource.org/wiki/Das_Manifest_zur_Brechung_der_Zinsknechtschaft (accessed July 21, 2022).

Federici, Silvia. *Caliban and the Witch: Women, the Body and Primitive Accumulation*. London: Penguin, 2021.

Feldman, Gerald D. *The Great Disorder: Politics, Inflation, and Society in the German Inflation, 1914–1924*. New York: Oxford University Press, 1997.

Feuchtwanger, Lion. *Success: Three Years in the Life of a Province*. Trans. Willa and Edwin Muir. London: Martin Secker, 1930.

Fleckner, Uwe, Martin Warnke, and Hendrik Ziegler, eds. *Handbuch der politischen Ikonographie*. Munich: Beck, 2011.

Foster, John Bellamy. "Marx's Theory of Metabolic Rift. Classical Foundations for Environmental Sociology." *American Journal of Sociology* 105, no. 2 (1999), 366–405.

Foster, John Bellamy, and Brett Clark. "The Robbery of Nature." *Monthly Review*, July 1, 2018, https://monthlyreview.org/2018/07/01/the-robbery-of-nature/ (accessed August 28, 2019).

Freud, Sigmund. "Character and Anal Eroticism." In *Collected Papers*, vol. 2, trans. Joan Riviere, 45–50. London: Hogarth, 1946.

Friebel, Alexander. "Ohne Papier keine Zeitung: Die Erfindung des Holzschliffpapiers als Meilenstein in der Entwicklung des deutschen Pressewesens." *Jahrbuch für Kommunikationsgeschichte* 3 (2001), 132–156.

Gabriel, Gottfried. *Ästhetik und Rhetorik des Geldes*. Stuttgart: Frommann-Holzboog, 2002.

Gelderloos, Carl. "Simply Reproducing Reality—: Brecht, Benjamin, and Renger-Patzsch on Photography." *German Studies Review* 37, no. 3 (2014), 549–573.

Gerster, Ulrich. "Kontinuität und Bruch. Georg Schrimpf zwischen Räterepublik und NS-Herrschaft." *Zeitschrift für Kunstgeschichte* 63, no. 4 (2000), 532–557.

Geyer, Martin H. *Verkehrte Welt. Revolution, Inflation und Moderne: München 1914–1924*. Göttingen: Vandenhoeck & Ruprecht, 1998.

Gies, Horst. *Richard Walther Darré: Der "Reichsbauernführer," die nationalsozialistische "Blut und Boden"-Ideologie und Hitlers Machteroberung*. Vienna: Böhlau Verlag, 2019.

Glaser, Curt. "Vom Graphik-Sammeln." *Das Kunstblatt* 3 (1919), 321–330.
Goethe, Johann Wolfgang von. *Faust: Erster und zweiter Teil*. Munich: Deutsche Taschenbuch Verlag, 1997.
Goethe, Johann Wolfgang von. *Faust: Part One*. Trans. David Luke. Oxford: Oxford University Press, 2008.
Goethe, Johann Wolfgang von. *Faust: Part Two*. Trans. David Luke. Oxford: Oxford University Press, 1994.
Goll, Ivan. "Extracts from Ivan Goll, Sodom and Berlin (1929)." Trans. Donald Nicholson-Smith. *The Brooklyn Rail*, 2006, https://brooklynrail.org/2006/02/fiction/extracts-from-ivan-goll-sodom-and-berlin-1929 (accessed March 10, 2022).
Goux, Jean-Joseph. *Symbolic Economies: After Marx and Freud*. Trans. Jennifer Curtiss Gage. Ithaca, NY: Cornell University Press, 1990.
Goytisolo, Juan. *State of Siege*. Trans. Helen Lane. London: Serpent's Tail, 2003.
Grabowski, Hans-Ludwig, and Wolfgang Haney, eds. *"Der Jude nahm uns Silber, Gold und Speck …": Für politische Zwecke und antisemitische Propaganda genutzte Geldscheine in der Zeit der Weimarer Republik und des Dritten Reichs*. Regenstauf: Battenberg Gietl Verlag, 2015.
Green, Malcolm, trans. *Blago Bung Blago Bung Bosso Bataka! First Texts of German Dada by Hugo Ball, Richard Huelsenbeck, Walter Serner*. London: Atlas, 1995.
Grosz, George. "Statt einer Biographie." *Der Gegner* 1, no. 3 (1920), 68–70.
Guattari, Félix, and Gilles Deleuze. *A Thousand Plateaus: Capitalism and Schizophrenia*. Trans. Brian Massumi. Minneapolis: University of Minnesota Press, 1987.
Guttsmann, W. L. *Art for the Workers: Ideology and the Visual Arts in Weimar Germany*. Manchester: Manchester University Press, 1997.
Hablik, Wenzel. "Die freitragende Kuppel." *Frühlicht* 3 (1921), 173–178.
Haney, David H. *When Modern Was Green: Life and Work of Landscape Architect Leberecht Migge*. London: Routledge, 2010.
Hausmann, Raoul. "Return to Objectivity in Art." In *Dada Almanac*, ed. Richard Huelsenbeck, 151–156. London: Atlas Press, 1998.
Haxthausen, Charles W. "Bloody Serious: Two Texts by Carl Einstein." *October* 105 (2003), 105–118.
Hayek, F. A. "The Use of Knowledge in Society." *American Economic Review* 35, no. 4 (1945), 519–530.
Heinrich, Michael. *An Introduction to the Three Volumes of Karl Marx's Capital*. Trans. Alexander Loscasio. New York: Monthly Review Press, 2012.
Heise, Nele. "Das Bauhaus in allen Taschen: Notgeldscheine als Vorboten der Neuen Typografie." In *bauhaus-kommunikation: Innovative Strategien im Umgang mit Medien, interner und externer*

Öffentlichkeit, ed. Patrick Rössler, 265–280. Berlin: Gebr. Mann Verlag, 2008.
Herf, Jeffrey. *Reactionary Modernism: Technology, Culture, and Politics in Weimar and the Third Reich*. Cambridge: Cambridge University Press, 1984.
Hethey, Frank. "Ein Oberlehrer als Geheimbündler." *WK Geschichte*, 2021, https://wkgeschichte.weser-kurier.de/ein-oberlehrer-als-geheimbuendler/ (accessed August 25, 2022).
Hollier, Denis. *Against Architecture: The Writings of Georges Bataille*. Trans. Betsy Wing. Cambridge, MA: MIT Press, 1989.
Hörisch, Jochen. *Heads or Tails: The Poetics of Money*. Trans. Amy Horning Marschall. Detroit: Wayne State University Press, 2000.
Hruska, Libby, ed. *German Expressionism: The Graphic Impulse*. New York: Museum of Modern Art, 2011.
Hugo, Victor. *Les misérables*. Trans. Norman Denny. London: Penguin, 1982.
Jameson, Fredric. *The Prison House of Language: A Critical Account of Structuralism and Russian Formalism*. Princeton, NJ: Princeton University Press, 1972.
Jefferies, Matthew. "Die Schöne Heimat? Depictions of Germany in a Popular Photobook from the Second Empire to the Federal Republic." *New German Critique* 46, no. 2 (2019), 35–63.
Joselit, David. *After Art*. Princeton, NJ: Princeton University Press, 2013.
Jünger, Ernst. *The Worker: Dominion and Form*. Trans. Laurence Paul Hemming and Bogdan Costea. Evanston, IL: Northwestern University Press, 2017.
Kaes, Anton. "Die ökonomische Dimension der Literatur: Zum Strukturwandel der Institution Literatur in der Inflationszeit (1918–1923)." In *Konsequenzen der Inflation*, ed. Gerald D. Feldman, 307–329. Berlin: Kolloqium Verlag, 1989.
Kaes, Anton, Martin Jay, and Edward Dimendberg, eds. *The Weimar Republic Sourcebook*. Berkeley: University of California Press, 1994.
Kafka, Ben. "Review: Jussi Parikka's *Geology of Media*." *Artforum*, November 2015, https://www.artforum.com/print/201509/jussi-parikka-s-geology-of-media-55519 (accessed December 18, 2019).
Kandinsky, Wassily. *Über das Geistige in der Kunst*. Bern: Benteli Verlag, 2009.
Kemp, Wolfgang. *Wir haben ja alle Deutschland nicht gekannt: Das Deutschlandbild der Deutschen in der Zeit der Weimarer Republik*. Heidelberg: Heidelberg University Press, 2016.
Klossowski, Pierre. *Living Currency*. Trans. Nicolae Morar, Vernon C. Cisney, Paul Foss-Heimlich, and Daniel W. Smith. London: Bloomsbury Academic, 2017.
Kluge, Alexander, and Oskar Negt. *Public Sphere and Experience: Toward an Analysis of the Bourgeois and Proletarian Public Sphere*.

Trans. Assenka Oksiloff, Jamie Owen Daniel, and Peter Labanyi. Minneapolis: University of Minnesota Press, 1993.

Korff, Gottfried, ed. *Kasten 117. Aby Warburg und der Aberglaube im Ersten Weltkrieg*. Tübingen: Tübinger Vereiningung für Volkskunde, 2007.

Kracauer, Siegfried. "Notgeld und Kleingeld." In *Siegfried Kracauer Werke*, ed. Inka Mülder-Bach, 5.1. Berlin: Suhrkamp, 2011.

Kracauer, Siegfried. "Wiederkehr der Toten?" In *Werke 5.1. Essays, Feuilletons, Rezensionen. 1906–1923*, 691–693. Berlin: Suhrkamp, 2011.

Krauss, Rosalind E. *The Picasso Papers*. New York: Farrar, Straus and Giroux, 1998.

Kuhn, Alfred. "Über das Sammeln von Graphik." *Kunstchronik und Kunstmarkt* 30 (1923), 594–597.

Künzel, Christine. "'[D]ie dunkle Schlange des lügnerischen Papiergelds': Anmerkungen zur Ästhetik und Rhetorik von Papiernoten in der großen Inflation (1918–1923)." In *Bild Medium Geld: Bildkulturen und Medienreflexionen des Monetären*, ed. Judith Ellenbürger and Felix Gregor, 79–94. Paderborn: Wilhelm Fink, 2019.

Kurlander, Eric. "Hitler's Monsters: The Occult Roots of Nazism and the Emergence of the Nazi 'Supernatural Imaginary.'" *German History* 30, no. 4 (2012), 528–549.

Laube, Gisbert. *Der Reichskunstwart: Geschichte Einer Kulturbehoerde 1919–1933*. Frankfurt: Peter Lang, 1997.

Lauenburger, Erich. "Papiernot—Papierverschwendung." *Das Plakat* 10, no. 1 (1919), 89–90.

Liao, Shannon. "Amazon Warehouse Workers Skip Bathroom Breaks to Keep Their Jobs, Says Report." *The Verge*, 2018, https://www.theverge.com/2018/4/16/17243026/amazon-warehouse-jobs-worker-conditions-bathroom-breaks (accessed October 8, 2019).

Lindman, Kai. *Celler Notgeld. Notgeldscheine des 20. Jahrhunderts in Stadt und Kreis Celle*. Celler Beiträge zur Landes- und Kulturgeschichte. Celle: Shriftenreihe des Stadtarchivs Celle und des Bomann-Museums, 1992.

Linse, Ulrich. *Barfüssige Propheten: Erlöser der zwanziger Jahre*. Berlin: Siedler, 1983.

"Lockstedter Lager. Eine Notgeld-Moritat." *DENK MAL!*, https://www.denk-mal-gegen-krieg.de/assets/Uploads/Lockstedter-Lager-eine-Notgeld-Moritat-uberarbeitete-Fassung.pdf (accessed July 9, 2022).

Lukács, Georg. *The Destruction of Reason*. Trans. Peter Palmer. London: Merlin Press, 1980.

Lukács, Georg. *History and Class Consciousness: Studies in Marxist Dialectics*. Trans. Rodney Livingstone. Cambridge, MA: MIT Press, 1971.

Lukács, Georg, Bertolt Brecht, Ernst Bloch, Walter Benjamin, and Theodor W. Adorno. *Aesthetics and Politics*. London: Verso, 2006.

Maibaum, Katrin, and Katharina Gräber. *Wenzel Hablik—expressionistische Utopien: Malerei, Zeichnung, Architektur*. Munich: Prestel, 2017.
Makela, Maria. "Making Lemonade out of Lemons: Merz and Material Poverty." *Art History* 42, no. 4 (2019), 652–677.
Mann, Thomas. "Inflation: The Witches Sabbath: Germany 1923." *Encounter* 44, no. 2 (1974), 60–64.
Marc, Franz. "Die Neue Malerei." *Pan* 2, no. 16 (1912), 468–471.
Marx, Karl. *Capital*, vol. I. Trans. Ben Fowkes. London: Penguin, 1976.
Marx, Karl. *Capital*, vol. III. Trans. David Fernbach. London: Penguin, 1991.
Marx, Karl. *Economic and Philosophic Manuscripts of 1844*. Trans. Martin Milligan. Mineola, NY: Dover, 2007.
Maynes, Erin Sullivan. "Making Money: Notgeld and the Material Experience of Inflation in Weimar Germany." *Art History* 42, no. 4 (2019), 678–701.
Mehl, Manfred. *Deutsche Serienscheine von 1918–1922*. Regenstauf: Gietl Verlag, 1998.
Melville, Herman. *Billy Budd, Sailor and Selected Tales*. Oxford: Oxford University Press, 2009.
Meyrink, Gustav. *The Golem*. Trans. Mike Mitchell. Sawtry: Dedalus, 1995.
Mühlen, Hermynia zur, and George Grosz. *Was Peterchens Freunde erzählen: Märchen*. Berlin: Malik Verlag, 1921.
Müller, Michael. "The Dictate of Coldness: Critique from the Left, 1919–1933." In *Bauhaus Conflicts, 1919–2009: Controversies and Counterparts*, ed. Philipp Oswalt, 50–65. Ostfildern: Hatje Cantz, 2009.
Nachtigall, Jenny. "Life." In *Kunst und Politik: Jahrbuch der Guernica-Gesellschaft 21. Keywords for Marxist Art History Today* (Göttingen: Vandenhoeck & Ruprecht, 2019), 77–86.
Nachtigall, Jenny, and Kerstin Stakemeier. "Lu Märten: An Introduction to Four Texts." *October* 178 (2021), 3–14.
Negt, Oskar, and Alexander Kluge. *History and Obstinacy*. Trans. Richard Langston, Cyrus Shahan, Martin Brady, Helen Hughes, and Joel Golb. New York: Zone Books, 2014.
Niebisch, Arndt. "Excess-Zero: Dada and the Logic of Inflation." *Rheinsprung 11: Zeitschrift für Bildkritik*, 2013, https://rheinsprung11.unibas.ch/ausgabe-05/thema/excess-zero-dada-and-the-logic-of-inflation/ (accessed January 7, 2020).
Nigel Dodd. *The Social Life of Money*. Princeton, NJ: Princeton University Press, 2014.
Nippa, Annegret. *Bruno Taut: Eine Dokumentation. Projekte—Texte—Mitarbeiter*. Magdeburg: Landeshauptstadt Magdeburg, 1995.
No Relief: Denial of Bathroom Breaks in the Poultry Industry. Oxfam America, 2016, https://www.oxfamamerica.org/static/media/files/No_Relief_Embargo.pdf.

Noys, Benjamin. “Georges Bataille’s Base Materialism.” *Cultural Values* 2, no. 4 (1998), 499–517.
“Nr. 378. Sitzung des Reichsbankkuratoriums: Wirtschaftliche und finanzielle Lage des Reiches.” Bundesarchiv (Historische Kommission bei der Bayerischen Akademie der Wissenschaften und das Bundesarchiv, 1922), https://www.bundesarchiv.de/akten reichskanzlei/1919-1933/0000/wir/wir2p/kap1_1/kap2_143/para3 _1.html (accessed July 15, 2022).
Oppenheimer, Paul, trans. *A Pleasant Vintage of Till Eulenspiegel.* Middletown, CT: Wesleyan University Press, 1972.
Ostwald, Hans. *Sittengeschichte der Inflation.* Berlin: Neufeld & Henius, 1931.
Otto, Elizabeth. “A ‘Schooling of the Senses’: Post-Dada Visual Experiments in the Bauhaus Photomontages of Laszlo Moholy-Nagy and Marianne Brandt.” *New German Critique* 36 (2009), 89–131.
Papapetros, Spyros. “Malicious Houses: Animation, Animism, Animosity in German Architecture and Film—From Mies to Murnau.” *Grey Room* 20 (2005), 6–37.
Papapetros, Spyros. *On the Animation of the Inorganic: Art, Architecture, and the Extension of Life.* Chicago: University of Chicago Press, 2012.
Penner, Barbara. *Bathroom.* London: Reaktion Books, 2013.
Potts, Alex. “Labour.” In *Kunst und Politik: Jahrbuch der Guernica-Gesellschaft. Schwerpunkt: Keywords for Marxist Art History Today*, 69–75. Göttingen: Vandenhoeck & Ruprecht, 2019.
Powers, Michael. “Red Fairy Tales and Non-Anthropocentric Solidarity: Hermynia zur Mühlen, Ernst Bloch, and Siegfried Kracauer.” *German Quarterly* 94, no. 2 (2021), 208–218.
Priddat, Birger P. “‘Geist der Ornamentik,’ Ideogrammatik des Geldes: Allegorien bürgerlicher Zivilreligion auf Banknoten des 19. und 20. Jahrhunderts.” In *Kapitalismus als Religion*, ed. Dirk Baecker, 19–34. Berlin: Kulturverlag Kadmos, 2009.
Redslob, Edwin. “Banknoten-Stil.” *Vossische Zeitung* (Berlin), March 4, 1921, 2.
Reschke, Wolfgang. “Notgeld in Kreis Steinburg von 1914 bis 1923.” In *Steinburger Jahrbuch 1986: Geldgeschichte, Wirtschaft und Sparkassenwesen*, ed. Alexander Ritter and Peter Fischer. Itzehoe: Heimatverbandes für den Kreis Steinberg, 1985.
Rigby, Ida Katherine. “German Expressionist Political Posters 1918–1919: Art and Politics, a Failed Alliance.” *Art Journal* 44, no. 1 (1984), 33–39.
Ringer, Fritz. *The Decline of the German Mandarins: The German Academic Community, 1890–1933.* Cambridge, MA: Harvard University Press, 1969.
Roberts, William Clare. *Marx’s Inferno: The Political Theory of Capital.* Princeton, NJ: Princeton University Press, 2016.

Rose, Gillian. *The Melancholy Science: An Introduction to the Thought of Theodor W. Adorno*. London: Verso, 2014.
Rosler, Martha. "Culture Class: Art, Creativity, Urbanism, Part II." *E-Flux*, March 2011, https://www.e-flux.com/journal/23/67813/culture-class-art-creativity-urbanism-part-ii/ (accessed October 29, 2019).
Rössler, Patrick. *Herbert Bayer: Die Berliner Jahre—Werbegrafik 1928–1938*. Berlin: Vergangenheitsverlag, 2013.
Rowley, Eric. *Hyperinflation in Germany: Perceptions of a Process*. Aldershot, UK: Scolar Press, 1994.
Schlaffer, Heinz. *Faust zweiter Teil: Die Allegorie des 19. Jahrhunderts*. Stuttgart: Metzler, 1981.
Schmalenbach, Werner. *Kurt Schwitters*. London: Thames and Hudson, 1970.
Scholz, Georg. *Schriften, Briefe, Dokumente*. Ed. Karl-Ludwig Hofmann and Ursula Merkel. Karlsruhe: Info Verlag, 2018.
Schröter, Jens. "Das Geld und die Medientheorie." *Zeitschrift für Medienwissenschaft* 10, no. 18 (2018), 59–72.
Schuetzinger, Hermine C. "Künstlerisches Kriegsnotgeld." *Das Plakat* 10, no. 1 (1919), 60–66.
Schwartz, Frederic J. "Aby Warburg and the Spirit of Capitalism." In *Renew Marxist Art History*, ed. Warren Carter, Barnaby Haran, and Frederic J. Schwartz, 117–137. London: Art/Books, 2013.
Schwartz, Frederic J. *Blind Spots: Critical Theory and the History of Art in Twentieth-Century Germany*. New Haven: Yale University Press, 2005.
Schwartz, Frederic J. *The Werkbund: Design Theory and Mass Culture before the First World War*. New Haven: Yale University Press, 1996.
Schwitters, Kurt. *Das literarische Werk*. Ed. Friedrich Lach. 5 vols. Cologne: DuMont Buchverlag, 1981.
Shell, Marc. *The Economy of Literature*. Baltimore: Johns Hopkins University Press, 1993.
Shell, Marc. "The Issue of Representation." In *The New Economic Criticism*, ed. Martha Woodmansee and Mark Osteen, 44–64. London: Routledge, 1999.
Simmel, Georg. *The Philosophy of Money*. Trans. Tom Bottomore, David Frisby, and Kaethe Mengelberg. Abingdon, UK: Routledge, 2011.
Simmons, Sherwin. "Advertising Seizes Control of Life: Berlin Dada and the Power of Advertising." *Oxford Art Journal* 22, no. 1 (1999), 119–146.
Simmons, Sherwin. "Kitsch oder Kunst? Kokoschka's *Der Sturm* and Commerce in Art." *Print Collector's Newsletter* 23, no. 5 (1992), 161–167.
Speelmans, Beatrice. "Anomic Speculation: The Cultural Logic of Tokenisation. An Investigation of Notgeld, Complimentary Local Currencies and Non-Fungible Tokens." MA thesis, Courtauld Institute, 2021.

Spengler, Oswald. *The Decline of the West. Complete in One Volume*. Trans. Charles Francis Atkinson. London: George Allen & Unwin, 1934.

Steiner, Rudolf. "Agriculture Course, Lecture II." Trans. George Adams. *Rudolf Steiner Archive*, 1924, https://rsarchive.org/Lectures/GA327/English/BDA1958/19240610p01.html (accessed September 15, 2022).

Steinitz, Kate. *Kurt Schwitters: A Portrait from Life*. Berkeley: University of California Press, 1968.

Steyerl, Hito. *Duty Free Art: Art in the Age of Planetary Civil War*. London: Verso, 2017.

Stoltzenberg, Dietrich. *Fritz Haber: Chemist, Nobel Laureate, German, Jew*. Philadelphia: Chemical Heritage Press, 2004.

Szendy, Peter. *The Supermarket of the Visible: Toward a General Economy of Images*. Trans. Jan Plug. New York: Fordham University Press, 2019.

Te Heesen, Anke. *The Newspaper Clipping: A Modern Paper Object*. Trans. Lori Lantz. Manchester: Manchester University Press, 2014.

Theweleit, Klaus. *Male Fantasies*, vol. 1: *Women, Floods, Bodies, History*. Trans. Chris Turner, Erica Carter, and Stephen Conway. Minneapolis: Minnesota University Press, 1987.

Tucker, Robert C., ed. *The Marx-Engels Reader*. New York: W. W. Norton, 1978.

Uebe. "Das neue Notgeld der Stadt Osterfeld." *Das Notgeld* 4, nos. 9–10 (1922), 204–205.

"Verschiedenes Geld." *Itzehoer Nachrichtung*, April 21, 2021, 2.

Vishmidt, Marina. *Speculation as a Mode of Production: Forms of Value Subjectivity in Art and Capital*. Leiden: Brill, 2019.

Vogl, Joseph. *The Specter of Capital*. Trans. Joachim Redner and Robert Savage. Stanford, CA: Stanford University Press, 2015.

Warnke, Martin. *Political Landscape: The Art History of Nature*. Illustrated edition. London: Reaktion Books, 1994.

Weber, Max. "Science as a Vocation." In *From Max Weber: Essays in Sociology*. Ed. and trans. H. H. Gerth and C. Wright Mills, 129–156. London: Routledge, 2009.

Wegener, Franz. *Der Alchemist Franz Tausend: Alchemie und Nationalsozialismus*. Gladbeck: Kulturfoerderverein Ruhrgebiet, 2013.

Weidinger, Alfred, Marcus Andrew Hurttig, and Fabian Müller, eds. *Karl Hermann Trinkaus: Bauhaus—Der neue Mensch*. Vienna: Verlag für moderne Kunst, 2019.

Weinstein, Joan. *The End of Expressionism: Art and the November Revolution in Germany, 1918–19*. Chicago: University of Chicago Press, 1989.

Weissberg, Liliane. "Notenverkehr: Antisemitische Motive und Texte auf dem Notgeld der 20er Jahre." In *Abgestempelt! Antisemitische Bildpostkarten 1885–1945*, ed. Fritz Backhaus, 276–283. Heidelberg: Umschau/Braus, 1999.

Wenzel, Manfred. "Der Ilmenauer Bergbau und sein Einfluß auf Goethe als Dichter und Naturforscher." *Medizinhistorisches Journal* 22, no. 1 (1987), 3–27.

Werckmeister, O. K. *The Making of Paul Klee's Career, 1914–1920*. Chicago: University of Chicago Press, 1989.

Werckmeister, O. K. "The Turn from Marx to Warburg in West German Art History, 1968–1990." In *Marxism and Art History: From William Morris to the New Left*, 213–220. London: Pluto Press, 2006.

Westheim, Paul. "Kunst als Sachwert." *Das Kunstblatt* 7 (1923), 229–231.

Westheim, Paul. "Die Landschaft." *Das Kunstblatt* 4 (1920), 7–19.

Whyte, Iain Boyd, ed. and trans. *The Crystal Chain Letters: Architectural Fantasies by Bruno Taut and His Circle*. Cambridge, MA: MIT Press, 1985.

Widdig, Bernd. *Culture and Inflation in Weimar Germany*. Berkeley: University of California Press, 2001.

Wiggershaus, Rolf. *The Frankfurt School: Its History, Theories and Political Significance*. Trans. Michael Robertson. Cambridge: Polity Press, 1993.

Wingler, Hans. *The Bauhaus: Weimar, Dessau, Berlin, Chicago*. Cambridge, MA: MIT Press, 1978.

Wirthmann, Hans-Joachim. *Notgeldscheine von Heinz Schiestl*. Lohr am Main: Geschichts- und Museumsverein Lohr am Main, 2007.

Zeller, Christoph. "Aus Müll Gold gesponnen: Kurt Schwitters' Merzkunst und die Inflation." *German Studies Review* 31, no. 2 (2008), 345–367.

Zentralamt der Dadaismus. "Legen Sie Ihr Geld in dada an!" *Der Dada* 1 (1919), 7–8.

Zhu, Xiaojue Michelle. "A Re-Examination of the City-Country Dichotomy in Weimar Germany: Georg Scholz's Industrial Farmers (1920)." *Immediations* 18 (2021), https://courtauld.ac.uk/research/research-resources/publications/immeditations-postgraduate-journal/immediations-online/immediations-no-18-2021/a-re-examination-of-the-city-country-dichotomy-in-weimar-germany-georg-scholzs-industrial-farmers-1920/ (accessed April 4, 2022).

Zweig, Arnold. "Der Angriff der Gegenstände." In *Essays. Zweiter Band. Krieg und Frieden*, 57–62. Frankfurt: Fischer, 1987.

Image Credits

Unless stated otherwise, all images are from the author's collection.

akg-images: page 86
Hans-Ludwig Besler: pages 125, 149 (bottom)
bpk/Kunstbibliothek, SMB, Photothek Willy Römer/Willy Römer: page 11
bpk/Sprengel Museum Hannover/Michael Herling/Aline Gwose: page 98
Nathaniel Butler: pages 89 (bottom), 143 (top), 144 (both), 155, 191, 201
Centre Pompidou, MNAM-CCI, Dist. RMN-Grand Palais/image Centre Pompidou, MNAM-CCI: page 8
© DACS 2022: pages 102, 103, 104, 105
Deutsche Bundesbank: page 203
© Estate of George Grosz, Princeton, NJ/DACS 2022: pages 70–71, 80, 139
Fitzwilliam Museum, Cambridge: pages 12, 31, 55, 74, 89 (top), 120–121, 131
Giesecke+Devrient Geldscheinsammlung: pages 61, 62, 190, 194, 212–213
David Haney: page 209
The Israel Museum. Collection Schwartz, courtesy Mudima, Milan, Italy, Luisa Ricciarini/Bridgeman Images: page 101
Ketterer Kunst, Munich: pages 226, 227, 228, 229
Kosmos/von Debschitz, fritz-kahn.com: page 207
Kurt Schwitters Archive, Sprengel Museum Hannover: page 99
Ogmios: page 183
Tilman2007: page 182
Von der Heydt-Museum Wuppertal. Photo: Antje Zeis-Loi, Medienzentrum Wuppertal: page 50
Warburg Institute, London: frontispiece and pages 10, 13, 33, 41, 44 (both), 45, 53 (both), 56, 57, 58, 72, 82–83, 130, 136, 143 (bottom), 170
Wenzel-Hablik-Foundation, Itzehoe: pages 7, 214

Index

The MIT Press would like to thank the anonymous peer reviewers who provided comments on drafts of this book.

The generous work of academic experts is essential for establishing the authority and quality of our publications. We acknowledge with gratitude the contributions of these otherwise uncredited readers.

This book was set in Haultin by the MIT Press. Printed and bound in Canada.

Library of Congress Cataloging-in-Publication Data
Names: Wilkinson, Tom, author.
Title: Emergency money : Notgeld in the image economy of the German inflation, 1914–1923 / Tom Wilkinson.
Description: Cambridge, Massachusetts : The MIT Press, [2023] | Includes bibliographical references and index.
Identifiers: LCCN 2022061584 | ISBN 9780262546805 (paperback)
Subjects: LCSH: Emergency currency—Germany—History—20th century. | Inflation (Finance)—Germany—History—20th century. | Art and society—Germany—History—20th century.
Classification: LCC HG353.3 .W55 2023 | DDC 332.4/1420943—dc23/eng/20230309
LC record available at https://lccn.loc.gov/2022061584

10 9 8 7 6 5 4 3 2 1

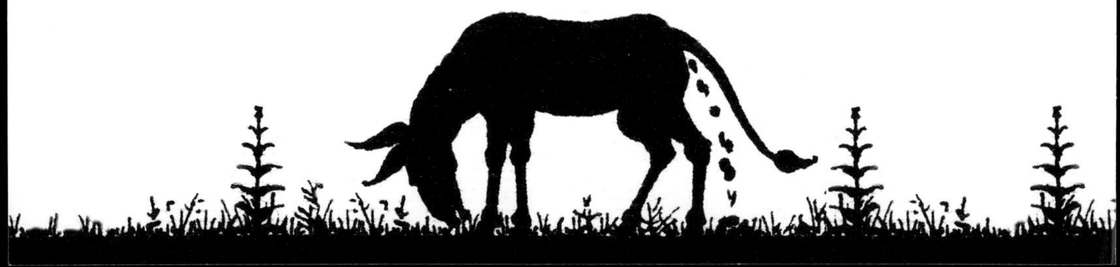